«Brave and noble elephant! We entreat you to banish every wish to stay in the forest.»

SIAMESE BRAHMINIC CHANT

«BANGKOK! I THRILLED. I HAD BEEN SIX YEARS AT SEA, BUT HAD ONLY SEEN MELBOURNE AND SYDNEY, VERY GOOD PLACES, CHARMING PLACES IN THEIR WAY – BUT BANGKOK!»

JOSEPH CONRAD

«BANGKOK HAS BEEN APTLY STYLED THE
'VENICE OF THE EAST,' FOR ITS
THOROUGHFARES AND HIGHWAYS OF
TRAFFIC ARE SIMPLY INTERSECTING
CANALS AND BRANCHES OF THE RIVER;
AND THE MAJORITY OF THE HOUSES ARE
EITHER FLOATING, BUILT UPON RAFTS,
OR UPON PILES ON THE SIDES OF THESE
WATERWAYS.»

FRANK VINCENT

NUMEROUS SPECIALISTS AND ACADEMICS HAVE CONTRIBUTED
TO THIS GUIDE. SPECIAL THANKS TO WILLIAM WARREN
DAVID STONE AND LUCA INVERNIZZI TETTONI.

CONTRIBUTORS
Anuar Bin Abdul Rahim, Dieter Ande, Osman Asari, Martine Buysschaert,
Jimmy Chan, Michel Chantraine, Cheong Yim Mui, Julia Davison, Xavier
Demangeon, M.L. Triyosudh Devakul, Armelle Dupont, Bruce Granquist,
Christine Hawixbrock, Luca Invernizzi Tettoni, Claude Jacques, Kang Nee,
Christine Lorian, Hansjorg Mayer, Brigitte Moriset, Kittisak Nualvilai,
Maurice Pommier, Seah Kam Chuan, Soon Ching Yee, David Stone, Tan Seok
Lui, Tan Tat Ghee, William Warren, Manfred Winkler, Paul Yip.

WE WOULD ALSO LIKE TO THANK
Stefan B. Polter and Sarah Anderson

PRACTICAL INFORMATION TRANSLATED BY NATHALIE PHAN
EDITED AND TYPESET BY BOOK CREATION SERVICES, LONDON
PRINTED IN ITALY BY EDITORIALE LIBRARIA

EVERYMAN GUIDES
PUBLISHED BY DAVID CAMPBELL PUBLISHERS LTD, LONDON

© *1993 David Campbell Publishers Ltd*

© *Editions Nouveaux-Loisirs, a subsidiary of Gallimard, Paris*

ISBN 1-85715-826-1

THAILAND

EVERYMAN GUIDES

CONTENTS

11

HOW TO USE THIS GUIDE

The symbols at the top of each page refer to the different parts of the guide.

■ NATURAL ENVIRONMENT

● UNDERSTANDING VENICE

▲ ITINERARIES

◆ PRACTICAL INFORMATION

The itinerary map shows the main points of interest along the way and is intended to help you find your bearings.

The mini-map locates the particular itinerary within the wider area covered by the guide.

CANNAREGIO

The gateway to Venice, after all, is neither the station nor the Piazzale but the Grand Canal behind us, churned by propellers, turbulent as a great river.
Fernand Braudel, *Venice*

Santa Lucia Station.

Immediately outside the railway station lies Cannaregio, the first of the six *sestieri* of Venice. Situated at the north-west end of the city, this is the second largest *sestiere* after Castello ▲ 155, covering an area of 150 hectares. Nearly a third of the population of Venice is concentrated here, amounting to more than twenty thousand people. There are two theories about the origin of the name Cannaregio; according to one, it comes from *Canal regio* (the Royal Canal), meaning to one, Secundo (which used to provide convenient access to the city from the mainland, by once bridging the lagoon canal of San broad waterway which provided convenient access to the city from the mainland, by once bridging the lagoon (other hypothesis is that the word derives from the reeds and of straight, parallel canals. In this case, a system comes which used to abound in this area. In this case, a system southwards and linked by calli, criss-cross this road of workmen's houses interspersed with magnificent palaces. To the south, behind the palaces of the Grand Canal, 15 feet wide. street known as the Strada Nuova was built at the end of the last century. Now pedestrianized, this street runs from the station to the Campo Santi Apostoli, crossing the *sestiere* from one side to the other as it goes. Few people lived in this *sestiere* where names as 11th century, and it seems to have taken form only gradually, as the process of draining and consolidating the site progressed. From the 15th century onwards, Cannaregio was a definable quarter, though it was still peripheral to Venice proper. Before the railway bridge and the station were built, manufacturing was the principal industry in the district, despite attempts to create a new area of growth with the Fondamenta Nuove. A similar project in the 16th century, the draining of the Sacca della Misericordia, was also never realized.

THE GATEWAY TO VENICE ★

PONTE DELLA LIBERTA. Built by the Austrians 50 years after the Treaty of Campo Formio in 1797 ● 34, to link Venice with Milan. The bridge ended the thousand-year separation from the mainland and shook the city's economy to its roots as Venice, already in the throes of the industrial revolution, saw its dependence on the mainland grow out of all recognition.

SANTA LUCIA STATION. The present station dates from 1955, but still bears the name of the Renaissance church demolished in 1861 to make way for it. Opposite is the green dome of the Church of San Simeone Piccolo.

✹ Half a day

BRIDGES TO VENICE
The Austrians conceived a project for a bridge between Mestre and Venice as early as 1814. It was not until 1846 that construction of the Ponte della Liberta was finally begun. The span of the viaduct was almost 11,500 feet, and it included 222 stone arches. On April 25, 1933, the Ponte della Liberta was opened, built by the engineer Umberto Fantucci, this bridge was intended for use by motor cars.

★ The star symbol signifies that a particular site has been singled out by the publishers for its special beauty, atmosphere or cultural interest.

● ▲ ■ ◆
The symbols alongside a title or within the text itself provide cross-references to a theme or place dealt with elsewhere in the guide.

At the beginning of each itinerary, the suggested means of transport to be used and the time it will take to cover the area are indicated:
- 🚤 By boat
- 🚶 On foot
- 🚲 By bicycle
- ✹ Duration

PONTE DELLA LIBERTA. Built by the Austrians 50 years after the Treaty of Campo Formio in 1797 ● 34, to link Venice with Milan. The bridge ended the thousand-year separation from the mainland and shook the city's economy to its roots as Venice, already in the throes of the industrial revolution, saw

✹ Half a day

BRIDGES TO VENICE

NATURE

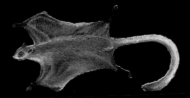

RED RHODODENDRON

Much of Thailand's natural heritage is due to the shape of the country, a stretched ribbon of land over 900 miles long, spanning both seasonally dry zones and habitats where rain falls throughout the year. The present-day Thai landscape has been molded by the actions of various colonists in the past, with farming being the most important influence. About 20,000 square miles of the country are set aside as conservation areas (for example, northeast Thailand national parks ▲ *238–40)*, many of which are open to the public, offering visitors an opportunity to encounter a wide range of plants and animals within a natural environment.

Tropical rain forest

Savanna

Monsoon forest

KOUPREY
Once a widely distributed species, the kouprey is today one of the most seriously threatened large mammals in the world.

BARKING DEER
Also called *muntjac,* these solitary animals are found in woodlands, rain forests and monsoon forests with dense vegetation.

MIXED DECIDUOUS FOREST
It supports a great proportion of the country's interesting and varied wildlife.

BANTENG
The banteng is a species of wild ox native to Southeast Asia.

UNDERWATER WORLD

TROPICAL RAIN FOREST
It is one of the richest ecosystems on the planet today.

MANGROVES
Coastal mangrove formations help protect shorelines from erosion and also provide a safe haven and nursery ground for a huge variety of fish species.

RIVERINE GRASSLANDS
Open patches of riverine grassland and savanna are important feeding and browsing areas for many forest herbivores. Many areas of grassland were formerly forested but regular outbreaks of fire prevent woody regeneration of these areas.

MONITOR LIZARD
The monitor lizard is a diurnal species that feeds on insects, eggs, fish, other lizards, snakes, nestling birds and small mammals.

GLORIOSA SUPERBA

HORNBILL
The strong and often ornate beak of the hornbill is perfectly molded for picking and cracking large fruit and seed pods from a wide range of forest plants.

LEAF MONKEY (1) AND GIBBON (2)
These primates dwell in the forest canopy and feed on fruit and leaves. The leaf monkey has a large, especially adapted stomach similar to that of a cow.

ASIAN BLACK BEAR
The Asian black bear is a forest dweller that feeds mainly on nuts and fruit, as well as ants, insect larvae and carrion.

MONTANE EVERGREEN FOREST
This is typified by an open canopy with trees festooned in lichens and epiphytes. Trees are also much shorter and less straight when compared with those of lowland forest.

HILL EVERGREEN RAIN FOREST
Climbing from montane evergreen forests, an unclear transition zone of slightly smaller trees that are widely spaced apart lies at an altitude of 2,300–2,600 feet above sea level.

EVERGREEN RAIN FOREST
True evergreen rain forest exists only in the extreme southern region of peninsular Thailand, near the Malaysian border.

WILD GINGER
One of a large number of economically valuable plants that grow wild in the forests of Thailand, the wild ginger plant is believed to have a number of medicinal healing properties that are now being investigated.

FUNGI
As part of the nutrient recycling scheme of the natural forest, fungi play an essential role in all forests and woodlands.

DRY DECIDUOUS WOODLANDS
Extensive dry deciduous woodlands with some dipterocarp species still occur in the north and east of the country.

BAMBOO FOREST
Bamboo stands are present in monsoon forests and generally thrive in areas previously cleared by man, blocking out most growth beneath their lofty foliage.

GREEN PEAFOWL
The only viable population of green peafowls remaining in Thailand is found in the Huai Kha Khaeng Wildlife Sanctuary where about 300 birds gain refuge.

17

Tropical forests are like a kaleidoscope of different worlds. They cover a fifth of the earth's land surface and are home to about half of the known species of animal and plant life. The forests ▲ *238–40* are confined to a belt around the equator, where the stable climate, temperature and humidity permit a great diversity of vegetation and wildlife.

162 FEET

EMERGENT LAYER
The few emergent trees above the canopy are home to insectivorous bats and birds such as eagles and hornbills.

122 FEET

CANOPY LAYER
The canopy is a continuous layer of foliage about 22 feet deep that supports a broad variety of animals. Mammals like flying squirrels, gibbons and macaques feed **FLYING** on the rich supply **SQUIRREL** of fruit, leaves, bark and nuts.

PIG-TAILED MACAQUES
These are diurnal primates, living in groups of 15–30 animals, feeding on fruit, small vertebrates and insects. They are mostly found in hill forests.

Constant temperature and high humidity levels favor the growth of lianas, trailing vines, lichens and epiphytes.

FOLIAGE
The leaves of the canopy can change their positions in order to catch the maximum amount of sunlight. Their drip-tips allow the rain to drain away and the waxy coating is a protection against algae and moss.

79 FEET

UNDERSTORY
Mammals like the peculiar binturong, pangolin and civet move freely in the understory between the ground and the upper tree layer in search of morsels and a safe place to rest.

The buttress or stilt-like roots of the trees help support them in the shallow soil.

41 FEET

FOREST FLOOR
At the top of the food chain are predators such as tigers or leopards that stalk their wary prey in the shade of the lower canopy and the forest floor.

The dark forest floor is alive with communities of omnivorous insects such as ants and termites.

TAPIR
A shy forest-dweller, this herbivore is often found near quiet rivers and wallows, feeding on leaves and small trees.

GROUND
The plants, insects and fungi that dwell at ground level are fed upon by mammals and birds.

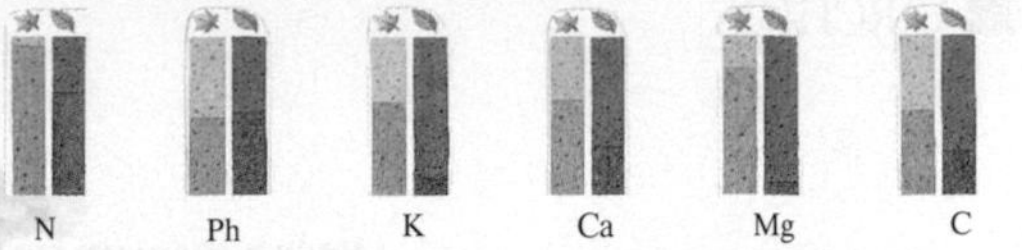

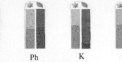

N   Ph   K   Ca   Mg   C

SILVER-EARED MESIA

BLACK-THROATED SUNBIRD

BINTURONG
Resembling a small bear, the binturong has a bushy, prehensile tail that enables it to feed in the trees as well as on the ground.

PALM CIVET
The agile small-toothed palm civet is a nocturnal species that searches for insects, fruit and small mammals in the branches of tall secondary forests.

SLOW LORIS
This is a solitary nocturnal primate with large eyes and a thickly furred body.

TIGER
This is the largest member of the cat family; fewer than 250 now survive in Thailand.

PANGOLIN
The scaly armor plating of the pangolin allows it to roll into a tight ball when threatened. It feeds exclusively on ants and termites.

NUTRIENT STORAGE
While in temperate forests a high proportion of nutrients is held in the soil (left-hand bar, above); in the poorer tropical soil, they are held in the biomass (right-hand bar, above). As the scarce soil nutrients are found near the surface, the roots of the trees seldom grow deeper than 26 feet.

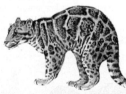

ELEPHANT
The largest land mammal in Thailand, the Asian elephant is now a rare sight, with fewer than 3,000 animals remaining. Most of them are found in the national parks of the northeast.

CLOUDED LEOPARD
Living in tall secondary forests, the clouded leopard is a nocturnal predator that feeds on pigs, deer, monkeys and smaller animals.

NUTRIENTS RECYCLING
Different forms of plants and animals have evolved in harmony on the forest floor to recycle decaying materials such as leaves and tree trunks, returning valuable nutrients back to the soil. In time these are taken up by other plants, sustaining the incredible diversity that exists in the forest and thereby continuing the natural cycle that began millions of years ago. The harmony and natural balance of this network is threatened by deforestation, shifting agriculture and human intrusions.

19

BROWN-THROATED SUNBIRD

The orchid family is the largest of the flower kingdom, with more than 35,000 wild species and as many hybrids. Thailand's tropical forests ▲ *238–40* and mangroves ■ *22–3* host an amazing diversity of both terrestrial and epiphytic species, presenting a vast array of shapes, sizes, vibrant colors and intoxicating perfumes. Breeders in orchid farms ▲ *290* continually produce new hybrid species using artificial cross-pollination and propagation methods. Their creations are in great demand for the international cut flower market.

VENUS' SLIPPER
This yellow terrestrial orchid is found growing at low altitudes in limestone crevices near the coastal areas of Thailand, southern Burma and Cambodia.

CORYBAS
This terrestrial orchid named after the *Corybas*, the dancing priests of Phrygia, because of its helmet-shaped sepals, lives in the dark undergrowth of the rain forest. It thrives on the abundant supply of moisture and nutrients of the forest soil.

CYMBIDIUM SIAMENSIS
Cymbidium orchids, from the Greek word *kymbion,* which means boat-shaped, were praised by Confucius as the "queen of all flowers." Although such orchids occur all over Asia, this particular ivory species is native to Thailand where it grows at altitudes of between 1,000 and 2,500 feet.

GARDENS IN THE AIR
Falling organic litter lodged between the tree branches forms a rich soil in which epiphytic plants such as bromeliads and orchids grow. Orchids are non-parasitic species. Their elaborate structure allows them to make the most of the supply of rainwater and nutrients without damaging their host plants.

Sepal
Petal
Anther cap
Labellum

VANDA COERULEA
This spectacular blue orchid native to Thailand belongs to the Vanda family. It grows at high altitudes between 3,300 feet and 4,600 feet, and can be found in the mountains around Chiang Mai ▲ 290.

SUNBIRDS
In their search for nectar, sunbirds carry pollinia from flower to flower thus acting as pollinating agents.

PSEUDO-COPULATION
Some orchids produce an aroma similar to that of female organs of insects, thus deceiving their pollinators. Lured into mating with the flower, the insect shakes the pollinia out of the anther cap, involuntarily causing pollination.

POLLINATION
Bees and wasps are the most common pollinators of wild orchids. When the insect lands on the labellum, the pollinia adheres to its body. It is then transferred to other flowers.

AERIDES ODORATUM
The poetical name of this orchid, "children of the air", refers to its epiphytic habit. Also known as the "foxtail orchid," this fragrant flower comes in various shades of ivory, magenta and pink.

BULBOPHYLLUM CONCINNUM
A common sight in mangroves and wetlands, this flower belongs to the largest group of orchids. Its rhizomes creep on tree roots and branches, producing clusters of golden spiky petals.

CATTLEYAS
This variety of orchids, named after William Cattley, the first horticulturist successfully to grow epiphytic orchids in England, is the most popular orchid in cultivated collections. Orchidists and breeders, artificially cross-pollinating species within a genus or intergenetically, can create the most dazzling hybrids, many of which are developed for the cut flower market.

DENDROBRIUM TRIGONOPSIS
As indicated in its name *dendrobrium* from the Greek word *dendron* (tree), this aerial species grows on trees. Though its habitat ranges from the tropical forests of Malaysia to the snow-covered peaks of the Himalayas, this flower is mostly found in the depth of the jungles of Thailand, Burma and Laos.

Mangroves and intertidal mudflats are of great conservation value in Thailand, helping sustain valuable inshore fisheries and protecting the coast from erosion. With a constant supply of water, sunlight and nutrients the rate of growth of mangrove trees is very fast. The most extensive and species-rich mangrove ecosystems are found along the west coast of the peninsula ▲ *218–19, 220, 224*. There are also several important mangroves and mudflats on the east coast, as well as in the inner gulf, although large areas have been converted to prawn ponds. The total area of mangrove forest is about 2,300 square miles most of which are along the west coast.

The fruit of the Nipa palm is edible. The Nipa borders waterways in the mangrove deltas off the open sea and usually covers much of the swamp area.

Hardy fruits of *Amoora calcullata* and *Xylocarpus gremata*. There are few flowers or fruits in the mangrove forest.

Crab-eating macaques are one of the numerous mammal species living in this environment.

Charcoal making is one of the many threats facing the coastal mangrove forest. Shrimp farming is another.

Free form furniture, made from the roots of the mangrove.

Cross-section of the mangrove coastline. The swamps are criss-crossed by tidal channels, which are often bordered by the Nipa palm. The mangrove's enormous root systems are the dominant feature of the habitat. It extends to the low tide mark, below which the roots cannot obtain enough oxygen for growth. Where the ground rises above high tide mark level away from the open sea, the surroundings gradually assume the character of lowland rain forest.

A mangrove coast in southern Thailand, covering sinking limestone ranges millions of years old. As the sea level changes, the mangrove forest cover advances or retreats.

The Brahmini kite circles above the mangrove.

This large estuarine crocodile is rarely seen. Forest clearance and aquaculture projects are responsible for its dwindling numbers ▲ 191.

The mangrove snake is particularly adapted to this unusual habitat and is found just above the water level.

The collared kingfisher (1), gray heron (2) and little cormorant (3) are bird species common in the coastal swamps and mud flats.

Rhizophora mucronata produces pointed spikes (right) that form effective instant seedlings. Equipped with tiny leaves at the top end, they drop off the parent into the mud below and take root at once. Apart from this unusual mode of propagation, *Rhizophora mucronata* produces conventional seeds as well.

Below the water level, the mud and the roots give shelter to a plethora of marine life, including fish, crabs and molluscs.

■ RICEFIELDS

CRIMSON HERON

An extraordinary amount of human energy is invested in producing the rice crop throughout the year. Rice plays an important role in the daily lives of the people, providing the staple diet for the Thai population as well as being a major export crop. Many cultural rituals are closely tied to the cultivation of rice and complex calculations are made to predict forthcoming rainfall patterns and the bounty of future crops. Little has changed in the ricefields of Thailand ▲ *246–7* over the centuries and, in addition to providing an important wildlife refuge for a large number of species, they also remain a source of great spiritual and intellectual inspiration.

PAPAYA TREES
All available land is cultivated. Papaya and banana trees are frequently planted on the verges of the ricefields.

BEAST OF BURDEN
Although mechanical means of plowing ricefields are now available, most farmers still prefer traditional means of cultivation involving the use of the water buffalo as a general beast of burden. Known locally as the "Asian tractor", the water buffalo is also an important source of milk and meat for many people. Its hide is used in clothing and its dung is collected as a fertilizer or as a source of fuel for burning.

1. PREPARING THE LAND
The farmer and the water buffalo drag a heavy plow to loosen up the water-logged soil, and their trampling actions also help to redistribute the valuable nutrients stored in the soil. Prior to planting, a heavy log is pulled across the muddy base to prepare a firm bed for the young seedlings.

LIFE AT THE WATER'S EDGE
The ricefield provides an ideal habitat for reptiles, fish and amphibians. Many of the fields are deliberately stocked with carp and catfish, which feed on decaying plants, algae and insect larvae. Frogs also help control the level of harmful insects, thereby eliminating the use of costly and often destructive pesticides.

2. TRANSPLANTING THE SEEDLINGS
Once the ricefield has been flooded and suitably prepared, bunches of bright green seedlings are transplanted from the tiny nursery beds where they were raised. This work is done entirely by hand, people laboring all day to set out row upon row of tender young plants. The softened mud base facilitates the planting process and seedlings quickly take root in this habitat.

The bright green seedlings clustered in ricefields prior to transplanting and the sun-drenched fields of rice that await harvesting are familiar sights in Thailand.

BIRDS OF THE RICEFIELDS

The ricefields provide a rich feeding haven for a variety of birds. Some of the most common of these are the munias, a group of small, seed-eating birds that feed on ripening rice. These, in turn, attract aerial predators such as the black-shouldered kite and marsh harrier, which may also feed on amphibians such as frogs.

EGRETS AND HERONS

The rich aquatic and terrestrial life of the ricefields attracts large numbers of herons and egrets in all seasons. Although egrets and herons usually feed alone, they often roost together, which probably assists in detecting predators ▲ 208.

3. RIPENING

Through careful management of the water level, the plants flourish, grain heads develop and swell as the sun ripens the swaying stalks. This stage of growth is the least demanding in terms of labor input, but there are always water levels to be controlled, dykes to be repaired and nursery beds to be tended elsewhere in the ricefields.

COMB DUCK

The comb duck is a frequent visitor to ricefields and it nests on the edges of wooded marshland. It flies with broad wing beats.

HARVESTING THE RICE AND THRESHING

The long stalks of ripe corn are harvested and then beaten over a drum to dislodge the grains from the chaff. Winnowing sifts off any remaining waste while the plump rice grains are dried in the sun before being stored.

4. HARVESTING

The harvesting of a paddy crop marks the end of a long period of hard labor and no time is lost in cutting the ripened golden stalks lest wild animals or inclement weather threaten to destroy the season's efforts. Rice stalks are harvested using a sharp sickle; the cutter lays the stalks tenderly on the ground in his wake. Later these will be collected and stacked, prior to threshing.

PESTS IN THE RICEFIELDS

The ricefield mouse and rat are common inhabitants of all ricefields and open grasslands, feeding on fallen grain, seeds and insects. The rat may also feed on rice plants and may be a pest in granaries where the dry grain is stored.

TRADITIONAL SILK LOOM

Several spectacular species of butterfly are found in the mountain ranges of north and northwest Thailand, near Chiang Rai, Pai, Mae Hong Son, and in the national park northwest of Chiang Mai ▲ 273. In the cultivated zones, ricefields and rubber plantations, few species have survived the process of deforestation. The entire zone from Lampang to Chiang Mai is undergoing reforestation but the plant species being used do not produce a habitat favorable to the reestablishment of butterfly species. Certain "cosmopolitan" species of butterfly can travel for miles across oceans. The first explorers to arrive in Siam found several well-known European, African and North American species.

15–18 d
Ecdysis

10–12 da
Hatching

ATROPHANEURA POLYEUCTES
A jungle butterfly that sometimes ventures into towns and villages.

STICOPHTALMA CAMADEVA
This is the biggest diurnal butterfly in Thailand and South East Asia with a wing span of 5.6 inches.

TROIDES AEACUS
The *Troides aeacus* reigns in the north. Its caterpillar deters birds and insectivorous reptiles by living on a poisonous liana, the *aristoloche,* which protects it against predators. This butterfly has recently been designated an endangered species.

PAPILIO ARCTURUS
The black part of the wings of the *Papilio arcturus* looks as though it is sprinkled with emerald dust. This spectacular butterfly can often be seen along mountain tracks.

ACHERONTIA LACHESIS
The *Acherontia lachesis,* which lives in the northern mountains, is the Thai cousin of the European "death's head hawk moth" (*A. atropos*). It is a nocturnal butterfly and will risk its life to penetrate beehives to gorge itself on the honey.

BHUTANITIS LIDDERDALI
This butterfly is from the northern mountain valleys. At rest, its hind wings are covered by the fore wings, hiding their magnificent colors and allowing the insect to blend with its surroundings.

TERINOS CLARISSA
The *Terinos clarissa* belongs to the *nymphalides* family. This small butterfly is mauve, varying in shade with the angle of vision. It flies discreetly close to the ground in the deep forest and at rest it is camouflaged against the vegetation.

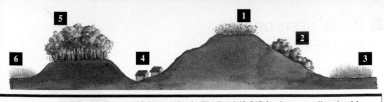

4–6 days
Silk spinning

**LIFE CYCLE
OF THE
MULBERRY
BOMBYX**

4–12 days
Pupation

days
genesis

1. Doi Inthanon, highest point in Thailand (8,547 feet), poor soil and cold climate where small mountain butterflies are found.

2. Chedi (6,600–8,250 feet), few cultivated areas and little highland forests. Habitat of small butterflies.

3. Chiang Mai plains, *pierides* and swallow-tail butterflies.

4. Mae Chaem, cultivated valley (1,580 feet) with a wide range of butterflies within the low vegetation.

5. Mae Surin rain forest (330–4,950 feet), privileged home to the most beautiful specimens in Thailand.

6. Khun Yuan (1,650–3,300 feet), a zone where rain forest butterflies live side by side with the small valley species.

THE SILK INDUSTRY

The silk industry in Thailand is now located mainly in the northeast of the country. The larvae of the *Mulberry bombyx*, probably the best-known Thai moth, produce silk. This moth does not exist in the wild. Having long been domesticated, it has even lost the ability to fly.

After ecdysis the silkworms are placed on bamboo trays, known as *jo*, where they secrete a fibrous slime that protects them until metamorphosis.

A mural painting from Wat Phumin in Nan Province, showing a Lanna lady selecting spools of yarn while working at a Thai frame loom.

The filaments are spun and eventually skeins are produced. Each cocoon yields about 2,000 feet of usable thread (*mai luad*), although in total a mature cocoon can contain over 1 mile of thread in about 30 layers. Silk made from thread still coated with sericin is called raw silk. Natural silk or *tussah* is the silk produced by undomesticated caterpillars living in trees.

Cocoons are taken from the *jo* and boiled to remove the sticky sericin coating the silk filaments.

The raw thread is bright yellow. Before weaving it is washed first in a herbal mixture made from the bark and leaves of the banana tree, and then in a *ke* solution made from a thorny vine that is commonly found on hillsides, then dyed. Traditional dyes used include lac, indigo, krajai berries and thalang roots. To the east of Chiang Mai, on the way to Charoen Muang, it is possible to visit a *magnanerie* (silkworm rearing house) and to taste chrysalides which have been grilled after the removal of their silk filaments.

■ BIRDS' NESTS OF SOUTHERN THAILAND

Thailand is one of the major producers of edible birds' nests, a delicacy in Chinese cuisine dating as far back as the Ming and Qing dynasties of the 17th century. The swiftlets (*nok kin lom*) nest in caves along the southwestern coast and on the offshore islands ▲ *215, 223*. They find their way by echolocation. A series of up to 20 audible clicks per second is emitted and the echoes reflecting off the walls enable the birds to maneuver in the darkness. Already an expensive delicacy, these birds' nests could become more expensive as overcollection threatens the normal cycle of nest building.

TYPES OF NESTS
The black nest swiftlet (*Aerodramus maximus*) uses its black feathers to build nests, hence the name "black nests." In contrast, the white nest swiftlet (*Aerodramus fuciphagus*) builds its nest wholly with saliva.

GRADES OF BIRDS' NESTS
The price of edible birds' nests varies according to their quality. White nests, wholly made of saliva, are more expensive. The best birds' nests are the first ones built during the breeding season. Thicker and translucent white, they expand to almost 20 times their volume upon soaking. Second and third nests are of lower grade, appearing dirtier and thinner.

COLOR AND QUALITY
Some supposedly high-quality nests are reddish. However, the coloration bears no relation to blood and may have leached into the nest from the substrate.

NEST COLLECTING TOOLS

COLLECTING BIRDS' NESTS
In Thailand this is carried out between February and July. Three collections are made each breeding season. Birds' nests are usually found in the lofty and dark interiors of caves. The nest collector, armed with a small torchlight and rope, stealthily climbs up the bamboo stilt that leads him to the nest ▲ *215*.

CAVES

Besides the swiftlets, an interacting community of animals known as troglodytes may be found in the caves. Bats are abundant. Both bats and swiftlets produce guano, which is fed upon by insects such as moths and cockroaches. These insects in turn provide food for other predators such as bugs, centipedes and geckos. The most common predators of the swiftlets and their nestlings are the snakes, hawks and eagles that hunt in the surrounding areas, and the egg-eating crickets.

EAGLE

CRICKET

DRY LONGAN

BUILDING THE NEST

The bird makes chewing and retching movements of the bill and throat, as the saliva is regurgitated and worked around the mouth. Saliva is smeared on the edge of the nest with the sides of the bill. The nest takes shape as a pad of hardened saliva adhering to the wall. Subsequently a rim is added and material is laid down in layers until a small cup-shaped nest is finally formed.

DRY BABY ABALONE

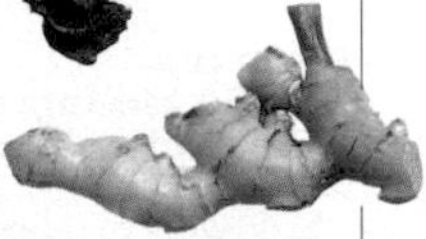

GINGER

HONEY ROCK SUGAR

RED DATES

ROCK SUGAR

SHARKS' FINS

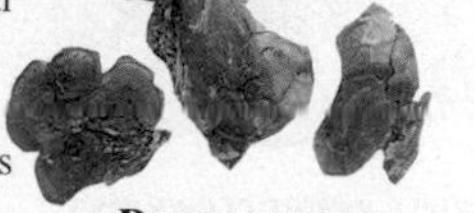

A SOUP TONIC

Bird's nest soup made with traditional ingredients has long been used as a tonic in Chinese medicine, and to protect the body against various ailments. Recent research on the nutritional value of birds' nests has shown the presence of a soluble glycoprotein that may promote growth, tissue repair and cell division within the immune system.

DRY SNOW FROG

■ CORAL REEFS

GREEN TURTLE
Green turtles are exploited for their shell,
flesh and eggs, and their numbers have
been decimated wherever they occur.

The coral reef ecosystem is one of
the richest habitats on earth. Coral
colonies are composed of countless
individuals – polyps – that feed on plankton.
Although coral reefs can cover a large area,
they grow very slowly: it may take 1,000 years
for a reef to grow just 3 feet. When corals
die, their skeletons remain and a new
generation of polyps can grow on top of
them. Each type of coral has its own
distinctive shape, adding further to the
splendor of the reef
ecosystem.

COACHMAN FISH
The name of this fish
derives from the long,
whip-like appendages
that often hang from
its dorsal fin.

SURGEON FISH
Originating in the
Indo-Pacific region,
this species is quite
aggressive.

EMPEROR FISH
This fish has one of the largest territories of all
coral-reef dwellers.

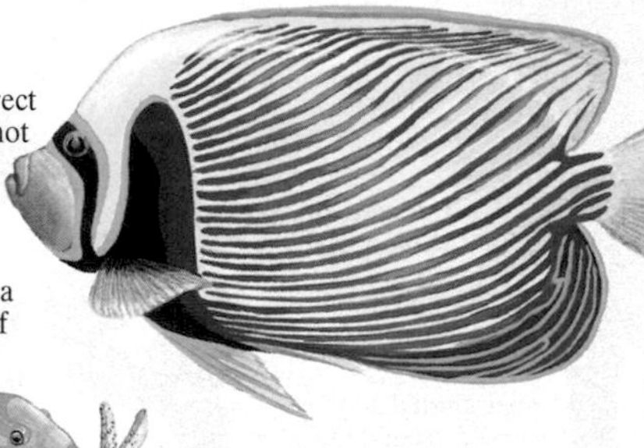

TRIGGERFISH
Its common name refers to an erect
spine in its dorsal fin, which cannot
be released until a second spine
(the trigger) is withdrawn.

PARROT FISH
Parrot fish have large scales and a
typically bird-like beak formed of
fused teeth.

CORAL REEFS AND POLYPS
Coral reefs provide an important source of
food and income to local Thais. A coral polyp is
a soft, almost transparent animal that builds its
skeleton outside its body. Polyps feed at night by
extending their tentacles, each of which is armed with a
series of stinging cells that paralyse any passing prey.
The moray eel is a key predator in the reef
ecosystem; it hides in crevices, lunging out to
seize unsuspecting fish.

TRIPLE BANDIT CLOWN FISH
This fish lives in close association
with sea anemones.

HISTORY

PEOPLE OF SIAM

Thailand is a mosaic of peoples and cultures, and yet it has never suffered any serious racial conflict. This may be due to the fact that the central Thai have ruled more by consensus than by force. The widespread practice of Theravada Buddhism has also promoted racial harmony.

THE THAIS. The Thais belong to the Tai group and migrated into the Chao Phraya River valley at the beginning of the first millennium. When they first arrived, the region was inhabited by Austro-Asiatic groups speaking

Mon and Khmer; the present-day Thais are the product of the assimilation and fusion of these three groups. Many Thais still live in southern China (particularly in Yunnan, Guangdong, and Guangxi). Today four subdivisions of Thais are recognized in the country: the central Thais (from the region between Sukhothai and Phetchaburi), who speak the standard Thai taught in schools; the Pak Isan Thais (a mixture of Thai and Khmer in the northeast), who also speak standard Thai; the Pak Tai Thais (south of Phetchaburi), who have a darker complexion and speak a dialect largely incomprehensible to central Thais; the northern Thais, who speak a different dialect and who are a fusion of Thai immigrants with Karens and Lawas (Austro-Asiatic). Each of these groups had largely independent histories until recent centuries.

THE CHINESE. As traders, the Chinese arrived long before the Thais. They settled more permanently, at first in coastal cities in the south and then in other areas. The peak period of Chinese migration was in the 19th and early 20th centuries, and they now form a substantial part of most urban populations. Thanks to extensive assimilation, it is difficult to distinguish them as a separate ethnic group.

THE LAOS. Much of the northeast is inhabited by groups of Lao-speaking people – Lao Wieng, Yuai, Yo, Lao Kao and Phutai – who migrated (some were forcibly moved) mostly during the last century and are today among the poorest in the country. Like the Thais, they belong to the Sino-Tibetan group. They are renowned for their weaving skills, and some groups were once distinguished by their dress, rather like today's hill tribes; these elaborate costumes can still be seen during village festivals. Though Buddhist, many still practice older animistic rituals.

THE KHMERS. Khmer-speaking people are also numerous in some parts of the northeast, particularly in Surin province near the Cambodian border. Most of them migrated during the 19th century when Siam occupied a large part of Cambodia. The recent war in Cambodia has driven millions of Khmer refugees into Thailand but many of them are being gradually repatriated.

LANGUAGE
Eighteen million people in Thailand speak Lao.

THE SHANS. The Thai Yai (right), called the Ngiaw by the Thais, belong to the Tai linguistic family and migrated from the Shan states of Burma in the 19th century. Today the Shans are scattered throughout the north, especially in Mae Hong Son and Mae Sariang.

THE MUSLIMS. Thailand's largest religious minority, Muslims are concentrated mainly in the southernmost provinces of Narathiwat, Pattani, Yala and Satun. Most are of Malay descent and speak Malay as well as Thai. Ninety-nine percent of the Muslim population are Sunni Muslims, while the remaining one percent are Shi'ite. Those Muslims who are not Malaysians are probably descendants of Persian, Middle Eastern and Indian traders (left) who had settled in Siam during the Ayutthaya and early Bangkok periods.

MUSLIMS
Approximately 2 million Muslims live in Thailand. There are about 2,000 mosques in the country.

THE MONS. These people, who live mostly in Nakhon Pathom, Samut Songkram and Samut Prakan, are not ancestors of the ancient Mon culture that once ruled over portions of central Thailand, but relatively recent Buddhist immigrants from Burma.

A Karen with traditional pendants.

HILL TRIBES. The majority of the hill tribes ▲ *284, 294–301* in northern Thailand are relatively recent immigrants to the region. Only the Karens and the Lawas (right) were settled in the country prior to the arrival of the Thais. The hill tribes form a minority. In 1983, their total population was only about 416,000. Apart from the Karens and the Lawas, this group also includes the Miens, Lisus, Lahu Shis and the Blue and White Hmongs. While aspects of religions such as Christianity, Buddhism and Islam have been adopted by some hill tribe people, animism is still much in evidence.

PREHISTORY

ROCK PAINTINGS
Several caves or rock faces are decorated with paintings from simple handprints to complete tableaux showing scenes of hunting, fishing and dancing. These could date back to the 4th century BC. Some are easily accessible, like those at Khao Chiang Ngam, 124 miles from Bangkok on the road to Khorat.

PLEISTOCENE. Evidence of Pleistocene cultures, dating from 600,000–130,000 BC, have been found in various parts of Thailand, from Lampang in the north to Krabi in the south. The earliest implements found were pebble tools, followed by early flake tools (300,000–290,000 BC), then by Proto-Hoabinhian pebble tools (140,000–13,000 BC)

TRIPOD
(c. 2000 BC)
This pottery tripod was found at Ban Kao, in the

Kanchanaburi province. It was probably copied from a tin prototype, and is reminiscent of the Chinese bronzes of the Han dynasty.

HOABINHIAN. This term was coined by a French archeologist in Vietnam in the 1920's and covers a period from around 120,000 –2000 BC. The earliest Hoabinhian tools in Thailand were found in caves in Mae Hong Son and Kanchanaburi. In the former, the American archeologist Chester Gorman found tools and seeds of various cultivated plants including betel nut, black pepper, bottle gourd and cucumber. These have been dated by carbon-14 tests to as far back as 9700–6000 BC, far earlier than previously suspected. More sophisticated tools like the polished adze and the edge-ground knife appeared in the cave around 6800 BC Pottery has also been found at the same level.

3000 BC
First civilizations in Mesopotamia.

2700–2300 BC
Egyptian pyramids of Kheops, Khephren and Mykerinos built.

1765–1122 BC
Shang Dynasty.

566–486 BC
Buddha.

219 BC
Hannibal crosses the Alps.

BAN CHIANG ▲ *229*. The discoveries of a prehistoric culture at Ban Chiang, in the northeastern province of Udon Thani, have aroused considerable archeological controversy, with some historians questioning the early dates originally ascribed to the appearance of copper and bronze. Most now accept that the initial dating of 4000 BC is too early but still maintain that the two metals could possibly be dated to between 2500 BC and 2000 BC – later than their first appearance in the Middle East but approximately contemporaneous with copper in China – and that Thailand had a true Bronze Age. Painted pottery found in the burial sites at Ban Chiang and elsewhere in the northeast was produced relatively late in the culture's history, between 1000 BC and 500 BC. The most recent level of the Ban Chiang excavation is dated at around 250 BC.

THE INDIAN INFLUENCE. In the 1st century AD, Indian merchants began arriving in peninsular Thailand in search of new products to trade. They brought with them Indian ideas of art, architecture, religion and government that dominated the south over the next five centuries and later spread to other parts of the country. At first Hindu images were produced, but, from the 5th century onward, Buddhist images appeared in greater numbers, reflecting this new religion, which also came from India.

SRIVIJAYA ▲ *200*. Beginning in the 8th century AD a new, more warlike empire called Srivijaya was established in the southern peninsula, originating from Sumatra. It remained the principal force in the region until the 13th century. Many historians disagree about the exact center of the empire, but one of its important centers was Ligor, or Nakhon Si Thammarat. Wholly Hindu at first, Srivijaya later also practiced Mahayana Buddhism and beautiful images were created for both religions.

DVARAVATI ▲ *158, 160*. What is traditionally called the Dvaravati Period extends from the 7th to 11th centuries AD; a more accurate name might be Mon, for during this period, several Mon kingdoms rose in central Thailand, first at U Thong near the subsequent Thai capital of Ayutthaya, and later at Lopburi and Nakhon Pathom. All three were centers of Theravada Buddhism, the sect eventually adopted throughout the country. The Mons eventually succumbed to the more powerful Khmers.

KHMER EMPIRE. In the 7th century AD the rising Khmer Empire began to extend its power over the northeastern region. By the 11th century it had reached the Chao Phraya River valley. The great period of Khmer monument building commenced with the reign of Suriyavarman I (AD 1002–50) ▲ *230*. The principal religion in the early centuries was Hinduism, which was replaced with Mahayana Buddhism by the late 12th century. Khmer power began to wane in the 13th century.

MIGRATION OF THE THAIS. It is thought that in the 11th century AD Thais migrated in large numbers from Yunnan in southern China, driven by a desire for greater independence and better farmland. They formed two groups of kingdoms, in the north near the Mekong River and further south at the edge of the Chao Phraya River valley.

27 BC–AD 14
Foundation of the Roman Empire.

AD 330
Foundation of Constantinople.

Votive tablet of the Srivijaya era.

AD 348
Buddhist settlements at Dunhuang.

AD 395
Fall of the Roman Empire.

AD 518–907
Tang Dynasty.

AD 571–632
Mohammed

WHEEL OF THE LAW
This wheel dates from the 7th century and is a symbol of the law taught by Buddha.

AD 762
Foundation of Baghdad.

AD 800–14
Reign of Charlemagne, Holy Roman Emperor.

AD 960–1274
Sung Dynasty.

AD 1066
The Norman Conquest in England.

AD 1096–9
The First Crusade.

Soldiers and elephants, in celadon, from the Sukhothai era.

THE SIAMESE KINGDOM

POWER STRUGGLE IN SUKHOTHAI.
In the first half of the 13th century, probably in the 1240's, a Thai chieftain later known as King Intradit joined forces with several other groups, overthrew the Khmer overlord at Sukhothai ▲ 251, 254, and established an independent Thai kingdom of the same name. Sukhothai remained small under its first two rulers; it expanded dramatically, however, during the reign of King Ramkhamhaeng (left), exerting either direct or indirect power over much of present-day Thailand through force and strategic alliances. Ramkhamhaeng is also credited with devising the Thai alphabet as well as a paternalistic system of monarchy that is regarded as ideal even to this day. Aside from its political achievements, Sukhothai is also remembered for its superb Buddhist art and architecture, which were distinctively Thai, and which are still considered the finest ever created in the country. Also notable were the beautiful ceramics produced first at Sukhothai and later at the satellite city of Si Satchanalai. Sukhothai's empire began to fall apart rapidly after Ramkhamhaeng's death and by 1320 it had once more become a small kingdom of little regional significance. By 1378 it had become a vassal state of Ayutthaya.

THE RISE OF AYUTTHAYA. Ayutthaya was founded on the Chao Phraya River by King Ramathibodi in 1350. Over the next four centuries, it grew from a small, fortified city into one of the great capitals of the region, its power reaching far beyond the fertile river valley. The capital fell to the Burmese in 1569, but less than two decades later regained independence under the able leadership of the future King Naresuan, who proceeded to extend its rule over most of the southern peninsula, the north, and both Cambodia and Laos. Relations with Europe began with a treaty between Siam and Portugal in 1516. The Dutch received permission to build a trading station in 1604, followed by the British in 1612. By King Narai's reign in 1656, Ayutthaya already had a cosmopolitan population of nearly a million. The first French Catholic missionary arrived in Ayutthaya in 1662, joined by others two years later. Given land on which to build churches and schools by King Narai, they became an important force in relations between the two countries. The first Thai embassy sent to France was lost at sea in 1681, but a second arrived safely in 1684 and formally requested a French mission to Ayutthaya. The first of these missions arrived in

1685, headed by the Chevalier de Chaumont; a second arrived two years later. A Thai embassy accompanied the first on its return to France, and was received at the court of Louis XIV. Following the death of King Narai in 1688, conservative elements assumed control and expelled many Europeans during the latter part of Ayutthaya's rule ▲ 242–3.

THE FALL OF AYUTTHAYA.

Shortly after King Ekatat assumed the throne in 1758, Ayutthaya was attacked once more by the Burmese under King Alaungpaya. A second invasion led by Alaungpaya's son, Hsinbyushin, succeeded in capturing Ayutthaya, after a siege lasting more than a year. The city was burned and looted by the victors and more than 30,000 of its inhabitants were taken to Burma. Son of a Chinese father and a Thai mother, the future King Taksin was a military officer at the time of Ayutthaya's fall. Within seven months he managed to rally Thai forces, expel the Burmese from the ruins of the city, and establish a new capital at Thonburi, further down the Chao Phraya River.

THE CHAKRI DYNASTY.

In March 1782 a revolt broke out against King Taksin ● 39 ▲ 262, who was thought to have become insane. He was replaced by a prominent military commander who, as King Rama I, founded the Chakri Dynasty and, for strategic reasons, moved the seat of government across the river to a small trading port known as

Bangkok. King Rama IV, or King Mongkut (r. 1851–68, left), is best known as the hero of *The King and I*. To the Thais, however, he is remembered as one of the most far-sighted Chakri rulers, who negotiated important treaties with European powers, introduced modern sciences, and set his kingdom on the path to reforms that undoubtedly helped save it from the colonial fate that befell all its immediate neighbors. During his reign from 1868 to 1910, King Rama V (below), or King Chulalongkorn as he is better known, carried his father's reforms further. He abolished slavery, reorganized the governmental system, and built the first railways. The first Thai king to visit European capitals, Rama V also sent most of his sons abroad for further education. Though forced to concede a considerably large sector of Thai territory to France and England, Rama V was able to preserve his country's independence.

1762–96
Reign of Catherine II of Russia.

1787
American Constitution drafted.

1789
The French Revolution.

1804–14
Napoleon Bonaparte, Emperor.

1868–1912
Meiji Period in Japan.

1869
Suez Canal opened.

RAMA V SURROUNDED BY HIS FAMILY
This portrait is in the Western style.

37

THE LANNA KINGDOM

6TH CENTURY AD
Arab invasions.

571–632
Mohammed.

982
Erik the Red discovers Greenland.

A Bodhi tree at the Pong Yang Kok wat in Lampang Luang.

1099
The First Crusade – Jerusalem taken.

1325
Foundation of Tenochtitlan by the Aztecs.

1453
Constantinople taken by the Turks.

1497
Vasco da Gama discovers sea route to India.

The Ched Yod wat at Chiang Mai, built in 1455.

Northern Thailand, which has a history largely independent from the rest of the country, appears to have been populated by different groups of Thais, who assimilated with local inhabitants and settled in the fertile valleys of the north around the first millennium. Present-day Chiang Saen was the seat of the Ngong Yang kingdom, and was one of the main centers. Chiang Saen ▲ *302* and Payao, another center, were both in contact with India, through Burma, and traded with the Srivijaya empire. The decline of the latter led to the emergence of a trade route to China and ultimately to the birth of a powerful kingdom in the north.

HARIPUNCHAI (LAMPHUN) ▲ *274–5.* Mon immigrants from the Dvaravati kingdom of Lopburi founded the city of Haripunchai in the 7th century, as well as a string of fortified towns around it. Devout Buddhists, the Mons were a key force in the conversion of the Thais in the north and Haripunchai remained an important cultural center for centuries.

KING MENGRAI. Unification of the small northern principalities was achieved by King Mengrai, a Ngong Yang chief of mixed Thai and Lawa blood. Embarking on a grand scheme for conquering the whole region, he founded Chiang Rai ▲ *292*, seized Haripunchai in 1292, annexed Payao and, in 1296, founded his new capital of Chiang Mai. He thus established the powerful Lanna kingdom, which was to last for 600 years before being annexed by Siam. For a considerable period, toward the end of the kingdom, it was in effect under Burmese or Central Thai control ▲ *262, 267.*

THE GOLDEN AGE OF LANNA. The 15th century saw the flowering of the Lanna kingdom, which was powerful enough to host an international Buddhist gathering in 1455. Trade, art and education flourished, despite the occasional feudal battles between vassals and princes. The west bank of the Mekong (today parts of Laos, Burma and Thailand) was also ruled by the King of Lanna.

THE BURMESE INVASION. Quarrels over the possession of

a powerful talisman, an image of the Buddha, led to a Burmese invasion in 1558 and Lanna became a vassal state of the King of Pegu, governed by Burmese-appointed rulers. King Naresuan of Ayutthaya, fighting the Burmese who had invaded Siam, expelled these rulers from Lanna in 1598 and for the next 17 years Ayutthaya remained the dominant power in the north.

THE BURMESE ERA. In 1615, the Burmese King of Ava reestablished control over Lanna, which lasted for more than a century. Actual Burmese presence in the north, however, remained minimal and had very little effect on most of the population. The darkest period in the history of the north began with the rebellion of General Thip, who defeated a Burmese army and proclaimed himself King of Lampang in 1727. His successors eventually ruled in the 19th century, but before that, the King of Ava sent army after army into Lanna and Siam. After the fall of Ayutthaya, Kawila of Lampang and King Taksin of Thonburi joined forces against the Burmese. Having reconquered Chiang Mai in 1776, however, the Thais were forced to abandon the impoverished city. Lanna and Laos were decimated by the endless war; towns such as Chiang Saen, Luang Prabang and Vientiane, previously spared by the Burmese, were destroyed by the Thais to prevent their recapture. The strain, accumulated over many hard-fought battles, took its toll on Taksin and affected his mental health. He became eccentric and cruel toward his subordinates. In 1782, an élite group of officials led by Phya San rebelled, forcing Taksin to abdicate.

THE 19TH CENTURY. Independent but impoverished, 19th-century Lanna was governed by the family of Kawila ▲ 279, nominally a vassal of Thailand, but in fact autonomous. Not until 1874 was a Thai High Commissioner sent to administer the north and during the reign of King Rama V the region was slowly incorporated into the Thai kingdom. Laos, east of the Mekong, annexed by King Rama I during the Burmese War, was ceded to France in 1893, following a show of force by gunboats.

The old walls of Chiang Mai.

1588
Spanish Armada defeated.

1733
John Kay invents flying shuttle.

1769
Richard Arkwright erects spinning mill.

A BURMESE PRINCE
Mural painting at Lampang (left).

1837–1901
Reign of Queen Victoria.

1894
Japan declares war against China.

Chao Kaew Nawarat, last king of Chiang Mai (1911–39).

39

CONTEMPORARY HISTORY

In 1910, at the time of King Rama V's death, Thailand had become a modern nation recognized by the Western world, its boundaries apparently more or less secure. The following 80 years, however, were to be turbulent and marked by momentous events both inside the country and beyond.

FROM RAMA VI TO MODERN LEADERS. The first Thai ruler to be educated abroad, King Rama VI continued many of the reforms initiated by his father. In 1913, a law was passed requiring Thai citizens to have surnames for the first

time; the first university, Chulalongkorn, was established in 1917; the country entered World War One on the side of the Allies; and unequal treaties with Western powers were renegotiated in Thailand's favor.

END OF THE ABSOLUTE MONARCHY. King Rama VI's successor, Rama VII (above and below), inherited numerous economic and social problems. On June 24, 1932, a small group of foreign-educated military officers and civil servants staged a coup d'état calling for a constitutional monarchy. The king, who had already been thinking along such lines himself, granted their request. Later, he became disillusioned and abdicated in 1935, spending the rest of his life in England. Prince Ananda Mahidol, then a boy of 10, was named his successor and a regency council was appointed until he completed his studies in Switzerland.

POWER STRUGGLES. The two dominant figures in Thai politics during the 1930's were Luang Pibulsonggram, later known as Field Marshal Pibul, and Dr Pridi Panomyong. Both men were educated in France. These two leaders held

different views on many issues and were in frequent conflict. By the end of the decade, Pibul had become the country's Prime Minister and Dr Pridi had held several senior posts, including that of Minister of Foreign Affairs.

THE PACIFIC WAR. In 1940, following the fall of France, skirmishes broke out along the borders of Thailand and Indo-China which resulted in the return of areas in Laos and Cambodia to Thailand the following year. Upon the outbreak of the Pacific War on December 8, 1941, Japan demanded free passage through southern Thailand for its attack against British territories. Unable to resist, Pibul granted permission and, further, issued a declaration of war against Great Britain and the United States in January 1942. A Free Thai underground movement was organized by Pridi during the war, not only bringing him back to power but also enabling Thailand to avoid being treated as an enemy nation following Japan's defeat.

THE NEW KING. On June 9, 1946, the young King Ananda (right) was found shot dead in his room at the Grand Palace during a visit from Switzerland. His younger brother thus came to the throne as King Bhumibol Adulyadej, Rama IX, in circumstances that were both tragic and politically explosive.

TUMULTUOUS TIMES. The next three decades saw a number of coups and counter-coups. Accused of complicity in the death of the king, Pridi was forced into exile by Pibul. Though Pridi attempted two comebacks, in 1949 and 1951, both ended in failure and he retired first to China and finally to France. Pibul remained in power until he, too, was overthrown by Field Marshal Sarit Thanarat in 1957. In October 1973 Thai students staged a series of massive demonstrations that overthrew the military government and sent its leaders into exile. Three years of chaotic democracy ensued, but in 1976, alarmed by the unrest and by the fall of Indo-China to communists, rightist elements returned to power in a violent coup in which several hundred students were killed.

A UNIQUE MONARCHY. One of the outstanding forces in contemporary Thailand is the monarchy that has evolved under King Bhumibol Adulyadej (below) following his official coronation in 1950. Though theoretically operating under constitutional limitations similar to those that apply in England, the king has achieved an imposing moral authority rivaling that of his absolute ancestors, largely through an extensive network of royally initiated programs aimed at rural development. Today the king and other members of the royal family spend much of the year outside Bangkok, overseeing such projects as crop substitution for northern hill tribes to replace their traditional opium poppy and improved water resources in the arid northeast. The great respect earned through these endeavors has enabled the king to act as a decisive mediator in times of severe civil unrest, particularly during the student revolution of 1973 and, even more dramatically, during the recent upheaval of 1992 when he made an unprecedented television appearance to effect a compromise between the opposing groups.

1941
Japanese attack on Pearl Harbor.

1945
Atomic bomb dropped on Hiroshima. End of World War Two.

1947
Indian Independence.

1948
Assassination of Mahatma Gandhi.

1950–3
Korean War.

1953
Edmund Hillary and Sherpa Tenzing reach summit of Everest.

1958
Treaties establishing EEC come into force.

1963
Assassination of John F. Kennedy.

1969
First men land on the moon.

MODERN THAILAND. Thailand's recent history has been marked by further military coups, successful and otherwise, but it has also enjoyed steady economic and social progress, particularly during the eight-year premiership of General Prem Tinsulanonda (1979–88). The local communist insurgency, at its strongest in the 1970's, has largely ended, relations with neighboring countries have been improved, and democratic institutions have gained increasing support among the general population. At the same time, Thailand has achieved the status of a "Newly Industrialized Country", with manufactured exports now exceeding agricultural produce in terms of national revenue.

1975
End of Vietnam War.

1979
Phnom Penh, capital of Cambodia, falls to the Vietnamese.

1989
Berlin Wall is demolished.

1990
Iraq invades Kuwait.

There was an apparent setback to national development in May 1992, when bloody riots forced the resignation of the non-elected Prime Minister General Suchinda Kraprayoon and damaged the country's international image of stability. On the other hand, many knowledgeable observers saw this as an encouraging sign that middle-class Thais are no longer willing to accept traditional military dominance in political affairs and thus feel that Thailand will continue to expand its role as a regional power.

The election on September 13, 1992 was a crucial test for Thai democracy. However, the five-party coalition, formed on September 20, consisted of the same partners proposed by Chuan Leekpai, head of the Democratic Party, three months before the election. One important consideration for the new government, following bad press resulting from the 1992 riots and longer-standing worries over Thailand's sex industry and AIDS, is for it to regain international confidence in the tourism industry and further promote the supply of foreign investment. Both factors are crucial to Thailand's future economic growth. The new government is also expected to concentrate on anti-corruption measures and, provided new Prime Minister Chuan Leekpai can keep the faith of the Thai people, the military arm of the law will probably desist from interfering in domestic politics.

1991
Operation Desert Storm liberates Kuwait.

1992
Bill Clinton (Democrat) elected President of the United States.

ARTS AND TRADITIONS

The primary aim of Buddhists is to overcome the suffering of this world by salvation through enlightenment. Mahayana (Greater Vehicle), or northern Buddhism, is found in China, Korea and Japan. Theravada, or southern Buddhism, the only surviving school of the Hinayana (Lesser Vehicle) system, originated in Sri Lanka and incorporates elements of Hinduism and local beliefs. It predominates in Thailand, Burma, Laos and Cambodia.

WHEEL OF THE LAW
Known as *dharmacakra*, the wheel symbolizes the living nature of Buddhist teachings, the perpetual changing of all objects and beings, and the constant quest for salvation. The deer refers to a deer park near Benares, where Buddha preached his first sermon, "setting in motion the Wheel of the Law."

DIVINE KING
This bejeweled image of Buddha shows the identification of Buddhahood with kingship in Cambodia, where under Jayavarman II, Mahayana Buddhism was declared the state religion. This *devaraja* (divine king) cult was introduced by Jayavarman II in the early 9th century and influenced Buddhist iconography in the 11th century when the Central Plains of Siam were under Khmer rule.

A SYMBOLIC ACT
Siddhartha Gautama (563–483 BC), the founder of Buddhism and better known as Sakyamuni or Buddha, was educated as an Indian prince. One day he rode from his palace accompanied by his groom, Chana, while the gods muffled the sound of the hooves with their hands. In the countryside, he cut off his long hair and beard, and donned plain clothes to symbolize his renunciation of the world and decision to become an ascetic.

"MUDRA"
Mudra are the hand gestures found in Buddhist iconography. This 14th-century image of Buddha shows the *bhumisparsa mudra* (touching the earth), made when Sakyamuni called the earth to witness his attainment of Buddhahood.

BODHI TREE

The tree under which the future Buddha obtained full enlightenment was a fig (*Ficus religiosa*). There he sat, vowing not to move until he had gained enlightenment, successfully resisting Mara's assaults. Many temples in Thailand were built around sacred Bodhi trees brought back as cuttings from India by pilgrims.

MERCIFUL BODHISATTVA

Avalokitesvara is one of the most popular Bodhisattvas, who sees all the misery of the world and treats it with compassion, and is often depicted with 11 hands and 1,000 arms, each symbolizing one aspect of the help he can provide.

BODHISATTVAS

In Theravada Buddhism, only a chosen few can ever reach full enlightenment and terminate the chain of rebirths. However, in Mahayana Buddhism, Bodhisattva intercessors and enlightened individuals voluntarily postpone their own nirvana indefinitely in order to devote themselves to the salvation of mankind.

VICTORY OVER MARA

Mara, the god of death, tried to prevent Sakyamuni's salvation, fearing that his own kingdom of deaths and rebirths would be in peril. He vainly attempted to dislodge Sakyamuni from his meditations by sending an army of demons and by tempting him with his beautiful daughters and their voluptuous dancing. But when Sakyamuni performed the earth-touching *mudra*, and the earth trembled, Mara fled.

MEDITATION

It is one of the many ways of reaching enlightenment, a state that can be described in Buddha's own words: "There is a sphere which is neither earth, nor water, nor fire, nor air, which is not the sphere of the infinity of space, nor the sphere of the infinity of consciousness, the sphere of nothingness, the sphere of neither perception nor non perception, which is neither this world nor the other world, neither sun nor moon. I deny that it is coming or going, enduring, death or birth. It is only the end of suffering."

● BUDDHISM IN THAI LIFE

Thailand is one of the most strongly Buddhist countries in the world; 95 percent of the population practice Theravada Buddhism (a branch of Hinayana Buddhism). As Buddhism is the state religion, the King has the right to appoint the supreme patriarch of the *sangha* (Buddhist clergy). General awareness of the way of life of the *sangha* is strong, half the male population has gone through a period of monkhood in their lifetime. Monks are highly revered. In towns and villages the wat (temple) is the heart of social and religious life.

ROLE OF A MONK

Some monks pass their time studying Buddhist scriptures and practicing meditation. Many others, however, perhaps the majority, play an active role in daily life, sometimes as teachers, sometimes as advisors in village disputes. Monks are called on, too, to preside over a wide variety of ceremonial occasions, from funerals to the opening of a new business.

RENUNCIATION OF WORLDLY GOODS

This 19th-century photograph reflects the typical life of monks, who in following the footsteps of Prince Siddhartha, renounce material possessions, pain and passion in pursuit of enlightenment.

ACQUIRING MERIT

Thai Buddhists acquire merit through a number of traditional acts. The most common is offering food to monks in the early morning, while others include presenting robes and other necessities to monasteries, releasing caged birds, and building new temples.

MEDITATION

The purpose of meditation is to cleanse the mind of irrelevant thoughts and enhance concentration on the central aim of achieving nirvana. There are a variety of schools, with different teachers and methods, all with the same ultimate purpose.

BUDDHIST ART

Buddhism has been the greatest source of inspiration in Thai art, producing not only countless images but also temples and their elaborate decorations. The purpose is not to create objects of beauty but to express the piety of the artist and thus gain merit.

MONKS AS TEACHERS

For centuries the only schools in Thailand – necessarily limited to boys – were those in temples, where monks offered instruction in secular as well as religious matters. Despite the growth of state education, senior priests are still regarded as scholarly sources of wisdom; their philosophical books are widely read and they are often consulted in times of crisis.

ORDINATION

At some point in his life, generally just before he marries and starts a family of his own, a young Thai may undergo training as a monk, often for three months during the rainy season. In villages, the entire population takes part in the ordination ceremony, which involves both religious solemnity and enthusiastic celebration ▲288. The *nak*, or future novice, has his head shaved and is dressed in white

robes symbolizing purity; carrying an incense stick, a candle and a flower, he is then carried in a gala procession to the temple, where the ordination ceremony is conducted by resident monks.

47

Short-lived though they may be, traditional Thai flower arrangements qualify as genuine works of art. The object is not to reflect nature but to fashion something that, at first appearance, could hardly be less natural; Thai flower arrangements are often reminiscent of the complex patterns on painted porcelain or intricately set pieces of jewelry. Women of the royal court were celebrated for their skill at producing such creations and the art still continues today in numerous offerings for both religious and secular occasions ▲ 265.

"BAI-SRI"
Bai-sri are special creations used in a number of Thai ceremonies. These are based on a structure of deftly folded banana leaves, which are then further adorned with such flowers as jasmine and sometimes food. *Bai-sri cham*, for instance, has a central banana-leaf cone filled with cooked rice topped by a hard-boiled egg; surrounding it are other cones decorated with various flowers. This is often given as a token of respect by a student to a teacher or presented as a good-luck offering to infants.

GIFT PRESENTATION
Flowers and garlands are used to embellish gifts. This beautiful flower arrangement covers robes and items presented to monks on special occasions.

"JAD PAAN"
Jad paan, or bowl arrangements, are also called *poom*, because of the traditional rounded pyramidal shape, which resembles a budding lotus. The core, 4 to 8 inches high, is made of moistened earth, sawdust, or styrofoam. The entire core is tightly embedded with flowers which resemble multi-colored pieces of porcelain. Bowl arrangements are often used in wedding ceremonies, when they are placed beneath the hands of the bride and groom, to receive holy water poured by the guests.

"MALAI"

Exquisitely fashioned *malai*, or garlands, play an important part in Thai social and religious life. In the most common kind, fragrant white jasmine buds are threaded thickly together, with accents of color provided by other flowers such as roses, marigolds and orchids. There are also highly complex versions requiring many hours of work. Nearly everyone who visits a shrine brings a *malai* as an offering to the resident spirit. Taxi drivers hang a garland from the dashboard to avoid accidents, and Buddhist altars in Thai homes receive a fresh one daily. You are also likely to be given a *malai* if you move into a new house, get engaged, or depart from or arrive at a party.

BASIC "KRATHONG"

Krathong, the elegant little boats set adrift on waterways during the Loy Krathong festival ● 73, belong to the *bai-sri* category, the base being composed of banana leaves folded to resemble an open lotus blossom. This is then decorated with flowers, incense sticks and lighted candles and sent out as an offering to the water spirits on the night of the full-moon in the 11th lunar month, usually in late October or early November. In recent years, *krathong* have been made of colorful papers arranged around a base of styrofoam.

ORNATE "KRATHONG"

According to legend, Loy Krathong originated in Sukhothai ▲ 251, 265, as a palace pastime in which royal ladies competed to see who could produce the most spectacular *krathong*. The same sense of competition remains today, with some creations towering more than 3 feet high in a variety of fantastic shapes. Prizes are awarded to the most imaginative.

49

A wide variety of traditional Thai occasions call for an offering of one kind or another. Some are secular: an auspicious birthday celebration, greeting an honored guest or the opening of a business. By far the greatest number, however, are religious in nature, presented during special merit-acquiring rituals and almost any visit to a Buddhist temple or shrine. The composition of such an offering varies considerably and may range from flowers and symbolic items to food and paper money – all, of course, arranged attractively.

BASIC OFFERINGS
The basic offering made to images of Buddha and on ceremonial occasions consists of incense sticks, candles and flowers, usually lotus buds. The first symbolizes life's fragrance, the second suggests its transitory nature, and the third is a reminder of the impermanence of beauty – all significant concepts in the Buddhist faith.

MONEY TREES
Thod kathin, held at the end of the annual Rains Retreat, are ceremonies in which groups visit temples to present various necessities to the resident monks. Besides new robes and Buddhist literature, offerings may include financial donations, in which case the money is elegantly arranged in the form of a tree that is proudly carried in a gala procession to the monastery. Such trees are often displayed for several days in front of the house of the donor, and anybody can join the merit-acquiring ceremony by adding their own contribution to the tree.

MEALS FOR MONKS
On Buddhist holy days the laity often offers the midday meal to monks at a temple as a means of acquiring. Much care goes into the presentation of the various dishes, which are traditionally displayed on shaped banana leaves and decorated with fresh flowers and delicately carved fruits.

Far older than Buddhism in Thailand is belief in spirits, as well as various gods and demigods. There are spirits who guard individual pieces of land, for instance, and others who watch over villages and capital cities or make their home in trees and caves. The general term for such invisible beings is *phi* ▲ *291*, but special names are given to many who enjoy demigod status. To avoid difficulties and ensure harmony and prosperity, all must be placated, sometimes with a special abode of their own, always with carefully prepared offerings. Such animistic beliefs do not clash with Buddhism; rather they coexist comfortably and often overlap in ways mystifying to outsiders.

DAILY PLACATIONS
To promote harmony and goodwill, the guardian spirit is placated with daily offerings by household members, the most basic being fragrant incense sticks, candles and flowers. Employees and shopkeepers regularly present offerings at the spirit house of their workplace while actors and dancers do so before a performance. Chinese shopkeepers usually have a spirit house for the local spirits and a small shrine painted in red, dedicated to the Taoist gods.

SPIRIT HOUSES
The guardian spirit of a particular compound, whether residential or commercial, is generally provided with a small house on the property; the exact site must be determined by an expert and has nothing to do with esthetic considerations. Elevated on a post, the houses come in a wide variety of forms, some simple wooden replicas of a traditional Thai dwelling, others ornate cement creations that resemble miniature Buddhist temple buildings down to the smallest decorative detail.

ELABORATE OFFERINGS
Spiritual abodes in wealthier compounds are lavishly supplied with a variety of elaborate offerings. In addition to small dolls to symbolize attendants, these may include floral displays, fresh fruits, and culinary delicacies ranging from sweets to full meals, carefully arranged on plates.

The elephant, which once roamed wild in large numbers in Thai forests, has played an important cultural and economic role since the early days of the kingdom ▲ 229. "White elephants" were revered as symbols of royalty; the Thai national flag used to show a white elephant on a red background, until the adoption of the present striped flag in 1917. The kings and princes of Ayutthaya rode into battle on war elephants, and King Rama IV of Bangkok in a letter offered a supply of the animals to US President Buchanan. In the past and to some degree at present, elephants, valued for their skill and their might, provided the main work force in the teak forests of the north.

ELEPHANT TUSKS
While their collection is deplored by environmentalists today, elephant tusks were treasured possessions in the past; some, like the ones shown above, were carved with Buddhist motifs, while others were mounted for display in palaces.

SOUTHERN ROUNDUP
In southern Thailand, as elsewhere, wild elephants were captured by driving them with drums, trumpets and gunfire into stockades, where they were tamed and trained.

TRAINING MANUALS
As far back as 2,000 years ago, Sanskrit manuals outlined precise procedures for capturing and, most importantly, training wild elephants. The manuscript book shown above, written during the reign of King Rama II, undoubtedly drew on these ancient sources, as well as on the practical experience of Thai trainers. While force was sometimes required, the most important part was winning the animal's confidence and affection.

ELEPHANTS IN WAR

Their value in war may well have been a major catalyst in the taming of elephants. About 22,000 supposedly took part in ancient Indian battles, leading the charge, and a 16th-century Burmese invasion force against Ayutthaya consisted of 300,000 men, 3,000 horses and 700 elephants. One of the most celebrated encounters in Thai history was an elephant-back duel between the Ayutthayan King Naresuan and a Burmese Crown Prince in 1592, resulting in victory for Naresuan.

ELEPHANTS IN HUNTING

Kings and royal princes often rode on elephants while hunting, as seen in this illustration from an ancient manuscript.

MYTHICAL ELEPHANTS

Elephants figure not only in Buddhism but also in Hindu mythology. The three-headed Erawan, for example, is the mount of the god Indra, while the *gajasingha* was a lion with the head of an elephant and Ganesha was the elephant-headed son of Shiva and Parvati, regarded as the god of arts or knowledge.

HOWDAHS

Howdahs, or elephant chairs, came in a wide variety of forms. Some were relatively simple wooden seats secured to the animal's back with leather straps, while those for royalty could be ornate, comfortably appointed palanquins. Palaces had special platforms for mounting and descending.

THE WHITE ELEPHANT

White elephants – actually a silvery gray – were revered as auspicious symbols by rulers in the past. Even today, when one of these rare animals is discovered in Thailand, it is presented to the king and kept in a special enclosure at Chitralada Palace, the royal residence. Ten have been found so far during the reign of King Rama IX.

An aspect of Ayutthaya noted by almost every early European visitor was the spectacle of the ornately carved and gilded royal barges, sometimes hundreds of them rowed by chanting oarsmen in elaborate costume. The custom was continued in Bangkok, where new barges were built by King Rama I and used to deliver offerings to monasteries along the river. After a long period of disuse following the end of the absolute monarchy in 1932, the elegant craft have been restored or entirely rebuilt during the present reign and processions have been held on several occasions, most notably during the Bangkok bicentennial celebrations in 1982.

EKACHAI BARGE
There are two Ekachai barges in the procession, used to carry religious items. The prows are stylized horns of *hera*, or horned dragons, the bodies of which are painted in gold-and-black lacquer.

SUPHANAHONGSA
The most important of the barges is the Suphana-hongsa or Golden Hansa – the mythical, swan-like mount of Brahma – in which the king rides ▲ *174*. The present one, built by King Rama VI in 1911, is made from a single teakwood trunk, 150 feet long and over 10 feet wide at the beam; a full crew consists of fifty oarsmen, two steersmen, two officers fore and aft, one standard-bearer, one signalman, one chanter and seven royal insignia bearers.

ADORNMENT
Intricately woven floral wreaths, resembling thick bejeweled necklaces, adorn the prows of the barges during a procession.

CLASSIC FORMATIONS

The royal barge procession held in 1982 was based on the formation shown in a 19th-century manuscript, probably a copy of a much earlier one. The procession extended for 3,220 feet and involved a total of 51 principal barges, all richly decorated, and 2,192 men. In addition, there were numerous smaller craft, known as *rua dang* and *rua saeng*, which acted as outer escorts and attendants; most of these were plain, with slightly raised stem and stern pieces, though a few performed special duties and were decorated with gold leaf. The crews consisted of officers and men of the Royal Thai Navy, who were carefully trained in traditional ways of propelling the long boats.

GUNBOATS

In early times, the barges were used in fighting. They were manned by crews of 60 to 70 oarsmen, or *rua chai*. Later they were armed with cannons protruding through the prow, which subsequently began to be decorated with figureheads from mythology, partly, perhaps, for identification but also to bring good fortune in battle.

EARLY IMPRESSIONS

The first visual impressions of the royal barges, in the 17th century, came in the form of sometimes fanciful engravings that accompanied books written by members of the two French embassies that came to the court of King Narai.

BOAT SONGS

"It was a breathtaking sight," wrote Father Guy Tachard, a Jesuit priest who witnessed a royal barge procession in late 17th-century Ayutthaya. "The sound of traditional chanting reverberated along both banks of the river which were crowded with people waiting to see the spectacular event." The rhythmic barge songs still survive, varying in pace to match the different speeds and strokes of the oarsmen.

"They wear few clothes," wrote Simon de la Loubère of the ordinary Thais he saw in 17th-century Ayutthaya, "not so much by reason of the heat as by the simplicity of their manners." In everyday traditional life, the only apparel for both men and women was a length of homespun cotton that could be worn as skirt or trousers. Silk was reserved for royalty ▲ 228. Despite the growing popularity of Western fashions, many people in the countryside still regard the old-style dress as being more suited to their ways of life.

"JONGKRABANE"
The *jongkrabane* ● 105, a length of cloth was wrapped around the waist then pulled through the legs and secured at the back, was popular with women in the past. A similar fashion worn by men was called a *pannung*.

ADORNMENT
Elegant jewelry – gem-studded brooches, buckles, pendants, tiaras, heavy gold belts and body chains – has been worn in Thailand since the Dvaravati period. An innovation of the Ayutthaya period was the wearing of particular colors

on different days of the week: red for Sunday, yellow for Monday, pink for Tuesday, green for Wednesday, orange for Thursday, blue for Friday, and purple for Saturday.

MENSWEAR
Traditionally, Thai men wore only a sarong, sometimes pulled between the legs to form pantaloons. This fashion survives today in the all-purpose length of cotton called a *phakoma* ▲ 271, which can also be used as a head-covering, a wash cloth, or an impromptu tent for a siesta in the ricefields.

PRINTED FABRICS

In the late Ayutthaya and early Bangkok periods, some pieces of cloth used by the aristocracy, both silk and cotton, were printed in India, using Thai motifs (above) that denoted various degrees of rank. The most popular of these was called *pha lai-yang*, or "designed cloth," and had to meet stringent esthetic requirements; less prized varieties were called *pha lai-nok-yang*, "cloth not according to design," and *pha liang-yang*, "copied design."

"MOR HOM"

A basic item of attire for most Thai farmers is the loose cotton shirt called *mor hom*, traditionally fastened with string at the front. These are dyed dark blue with indigo and worn by both men and women, often with a broad-brimmed hat of woven palm leaf to ward off the sun.

HAIRSTYLES

In former times, Thai men and women cut off almost all their hair except for a growth on the crown, as shown in the above detail from an early 19th-century mural; the remaining hair was compared to a lotus flower. Sometimes after childbirth or on the death of a close relative, women shaved their heads as completely as men did when entering the monkhood. Even today, older countrywomen often wear their hair closely cropped like a man's.

NORTHEASTERN ELEGANCE

In northeastern Thailand, where a sizeable part of the population is ethnically Lao, numerous striking costumes can be seen, particularly during festivals, when the best clothing is brought out. Lao embroidery is a notable skill of the region and is used to adorn sarongs as well as *sabai;* the latter are long pieces of cloth about a foot wide that are draped diagonally over the shoulder and fall to the waist.

NORTHERN "PASIN"

In northern Thailand *pasin,* as women's sarongs are called, have horizontal stripes and richly decorated areas at the bottom; on silk *pasin* the decorations are often in gold brocade, a craft for which the region is noted. Certain bright color combinations are deemed appropriate only for young, unmarried girls, while older women wear more subdued hues like dark blue and purple. Extending almost to the ankles, *pasin* are worn tightly tucked around the waist and often further secured with a belt.

TATTOOS

Tattoos are worn by Thai men less for esthetic purposes than to ward off a variety of dangers and bring good fortune; on some men of the far north

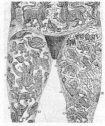

elaborate designs of auspicious animals once covered large areas of the body, almost like a suit of clothing. The practice has declined in modern times, but still it has its adherents and master tattooists command great respect from believers.

Thai royal attire was designed to impress, particularly on ceremonial occasions when the king, sitting high on his throne, wore so many ornaments and jewel-encrusted robes that he resembled a statue more than a living man.

Royal children wore similarly elaborate clothing on important occasions, such as the top-knot cutting ceremony when they came of age. The costumes of court officials – including the patterns of the silk they wore and the accessories they carried – usually varied according to their rank.

Each costume was strictly prescribed by royal order.

A KING IN STATE

Despite a few Western innovations, full ceremonial dress for royalty has changed remarkably little from the ancient past, as demonstrated in this photograph (left) of King Rama VI (1910–25). Prominent among its features are the tiered Great Crown of Victory with wing-like appendages on either side, a tight-fitting, high-necked tunic and trousers of gold-brocaded silk, special slippers and a richly embroidered and bejeweled robe. Some of the same features can be seen on images of the Buddha in royal attire made in the late Ayutthaya and early Rattanakosin periods.

DRESSED FOR THE OCCASION

At important ceremonies, princes would wear clothing and jewelry similar to that of their elders.

> «HIS COSTUME CONSISTED OF A PAIR OF TROUSERS, A SHORT
> BROWN JACKET OF SOME THIN MATERIAL, AND SLIPPERS;
> ON HIS HEAD HE WORE A LITTLE COPPER HELMET…
> AND AT HIS SIDE, A RICH SABRE.» HENRI MOUHOT

TONSURE CEREMONY
In the past, both boys and girls had shaven heads except for a tuft of hair on the crown. The cutting of this top-knot marked their official coming of age and, especially in the palace, was accompanied by elaborate ceremonies that extended over several days.

A ROYAL PRINCE
Royal princes of the mid-19th century wore rich gowns and sarongs of silk, the patterns of which were forbidden to those of lesser rank. Imported cloth from China and Japan was highly esteemed because of its comparative rarity, but Cambodian and Laotian silks were also prized. The gilded, broad-brimmed hat came into fashion during the Ayutthaya period, probably as a result of foreign influence.

A KING AND QUEEN
It was during the reign of King Rama IV, shown here with one of his queens, that Western fashions first appeared in royal circles. When British photographer John Thompson was invited to take some royal photographs in 1865, the King posed for one in "a sort of French Field Marshal's uniform" as well as others in more traditional dress.

WESTERN INFLUENCE
Western dress became widespread under King Rama V, shown on the right, the first Thai ruler to travel abroad and experience European culture at first hand. Men of the court adopted European suits and uniforms so enthusiastically that within a short time the old Thai costumes had virtually disappeared in palace circles.

ROYAL REGALIA
The royal regalia, received by each king on his coronation, include a number of swords, jeweled slippers, a fan and a staff, among other items, most dating back to the first Chakri ruler.

ROYAL WOMEN
The women of King Rama V's court were inspired by the fashions of England's Queen Alexandra, particularly her blouses with puffed sleeves. Sometimes these were worn with cumbersome Victorian skirts, sometimes with more graceful Thai *pasin*, or sarongs.

● SPECIAL ATTIRE

As well as the clothing already described as being worn by royalty and ordinary people, both past and present, there is another category in Thailand: that of special attire, real and imagined. The real includes the saffron robes prescribed for monks, a familiar sight in and out of Thailand's numerous temples, as well as certain military uniforms and costumes for special ceremonies. The imaginary takes in most of the early Western views of Thailand and its people, some recorded on the scene but many executed later by artists more influenced by fantasy than by a desire to portray reality.

A MONK'S ROBES
After ordination, a monk discards the clothing of the outside world and adopts priestly robes made of saffron-colored cotton cloth. These consist of three pieces of cloth, one worn sarong-like around the waist, another as a shoulder sash, and a third long enough to envelop the entire body. Only the first two are worn inside the monastery. New priests are instructed in the prescribed way of tying the robes. Vegetable dyes were traditionally used, but today most cloth is dyed with chemicals.

A MONK IN FULL ROBES
This old engraving shows a monk wearing the full set of three robes and standing near one of the gilded, tiered parasols seen in Buddhist temples.

SOLDIERS
Military uniforms have changed considerably over the years, becoming more Westernized. The soldier shown above is wearing one favored in late Ayutthaya and early Bangkok.

CEREMONIAL COSTUME
The figure on the right is dressed in one of the ornate costumes worn during the plowing ceremony, an ancient Brahminic ritual that originated in Ayutthaya to mark the beginning of the rice-planting season. It is similar to a court costume, consisting of a tall hat, richly brocaded tunic and pantaloons, and a semi-transparent gown trimmed with gold brocade. The ceremony was revived by the present king and is held annually in Bangkok during May at Sanam Luang, across from the Grand Palace.

THE AMBASSADOR'S HAT
In 17th-century French engravings of Ayutthaya, Thais are often shown wearing what some called the "ambassador's hat," known thus because it was worn by the three ambassadors who were received at Versailles. In reality, such a costume was never worn by commoners.

THE ORIGINAL HAT
An original specimen of the ambassador's hat is preserved at Lopburi National Museum.

A MANDARIN
The figure, from Simon de la Loubère's account of his visit to 17th-century Ayutthaya, is labeled "A Siamese Mandarin" and shows a silk *pannung* tucked between the legs, a blouse and an ambassador's hat.

AMBASSADOR'S ATTIRE
One of the ambassadors who were received by Louis XIV in Paris is shown above.

THAI AMBASSADORS AT VERSAILLES
The three Thai ambassadors who were received by Louis XIV in 1686 at Versailles caused a sensation, because of the lavish gifts they brought and also because of their exotic dress. Thai motifs appeared on French textiles and tapestries and their fancy costumes became the subject of endless engravings and calendars.

The earliest Thai musical instruments were given names that reflected the sounds they made, such as *krong*, *chap*, *ching*, *so* and *khong*. Later more complex instruments were created, many adapted from foreign cultures like Indian and Khmer. During the Ayutthaya period, an instrumental ensemble was composed of four to eight musicians; this was expanded to twelve in the early Bangkok reign of King Rama II. There are now about fifty different types of Thai musical instruments, including many regional variations. Music accompanies most traditional Thai occasions, from the classical dance festivals to folk theater and boxing matches.

XYLOPHONE

Closely akin to the Western xylophone is the instrument called *ranad*, one of the six basic components of most musical groups that accompany classical dancing and many ceremonies. The *ranad* comes in a number of types, some slightly curved and others flat, producing different tones. Its musical purpose is usually to produce variations on the principal melody and the rhythm. The keys are made of bamboo or seasoned wood mounted on a wooden frame.

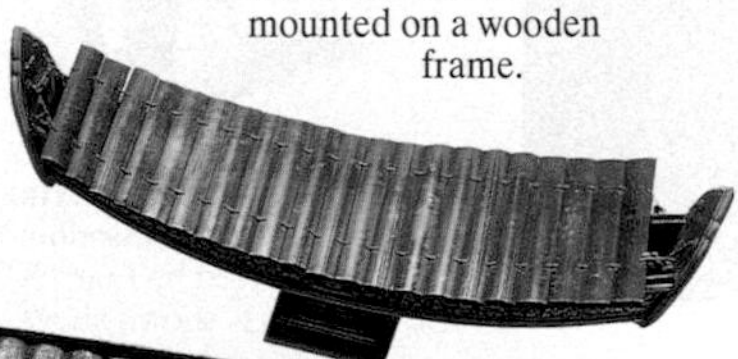

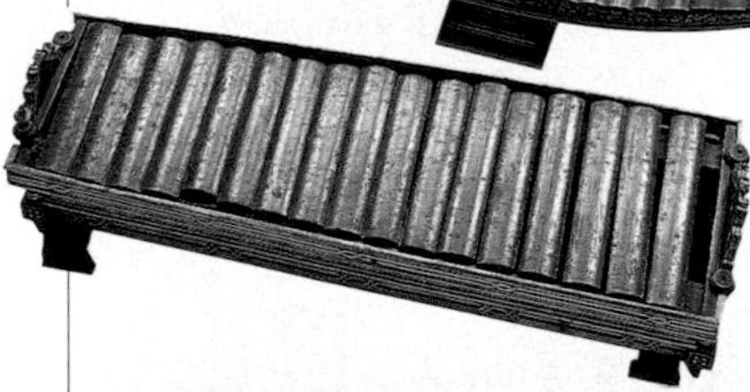

AN EVOLVING ART

Music dates back to the earliest days of the kingdom, as suggested by the stucco frieze below showing a group of musicians in the Dvaravati period (7th–11th century). Dvaravati instruments, the result of Indian influence, were adopted by the Thais, who went on to produce a number of new instruments. These are mentioned in the *Tribhumikatha*, one of the first books written in Thai, as well as on a stone inscription attributed to King Ramkhamhaeng of Sukhothai.

THE LONG DRUMS

The beat of a drum is essential to Thai music, providing a rhythmic excitement that rises and falls. In small ensembles, the most common type is the relatively small, double-ended *klong tad thapon*, but in the north huge drums called *klawng yao*, often several yards long and requiring several men to carry them, are frequently heard at festivals.

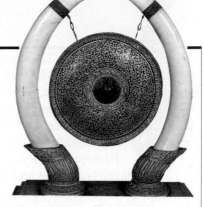

GONG

Large gongs ▲ *274* are often elaborately mounted, like the one above, which is suspended between a pair of elephant tusks. Smaller versions are used in most ensembles, along with xylophones, drums, the oboe-like *pinai*, the circular *khong wong yai*, and a set of small cymbals called *ching lek*. In addition to the role they play in music, gongs were traditionally struck to announce important events.

"KHONG WONG"

Known as *khong wong lek* (small) or *khong wong yai* (large) depending on their size, these consist of a circular series of small gongs suspended on a rattan frame and provide the melody in a Thai musical performance. There is no doubling in parts, so if two are involved only one plays the melody while the other plays variations.

ENSEMBLE

A typical small musical ensemble is called a *phipat* band. The majority of the instruments are percussive but there is always at least one reed, the *pinai*, which sounds somewhat like a bagpipe. In the illustration above, the man on the right is using a flute-like instrument composed of varying lengths of hollow bamboo; this is most often heard in the northeast and is of Lao origin.

STRINGED INSTRUMENTS

The *chakhay* is a thick-necked guitar-like instrument requiring great skill, it is heard only in larger orchestras and played on a low table, almost always by a woman. Another popular traditional Thai stringed instrument is the *saw sam sai*, a fiddle composed of a triangular coconut shell, an ivory neck, and three silk strings; King Rama II was a noted *saw sam sai* performer, so enthusiastic that he exempted from taxation all plantations that grew the triangular coconuts needed for its manufacture.

The classic Thai theater is the *khon*, a masked drama performed in dance and gesture at the royal court; it probably originated in Indian temple rituals and came to Thailand by way of Indonesia. The story lines are drawn from the *Ramakien*, the Thai version of the Indian *Ramayana*. During the Ayutthaya period, men played both male and female roles because the movements were thought too strenuous for women to perform, though by the early 19th-century Bangkok period both men and women were appearing on the stage together. All records of the story were lost with the destruction of Ayutthaya in 1767; King Rama I of Bangkok, together with literary members of his court, wrote a new version in 1798 and later additions were made by King Rama II.

THE "RAMAKIEN"

The *Ramakien* ▲ *151*, on which the *khon* is based, is an epic account in lyrical verse of the triumph of good over evil. The hero is Phra Ram, a king of Ayutthaya and also a reincarnation of the god Vishnu. His consort, Nang Sida, is abducted by the wicked King Thotsakan of Longka (Sri Lanka) and the lengthy drama recounts the ultimately successful efforts of the King and his brother Phra Lak, assisted by the clever monkey-god Hanuman, to rescue her. Performances were often staged on two consecutive nights for a total of more than 20 hours; a *khon* staging of the entire *Ramakien* would require 311 characters and take more than a month of continuous performance.

"KHON" TROUPES

Khon performers are trained from early childhood in the dance steps and gestures which require considerable physical strength and agility. A royal troupe was part of the palace retinue in both Ayutthaya and early Bangkok; later, a number of high-ranking princes had troupes of their own.

NARRATION

Narrative verses accompany *khon* performances. The verses are recited or sung either by a chorus or by a

single narrator sitting with a musical ensemble consisting of woodwinds, gongs, drums and other traditional instruments.

MASKS

Khon masks are creations made of lacquered papier mâché, decorated with gold and jewels, reflecting the personalities of the characters being portrayed.

THEATERS

Traditional *khon* performances were presented by torchlight in palace halls and courtyards with no complicated scenery to distract from the characterizations. Gradually, however, they moved outside the palaces in the early Bangkok period and could be seen in public theaters especially erected for the purpose during festivals and ceremonies. The shorter version of the *Ramakien* written by King Rama II is the most popular, and only selected episodes are offered to contemporary audiences. Even these are comparatively rare, however; the average visitor sees only brief excerpts performed between courses at Thai restaurants catering for tourists.

GESTURES

The familiar story is told through stylized postures and gestures, which express action, thought and feeling. Anger is shown by stamping a foot, Raising the upper lip with a pinch of the fingers conveys a smile and, thus, pleasure. Stiffening of the body with a certain arm motion suggests ambition, while supporting the brow bending and with one hand expresses sorrow. Discriminating audiences decipher the most subtle gestures and evaluate a performance on the basis of them.

COSTUMES

Khon costumes are made of heavy brocades decorated with costume jewelry and closely resemble the dress of royalty and celestial beings in classical Thai mural paintings. The major characters are identifiable by the color of their dress; Phra Ram, the hero, wears deep green, while his brother Phra Lak wears gold and the monkey-god Hanuman wears white. Phra Ram, Phra Lak and Nang Sida usually do not wear masks; Thotsakan, the villain, has a green mask on which small faces are painted to indicate that he is a 10-headed demon and Hanuman, a white simian one with a mischievous expression. Green masks denote high rank and purple and blue masks are for minor characters.

When the *khon* moved outside the limited
confines of the royal palace and became
part of the popular culture, it did so in a form known as *lakhon*.
This is less formal and the movements are less angular, more
graceful and sensual. The stories are drawn not only from the
Ramakien but also from a collection of morality tales called the
Jataka and from a Javanese historical romance known in Thai as
Inao. *Lakhon* is subdivided into several variations, the three
major ones being *lakhon chatri*, *lakhon nok* and *lakhon nai*;
another form of popular theater, relying more on social satire
and pantomime than on pure dance, is the *likay*.

ACTORS

Unlike *khon*, skilled *lakhon* and *likay* performers
are able to earn a living from their talents
outside places mainly limited to tourists. There
are resident troupes of female *lakhon* dancers
at nearly every major shrine, for example, and
their services are often called upon by people
wishing to thank the resident deity for
answered prayers; *lakhon* dancing is also often
a feature of festivals
and private
entertainments.
Similarly, *likay*
troupes
tour the country
presenting their shows at
fairs held in towns and
villages, some of the
performers
becoming major
stars among
rural
audiences.

"MANORA"

One of the principal
sources of *lakhon chatri*
is a Javanese romance
called *Manora*, in which
the heroine is half-
human and half-bird.
Long, curving metal
extensions (below) amplify
her graceful fingers.
Simpler performances of
lakhon chatri can be seen
regularly at popular shrines
in Bangkok such as the *lak
muang* (the city's
foundation stone)
and the one near the
Erawan Grand
Hyatt Hotel, where
supplicants whose
wishes have been
granted pay
resident troupes
of dancers to
perform.

> «THE GREATER PART OF THE PERFORMANCE CONSISTED OF
> MERELY TWISTING THE FINGERS AND HANDS AND ARMS IN SUCH
> POSITIONS AS TO MAKE THEM APPEAR OUT OF JOINT.»
>
> CARL BOCK

GRACEFUL FINGERS
In *lakhon* performances, especially those by women, the hands are particularly expressive, assuming gestures that

are only possible after years of training. The use of long metal nails, which originated in southern Thailand with the *Inao*, can now be seen in other parts of the country; one of the best-known variations is the romantic fawn *lep*, or "nail dance," a mainstay of northern celebrations.

THEATER TRAINING
Training for the Thai dance begins at an early age, with boys and girls at first learning to move their heads, bodies, limbs and fingers to music. Only later do they begin to practice the sixty-eight separate movements that comprise the more intricate alphabet of the dance, each movement having a picturesque name such as "the bee caressing the flower" or "the stag walking in the forest."

"LIKAY"
Likay performances can be seen at most Thai temple fairs. This combines a burlesque of *lakhon* with low comedy, the plots vaguely follow classical lines, with traditional characters, but much of the humor is spontaneous, involving double meanings and puns as well as allusions to local scandals and prominent figures.

Puppets were once an important part of traditional Thai theater. Predating both the *khon* and the *lakhon* was the shadow play, subdivided into *nang yai* and *nang talung*. Introduced from the Sumatran empire of Srivijaya, this was a form of entertainment in 17th-century Ayutthaya. Also seen were *hun* marionettes, little carved figures that enacted classical stories in the royal court. A popular version was *hun krabok* ("rod puppets"), similar to Punch and Judy puppets.

"HUN KRABOK"
A variety of *hun* marionette, *hun krabok* have detailed wooden heads and costumes that conceal a central rod; there are no arms or legs, only hands operated by two sticks hidden within the robe. Chakraphand Posayakrit, a contemporary artist, has fashioned a beautiful new set, which can be seen in occasional performances.

PUPPET DRAMA
Puppets were often dressed in the same costumes and masks found in *khon* dances, though some were used to perform Chinese dramas and were appropriately attired; considerable skill was required to paint the miniature faces and create the accessories. Puppet theater was a palace diversion and because of its slow pace never became widely popular outside.

"NANG YAI"

In *nang yai*, or "big *nang*," the cowhide shadow-play figures are huge, up to 6 feet tall and intricately designed, depicting characters from the *Ramakien* and other classical romances. Each is mounted on two sticks and held behind a brilliantly backlit white screen by bearers who dance their parts to the accompaniment of music and choral singing. Some scholars believe the movements of the bearers later evolved into a stylized dance and eventually led to the *khon* masked drama.

A DECLINING ART

A common form of night-time entertainment in the royal court of Ayutthaya, *nang yai*'s appeal gradually declined, because of the popularity of the *khon*.

"NANG TALUNG"

Nang talung is a more popular version of the shadow-play found at festivals in southern Thailand. The figures are smaller and have one or more moveable parts such as a chin or an arm. Concealed behind the screen along with the manipulators are singers and comedians whose witty contributions to the performance probably account for the continuing popularity of the form.

SHADOW-PLAY FIGURES

Shadow-play figures are carved from the hides of water buffaloes or cows that have been soaked, dried and scraped, then darkened with charcoal or tinted with herbs and berries.

"HUN LEK"

Hun lek, small *hun* marionettes, date from the reign of King Rama V; they were modeled either on characters from the *khon* or from Chinese dramas and manipulated by concealed threads pulled from below rather than from above. These puppets have almost vanished from Thailand's art scene, though one superb set can be viewed at Bangkok's National Museum.

Sanuk, a Thai term usually translated as "fun," is a much-valued pursuit and covers a wide range of activities. Prominent among them are various traditional sports that, despite such innovations as Western football and bowling, have never lost their appeal to the vast majority of Thais, especially in rural areas. During leisure time, almost any open field or festival offers a display of some kind, from the balletic ferocity of Thai-style boxing to more esoteric amusements such as a struggle between two giant horned beetles or multicolored Siamese fighting fish.

"TAKRAW"

In its traditional form, the game of *takraw*, which is also popular in neighboring countries such as Malaysia, involves keeping a hollow rattan ball aloft as long as possible. The circle of players can use their feet, knees, elbows and head but not their hands. Groups of young men start a casual *takraw* game almost anywhere during a break from work or school, demonstrating remarkable grace and footwork.

PROFESSIONAL "TAKRAW"

Over the years, more professional forms of *takraw* have evolved, using nets to separate opposing teams or high baskets through which the ball must be sent, along with strict rules of play. *Takraw* competitions of this kind are often held in Bangkok at Sanam Luang and also at the Asian Games.

BEETLE BATTLES

The large male horned beetle, commonly found in the Thai countryside, becomes aggressive when confronted by another member of his sex in the presence of a female. The ensuing battle, which ends when one of the contestants is overturned, is a popular spectator sport in villages, with wagers on the outcome.

"CHULA" KITES

The detail above, from an old mural painting, shows a *chula,* or "male", kite caught on a temple roof. On breezy afternoons during the hot season, kites of all kinds can be seen in the sky above Sanam Luang, the great oval field across from the gold spires of the Grand Palace.

KITE-FIGHTING

Kite-fights in Thailand are actually a symbolic battle of the sexes. The "female" is a small diamond-shaped kite called a *pukpao,* while the "male", called a *chula,* is a huge star-shaped creation that requires teams of up to seventy men to send it aloft and maneuver it. The object is for one of the *chula* to snare a *pukpao* with a bamboo hook and bring it down in "male" territory; alternatively, the more agile *pukpao* often succeed in looping their lines around a *chula* and bring it crashing to earth on their side of the field.

THE MARTIAL ARTS

As this old illustrated manuscript shows, boxing was an important part of self-defense. In the old days, no gloves were used and both hands and feet were bound in cloth that often contained bits of ground glass for added effect. Several Ayutthaya kings were famed for their skill in this graceful yet lethal art.

THAI BOXING

In modern Thai-style boxing, gloves are used but in most other ways it is similar to the sport of the past. Any part of the body, except the head, can be used as an offensive weapon and any part, including the head, is a fair target. The foot is the most effective of all, usually swung in a wide arc at lightning speed.

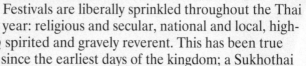

Festivals are liberally sprinkled throughout the Thai year: religious and secular, national and local, high-spirited and gravely reverent. This has been true since the earliest days of the kingdom; a Sukhothai stone inscription, describing an annual merit-acquiring event, says, "They join together in striking up the sound of musical instruments, chanting and singing. Whoever wants to make merry, does so; whoever wants to laugh, does so." Today Thais seize almost any occasion for a chance to don their best clothes and celebrate, whether it be one of the several milestones in the Buddhist calendar or merely some notable village event.

PLOWING CEREMONY
The royal plowing ceremony, an ancient Brahminic ritual marking the start of the rice-planting season, had been allowed to lapse for many years when it was revived by the present king in 1960. Held every May at Sanam Luang, across from the Grand Palace, it is a colorful event that climaxes with a prediction of the coming harvest for Thailand's farmers.

ROYAL HOLIDAYS
Many of Thailand's annual events celebrate the monarchy and involve lavish public decorations as well as festivities. These include the birthdays of the King (December 5) and the Queen (August 12), the date of the founding of the present Chakri Dynasty (April 6), Coronation Day (May 5), and Chulalongkorn Day (October 23), which honors the dynasty's beloved fifth ruler.

ROCKET FESTIVAL
Known as *bun bang fai*, northeastern rocket festivals combine Brahminic, Buddhist and animist elements and are basically concerned with bringing rain through the firing of homemade skyrockets and high-spirited village merrymaking that go on for two days.

CANDLE FESTIVAL

The beginning of Buddhist Lent, or Phansa, during July, is observed in the northeastern city of Ubon Ratchathani with the Candle Festival, when hundreds of beautifully carved candles, some several feet tall, are carried in gala parades before being presented to local temples.

SONGKRAN

Officially, Thailand begins the new year on January 1; at the same time, however, the old solar New Year, called Songkran, continues to be a major two-day celebration in mid-April. This is a typically Thai blend of solemn ritual and riotous festival. Offerings are brought to various temples, where both the abbot and the principal Buddha images are anointed with lustral water, while homes are given a thorough cleaning and homage paid to senior family members. Outside, pleasure reigns in the form of lavishly decorated parades, beauty contests, and buckets of water cheerfully thrown at anyone passing in the streets ▲ 265, 268.

LOY KRATHONG

Perhaps the loveliest of Thai festivals, Loy Krathong honors the water spirits through the launching of little candlelit boats, or *krathong*, in ponds and waterways all over the country. This occurs on the night of the full moon in the 11th lunar month, usually November, when the rivers and canals are at their highest ● 49 ▲ 251, 268, 288.

BUDDHIST OBSERVANCES

This detail from a mural painting shows the making of miniature sand chedis ● 98, or chedi *sai*, in temple compounds during the celebration of Songkran, the traditional New Year; the act reflects the origins of the oldest form of Buddhist monument. The importance of Buddhism can be discerned in many festivals.

73

Of all traditional Thai crafts, none plays a more significant and continuing role than baskets ▲ *273*. Made from a variety of easily obtainable materials – bamboo is the most common but certain reeds, grasses, palms and even ferns are also used – they were born of rural necessity and serve a wide range of needs: catching and keeping fish, carrying rice, storing household goods and steaming food, to mention only a few. Such baskets are basically utilitarian; at the same time, however, many of them display an undeniable elegance of form and delicacy of workmanship that raises them to the level of genuine folk art.

WATER BASKET
This ingenious device (called *mah* or *timah*), made with palm leaves and fitted with a wooden handle, is found in the south. Water can be scooped from a pond or, with the aid of a rope, drawn from a well.

SEED CONTAINER
Made of lacquered basketry to make it waterproof and also deter insect pests, this seed container is also decorated with stylized motifs and an outside frame of bamboo slivers. It is used in the north for storing seeds that will be sown during the next planting season.

RICE BASKET
Known as a *krabung*, this sort of basket is found in all regions of the country. It is neatly woven with bamboo supports up to its widest part and is used for measuring and carrying rice; four loops on the sides enable it to be strung on a carrying pole. *Krabung* may vary in shape from area to area.

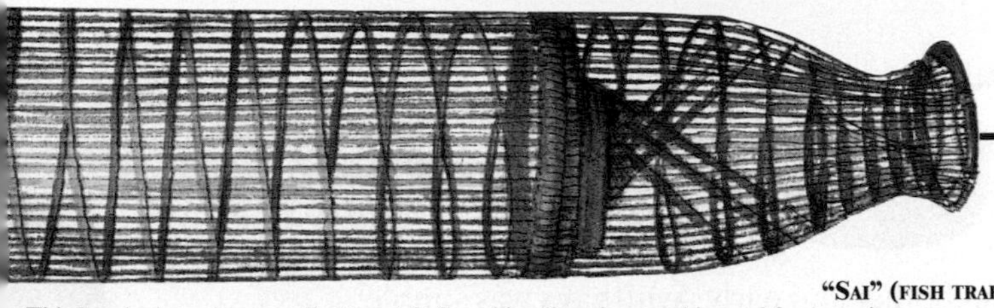

"SAI" (FISH TRAP)

This bomb-shaped trap, called a *sai*, is found in all regions and is used for trapping prawns or small fish, which swim into the opening and are prevented from escaping by bamboo slivers around the inside of the mouth. The average length is around 3 feet. Such traps are placed in ponds or rivers, and are usually fastened to stilts for locating purposes.

GLUTINOUS RICE BASKETS

Baskets like these are common in northern and northeastern Thailand, where they are used by farmers as a kind of lunch pail to carry glutinous rice with them when they go to work in the fields. The wooden foot keeps the basket raised from the ground, while the cord makes it easy to transport; the contrasting weaves add an esthetic touch.

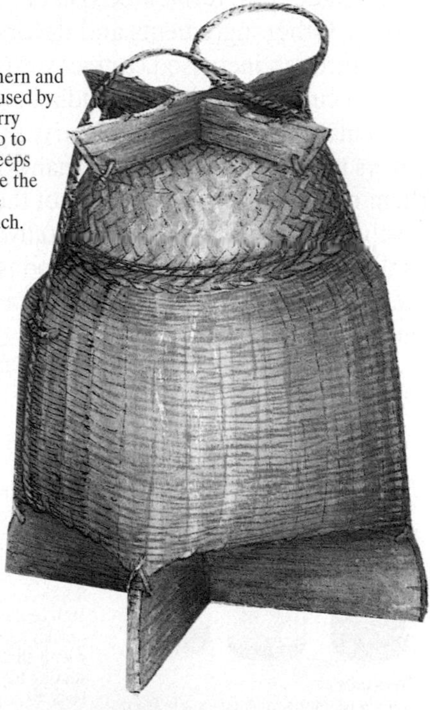

DUCK-SHAPED CONTAINER

All over Thailand, one can spot narrow-necked baskets like the one shown below, cleverly designed to keep a trapped fish alive while preventing it from escaping. The loose string attached at the neck makes it easy to carry.

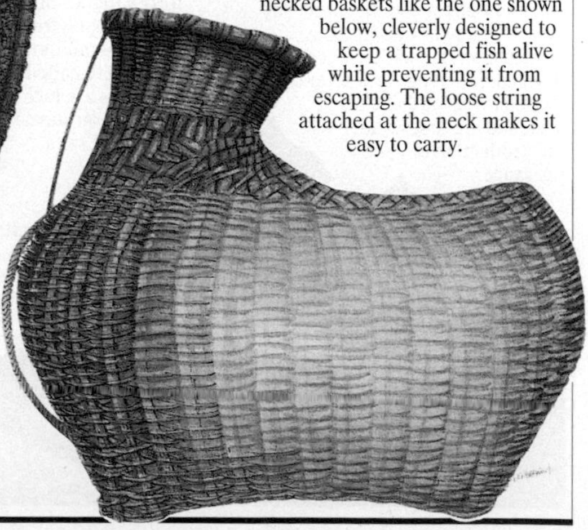

"SARB" (FISH TRAP)

This kind of fish trap is normally found in the northeast and is about 3 feet long. It is placed in streams and irrigation systems supplying the ricefields ▲ 24–5, where it is left to trap any fish that might pass when the ricefields are flooded.

75

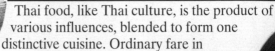

Thai food, like Thai culture, is the product of various influences, blended to form one distinctive cuisine. Ordinary fare in Sukhothai and early Ayutthaya was simple: mainly fish, fresh or dried, mixed with rice, vegetables, a few spices, and a salty sauce made from fermented fish or shrimp. Other ingredients and flavors came through increased contact with foreign cultures, China and India in particular, and also Europe. Today it covers a wide range of dishes, many of them regional specialties; those of the northeast, for instance, are generally regarded as the spiciest; in the south seafood is plentiful and Muslim specialties appear on the menu.

CHILLIES

Chillies, known in Thai collectively as *prik*, were introduced to Asia by the Portuguese from South America in the 16th century and quickly spread so widely that their searing flavor is now basic to numerous cuisines. Thai cooking employs over forty varieties of chilli, ranging from large and mild to tiny bombshells called *prik-kee-nu*, which translates as "mouse-dropping pepper," on account of their shape.

FISH SAUCE

Nam pla is a pungent sauce made from fermented fish, served as a salt substitute in early Thai cooking and still an essential condiment on any table. A number of brands are available on the market, each with its devoted adherents, and several coastal towns on the Gulf of Thailand are famous for the production of the sauce.

ROYAL CUISINE

Thai food that is prepared and served with enhanced elegance is often referred to as "royal cuisine" since it is supposed to have been inspired by palace chefs. Fruit and vegetables are carved into exquisite shapes, with colors and textures carefully matched, turning each dish into edible art.

STICKY RICE

A glutinous variety of rice, or *khao niaow*, is the staple in north and northeastern Thailand, largely due to the influence of neighboring Laos. Traditionally, this is rolled into small balls with the right hand and then dipped into the various liquid dishes. Special woven bamboo baskets are used to serve the rice at tables and to carry it into the fields by working farmers.

A THAI MEAL

A Thai meal, even in rather grand households, is an informal affair. Steamed rice forms the centerpiece – loose-grained in most parts of the country, glutinous in the north and northeast – and the other dishes are placed around it, to be eaten in any order a diner prefers. There may be many or few of these, depending on economic status, but there is usually some kind of curry, a soup and a spiced salad, along with fish sauce, chopped chillies and other condiments, and fresh fruit as a dessert.

NOODLES

Originally introduced from China, noodles often take the place of rice in quick meals supplied by vendors and sidewalk food shops. They come in numerous sizes, the most common being made from rice, flour or mung beans.

FRESH SEASONINGS

Besides chillies, a number of fresh herbs and roots are regularly used in Thai cooking. Coriander leaves and lemon grass are two of the most popular, while others include root ginger, basil, galangal, garlic and the kaffir lime (both leaves and fruit).

DRY SPICES

Black pepper, used as a hot spice before the introduction of chillies, is still a popular dry ingredient. Among the others are crushed coriander seeds, turmeric, cinnamon, cloves and sesame seeds.

THAI FRUITS AND SWEETS

Thailand is blessed not only with a wide selection of delectable fruits but also with some of the best varieties to be found in Southeast Asia. There are more than two dozen kinds of bananas, including a small, finger-sized species noted for its sweetness, as well as mango, durian, pineapple, jackfruit, rambutan, mangosteen, melons, lychee, papaya, guava, fresh coconuts and countless others. Fruit frequently serves as the dessert course, but there are also other choices, including a variety of confections that are eaten as snacks between meals.

STREET SWEETS
Khanom is the general Thai word for "sweet," and many street vendors specialize in one kind or another to tempt passers-by. The woman shown above is preparing a popular delicacy known as *khanom krok*, in which a mixture of thick coconut milk, rice flour, eggs, and sugar is cooked on the spot in a special clay mold.

FRUIT AND VEGETABLE CARVINGS
The art of fruit and vegetable carving was a renowned skill among women of the royal palace and even today many otherwise ordinary dishes in restaurants are enhanced by a radish or spring onion transformed into an unexpected flower. In the hands of a true expert almost any firm-fleshed fruit becomes an object of extraordinary beauty.

PORTUGUESE INFLUENCES
The Portuguese were the first Europeans to open trade relations with Ayutthaya, in the 16th century. Among their cultural influences that still survive are a number of delicate sweets

based on egg yolks and sugar, sometimes spun into a mass of thin threads through a special device made for the purpose.

ORNAMENTAL FRUITS

On special occasions, miniature fruits called *look choop* are made from a mixture of mung-bean paste and sugar, then flavored with fragrant essences and realistically colored with food dyes. The creation of these requires considerable skill, and, like fruit and vegetable carving, was once associated with the women of royal and aristocratic households. Decorative baskets of the little fruits are often presented as gifts on birthdays and other celebrations.

COCONUT MILK

A number of Thai desserts consist of various ingredients in sweetened coconut milk. Thin glass noodles may be served in this way, as well as tapioca, rice-flour dumplings that resemble lotus seeds, and sweet blackened jelly cubes. These are often colored with shocking pink and green food dyes and served with ice.

SWEET SELECTION

Presentation is an important part of the appeal of Thai sweets. Coconut custards and jellies are often wrapped individually in banana leaves, which imparts a subtle flavor as well as serving as a useful container, while egg-yolk confections are rolled into golden balls and cakes are cut into varied shapes. Other popular ingredients include glutinous rice, sweet potatoes, pumpkin, palm sugar, slivers of fresh young coconut and mung-bean paste.

FRUIT AND FRUIT VENDORS

Few Thai street scenes would be complete without a fresh-fruit vendor; his moveable shop dispenses a selection of succulent pineapple, green mango, crisp guava (often dipped into a mixture of dried chillies and salt), banana fritters, prickly rambutans, ruby-red mangosteens, and juicy slices of chilled watermelon.

DURIAN

A controversial fruit among Westerners because of its distinct smell ("like rotten onions and stale cheese," one writer described it), the durian is highly prized by Thais, fetching high prices during its short fruiting season. The creamy flesh is usually eaten together with sweet sticky rice. Numerous hybrids have been produced by Thai growers, bearing such imaginative names as "Golden Pillow," "Frog" and "Transvestite," the last so called because its seeds will not germinate.

79

This spicy dish from central Thailand is typical of Thai cuisine with its use of *nam pla*, chillies and other spices and herbs such as coriander. *Kaeng* is a common type of dish meaning "with spicy gravy" and there are many variations on its basic theme. This particular dish can be made with chicken, pork or beef, and is always served with rice and sometimes with salted hard-boiled eggs.

INGREDIENTS
FOR KAENG PHED PED YANG

1 roast duck, boned and cut into small pieces
3 cups of coconut milk
½ cup water
2-3 tablespoons red chilli paste (see "Ingredients for Chilli Paste," opposite)
2 stalks lemon grass
5 small tomatoes
3 tablespoons *nam pla* (fish sauce)
½ cup peas
4 green or red chillies
10 leaves of Asian basil

RECIPE FOR CHILLI PASTE

Fry the cumin and coriander seeds for 1–2 minutes until golden brown.
Chop the dried peppers, shallots, garlic and galangal finely. Pound all the paste ingredients, including the fried cumin and coriander, until a smooth paste is obtained. Set the chilli paste aside.

RECIPE FOR KAENG PHED PED YANG

1. Cut the chillies and soak them in water for 10 minutes. Cut the tomatoes into halves. Leave the chillies and tomatoes to one side.

2. In a pan, add two thirds of the coconut milk to the water and bring it to the boil. Leave to simmer.

3. Add the chilli paste and stir well. Cook for a few minutes.

4. Add the pieces of duck to the warmed coconut milk and paste mixture. Turn up the heat and cook for 10 minutes.

INGREDIENTS FOR CHILLI PASTE
2 teaspoons cumin seeds
1 teaspoon coriander seeds
8 dried peppers
1 teaspoon salt
1 teaspoon dried lemon
grass
2 tablespoons chopped
shallots
1 teaspoon chopped
garlic
1 teaspoon galangal
1 teaspoon shrimp paste
2 teaspoons water

Mortar and pestle are
indispensable utensils in
Asian kitchens.

6. Serve *kaeng phed ped yang* with white rice.

5. Add the *nam pla*, peas, tomatoes
and chillies. When the peas are
cooked, add the remaining coconut
milk and bring to the boil. Scatter
the basil onto the dish and turn off
the heat.

An old engraving showing Thai
women seated round a mat, eating a
meal with their fingers.

81

Thai is a pentatonal language belonging to the so-called group of Ka-Tai languages that includes Shan and Khun in Burma, Thô in Vietnam, Buyi and Zhuang in Yunnan and Guizhou provinces of China, and long-extinct languages such as Ahom in Assam. Most of the words are monosyllabic. There are five main dialects in Thailand.

Literature is mostly written in the central dialect spoken in and around Bangkok. Due to the early importance of Buddhism, a strong Sanskrit and Pali influence can be felt in the vocabulary as well as in the syntax. One of the main difficulties in learning Thai lies in the various conversational styles. There are several speech levels in spoken Thai, which depend on age, sex and social factors. The first-person pronoun, for instance, can be rendered in numerous ways ranging from the very humble, when speaking to the king, to the most dismissive.

THAI ALPHABET

According to tradition, the first Thai alphabet was created in 1283 by King Ramkhamhaeng, Rama the Powerful of Sukhothai, who based it on Mon and Khmer versions of an old South Indian script. All these scripts are organized around a horizontal line that runs throughout the words. The script of modern Thai follows very strict phonological rules. It consists of 44 consonants and 32 basic vowels that cannot be used alone and are written in close relationship to the consonants in order to create syllables.

MANUSCRIPTS

Old Thai manuscripts were written on two kinds of material: *khoi* paper, made from the bark of a local tree, and palm leaf. To make the latter, the leaves of palm fronds were dried and trimmed to form flat sheets; the calligraphy was etched with a sharp needle and the surface rubbed with ink to fill in the engraved areas. Palm leaf books were used only for religious texts and were rarely illustrated. *Khoi* books consisted of sheets folded concertina-fashion into a series of panels. These were often illustrated and dealt not only with religious subjects but also, especially in early Bangkok, with such secular matters as anatomy, warfare, the martial arts and auspicious elephants.

ARCHITECTURE

1. TEMPLE
2. SCHOOL
3. MARKET AND
   SHOPHOUSES
4. HOUSES ON STILTS
5. VEGETABLE FARM

The typical Thai village is built along a waterway; these form the principal artery of communication in the countryside. Each village is self-contained, comprising a Buddhist temple, a school and a market. Usually, a cluster of Chinese shophouses make up the village market. To stay above floodwaters, many of the houses in the village are built on stilts.

The basic Thai house of the past, rarely seen today, was a simple structure of bamboo and thatch, raised off the ground for protection against floods and wild animals. Most family life took place on a veranda-like platform outside the one or two rooms that served as sleeping quarters. In time, this model evolved into more complex structures of wood, varying in both form and decoration to suit conditions in different regions but always retaining their essential simplicity.

FLOATING HOUSES
Early Bangkok had many floating shophouses, where the family lived and traded. The floorboards in such structures are loosely fitted to allow for movement as the water rises and falls.
▲ 141.

CENTRAL PLAINS HOUSES
The best-known traditional house style is found in the Central Plains. Elevated on stout round posts, it has steep roofs with curved bargeboards and paneled walls leaning slightly inward; the various components are prefabricated to enable easy dismantling and reassembly. The simplest house consists of a single unit with an outside veranda, while those accommodating larger families might have several separate units arranged around a central platform ▲ 246.

ROOF GABLE ("NGAO")
A distinctive feature of the Central Plains house is the elegant curved decoration at the ends of the peaked bargeboards surrounding the gables. Known as *ngao,* it evolved from Khmer architecture and appears in elaborate forms on religious buildings and palaces. A stylized version can also be seen in domestic houses.

PANELING
Paneled walls are a relatively recent addition to the Thai house.

GATE
Houses belonging to more prosperous families usually have a gate, often sheltered by a Thai-style roof that opens on to the central platform. A jar of water is placed at the bottom of the steps so that visitors and residents can wash their feet before ascending.

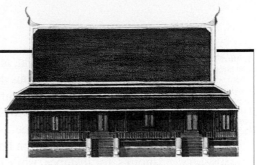

ROYAL HOUSES
Royal houses were similar in design to those of commoners except that they were generally closer to the ground and had more decorative features.

A famous example that survives from early Bangkok is the Tamnak Daeng, or "Red House," ▲ 157 now in the compound of the National Museum. Built by King Rama I as a residence for one of his queens, it was originally in Ayutthaya style but acquired more Rattanakosin elements during several moves. King Rama V presented the house to the museum as a reminder of an architectural style then becoming rare.

"SALA"
Sala, or pavilions, are open structures with characteristic Thai roofs where people relax and watch the world go by. They can still be seen in many parts of the country: near the entrance to temples, along roadsides and canals, and in several private compounds.

THE NORTHERN HOUSE
The northern Thai house differs significantly from its counterpart in the Central Plains. The walls lean outward, giving it a sturdier look, and windows are often smaller. A notable decorative feature, especially in the Chiang Mai area, are the V-shaped designs at the ends of the roof, called *kalae.* Some authorities believe they represent a pair of buffalo horns.

NORTHERN RICE BARN
A rice barn is a component of most traditional compounds in the northern region. Raised on pillars and with a ladder for access, it is a solid structure with few windows, used to store grain.

1. "BOT"
The bot, or ubosot, where new monks are ordained, is the most important building in the wat compound, though it may not be the largest or most impressive. It is always surrounded by eight boundary stones (*bai sema*) demarcating the consecrated area, which is outside the authority of any governing body.

The Thai temple, or wat, is actually a complex of buildings and religious monuments within a single compound, often varying in both age and artistic value, designed to serve a number of practical purposes in the surrounding community. One section houses the resident monks, for instance, while elsewhere there are structures for worship, for meetings, for education, for cremations, for enshrining relics and ashes of the deceased.

The focal point of village life, a wat is erected as an act of merit by the community as a whole or by a private patron and is best appreciated through an understanding of its different functions.

"VIHARN"
(NOT FEATURED)
The viharn is an assembly hall used by monks and the laity who come to hear sermons. The compound shown here is without a viharn; other compounds may have several. Viharns and bots are similar architecturally, only distinguishable by the presence of the *bai sema*.

2. "CHEDI"
A chedi, or stupa, is a reliquary monument where relics of the Buddha or the ashes of important people are enshrined. The chedi is often the main reason behind the construction of the wat compound.

3. BELL TOWER
Most wat compounds contain a bell tower. The bell is rung to summon resident monks to prayers in the late afternoon.

4. MONKS' QUARTERS
The monks' quarters in a wat consist of individual houses where the resident monks live, the largest unit being reserved for the abbot.

5. & 6. "HO TRAI"
Ho trai, or libraries, are usually built in the middle of a pond (5) or on a raised platform (6) to keep the manuscripts away from termites and other domestic pests.

7. "SALA KANPRIEN"
The *sala kanprien* usually serves as a meeting hall.

8. "SALA"
Other *sala* in the compound are used by visitors and pilgrims.

9. CREMATORIUM
Cremations are held in a tall, tower-like structure with steps leading to the area where the body is consigned to flames.

Thai architecture evolved from various cultural influences, adapted and subtly transformed into something distinctly different. The process began at Sukhothai, where the first models were stone-roofed Khmer temples and Mon structures. The Thais introduced wooden roofs and more ornamental features, such as colored tiles and ceramic adornments. Other architectural forms came from India, China and Sri Lanka. During the Ayutthaya period, Thai architecture achieved its own unique style.

SUKHOTHAI VIHARN
No Sukhothai-period viharns exist today in their original form, but as shown by this model displayed at the Sukhothai Archeological Park, they were rectangular, open-sided structures with sloping wood roofs in two sections, the lower part supported by pillars with lotus capitals. Ceramic decorations were liberally used ▲ *253, 254.*

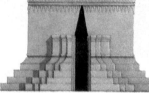

SUKHOTHAI MONDOP
Mondop, like this one at Wat Si Chum in Sukhothai, were cube-like structures, adapted from Sri Lanka through the Mons. The buildings, which had thick brick walls, were used to house an object of worship, such as a Buddha image or a sacred footprint. The name comes from the Sanskrit word *mandapa*, though in India the structure is designed either as an open hall or as a pavilion ▲ *253.*

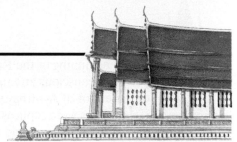

AYUTTHAYA TEMPLE BUILDINGS
Ayutthaya-style religious structures
▲ 245 were designed to impress with
their size and splendor.

A characteristic of the viharns and bots of the period
was a concave curve of the base called *thong sampao*.
Interiors tended to be dark, to emphasize the mystery
and royalty of the Buddha, while elaborate decorations
were used on the outside. The example shown above is
Wat Na Phra Meru, built in the 15th century and
restored by King Rama III of Bangkok.

**AYUTTHAYA-PERIOD
LIBRARY WINDOW**
This window of gilded
wood, adorned with inlaid
mosaic, is in an Ayutthaya-
period *ho trai*, or library;
the late 17th-century
structure was moved from
the old capital to Bangkok.

AYUTTHAYA-PERIOD DOORS
Shown here are doors at Wat
Yai Suwannaram in
Phetchaburi, which date from
the Ayutthaya period.
Beautifully carved and gilded,
they are particularly fine
examples of the graceful curves
that characterize Ayutthaya
style.

**AYUTTHAYA-PERIOD
SLIT WINDOWS**
Windows with narrow
openings, like the one
shown here from Wat Na
Phra Meru in Ayutthaya,
were of Khmer origin and
contributed to the darkness
of the interior.

THRONE HALL
Though the original has vanished, Ayutthaya's splendid Sampet
Prasat Throne Hall at the ancient city has been reconstructed from
its remains and from the evidence of records. It clearly shows the
ship-hull shape – a prominent feature then – that may have
symbolized a ship carrying Buddhist pilgrims to salvation.

LOTUS CAPITAL
Columns surmounted
by water-lily or lotus-
bud decorations
were common on
structures dating
from the Sukhothai to
Ayutthaya periods; in
Bangkok, the lotus
capital was replaced
entirely by the water-
lily motif. This
example is from the
Viharn Daeng in
Ayutthaya Province.

RATTANAKOSIN ARCHITECTURE

At the beginning of the Rattanakosin, or Bangkok, period, a conscious attempt was made to recreate the splendor of Ayutthaya. Some of the first buildings were replicas of former ones, with careful attention paid to every detail. Later Rattanakosin decorations became even more elaborate than those of Ayutthaya, influenced by Chinese motifs and love of color. Western influences became predominant under King Rama V, when foreign architects were brought in to design palace buildings and even temples reflected the new styles.

WAT PO
BELL TOWER
Covered with glazed tiles and adorned with pointed finials and ornate decorations, the bell tower at Bangkok's Wat Po ▲ 154 exemplifies all the best qualities of Rattanakosin art. The temple was a favorite with early Chakri rulers, particularly King Rama III.

WAT SUTHAT BOT
Built by King Rama I, founder of Bangkok, the finely proportioned bot of Wat Suthat is 264 feet long and stands on two terraces, adding to its imposing appearance.

WAT SUTHAT VIHARN
Wat Suthat viharn, one of the finest surviving structures of early Bangkok, has a double-layered roof and eight doors preceded by porticoes. The gables have magnificently carved decorations of various religious symbols, while the interior is divided into three sections by two rows of columns.

A colonnade surrounds the structure and bears the weight of the massive four-tier roofs. The interior is decorated with well-preserved mural paintings.

CHINESE INFLUENCE
Chinese architectural styles and decorations were popular during the reign of King Rama III, as can be seen in the viharn of Wat Tepidaram.

GATE OF WAT TEPIDARAM
Both Chinese and Western influences are revealed in the external walls of Wat Tepidaram, which are made of whitewashed brick and decorated with Chinese tiles and statues.

WAT SUTHAT DOOR
Leading to the bot enclosure, this door in Wat Suthat is framed with marble and displays the graceful curving lines typical of Rattanakosin.

WAT PHRA KEO WINDOW
Wat Phra Keo, enshrining the sacred Emerald Buddha and serving as the royal chapel, is the most splendid of all Rattanakosin temples, constituting a virtual textbook of classical architecture and decoration. The window shown above reflects the richness and intricate detail of its adornment.

WAT RAJABOPIT WINDOW
Wat Rajabopit, built by King Rama V, displays both traditional and Western styles. Windows like the one above are decorated with mosaics and carvings, and walls and pillars in the temple are covered with colored porcelain tiles.

WAT PHRA KEO mondop
The *mondop* at Wat Phra Keo, dating from the reign of King Rama I, is regarded as the most beautiful example of Rattanakosin architecture. Square-shaped and surmounted by a slender spire, it is supported outside by tall elegant columns and is covered with an incredible profusion of lavish decorations.

WAT BENCHAMABOPIT (MARBLE TEMPLE)
Popularly known as the Marble Temple, Wat Benchamabopit ▲ *179, 258* was built toward the end of King Rama V's reign and displays an eclectic blend of cultural influences. The walls are covered with marble brought from Carrara, Italy, while the yellow roof tiles are Chinese. The bot has stained-glass windows as well as massive marble Khmer-style *singha* (guardian lions), flanking the doors.

Religious architecture in the northern Lanna kingdom developed independently from that of Ayutthaya in the Central Plains and is linked more with the Thai people of Yunnan, the Shan states and Laos. Thanks to the surrounding teak forests, wood was used extensively in construction and also in decorative carvings to adorn temples. Old Lanna viharns were open, like those of Sukhothai, and the columns supporting the roof were often low.

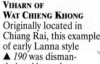

VIHARN OF WAT CHIENG KHONG
Originally located in Chiang Rai, this example of early Lanna style ▲ *190* was dismantled and brought to the ancient city outside Bangkok to be reassembled. Except for a brick base, the viharn is built entirely of wood, including wooden tiles, and is open on all four sides; low columns support the huge tiered roof.

VIHARN LAIKAM OF WAT PHRA SINGH
This early 19th-century viharn at Wat Phra Singh is possibly the finest example of late Lanna style surviving in Chiang Mai. It is a closed structure with brick walls and a wooden façade; guardian serpents stand on the entrance stairs ▲ *266*.

LIBRARY OF WAT PHRA SINGH
Wat Phra Singh's library is a small wooden building, raised on a high brick base, decorated with stucco deities. The library itself is adorned with intricate inlaid decorations and reflects pure Lanna style at its best ▲ *266*.

KU OF WAT PHRA THAT LAMPANG LUANG
A unique feature of Lanna architecture is the *ku*, a brick structure used to house the Buddha image. Similar to a chedi, it is gilded and placed inside a temple. The *ku* above is in Lampang province ▲ *276, 281*.

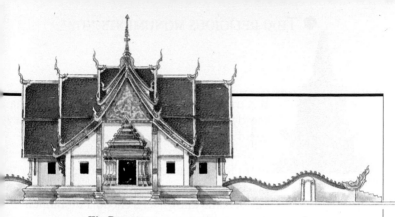

WAT PHUMIN

Wat Phumin in Nan province ▲ *285* was established in 1596 by a local ruler and restored in 1865 and 1873. Its main building, serving as both bot and viharn, is a unique structure built on a perfect cruciform plan, with four axial porches leading to four Buddha images placed in the center. On the interior walls are lively murals depicting the Jataka stories and painted about a hundred years ago. The stairways of two opposite entrances are flanked by *naga* with the tail at one doorway and the head at the other. The chapel has a five-tier roof, decorated with *naga* symbolizing the water flowing down from Mount Meru.

CEREMONIAL GATE, WAT SUAN DOK

Monumental gates, like this one at Wat Suan Dok in Chiang Mai, are typical of the north and were also a feature of now-vanished palaces. Wat Suan Dok was once a *wiang*, or fortified monastery, built on the site of a royal garden ▲ *269, 279*.

MONDOP OF WAT PONGSANUK TAI

This graceful *mondop* at Wat Pongsanuk Tai in Lampang ▲ *279* is a typical example of old Lanna style. Completely open on all sides, it has a tiered roof with false upper storics and a cage enclosing four Buddha images flanking a Bodhi tree. The decorations display a wit and ingenuity lacking in many modern temples of the region, which have been influenced by Bangkok tastes.

RELIQUARY CHEDI
A reminder of the original significance of the chedi is this example, made of limestone and standing 19 inches high; dating from the 7th and 8th centuries, it was found in Saraburi Province and is now in the National Museum.

It is traditionally claimed that, as the Buddha was dying, one of his disciples asked how they could remember him and his doctrines. He replied that they could make a mound of earth in which a relic of his body could be placed after his cremation. Thus began what has become known as a chedi, a monument that over the years became taller, narrower, and often of considerable size, used to enshrine relics of the Buddha or the ashes of important people, religious and royal. Chedis are found in every wat, often along with prangs, an older type of monument adapted from Hindu architecture, and introduced to Thailand by the Khmers.

SRIVIJAYA CHEDI
Chedis of the Srivijaya period, which lasted in the southern peninsula from the 7th to the 13th centuries, were built of brick and stucco and had strongly Javanese characteristics. The only surviving example in good condition is the one shown on the right, which stands on a square foundation and has four square tiers ascending in decreasing size; located at Wat Phra Boromathat in Chaiya ▲ *201*, it dates from the 8th century but has been restored several times, most recently in 1901 and 1930.

SUKHOTHAI LOTUS-BUD CHEDI
The monument after which Wat Chedi Chet Thaew is named was built during Sukhothai's classic period, in the mid-14th century, at the satellite city of Si Satchanalai. An almost identical copy of one at Wat Mahathat in Sukhothai, it has a lotus-bud finial, a feature unique to Sukhothai religious architecture and found on many monuments throughout the kingdom ▲ *256*.

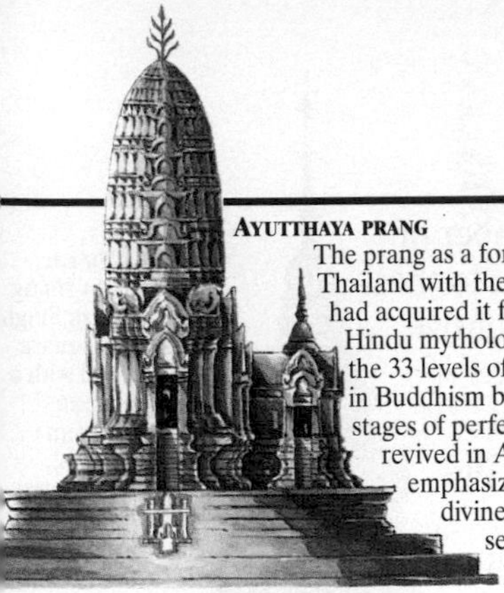

AYUTTHAYA PRANG

The prang as a form came to Thailand with the Khmers, who had acquired it from India. In Hindu mythology, it represents the 33 levels of heaven, which in Buddhism became the 33 stages of perfection. It was revived in Ayutthaya to emphasize the concept of divine kingship, as seen here in the prang of Wat Raja Burana ▲ 243, built of stuccoed brick and laterite in 1424. A rare collection of gold objects was found in 1957 in a large crypt beneath the prang.

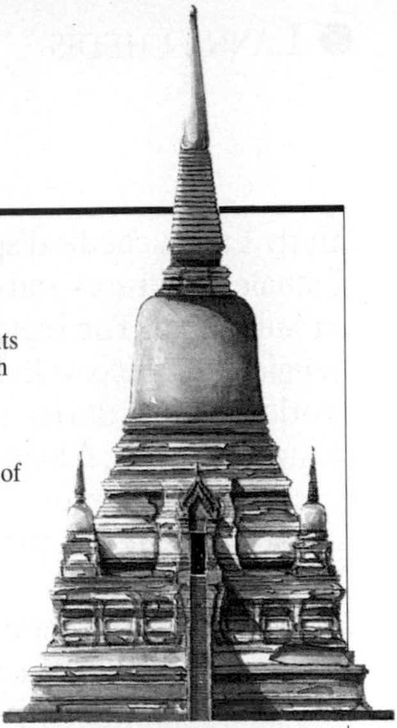

BELL-SHAPED CHEDI

The bell-shaped chedi originated in Sri Lanka and first appeared in Thai religious architecture during the Sukhothai period; it has been used since throughout Thai history up to the present. The one shown above, at Wat Yai Chai Mongkol in Ayutthaya, is 238 feet high, composed of brick and stucco, and was built by King Rama-thibodi in 1358 ▲ 245.

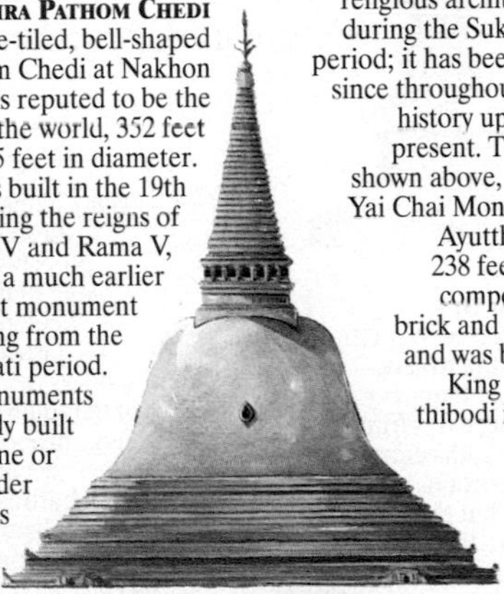

PHRA PATHOM CHEDI

The orange-tiled, bell-shaped Phra Pathom Chedi at Nakhon Pathom is reputed to be the tallest in the world, 352 feet high and 315 feet in diameter. It was built in the 19th century during the reigns of King Rama IV and Rama V, and encases a much earlier 132-foot monument dating from the Dvaravati period. Several monuments are similarly built around one or more older structures ▲ 186.

WAT ARUN

Wat Arun, or the Temple of Dawn, is one of Bangkok's major riverside landmarks ▲ 170. The central prang, 221 feet high, stands on a 122-foot base; originally only 50 feet high, it was raised to its present height during the reigns of King Rama II and Rama III. Stairways lead up at the four cardinal points, and there are smaller prangs at each of the four corners. All are decorated with multicolored ceramic.

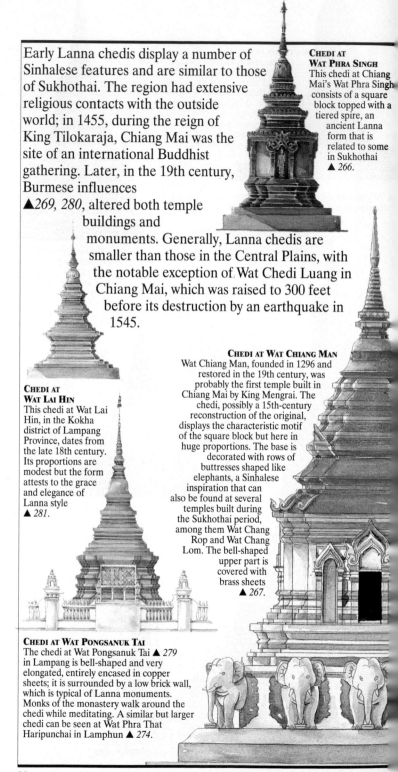

Early Lanna chedis display a number of Sinhalese features and are similar to those of Sukhothai. The region had extensive religious contacts with the outside world; in 1455, during the reign of King Tilokaraja, Chiang Mai was the site of an international Buddhist gathering. Later, in the 19th century, Burmese influences ▲269, 280, altered both temple buildings and monuments. Generally, Lanna chedis are smaller than those in the Central Plains, with the notable exception of Wat Chedi Luang in Chiang Mai, which was raised to 300 feet before its destruction by an earthquake in 1545.

CHEDI AT WAT PHRA SINGH
This chedi at Chiang Mai's Wat Phra Singh consists of a square block topped with a tiered spire, an ancient Lanna form that is related to some in Sukhothai ▲ 266.

CHEDI AT WAT LAI HIN
This chedi at Wat Lai Hin, in the Kokha district of Lampang Province, dates from the late 18th century. Its proportions are modest but the form attests to the grace and elegance of Lanna style ▲ 281.

CHEDI AT WAT CHIANG MAN
Wat Chiang Man, founded in 1296 and restored in the 19th century, was probably the first temple built in Chiang Mai by King Mengrai. The chedi, possibly a 15th-century reconstruction of the original, displays the characteristic motif of the square block but here in huge proportions. The base is decorated with rows of buttresses shaped like elephants, a Sinhalese inspiration that can also be found at several temples built during the Sukhothai period, among them Wat Chang Rop and Wat Chang Lom. The bell-shaped upper part is covered with brass sheets ▲ 267.

CHEDI AT WAT PONGSANUK TAI
The chedi at Wat Pongsanuk Tai ▲ 279 in Lampang is bell-shaped and very elongated, entirely encased in copper sheets; it is surrounded by a low brick wall, which is typical of Lanna monuments. Monks of the monastery walk around the chedi while meditating. A similar but larger chedi can be seen at Wat Phra That Haripunchai in Lamphun ▲ 274.

THAILAND AS SEEN
BY PAINTERS

The first Western impressions of Siam are found in early atlases and accounts of voyages and explorations. There are many interesting engravings that accompany the publications of the travels of French Jesuits and the two French embassies to Ayutthaya in 1685 and 1687. The flurry of diplomatic activities and the arrival in Paris of Siamese ambassadors increased the interest in this newly discovered exotic land. One of the most popular subjects was the grand parade of royal barges carrying the Chevalier de Chaumont and his retinue to the king's palace. While the original theme was engraved in the book by Father Guy Tachard, the subject was elaborated and developed in countless prints such as that

shown left (1). Royal elephants and their rich caparisons were another favorite subject (2). This image comes from La Loubère's works. Prints were rarely drawn first-hand and were produced from descriptions and sketches by missionaries. The Cabinet des Estampes in Paris preserves a collection of 33 watercolors that cover most of the themes depicted in the engravings. Reproduced here are a map of Ayutthaya (3) and two views (4 and 5) of the observatory that was constructed by King Narai and given to the Jesuits to pursue their astrological studies.

1	3
	4
2	5

ARUNOTHAI:
LIFE IN THE HAREM

The languid tempera ladies who appear on these pages are the work of Arunothai Somsakul, a contemporary Thai artist. He is inspired by his affection for the elegance of turn-of-the-century court life in Bangkok, which he portrays in a decadent, almost Symbolist manner. A large portion of Arunothai's output is manifestly erotic, and even his more decorous works are suffused with an air of almost palpable sensuality. The oblique looks and whispered conversations of the palace ladies suggest either intrigues or assignations, the imminence of scandal. Even the figures carved in relief on the walls seem privy to many an exciting secret. The concupiscent atmosphere is sometimes reinforced by the presence of small erotic embellishments hidden within the composition that go unnoticed at first – or even second – glance.

The figures conspire in detailed settings that accurately portray the objects of court life at the time. Specific situations are often recognizable: the Vimarn Mek Palace seen through the window behind the gossiping ladies, for example.

The paintings are, as is usual with Arunothai, set during the fifth reign, when Western fashions, often somewhat modified, were already being adopted by Bangkok society.

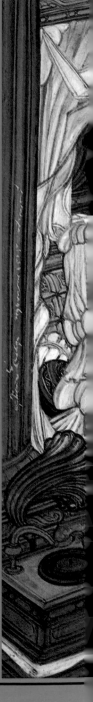

«THE NORTHERN SCHOOL IS CLEARLY DISTINGUISHED BY ITS VIVID
PORTRAYAL OF FAMILIAR SCENES CONVEYING A STRONG FEELING
OF INTIMACY.»

JEAN BOISSELIER

A record of the colorful mosaic of races and cultures of northern Thailand is preserved in the murals at Wat Phra Singh, Chiang Mai. The surviving Lanna murals are engaging portraits of life in the north, before the irresistible influence of the culture of Bangkok overwhelmed the more delicate Lanna traditions. The murals were probably painted by a local artist named Jek Seng, who completed them during the late 19th century. The changing fashions and growing cosmopolitanism of the period are depicted in a detail from a mural (1), where the man watching the buffaloes wears a Bangkok-style *pannung* ● 56, evidence that the culture of the capital was already spreading northward at this time. On the same mural, the lofty personages asking for directions are Shan, as is evident from the turbans and striped shawls they wear (2). Their Lue guide is heavily tattooed about the legs and loins and is armed with a red umbrella. The ladies of the market are more conservatively attired; their classic striped sarongs, bare bosoms and thin shoulder-cloths are typically Lanna (3). Life in a typical northern Thai house is also clearly shown (4).

1	3
2	4

«KHRUA IN KHONG, WITH ALL HIS INNOVATIONS, STRANGE
LIFESTYLE AND ODD AND FORCEFUL PERSONALITY, MAY BE
CONSIDERED THE FIRST ARTIST IN THE WESTERN MEANING
OF THE WORD IN THAILAND.»   PIA PIERRE

The lush green countryside of Thailand did not appear in Thai paintings until relatively late. The religious nature of the works and the flat two-dimensional style confined naturalistic elements to the role of embellishments, with which Thai artists filled up small empty corners of their compositions. The influence of Chinese landscape painting was first felt in the 19th century, gradually filtering into the work of Thai muralists and causing larger areas of their paintings to be treated as landscape. Even so, it was not until the advent of the artist-monk from Phetchaburi, Khrua In Khong ▲ 196, that the landscape per se became a subject in Thai art. An intimate of King Rama IV, Khrua In Khong found inspiration in the traditions of Western painting, which he discovered in the form of reproductions brought to Thailand by ambassadors and missionaries. Khrua In Khong introduced the concept of perspective to Thai painting; he also showed affection for the American neo-classical style of architecture, which made its earliest appearance in Thailand during the 19th century. Khrua In Khong added new colors to the Thai painter's palette, showing a clear preference for darker tones. The two images here of a river scene (1) and town life (2) were finished at Wat Bowornivet, Bangkok, around 1860, and are intended as figurative depictions of religious teachings. The metaphorical landscapes depicted are recognizably Thai; the abundance of water and rolling limestone hills in the background are almost certainly a remembrance of his native Phetchaburi. Khrua In Khong's stormy skies, however, are not particularly Thai; the treatment of clouds and sunlight effects owe a visible debt to the *Tempesta* of Giorgione, a work that was fresh in Khrua In Khong's mind at the time. The geometric perspective of some of the buildings is inspired by the *Flagellazione* of Piero della Francesca.

«THERE IT WAS…THE ORIENTAL CAPITAL WHICH HAD AS YET
SUFFERED NO WHITE CONQUEROR; AN EXPANSE OF BROWN
HOUSES OF BAMBOO…SPRUNG OUT OF THE BROWN SOILS ON THE
BANKS OF THE MUDDY RIVER.» JOSEPH CONRAD

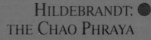

Following the expulsion of the French from Ayutthaya in 1688, a century of isolationism followed. During this time few foreigners visited Siam. As a result most of the atlases and books printed contained illustrations adapted from those of La Loubère and Father Guy Tachard. Normal relations with Western countries were resumed during King Rama IV's reign (1851–68) and Siam once again received the attention of writers and publishers, though still very few artists traveled in the country. One of the few artists to visit Siam was Eduard Hildebrandt (1818–69), who produced a series of watercolors of Bangkok and had them published as chromolithographs in his book, *Drei Reise um die Erde* (London, 1867). The two reproduced here show the banks of the Chao Phraya, which at that time was the main thoroughfare of the city. In the first painting, beyond the floating houses, Wat Arun, a famous landmark, can clearly be seen (1). The second provides a glimpse into one of the many floating shophouses that lined both banks (2). The Chinese temple behind would have been one of the few edifices at the time to be built of brick.

1
2

«I WILL LEAVE! STEAMSHIP WITH SWAYING MASTS, WEIGH ANCHOR
TOWARD EXOTIC NATURE.»

STEPHANE MALLARMI

By the turn of the century, in that period of revolutionary ideas that was to transform the art scene in the West, many artists felt a special fascination for the Orient and its exotic themes. However, only a few were able to experience at first hand the colors and atmosphere of the East. One artist who did was Galileo Chini (1873–1956). He was summoned to Bangkok in 1911 to

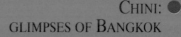
decorate the ceiling of the new throne hall there, which had recently been completed by Annibale Rigotti. Chini spent two and a half years in Siam, painting the vaulted ceiling of the throne room with friezes in the Secessionist style and large frescoes depicting the glory of the Chakri Dynasty. The artist's long, prolific career subsumed many crucial phases in the development of modern art: the Pre-Raphaelite movement, Secessionism, Symbolism and Divisionism. Underlying these explorations was a solid Florentine mastery of his craft. The friezes in Bangkok are among the most charming of Chini's paintings. However, the work he completed during the Siam years ranks among his finest in that period. The mood suggested in *Mesu the Performer* (1), a study of a Thai dancer against a stark black background, is almost erotic, with a touch of the Symbolist manner. Another of Chini's masterpieces is undoubtedly the *Chinese New Year Festival in Bangkok* (2), its phantas-magoric quality achieved through strength of color and diffused light from an apparent multiplicity of sources. A vague hint of the Futurist work of Boccioni is visible here. *Nostalgia by the River* (3), painted in 1913 in the Divisionist style, creates a suggestive mood around what has long been one of the most popular Thai themes among artists: the river with its decadent, sensual atmosphere.

Chini was fascinated by the elaborate costumes of the Siamese court and pursued his studies with a series of large temperas of figures which are almost scenographic cartoons rather than paintings. The Brahmins shown in the picture above are an exemplary study on white with the translucent and transparent nuances of their immaculate clothes rendered with luminous precision.

THAILAND AS SEEN
BY WRITERS

● The kingdom of Siam

Early accounts of Siam

AN IMPORTANT DOCUMENT

The kingdom of Siam had hardly any contact with the West until the 16th century; at least, no notable account of it is found in Western chronicles. Nicolò de' Conti (1395–1469) mentioned the kingdom of Siam, but never visited Ayutthaya, although he crossed the Tenasserim in 1420–30. The first travelers to give a full description of Siam and its inhabitants are the Portuguese. In 1511 Afonso de Albuquerque conquered Malacca, made it a Portuguese stronghold in the Far East, and at once set out to establish relations with all the neighboring peoples. The following is an extract from the instructions given by Afonso de Albuquerque to the ambassador Antonio Miranda de Azevedo in early January 1512, and is the first Western document to recognize the importance of Siam.

❝You shall tell the King of Siam that I am sure that he will rejoice with the destruction of the King of Malacca, with whom he has always been at war. Tell him that the King of Portugal will be very pleased that the Siamese ships and people will trade again with Malacca and that this was the main reason for which I took the city. And tell the King of Siam that if he needs the support of our fleet and our men to preserve his nation, I, as captain-general of the King of Portugal, will serve him in everything he will command.**❞**

Bras de Albuquerque, *Comentarios do Grande Afonso de Albuquerque*, Coimbra, 1923, Part III, Chapter XXXVI

THE KINGDOM OF SIAM

The following, written between 1513 and 1515, is from "A Suma Oriental" by Tomes Pires (1468–1522), who worked as a clerk in the Portuguese trading house in Malacca for over two years; while there is no evidence that he actually visited Siam, he talked with many who did and based this account on their reports. Pires was sent on important missions in India and China and following a series of misunderstandings was eventually imprisoned and killed by the Chinese at Canton. The memoirs of the first part of his adventurous life were first published in Italian by the Venetian scholar Ramusio, in the second half of the 16th century.

❝The kingdom of Siam is heathen. The people, and almost the language, are like those of Pegu. They are considered to be prudent folk counsel. The merchants know a great deal about merchandise…The kingdom is justly ruled. The king is always in residence in the city of Odia (Ayutthaya). He is a hunter. He is very ceremonious with strangers; he moves freely and easily with the natives. He has many wives, upwards of five hundred. On the death of the king a person of the royal blood, usually a nephew, the son of a sister, if he is suitable, and if not there are sometimes agreements and assemblies to decide who will be the best. Secrets are closely kept among them. They are very reserved. They speak with well-taught modesty…**❞**

Tomes Pires, *A Suma Oriental* Translated by Armando Cortesao, London 194–

VENICE OF THE EAST

Soldier, merchant and traveler, Fernão Mendez Pinto (1510–83) lived for many years in the East, writing a record of his pilgrimage in what is perhaps the most original work of this period of Portuguese expansion. A literary masterpiece, the "Peregrinação" was first published in Lisbon in 1614 and has been translated into Spanish, French and English. Fernão Mendez Pinto was in Siam twice in the mid-16th century. The following is extracted from a letter he wrote to the Fathers and Brothers of the Society of Jesus.

…In the Kingdom of Sornau which is called Siam where I was on two occasions I went to the city of Ayutthaya where the court of the King can be found, and I can state that it is the greatest affair that I saw in all those parts. This city is like Venice because one travels more by water than one does by land. I heard it be said by many that there were over two hundred thousand boats but I did not see a league's length of waterway which was so full that one could not pass; for many fairs are held on the rivers round the city and these are like the feasts of the idols. And to each one of these fairs come five hundred boats and at times over one thousand. The King is called Precaocale, which I have been told means the second person of God. No foreigners have been allowed to see his palaces except for the Ambassadors or those who are to become his vassals. On the outside the palaces are covered with metal and on the inside there is a great deal of gold. The King comes out two times in each year in order that all should see him and is accompanied by two hundred elephants on which are mounted many lords and captains, and he is accompanied by between five and six thousand guardsmen…He is carried on an elephant, sitting on a very ornate chair and one of his pages sits on the elephant's head carrying a gold rope in his hand. On his right hangs a bag full of coins which he distributes as alms.**"**

TRANSCRIBED IN *FERNÃO MENDEZ PINTO, SUBSIDIOS PARA A SUA BIOGRAFIA,*
BY CRISTOVÃO AIRES, LISBON 1904

DUBIOUS MORALS

Little is known of Thomas Herbert, an English adventurer who traveled around the world in the first half of the 17th century. The strange habits mentioned in the following extract, however, are not entirely fictional, and they are often mentioned by other contemporary authors.

"[The Siamese] have beene (in foregoing times) wicked Sodomites, a sinne so hateful to nature itselfe, that it aborres it; and to deterre these calamites, a late Queen commanded that all male children should have a Bell of gold (in it an Adders tongue dried) put through the prepuse, which in small time not only became not contemptible, but in way of ornament and for musick sake few now are without three or foure; so that when they have a mind to marry, he has his choice of what maid he likes, but beds her not, till the Midwife present a sleepie ophiated potion, during which the Bell is loosed from the flesh, and fastened to the fore-skin, which hinders not but titulates; the unguent is applied, and the cure is perfected. But to see a Virgin here, at virgins yeeres, is as a black Swan, in regards, in green yeeres they give the too forward maids a virulent drink; whose vertue (vyce rather) is by a strange efficacy to distend their mullebria so rapaciously that Bells and rope ring too easily: and which is worst (dull memory compels us to write it) the women here are not ashamed (the better to allure men from Sodomitry) to go naked to the middle, where with a fine transparent cobweb-lawn they are so covered, that by a base device is made to open as they go; so that any impure ayre gives all to mens immodest viewes, denudating those parts which every modest eye most scorns…**"**

THOMAS HERBERT, *SOME YEARS TRAVELS
INTO DIVERSE PARTS OF ASIA AND AFRIQUE,*
LONDON 1638

SUKHOTHAI

TEMPLES OF SUKHOTHAI

One of the greatest figures of the Portuguese Renaissance, João de Barros (1496–1570) was Factor of the House of India, 1533–67, and, as such, had access to sources and information about the overseas expansion of Portugal. He wrote the four "Decadas da Asia" ("Asian Decades"), first published in Lisbon between 1552 and 1615. Because of his impeccable style and the availability of abundant material, João de Barros is sometimes called the Portuguese Titus Livius. Sukhothai had lost its political importance when João de Barros wrote his "Decadas", but the fame of the city was obviously still alive, and the great temples were then still standing in all their magnificence.

"...In general, the Siamese are very religious and given to venerating God for they build many great magnificent temples, some of them of stone and mortar and others of bricks and mortar; in these temples they place images of human figures, of people whom they say are in heaven owing to their good deeds on earth, and they keep these images as a remembrance but they do not adore them. Among these images they have one made of clay, which must be about 50 paces long and which they call the Father of Men, and say that God sent it from Heaven, and that it was not made on earth, and that of the image some men were born, who were martyred in the name of God. The largest image made out of metal, of the many they have in that Kingdom, can be found in the Temple of the City of Sukhothai which they say is the oldest city in the Kingdom. This idol measures 80 palmos and there are a great number of smaller figures, down to human size. The Temples are large and sumptuous and the Kings spend much money on them and every King, a inheritor of the Kingdom, at once starts building a Temple in praise of God, and then builds two or three more, to which they bequeath great revenues.**"**

JOÃO DE BARROS, *DECADAS DA ASIA*
LISBON 177

PATTANI

THE QUEEN OF PATTANI

Pattani, a Malay kingdom on the coast of the Gulf of Siam, was from early times a vassal of Siam. The kingdom is often mentioned in ancient chronicles because of it importance as a trading post between Siam, China and the Indonesian archipelago. The Portuguese and the Dutch had their trade factories there. The following extract based on reports of contemporary travelers, is found in the "Pilgrimage" of Rev Samuel Purchas, a British erudite who compiled a geographical description of the world in the early 17th century.

"Patane is a City Southwards from Siam, chiefe of that Kingdome, whereto giveth name, in the height of seven degrees. The buildings are of Wood and Reede but artificially wrought. The Mesquit (for many of them are Mahumetanes) is of Bricke. The Chinois are more then the native inhabitants. Adulterie is here capital offence, the father of the malefactor being the Executioner, or his ne kinsman, if he be dead; yet is this vice common (notwithstanding this rigor) by reason of the womens unbrideled lust. The Kingdome hath bin governed many yeares by a Queene, who…keepes her selfe close at home among her women; of which some may not marry (but yet may doe worse) others may, having first obtained the Queen's licence. It is seldome that she is seene; yet sometimes she rideth on an Elephant in Progresse, for her recreation. And her Elephants, they have a device to take them in this sort. Some ride into the woods on a tame Elephant, and when they espice a wilde one, they provoke him to fight. Whilcs these are fastened in the encounter by the teeth or tuskes, each striving to overthrow the other, some come behinde the wilde Elephant, and fasten his hinder feet, and so either kill him for his teeth, or by famine tame him.**

SAMUEL PURCHAS, *PILGRIMAGE, OR RELATIONS OF THE WORLD AND THE RELIGIONS OBSERVED IN ALL AGES AND PLACES DISCOVERED FROM THE CREATION UNTO THE PRESENT*, LONDON 1617

THE END OF A WEALTHY KINGDOM

Pattani was eventually ravaged and destroyed by the Siamese and incorporated into the kingdom; its inhabitants were brought to Bangkok as slaves. This is what George Windsor Earl saw, two hundred years after Purchas' description.

**During many years the Siamese have been making annual excursions into the Malay Peninsula, apparently for no other purpose than to procure slaves. They ately took Queda, a town nearly opposite to Penang, the aggression being connived at, indeed materially assisted by the English, in consideration of some commercial advantages to be granted by the King of Siam.

Two junks, bringing the remainder of the inhabitants of Patani, arrived in the river during my stay. The decks of the junks could not contain these miserable captives, and platforms were erected on the outsides of the vessles for the purpose of affording greater space. These unfortunate creatures were tied hand and foot during the voyage, in order to prevent them from throwing themselves overboard, which many would have done had they been at liberty.…Many of the men were wounded, but no consideration was shewn them on that account, not even a bit of cloth being given to bind up their wounds. During the few days of their detention in the factory, numbers of them, particularly of the young children, died from want of food, and from the horrible state of disease which prevailed in consequence of the miseries which they had endured on the voyage. Those who survived were assigned away as slaves to the nobles, and were selected for removal with the utmost disregard to natural ties.**

GEORGE WINDSOR EARL, *THE EASTERN SEAS*, LONDON 1837, REPRINTED SINGAPORE 1971

AYUTTHAYA

THE PRESENTATION OF THE LETTER

Faced with a rebellious nobility and a growing Dutch naval presence in Asia, King Narai (1656–88) turned to the French. A 1684 embassy from Siam to the court of Louis XIV stirred up great interest in Paris and its court society, and led to a flurry of diplomatic activity. Ambassadors and members of the retinue published memoirs of their visits to Narai's great capital Ayutthaya, for a European audience that had only now discovered Siam. The first French embassy of the Chevalier de Chaumont in 1685 included Father Guy Tachard (1651–1712), a Jesuit priest whose book relates the diplomatic maneuvering that attended this contact between Europe and Asia.

❝It was a Surprise to the Ambassador, when he entered the Hall, to see the King so high above him, and he seemed somewhat troubled that he had not been told of it. When his Complement was made, the next thing he was to do in course, was to advance and present his Master's Letter to the King of Siam. It was agreed upon with the Lord Constance, that to show greater respect to the King's Letter, the Ambassador should take it from the Abbott de Choisi, who for that end should stand by his side during his speech, and hold the Letter in a golden Cup with a very long Foot. But the Ambassador perceiving the King to be so high above him, that to reach up to him he must have taken the Cup by the lower part of the Foot, and raised his Arm very high, thought that that Distance suited not with his Dignity, and that he ought to present the Letter nearer hand. Having a little considered, he thought it was his best Course to hold the Cup by the Boul, and to stretch his Arm but half out. The King perceiving the reason why he acted so, rose up smiling, and stooping with his Body over the Throne, met him half way to receive the Letter: He then put it upon his Head which was a Mark of extraordinary Honour and Esteem that he was willing to shew to the great that sent it.❞

FATHER GUY TACHARD, *A RELATION OF THE VOYAGE TO SIAM*, LONDON 168?

A VIEW OF AYUTTHAYA

After a somewhat scandalous youth, mostly spent as a transvestite in high Parisian social circles, the Abbé François de Choisy (1644–1724) became a Jesuit priest and went to Siam with the first French embassy in 1685 as assistant to its head, the Chevalier de Chaumont. The following view of Ayutthaya is from a memoir he published in the form of letters.

❝We went for a walk outside the town. I paused frequently to admire the great city, seated upon an island round which flowed a river three times the width of the Seine. There rode ships from France, England, Holland, China and Japan, while innumerable boats and gilded barges rowed by 60 men plied to and fro. No less extraordinary were the camps and villages outside the walls inhabited by the different nations who came trading there, with all the wooden houses standing o

M^{rs} LES AMBASSADEURS
DU ROY DE SIAM, ENVOYE
AU ROY LOUIS LE GRAND
EMPEREUR DES FRANCOIS
EN 1686.
A Paris rue St Jacques, à l'Image St François.

posts over the water, the bulls, cows, and pigs on dry land. The streets, stretching out of sight, are alleys of clear running water. Under the great green trees and in the little houses crowd the people. Beyond these camps of the nations are the wide rice fields. The horizon is tall trees, above which are visible the sparkling towers and pyramids of the pagodas. I do not know whether I have conveyed to you the impression of a beautiful view, but certainly I myself have never seen a lovelier one.**

ABBÉ DE CHOISY, *JOURNAL DU VOYAGE DE SIAM*, LONDON/PARIS 1687

ESTHETICS OF TEETH IN SIAM

"The Natural and Political History of the Kingdom of Siam", from which the following extract comes, was written by Nicolas Gervaise (1662–1729), a French priest who came as a missionary to Ayutthaya in 1683 and remained for four years; published in 1688, the book was used as a source by the better-known Simon de la Loubère.

One thing that the Siamese ladies cannot endure about us is the whiteness of our teeth, because they believe that the devil has white teeth, and that it is shameful for a human being to have teeth like a beast's. Therefore, as soon as the boys and girls reach the age of fourteen or fifteen, they start trying to make their teeth black and shiny. They do this in the following manner: the person whom they have chosen to render them this service makes them lie down on their back and keeps them in this position for the three days that the operation lasts. First, he cleans the teeth with lemon juice and then having rubbed them with a certain fluid which makes them red, he adds a layer of burnt coconut, which blackens them. The teeth are so weakened by the application of these drugs that they could be extracted painlessly and would even fall out if the patient risked eating any solids, so for these three days he subsists on cold soups, which are fed to him gently so that they flow down the throat without touching the teeth. The least wind could spoil the effect of this operation and that is why the patient stays in bed and makes sure that he is well covered until he feels that it is successfully accomplished…

NICOLAS GERVAISE, *THE NATURAL AND POLITICAL HISTORY OF THE KINGDOM OF SIAM*, LONDON 1688

A SIAMESE FESTIVAL

"A New Historical Relation of the Kingdom of Siam" by Simon de la Loubère, who led the second French embassy to Ayutthaya in 1687, is one of the most comprehensive sources of information about Siamese life and culture in the 17th century.

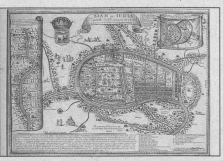

When the Waters begin to retreat, the People return them Thanks for several Nights together with a great Illumination; not only for that they are retired, but for the Fertility which they render to the Lands. The whole River is then seen covered with floating Lanterns, which pass with it. They are of different Sizes, according to the devotion of every particular Person; the variously painted Paper, whereof they are made, augments the agreeable effect of so many Lights. Moreover, to thank the Earth for the Harvest they do on the first days of their Year make another magnificent Illumination. The first time we arrived at Louvo [Lopburi today] was in the Night, and at the time of this Illumination; and we saw the Walls of the City adorned with lighten Lanterns at equal distances…

SIMON DE LA LOUBÈRE, *A NEW HISTORICAL RELATION OF THE KINGDOM OF SIAM*, LONDON/PARIS 1691

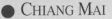

THE KINGDOM OF LANNA

THE CITY OF CHIANG MAI

Toward the end of the 19th century, Holt S. Hallett made an extensive trip through northern Thailand in search of a route for a British railway that would go from Burma, through upper Thailand, and eventually to China. The railway was never built but Hallett's account of his journey, entitled "A Thousand Miles on an Elephant in the Shan States", offers a rare view of a region visited by relatively few foreigners at the time. Here is an excerpt from his stay in Chiang Mai in 1876.

"It is a pretty sight in the early morning to watch the women and girls from the neighbouring villages streaming over the bridge on their way to the market, passing along in single file, with their baskets dangling from each end of a shoulder-bamboo, or accurately poised on their heads. The younger women move like youthful Dianas, with a quick, firm and elastic tread, and in symmetry of form resemble the ideal models of Grecian art...The ordinary costume of these graceful maidens consists of flowers in their hair, which shines like a raven's wing, and is combed back and arranged in a neat and beautiful knot; a petticoat or skirt, frequently embroidered near the bottom with silk, worsted, cotton, or gold and silver thread; and at times a pretty silk or gauze scarf cast carelessly over their bosom and one shoulder. Of late years, moreover, the missionaries have persuaded their female converts and the girls in their schools to wear a neat white jacket, and the custom is gradually spreading through the city and into the neighbouring villages...

After passing through the gates of the outer city we entered the market, which extends for more than half a mile to the gates of the inner city, and beyond them for some distance towards the palace. On either side of the main road little covered booths or stalls are set up; but most of the women spread a mat on the ground to sit upon, and placing their baskets by their side, expose their provisions upon wicker-work trays or freshly cut plantain-leaves...Passing from the outer into the inner town, we continued along the main road until we came to the enclosure wall of the palace grounds. The gate of the palace lies 1140 yards from the entrance of the inner town, and leads into an extensive court containing several buildings. The palace faces the gate, and is a substantial one-storied building slightly Chinese in aspect, with brick walls, plastered over with an excellent cement and a tiled roof. Ascending a flight of steps, paved with black tiles, we entered the audience-hall, which occupied the whole front of the building. The floor of the hall is inlaid with various woods, several chandeliers hung from the ceiling and the walls were papered like an English drawing-room, and adorned with long narrow gilt framed mirrors. The remainder of the furniture consisted of a lounge, an easy chair, a dozen drawing-room chairs, upholstered in green rep, and a small tea table. Through the doors leading into the private apartments some elegantly designed carved lattice-work partitions were seen, which served as screens in the interior of the palace.**"**

HOLT S. HALLETT, *A THOUSAND MILES ON AN ELEPHANT IN THE SHAN STATES*
LONDON 1891
REPRINTED BANGKOK 1988

STOICAL INDIFFERENCE

Carl Alfred Bock (1849–1932), a Norwegian naturalist of the positivist school, was an enthusiastic explorer and a prominent adventurer. Having acquired fame for his Borneo expeditions and published a book "The Head-Hunters of Borneo", Bock set out to explore northern Thailand at a time when the region was impoverished by continuous wars and misrule. Ever in search of the exotic and the sensational, Bock was often known to cast negative remarks on the natives, his judgment usually tainted by the desire to make his "adventures" seem a great deal more treacherous than they actually were.

"If a man's face is an index to his feelings, then the Laosians must be bereft of all capacity to appreciate any variety of mental emotions. It is the rarest phenomenon to see any change in their countenance or deportment, except – there is always one exception to every rule – when they are aroused to anger. This statement is more particularly true of the men, but even the women – demonstrative as the sex usually are – are seldom moved to either laughter or tears. Whatever news a Laosian may receive, whether of disaster or of joy, he hears it with a philosophic indifference depicted on his calm stoical countenance that a European diplomatist would give a fortune to be able to imitate. But when any sudden feeling of anger or any latent resentment is aroused, then the passion begins to display itself, if not in any great change of facial expression, at any rate in general demeanor, and in quick restless movements of impatience and irritation.

This natural stoical indifference to their surroundings is fostered by the influence of their religious belief, and by the general state of ignorance in which the people are kept, as well as by their isolation from the rest of the world. They are naturally lazy, and, with a fertile soil which provides them with all the necessaries of life without any appreciable effort on their part, their indolence is encouraged."

CARL A. BOCK, *TEMPLES AND ELEPHANTS, TRAVELS IN SIAM IN 1881–82*,
LONDON 1883

AN ASIAN ARCADY

THE LAND AND PEOPLES OF NORTHERN SIAM

THE GOLDEN TRIANGLE

Reginald Le May served for a time in the early years of this century with the British legation in Bangkok and later as Vice-Consul in the north; still later, he worked as an advisor to the Royal Siamese Government. "An Asian Arcady", from which the following comes, is an account of northern Thailand and of a 700-mile trip he took by elephant in 1914.

"Below my feet the river bank went sheer down for nearly fifty feet; the river itself was a mighty expanse of water flowing swift and clear, with just the top of an island showing, and far away on the other side the bank rose fully as high again, lined with row upon row of tall palms, looking like small shrubs in the distance. On the left, the river took a wide bend to the west, and on the right, another sweeping bend to the east, and in front the great gaunt hills rolled down to meet the river at either bend. This was the very apex of Siam. North lay British territory, the southern Shan states, and to the East, across the blue expanse, were the Lao states, which are now French soil. What a magnificent boundary to have for one's country! In full flood it must be a still more thrilling sight, but it is only in September or October, when the rains are nearly over and the northern rivers are beginning to rise, that one can see the river at its height. Once in about twenty years, the Mekhong overflows its banks, and when one thinks of their height and of the breadth of the river, the volume of water must be prodigious.... Chieng Sen is a mysterious old city, surrounded by a high, thick, strong wall with palisades on top of the brick, and deep trenches dug outside. How far the wall extends, and what area it embraces, it is difficult to say. The whole city is now so overgrown with plantations of teak, and thick secondary growth, that one cannot see more than twenty yards ahead, except in the main grassy track; but it must be of wide extent , for the District Officer told me that there are actually now tiger and other game living within the walls, and that he had recently fired several shots at a rhinoceros...

It is sad to contemplate a great city, which once contained seventy-five temples, deserted by all, and even its ruins lost in the jungle; but old Chieng Sen has little hopes of recovery now, for it lies off the main road and the cost of clearing the plantations and undergrowths of brushwood which now choke the city would be too great to repay the undertaking. How are the mighty fallen and the weapons of war perished! So the old city sleeps, a prey to the wild beast of the jungle and those craftier two-legged animals, who come to seek what they can find among the ruins which lie to hand.**"**

REGINALD LE MAY, *AN ASIAN ARCADY,* CAMBRIDGE 1926, REPRINTED BANGKOK 1986

BANGKOK

AN AUDIENCE WITH THE KING OF SIAM

After the assassination of Phaulkon and the expulsion of the French from Ayutthaya, Siam remained in almost complete isolation for nearly 150 years. Among the many unsuccessful delegations from the West was that of John Crawfurd, an Englishman. He came to the court of King Rama II in 1822. The following is an extract from Crawfurd's account of his first audience with the king.

"The curtain placed before the throne was drawn aside as we entered. The whole multitude present lay prostrate on the earth, their mouths almost touching the ground: not a body or limb was observed to move; not an eye was directed towards us; not a whisper agitated the solemn and still air....Raised about twelve feet above the floor, and about two yards behind the curtain alluded to, there was an arched niche, on which an obscure light was cast, of sufficient size to display the human body to effect, in the sitting posture. In this niche was placed the throne, projecting from the wall a few feet. Here, on our entrance, the King sat immovable as a statue, his eyes directed forwards. He resembled, in every respect, an image of Buddha placed upon his throne; while the solemnity of the scene, and the attitude of devotion observed by the multitude, left little room to doubt that the temple had been the source from which the monarch of Siam had borrowed the display of regal pomp.**"**

JOHN CRAWFURD, *JOURNAL OF AN EMBASSY FROM THE GOVERNOR GENERAL OF INDIA TO THE COURTS OF SIAM AND COCHIN-CHINA,* LONDON 1828, REPRINTED SINGAPORE 197

THE FLOATING CITY

Mrs Anna Leonowens, an English widow, arrived in Bangkok in 1862 engaged to teach English to some of King Rama IV's wives and children. She wrote two books about her experiences, "The English Governess at the Siamese Court" and "The Romance of the Harem", which later formed the basis of the popular musical "The King and I". Although her books, written in the style of the serial melodrama, are largely inaccurate, her description of Bangkok is quite realistic.

"The situation of the city is unique and picturesque. When Ayutthaya was 'extinguished,' and the capital established at Bangkok, the houses were at first built on the banks of the river. But so frequent were the invasions of cholera, that one of the kings happily commanded the people to build on the river itself, that they might have greater cleanliness and better ventilation. The result quickly proved the

visdom of the measure. The privilege of building on the banks is now confined to members of the royal family, the nobility and residents of acknowledged influence, political or commercial…At night the city is hung with thousands of covered lights, that illuminate the wide river from shore to shore. Lamps and lanterns of all imaginable shapes, colours, and sizes combine to form a fairy spectacle of enchanting brilliancy and beauty. The floating tenements and shops, the masts of vessels, the tall, fantastic pagodas and minarets, and, crowning all, the walls and towers of the Grand Palace, flash with countless charming tricks of light, and compose a scene of more than magic novelty and beauty. So oriental fancy and profusion deal with things of use, and make a wonder of a commonplace…

A double, and in some parts a triple, row of floating houses extends for miles along the banks of the river. These are wooden structures, tastefully designed and painted, raised on substantial rafts of bamboo linked together with chains, which, in turn, are made fast to great piles planted in the bed of the stream. The Meinam itself forms the main avenue, and the floating shops on either side constitute the great bazaar of the city, where all imaginable and unimaginable articles from India, China, Malacca, Burma, Paris, Liverpool and New York are displayed in stalls…

Naturally, boats and canoes are indispensable appendages to such houses; the nobility possess a fleet of them, and to every little water-cottage a canoe is tethered, for errands and visits. At all hours of the day and night processions of boats pass to and from the palace, and everywhere bustling traders and agents ply their dingy little craft, and proclaim their several callings in a Babel of cries. **"**

Anna Leonowens, *The English Governess at the Siamese Court*,
London 1870

THE WOMEN'S BURDEN

George Windsor Earl (1805–65) was a British officer in the Far East and Australia. Linguist, antiquarian and author, he wrote several books. His first work, and probably his best, "The Eastern Seas", recounts his travels in the Far East. The book stands out among contemporary literature for its acute judgment and sense of observation.

The Siamese empire is apparently on the decline, a circumstance which may be attributed to the ruinous wars in which it is continually engaged, and to the enormous church establishment. Every man is obliged to serve as a soldier when called for, and to bring with him provisions for his own subsistence sufficient for his supply for several months. Wars, therefore, entail little expense on the government which may account for the readiness with which they are undertaken. The men who are engaged in their usually inglorious campaigns, acquire habits of idleness which are never afterwards corrected, and consequently the support of these drones, and of the enormous mass of priesthood, falls entirely on the women. The body of Talapoins or priests is enormously disproportioned to the rest of the inhabitants. In Bangkok alone, their numbers exceed thirty thousand. Like lilies of the valley 'they toil not, neither do they spin,' but are idle consumers of the produce of the soil. They do not even cook their own provisions, not being permitted to do so by their creed, but the younger members of the community go from house to house to collect the viands which are bountifully supplied by the people. The Talapoins received a great accession to their ranks during a late period of scarcity, indeed it

123

must be a matter of surprise that all the males do not become members of the priesthood, since among the privileges of their order may be reckoned exemption from labour, taxation, and military service, while they are at liberty to retire from the office whenever they please; the mode of life, however, led by these lazy vagabonds is found to be so agreeable, that they rarely take advantage of the latter privilege. The males affect to consider the women in the light of an inferior order of beings, but these lordly personages seldom enter upon any undertaking of moment without first consulting their wives. The women indeed, may be said to compose the most important portion of the community. They transact the greater part of the mercantile business, and are the principal cultivators of the soil, cheerfully undertaking the most laborious employments in the support of their families. **"**

GEORGE WINDSOR EARL, *THE EASTERN SEAS,* LONDON, 1837
REPRINTED SINGAPORE, 1971

CONRAD ARRIVES IN BANGKOK

The future author Joseph Conrad (1857–1924) came to Bangkok in 1888 as a seaman named Josef Teodor Konrad Korzeniowski, to take his first command as captain of a ship called the "Otago". In "The Shadow-Line", he describes his arrival in the city.

"One morning, early, we crossed the bar, and while the sun was rising splendidly over the flat spaces of land we steamed up the innumerable bends, passed under the shadow of the great gilt pagoda, and reached the outskirts of the town...There it was, spread largely on both banks, the Oriental capital which had yet suffered no white conqueror; an expanse of brown houses of bamboo, of mats, of leaves, of a vegetable-matter style of architecture, sprung out of the brown soil on the banks of the muddy river. It was amazing to think that in those miles of human habitation there was not probably half a dozen pounds of nails...

Some of those houses of sticks and grass, like the nests of an aquatic race, clung to the shores, others seemed to grow out of the water; others again floated in long anchored rows in the very middle of the stream. Here and there in the distance, above the crowded mob of low, brown roof ridges, towered great piles of masonry, king's palace, temples, gorgeous and dilapidated, crumbling under the vertical sunlight, tremendous, overpowering, almost palpable, which seemed to enter one's

breast with the breath of one's nostrils and soak into one's limbs through ever pore of the skin. **"**

JOSEPH CONRAD, *THE SHADOW-LINE*
LONDON 198

MAUGHAM ON THAI TEMPLES

Somerset Maugham (1874–1965) was a doctor before he gained fame as a novelist and short-story writer. He served as a British agent in the two world wars. Maugham came to Thailand overland through Burma in 1923. The following extract from one of his travel books, "The Gentlemen in the Parlour", records his vivid impressions of Bangkok's famous Buddhist temples.

"They are unlike anything in the world, so that you are taken aback, and you cannot fit them into the scheme of the things you know. It makes you laugh with delight to think that anything so fantastic could exist on this sombre earth. They are gorgeous; they glitter with gold and whitewash, yet are not garish; against that vivid sky, in that dazzling sunlight, they hold their own, defying the brilliancy of nature

and supplementing it with the ingenuity
and the bold playfulness of man. The artists
who developed them step by step from the
buildings of the ancient Khmers had the
courage to pursue their fantasy to the limit; I fancy that art meant little to them,
they desired to express a symbol; they knew no reticence, they cared nothing for
good taste; and if they achieved art it is as men achieve happiness, not by pursuing
it, but by doing with all their heart whatever in the day's work needs doing. I do not
know that in fact they achieved art; I do not know that these Siamese wats have
beauty, which they say is reserved and aloof and very refined; all I know is that they
are strange and gay and odd, their lines are infinitely distinguished, like the lines of
a proposition in a schoolboy's Euclid, their colours are flaunting and crude, like the
colours of vegetables in the greengrocer's stall at an open-air market, and, like a
place where seven ways meet, they open roads down which the imagination can
make many a careless and unexpected journey.**

A WELCOME FROM MISS PRETTY GIRL

*A calling card was given to Somerset Maugham by a street tout during his visit to
Thailand in 1923. Reproduced here is its message, which was recorded in the same
book. The gentleman, incidentally, refused the invitation.*

**"Oh, gentleman, sir, Miss Pretty Girl welcome you Sultan Turkish Bath, gentle
polite massage, put you in dreamland with perfume soap. Latest gramophone
music. Oh, such service. You come now! Miss Pretty Girl want you, massage you
from tippy-toe to head-top, nice, clean, to enter Gates of Heaven.**

SOMERSET MAUGHAM, *THE GENTLEMEN IN THE PARLOUR*,
LONDON 1930

THE TEMPLE OF DAWN

*"The Temple of Dawn" was one of a cycle of four novels by the Japanese
author Yukio Mishima (1925–70), the last of which was completed just
before his ritual suicide in 1970. Much of the novel takes place in
Bangkok, shortly before and during World War Two; in this passage the
young hero visits Wat Arun, the Temple of Dawn, in the early morning:*

**"It was still darkish, and only the very tip of the pagoda caught the first rays of the
rising sun. The Thonburi jungle beyond was filled with the
piercing cries of birds...The repetitiveness and the
sumptuousness of the pagoda were almost suffocating.
The tower with its color and brilliance, adorned in
many layers and graduated toward the peak, gave one
the impression of so many strata of dream sequences
hovering overhead. The plinths of the extremely
steep stairs were also heavily festooned and each
tier was supported by a bas-relief of birds with
human faces. They formed a multicolored pagoda
whose every level was crushed with layers of dreams,
expectations, prayers, each being further weighted
down with still other stories, pyramid-like, progressing
skyward...With the first rays of dawn over the Menam
River,...thousands of porcelain fragments turned into so
many tiny mirrors that captured the light. A great structure of
mother-of-pearl sparkling riotously...The pagoda had long served as a morning bell
filled with its rich hues, resonant colors responding to the dawn. They were created...to
evoke a beauty, a power, an explosiveness like the dawn itself.**

YUKIO MISHIMA, *THE TEMPLE OF DAWN*,
NEW YORK 1973

A HUMORIST IN BANGKOK

S.J. Perelman, a leading American humorist, was a regular contributor to the "New Yorker" magazine as well as a playwright and the author of early film scripts for the Marx brothers. Shortly after World War Two he made a trip through Asia, which under the title of "Westward Ha!" became a bestseller; the following extract gives his impressions of Bangkok at a time when it was relatively untouched by mass tourism.

"From the very beginning I was charmed by Bangkok, and I propose to be aggressively syrupy about it in the most buckeye travelogue manner. I liked its polite, gentle, handsome people, its temples, flowers, and canals, the relaxed and peaceful rhythm of life there. Apart from its shrill and tumultuous central thoroughfare swarming with Chinese and Indian bazaars, it struck me as the most soothing metropolis I had thus far seen in the East. Its character is complex and inconsistent; it seems at once to combine the Hannibal, Missouri of Mark Twain's boyhood with Beverly Hills, the Low Countries, and Chinatown. You pass from populous, glaring streets laden with traffic into quiet country lanes paralleled by canals out of a Dutch painting; a tree-shaded avenue of pretentious mansions set in wide lawns becomes a bustling row of shops and stalls, then melts into a sunny village of thatched huts among which water-buffalo graze. The effect is indescribably pleasing; your eye constantly discovers new vistas, isolated little communities around every corner tempting you to explore them."

S.J. PERELMAN, *THE MOST OF S.J. PERELMAN*
NEW YORK, 197

THE COUNTRYSIDE AND THE CITY

Minfong Ho is a Singaporean, but she spent most of her childhood in Thailand, and was for many years a teacher at the University of Chiang Mai. Her first novel, "Rice without Rain", was based on her experiences in northern Thailand during the 1976 student uprising, and it describes the politicization of an impoverished northern Thai village by a group of idealistic young students. The novel opens with a scene from the ricefields.

"Heat the colour of fire, sky as heavy as mud, and under both the soil – hard, dry unyielding. It was a silent harvest. Across the valley, yellow ricefields stretched stopped and dry. The sun glazed the afternoon with a heat so fierce that the distant mountains shimmered in it. The dust in the sky, the cracked earth, the shrivelled leaves fluttering on brittle branches – everything was scorched. Fanning out in jagged line across the fields were the harvesters, their sickles flashing in the sun Nobody spoke. Nobody laughed. Nobody sang. The only noise was wave after wave of sullen hisses as the rice stalks were slashed and flung to the ground. A single lark flew by, casting a swift shadow on the stubbled fields. From under the brim of her hat, Jinda saw it wing its way west. It flew to a tamarind tree at the foot of the mountain, circled it three times, and flew away. A good sign..."

The 1976 student movement was put down by the army, with considerable violence. Many of the student leaders fled to the jungle to take up arms with the Communist Party of Thailand (CPT). But most soon found themselves at odds with the CPT's hierarchy. Through a skillful policy of coercion and reconciliation, the Thai government was able to diffuse the Communist threat, and bring the guerillas out of the hills. Today, members of the 1976 movement are among the professional middle classes of Bangkok, and it was this group's willingness to take risks that led to the eventual victory of the pro-democracy forces, after a bloody confrontation in Bangkok's Sanam Luang square in 1992.

MINFONG HO
RICE WITHOUT RAIN

from the author of
SING TO THE DAWN

' 'I am Jinda, daughter of Inthorn Sriboonrueng,' she began. To her surprise she found that her voice was steady. It reverberated from all corners of the square, and even from the wall of the temple. She felt awed that her voice could reach so far. She had practised the speech so many times that it had become automatic, and it flowed effortless from her now, separate and yet a part of herself. Like a kite with a lovely long tail, tugging its way upwards as she held the string, her words flew up. It was an exhilarating feeling, and Jinda's voice grew stronger with it. 'My father has farmed all his life,' she said, 'and yet he has never had enough to eat. Why?' She paused, and in that brief silence she felt that maybe, just maybe, she could help change a bit of Thailand after all. 'Because he has had to pay half of his harvest to the landlord, year after year. Flood or drought.'

'Commie bitch!' A shrill voice pierced the air.

Startled, Jinda stopped. Who had shouted that? Why?

Suddenly, a heavy object sailed towards her, landing where the shoe-shine boy had been. There was a loud explosion, and bits of dirt and glass shattered out. In the rolls of smoke which poured forth, people screamed, and started to run.

Ned grabbed the microphone from Jinda, and urged the crowd to be calm. 'Nothing serious has happened,' he announced. 'A small homemade bomb has just been tossed at us. This has happened in previous rallies. It hasn't hurt anyone. Do not panic, I repeat, do not panic. The speech will continue.'

But something was happening on the far side of the square. The soldiers in their olive green fatigues had fanned out in front of the ambulances, and were advancing towards the centre, pushing the crowd forward.

There was another explosion. It landed further away, but the bomb was deafening and devastating. As the smoke cleared, Jinda stared, stunned. At least five students sprawled motionless on the grass…that was when the distant gunfire started. At first Jinda did not know what it was, this sharp staccato rattle. Then she saw students dropping to their knees, in crumpled heaps, and she understood. **"**

MINFONG HO, *RICE WITHOUT RAIN*,
SINGAPORE 1986

BANGKOK NIGHTLIFE

Born in England, Pico Iyer wrote for "TIME" magazine. He has also written for the "Partisan Review", "The Village Voice" and the "Times Literary Supplement". He came to Thailand in the 1980's while gathering material for a travel book later published as "Video Night in Kathmandu", from which the following excerpt is taken.

'In seedy and improvident Manila, the bars were the fast-buck stuff of a puritan's nightmare; while in high-tech and prosperous Bangkok, they were quicksilver riddles, less alarming for their sleaze than for their cunning refinement, embellished by the country's exquisite sense of design, softened by the ease of Buddhism, invigorated by the culture of *sanuk* (a good time). In Manila girls tried to sell themselves out of sheer desperation; in Bangkok, the crystal palaces of sex were only extra adornments in a bejeweled city that already glittered with ambiguities…In Bangkok, moreover, the ambivalence of the girls only intensified the ambiguity of the bars…no gaze was direct, and no smile clear-cut in the city of mirrors. And the mirrors were everywhere: one-way mirrors walling the massage parlors, mirrors lining the ceilings of the 'curtain hotels,' mirrors shimmering in the bars, pocket mirrors in which each girl converted herself into a reflection of her admirer's wishes. Look into a bar girl's eyes, and you'd see nothing but the image of your own needs; ask her what she wanted, and she'd flash back a transparent 'up to you.' Everything here was in the eye of the beholder; everything was just a trick of the light. **"**

PICO IYER, *VIDEO NIGHT IN KATHMANDU*,
NEW YORK 1988

NAKHON PATHOM

THE WORLD'S BIGGEST PAGODA

Sunthorn Phu (1786–1856) is generally regarded as Thailand's greatest poet, the first to bring realism into Thai verse. Born shortly after the establishment of Bangkok as the capital, he was a particular favorite of King Rama II, during whose reign he wrote perhaps the most famous of his works, "Khun Chang and Khun Phan". Sunthorn Phu is also noted for his works in a Thai genre called the "nirat", a sort of travel poem that blends descriptions of actual places with meditations on life and love by the poet. The following is from his "Nirat Phra Pathom", about a journey to the famous chedi in what is today called Nakhon Pathom.

"At last, we arrive at the Pagoda of the Sleeping Buddha's Temple.
It stands alone and high on a hill;
Colossally solid like a parapet,
Mounted on a manmade promontory.
It was constructed with sharp corners, showing the front gable,
Covered with a thin sheet of tin up to the top,
Stretching staunch and seamless in brick-and-stucco walls,
Wrought with time-honored and meticulous workmanship.
We walk around the Pagoda at the base,
Seeing deer's traces and hearing wild cocks crowing.
The spot is overgrown with wild creepers,
Winding and sticking in a thick green cluster.
We see secluded cubicles built for monks
Who may take shelter in their pilgrimages.
We are moved by their ardent faith.
At the stairs, we gaze up the slope:
It's so steep that our faces remain upturned.
That must be the way to heaven when we die.
We make an effort to help one another upward.
Once reaching the upper level, we are high spirited.
Pity my sons who also come up.
They are not so tired as us adults, though.
We hold candles in reverential attitude
And walk clockwise around the Pagoda
Three times, according to ceremonious practice.
Then we sit down and pay respects.
We offer incense sticks, candles, and flowers,
Also the candles entrusted to us by many others.
The owners had already made their wishes.
May they keep their beauty to the end.
May they be happy, every one of them,
Until they become enlightened by faith.
I've brought these candles with a desire
To be related to them in every life to come.
May our mutual love materialize now
And, in the future, may it be complete.
I salute the Pagoda of the Holy Relics:
May the true religious live forever.
I make merit, so the Buddha helps me
Increase my power to attain enlightenment.
And I'd like my words, my book,
To preserve, till the end of time and heaven,
Sunthorn the scribe who belongs
To the King of the White Elephant. "

SUNTHORN PHU, *NIRAT PHRA PATHO*
TRANSLATED BY MONTRI UMAVIJA
BANGKOK 19

ITINERARIES

▲ Bangkok.

▲ Wat Phra Keo and Royal Palace, Bangkok. ▼ Lumpini Park and modern Bangkok.

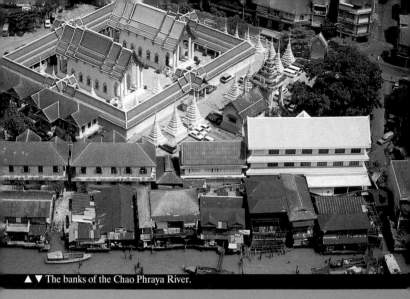

▲ ▼ The banks of the Chao Phraya River.

▼ Wat Thong Thammachat, Thonburi, in Bangkok.

▲ Phangnga Bay.

▼ Nai Han Beach, Phuket.

Kata Yai Beach, Phuket. ▼ Koh Phi Phi Le.

▲ Wat Phra Si Sanphet, Ayutthaya.

▲ Wat Mahathat, Sukhothai.　　　　　▼ Life on the river, Ayutthaya.

▲ Monks collecting alms in Chiang Mai. ▼ Duck farm, Singhburi.

▼ Floating market, Damnern Saduak.

BANGKOK

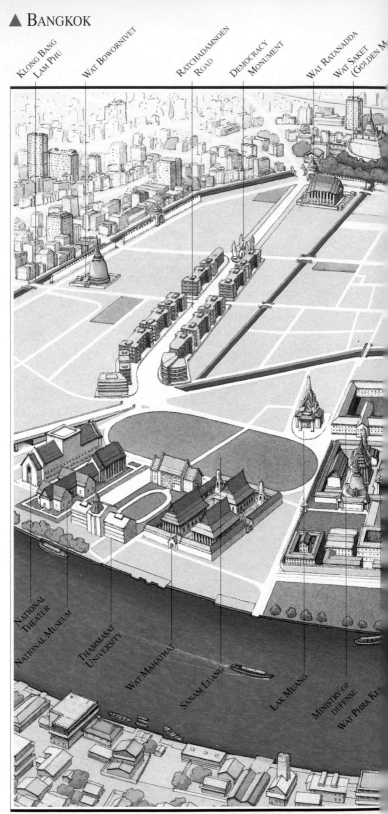

KLONG BANG LAM PHU

WAT BOWORNIVET

RATCHADAMNOEN ROAD

DEMOCRACY MONUMENT

WAT RATANADDA

WAT SAKET (GOLDEN M

NATIONAL THEATER

NATIONAL MUSEUM

THAMMASAT UNIVERSITY

WAT MAHATHAT

SANAM LUANG

LAK MUANG

MINISTRY OF DEFENSE

WAT PHRA KE

GIANT SWING

WAT SUTHAT

WAT RAJABOPIT

RAILWAY STATION

MEMORIAL BRIDGE

WAT ARUN

WAT RAJAPRADIT

ROYAL PALACE

WAT PO

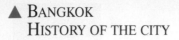

An early
view of
Bangkok from
the murals of
Wat Rajapradit,
painted in 1864.
Behind the roofs
of the Royal
Palace runs the
Chao Phraya,
lined with floating
houses on its banks.
Chinese shophouses
and Western-style
homes stand
among Thai
temples and
orchards.

Both literally and metaphorically, all roads in Thailand
lead to Bangkok (derived from *bang makok*, which means
"Village of the Wild Plum"), the center of almost everything:
of power both temporal and spiritual, of the ancient
monarchy, of commerce and communications, of higher
education and the arts, of that indispensable part of life the
Thais call *sanuk,* or "fun." It has a dynamic modern façade,
sprawling and often confusing to the newcomer, best
comprehended perhaps by looking back to the city's early
days.

THE FOUNDING OF BANGKOK

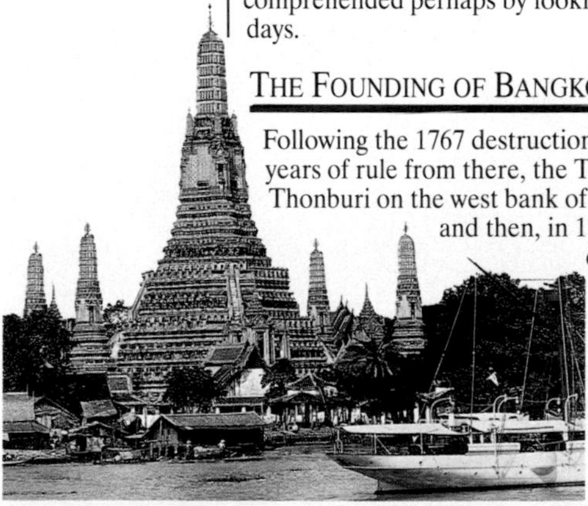

Following the 1767 destruction of Ayutthaya, after 400
years of rule from there, the Thai capital was moved first to
Thonburi on the west bank of the lower Chao Phraya River
and then, in 1782, to a small trading port
called Bangkok on the
opposite bank. King Rama
I, who decreed the move,
felt the position of the
new capital was more
defensible and that it
offered the space for a
capital worthy of the
Chakri Dynasty, which

« THE GENERAL APPEARANCE OF BANGKOK IS THAT OF A LARGE,
PRIMITIVE VILLAGE, SITUATED IN AND MOSTLY CONCEALED BY A
VIRGIN FOREST OF ALMOST IMPENETRABLE DENSITY.»

FRANK VINCENT, 1871

he had founded. He gave it a lengthy official title, which the
Thais have shortened to Krung Thep, "City of Angels," while
foreigners continue to use the old name; the period of Thai
history thus inaugurated is called Rattanakosin. As a
matter of interest, Krung Thep is adapted from its
actual name (listed in the *Guinness Book of
Records* as the world's longest place name):
*Krungthep Mahanakhon Bovorn Rattanakosin
Mahintharayutthaya Mahadilokpop
Noparatratchathani Burirom
Udomratchaniveymahasathan
Amornpiman Avatansathit
Sakkathattiya-avisnukarmprasit.*

RATTANAKOSIN ISLAND

The Grand Palace and its adjacent
royal chapel, the Temple of the
Emerald Buddha – both replicas of
Ayutthayan structures – were built
first on an artificial island created by
digging a canal where the river curved
sharply, a strategy that had been used at
Ayutthaya. Walled and fortified, the island
was the political and cultural heart of the
capital for more than a century. A group of
Chinese traders who had occupied the site were
moved outside the walls, where they formed the
nucleus of a flourishing community of narrow streets,
wharfs and warehouses that still exists. Spurred by
increasing trade with the outside world, relative political
stability and immigration (mainly Chinese), the city of
Bangkok expanded rapidly. Two new canals were excavated
and rows of floating houses ● 86 appeared on both banks of
the Chao Phraya, and ships began arriving from Europe as
well as neighboring countries. The floating houses served as
both shops and residences for most of the population. Not
until the 1820's did non-royal homes begin to appear on land,
the majority on the Thonburi side of the river. By the mid-
19th century, Bangkok had a population of 300,000 and was
well on its way to becoming a
major
metropolis.

**THE FOUNDER
OF BANGKOK**
King Rama I was a
former military
commander who
succeeded King
Taksin of Thonburi as
ruler in 1782; he also
began the Chakri
Dynasty, of which the
present king is the
ninth monarch. The
original buildings of
the Grand Palace, as
well as numerous
temples, date from
his seventeen-year
reign.

FLOATING HOUSES
Thousands of floating
houses, anchored to
stout posts, lined the
river and canals
of early Bangkok.

BANGKOK'S FIRST RICKSHAW

A wealthy Chinaman presented the first rickshaw to King Rama V in 1871; within a generation there were so many on the streets of Bangkok that, in 1901, a law was passed limiting their number. Automobiles arrived the following year. By 1908, there were over 300 cars; the invasion of this modern form of transportation spelled doom for the city's once numerous canals.

EARLY TIMES

Early Bangkok was a water-oriented city, with the river and an intricate system of canals, or klongs, serving as the means of communication. The first proper street appeared in 1862, during the reign of King Rama IV, and ran parallel to the river for a considerable distance. Along it were most of the embassies, trading companies and shophouses selling the latest imported goods. Soon roads began to radiate from the Chao Phraya, through former orchards and across ricefields, accommodating ever-growing numbers of rickshaws, carriages, trams and, in 1902, automobiles. King Rama V, inspired by his visits abroad attempted to create an orderly, European-style city in the Dusit district, with broad, tree-lined avenues and parks. But Bangkok resisted any such systematic planning; by World War Two it was sprawling in all directions from the original walled island. A building boom that started in the 1950's and continues to this day has transformed the capital almost beyond recognition to older Thais.

MODERN-DAY BANGKOK

Present-day Bangkok covers an area of some 600 square miles, on both sides of the river –forty-five times larger than its nearest provincial rival – and is home to an estimated seven million people, half of them below thirty years of age. (The exact population would be impossible to calculate; many are part-time laborers who come to work between farming chores, while others are still registered as residents of their hometowns despite years in the capital.) They live and work in a variety of centers, often commuting for several hours each day by bus, presently the city's only form of public transport. (Bangkok's public bus system, incidentally, is reputedly the largest in the world.) Government offices are concentrated mainly in the area around the Grand Palace and Ratchadamnoen Road, while Yaowarat Road and its environs are largely devoted to Chinese business firms and the powerful military has its headquarters behind high walls in the Dusit district. Silom Road has emerged as the financial district, with Patpong as a major attraction after nightfall; a number of leading hotels are also in this area. Though the streets off Sukhumwit Road comprise the prime residential district, new suburban housing estates can be found all around the city with shopping and recreational facilities constantly rising to meet the demands of their residents.

RECENT DEVELOPMENTS

The past decade or so has seen extensive construction along the Chao Phraya, especially on the Thonburi side, not only hotels but also residential condominiums for affluent Thais seeking a location more convenient to their offices. Nearly all of the country's major domestic and foreign businesses are located in Bangkok, along with the official residence of the royal family, government ministries, the most prestigious universities and preparatory schools, and the leading sports and cultural facilities. Thanks to this concentration of wealth and power, 90 percent of all the motor vehicles in the country are registered in the city, creating traffic congestion that an extensive network of overpasses and expressways has yet to solve. Though government policy encourages decentralization of industry into provincial areas, most of the modern factories are located in or near Bangkok, which is still the focus of the aviation, railway and communications systems, not to mention the extremely busy port of Klong Toey on the river, through which most of the country's imports and exports pass.

THAI TRAMS
Horse-drawn trams appeared on the streets of Bangkok in 1888; by the end of the century, the trams ran on electricity and continued to operate in decreasing numbers along New Road until the 1960's. The above painting, by contemporary artist Arunothai ● *102*, shows fashionably dressed tram passengers in the past.

CHINATOWN IN THE 1950'S
Yaowarat Road ▲ *176* is pictured in Chinatown during the 1950's, when trams were no longer the only public transport as buses were growing in popularity.

LATER PALACE BUILDINGS

The first Western-style buildings appeared in the palace enclosure during the reign of King Rama IV. These included a suite of rooms in the Siwalai Gardens, behind the Phra Maha Monthien, where the king lived and kept his collection of scientific instruments, and a tall structure with clocks on four sides. None of these remain today; they were torn down during the next reign, which saw the most extensive additions since the palace was built. King Rama V, the first Thai ruler to travel to Europe, ordered the construction of a new throne hall and royal residence. They were completed in time for the celebration of Bangkok's centenary in 1882.

AUDIENCE HALL
Thai kings since Rama V have traditionally received foreign ambassadors in the Central Audience Hall of the Chakri Maha Prasat, standing before a splendid wooden throne plated with silver and gold niello. On the walls are several large, European-style paintings of celebrated meetings between Thai ambassadors and King Louis XIV at Versailles.

CHAKRI MAHA PRASAT. Designed in neoclassical style by an English architect, the Chakri Maha Prasat was originally planned as a domed building, wholly Western in appearance; before completion, however, the dome was replaced with the older structures around it. The king and his principal queen moved to quarters on the upper floors of this structure and used the lower levels for state entertainment; a grand stairway reserved only for the king led down to the women's quarters behind the throne hall.

SIWALAI GARDENS. Also added most of the present buildings in now contains the Royal Boromphiman Mansion in the by a German architect as a Prince, and a few Western-style residences for queens and consorts in the Inner Palace. The gardens were used for receptions as well as a recreation area for the royal women and their children. Toward the end of his reign, King Rama V moved out of the Grand Palace to new

during the fifth reign wer the outer area, one of whic Household Bureau, th Siwalai Gardens, designe residence for the Crow

> «How can I describe the barbaric grandeur, the parade, the show, the glitter, the real magnificence, the profuse decorations of today's royal audience!»
>
> SIR JOHN BOWRING

quarters in the Dusit district but continued to use the older buildings for royal ceremonies, a tradition that was continued by subsequent rulers of the dynasty.

THE INNER PALACE. This was a secret world that much intrigued European visitors to Thailand in the 19th and early 20th centuries. According to Dr Malcolm Smith, an English physician who attended to King Rama V's principal queen and other royal patients, it "was a town complete in itself, a congested network of houses and narrow streets with gardens, lawns, artificial lakes and shops. It had its own government, its own institutions, its own laws and law courts. It was a town of women, one controlled by women. Men on special construction or repair work were admitted, and the doctors when they came to visit the sick. The king's sons could live there until they reached the age of puberty; after that they were sent to live with relations, or with the governors in the provinces. But the only man who lived within its walls was the king." At its peak, in King Rama V's reign toward the end of the 19th century, about 3,000 women lived in this part of the palace,

most of them servants or daughters of noble families who were sent here to learn various refined skills such as cooking, embroidery, and making floral wreaths. With the advent of royal monogamy in the next reign, the number steadily decreased as wives and princesses were allowed to move outside. A few stayed on, however, and the last resident died in the 1970's.

MUSEUMS IN THE PALACE COMPOUND

Just beyond the entrance is the Coins and Royal Decorations Museum. Early Thai coins and other items used as money are displayed here, in addition to medals and other decorations presented by Chakri kings for outstanding service, many of them set with precious stones. On the ground level of the Chakri Maha Prasat is a display of ancient weapons while near the Dusit Maha Prasat another museum contains stone inscriptions and palace decorations replaced during various renovations.

THE REGENT QUEEN
Queen Sowabha Phongsri, the principal queen of King Rama V, was the first of the royal wives to take up residence with the king outside the Inner Palace. She also served as regent during his trips abroad, and founded the first Thai girls' school and the Thai Red Cross, and, in general, was an important force in the liberation of Thai women from male domination.

THE TONSURE CEREMONY
One of the grandest rituals held in the Grand Palace was the Tonsure Ceremony, which marked the coming-of-age of children in the Inner Palace. After the tuft of hair was cut by Brahmin priests, the climax of a celebration that lasted several days, male children had to move out of the women's quarter to an outside residence.

145

The mythical half-bird, half-human *garuda* (above right) – legendary steed of the Hindu god Vishnu – is part of the royal insignia and appears among the decorations on many buildings within the palace compound.

As residence of the Lord of Life, as Thai kings are known, the royal palace has been the center of every capital in the country's history. The Grand Palace, surrounded by a high wall, covers nearly a square mile and, in its original form, was a conscious evocation of the one in Ayutthaya, divided into an outer part for government offices, a central portion containing the king's living quarters and audience halls, and an inner area for female members of the royal family and their attendants. Buildings were added to the palace compound by each of the first five Chakri rulers, particularly King Rama V, during whose reign Westernization was rapid.

The Dusit Maha Prasat depicted in a mid-19th-century engraving.

EARLY BUILDINGS

DUSIT MAHA PRASAT. Among the original palace buildings that still remain, though modified by later kings, is the Dusit Maha Prasat throne hall. Covered with four-tier tiled roofs and surmounted by a seven-tier gilded spire, it contains a blackwood throne inlaid with mother-of-pearl dating from the reign of King Rama I. The remains of kings, queens and royal family members are placed in the Dusit Maha Prasat prior to cremation. The building is open to the public.

THE PHRA THINANG APHONPHIMOK PRASAT. King Rama IV introduced Western architecture to the palace and was also responsible for one of its most beautiful traditional structures

King Rama V alighting at the Phra Thinang Aphonphimok Prasat pavilion at the turn of the century. The pavilion is a major attraction today.

the Phra Thinang Aphonphimok Prasat (right). This pavilion on the east wall surrounding the Dusit Maha Prasat was where the king changed his robes before descending a flight of steps to mount a

palanquin. The structure displays graceful elegance and a distinctive blend of simple with sumptuous decoration epitomizes classic Thai architecture. It was reproduced at the Brussels Exposition in 1958.

THE GRAND RESIDENCE GROUP. Also from the earliest period of the palace is a group of connecting buildings known as Phra Maha Monthien, "the Grand Residence." The first three kings of the dynasty lived in one of these, the Phra Thinang Chakraphat Phiman – Phra Thinang is a title bestowed on any structure (building, pavilion, throne and so on) used by a king. It contains the royal bedchamber and it is still traditional for new monarchs to spend a night here upon assuming the throne, symbolizing their assumption of residence in the palace of their ancestors. In front and connected by a flight of stairs is the Phra Thinang Phaisan Taksin, where coronation ceremonies are held. It also houses two historic thrones, the Royal Regalia, and a small, much venerated image called Phra Siam Thewathirat, regarded as the tutelary deity of the Thai nation. The first Chakri king is supposed to have made regular use of this hall and, when old, to have held private audiences from one of its windows with people in the courtyard below. From the Octagonal Throne on the east side, new kings formally receive the invitation to rule over the kingdom, while from the Phattrabit Throne on the west, they receive the Royal Regalia, consisting of the crown, a sword, a royal staff, a fan, a whisk made of yak's tail, bejeweled slippers, and the Great White Umbrella of State. In the northern wall of the Phaisan Taksin is a gate known as Thewarat Mahesuan, through which only the king, the queen, and the royal children may walk. This leads to the Phra Thinang Amarin Winitchai, originally the principal audience hall of the Middle Palace where officials of state and foreign ambassadors were received. Dominating this hall – the only one in the group now open to the public – is the Phra Thinang Busbok Mala, an open-pillar construction of ornately carved wood with a tiered roof, made during the reign of King Rama I; to the left and right of the base are lateral extensions that make the structure appear to be floating in the air. The whole rests on a gilded masonry dais that dates from the reign of King Rama III. Curtains were drawn to conceal the king when he entered from the Phaisan Taksin; when it was time for the audience a fanfare sounded, the curtains dramatically parted, and the ruler was revealed in all the magnificence of his Royal Regalia. The Phra Thinang Busbok Mala throne (above right) is reserved for kings and objects of veneration. It holds the urns containing the ashes of previous Chakri kings. From his place on the throne, the reigning Chakri king receives offerings and presides over the prayers of the royal family. Another throne in the building known as the Phra Thaen Sawetachat, is still used by the King for some of the investiture ceremonies as well as for the annual birthday audience.

View of the Phra Maha Monthien, a group of interlinked buildings known as "the Grand Residence" (above).

The Phra Thinang Busbok Mala throne, which contains funerary urns of the Chakri kings (below).

A large collection of ancient topiary – shrubbery trimmed into fancy shapes – adorns the front courtyard of the palace, a decorative technique that was probably inspired by plants in Chinese gardens.

WAT PHRA KEO

Wat Phra Keo, the Temple of the Emerald Buddha, serves as the royal chapel and as such is located in one corner of the Grand Palace compound; unlike other Buddhist temples, it has no resident monks.

THE EMERALD BUDDHA ▲ *170.* The fabled statue – the Phra Keo – was discovered when lightning struck an ancient stupa in northern Thailand in the early 15th century. Over the next five centuries, legends accumulated around the small seated image – 26 inches high and 19 inches wide at the lap span, actually carved from a semiprecious form of jade. It was enshrined in a number of northern cities and also, for more than 250 years, in Laos; the future King Rama I brought it back to Thailand after having destroyed Vientiane to take possession of it, and later made it the principal Buddha image of his new capital at Bangkok. The image is the most venerated of all the thousands in the country.

PALLADIA
The Emerald Buddha is the most eminent example of the Palladia, images reputed to be endowed with supernatural powers and considered protectors of a town, a king, or a dynasty.

Today the Emerald Buddha sits high atop an ornate throne of gilded wood in the bot of Wat Phra Keo,

«THE KING WAS THE DISK OF LIGHT AND LIFE.»
ANNA LEONOWENS

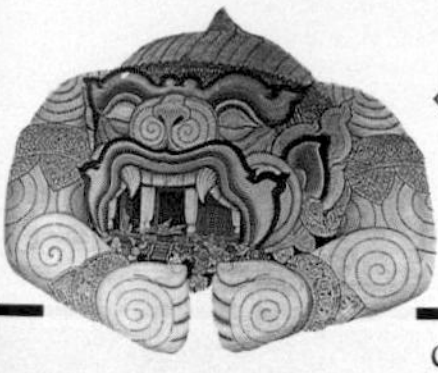

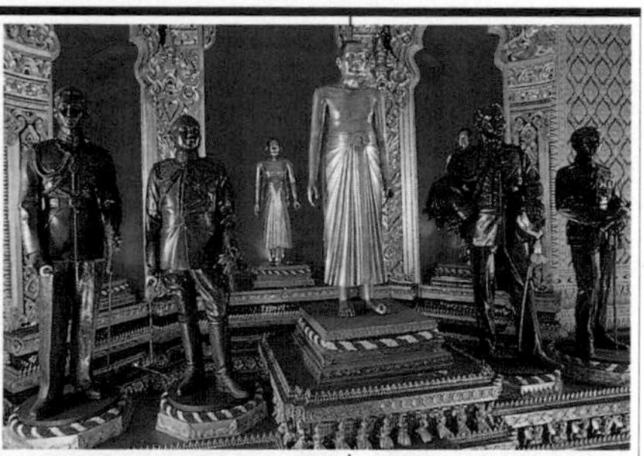

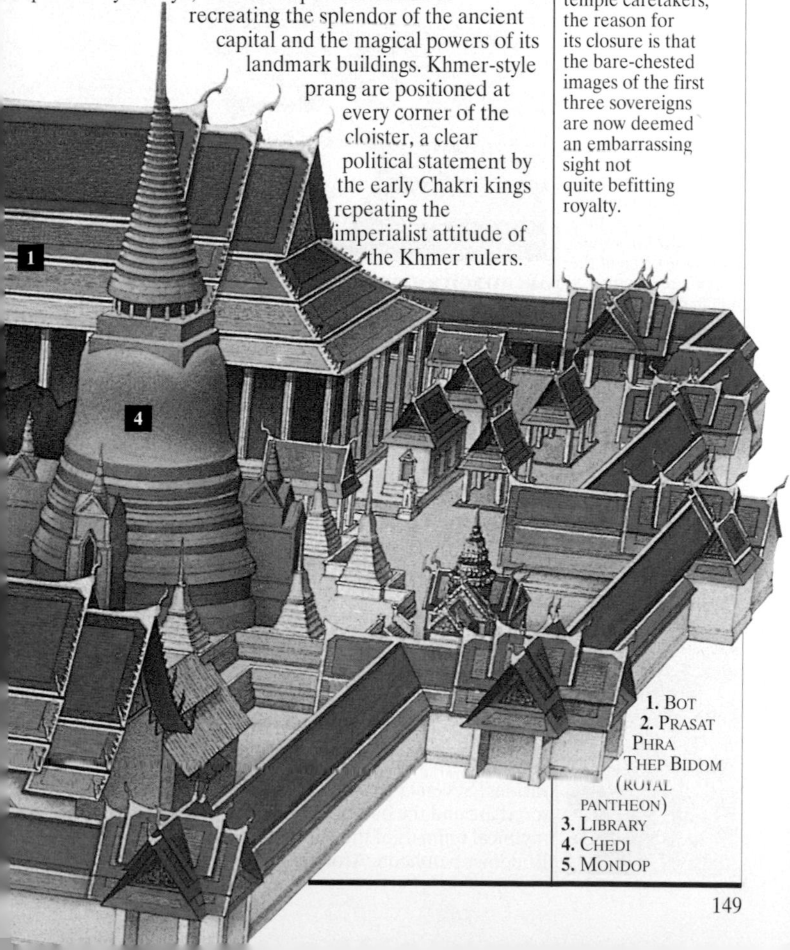

THE ROYAL PANTHEON
The reconstructed Prasat Phra Thep Bidom contains statues of previous Chakri kings. Usually closed, it is open to the public only on special occasions. According to temple caretakers, the reason for its closure is that the bare-chested images of the first three sovereigns are now deemed an embarrassing sight not quite befitting royalty.

constructed by King Rama I but extensively refurbished and added to by later kings. The carved gable boards of the building show the god Vishnu astride a *garuda* ▲ *146*, while the outer walls are richly decorated with gilded stucco and glass mosaics. Three times a year, at the beginning of each season – cool, hot and rainy – the robes of the image are changed in an elaborate ceremony presided over by the king; countless ordinary Thais also come regularly to make offerings at the temple and pray for various wishes to be granted.

OTHER BUILDINGS. On the side of the bot, also aligned on an east-west axis, are three elaborate buildings set very close to each other: the Prasat Phra Thep Bidom, reconstructed by Rama V, and converted by Rama VI into the royal pantheon; a library in the shape of a square *mondop* ● *90*, a replica of the Temple of the Buddha's Footprint in Saraburi; and a gilded chedi built with a design similar to those of Wat Si Sanphet in Ayutthaya, with the explicit intention of recreating the splendor of the ancient capital and the magical powers of its landmark buildings. Khmer-style prang are positioned at every corner of the cloister, a clear political statement by the early Chakri kings repeating the imperialist attitude of the Khmer rulers.

1. BOT
2. PRASAT PHRA THEP BIDOM (ROYAL PANTHEON)
3. LIBRARY
4. CHEDI
5. MONDOP

MYTHOLOGICAL CREATURES
Many of the divinities whose statues adorn the compound of Wat Phra Keo are of Hindu origin, further evidence of the blending of Buddhism with other religions. Some are fabulous animals that inhabited an imaginary forest in the Himalayas called the Himavat (the Himaphan in Thai). These include the *tantima* bird, a strange creature with a cock's comb and a parrot-like beak; the more graceful, swan-like *hong,* often at the top of a pole with a bell in its beak; and the elegant bird-humans, the *kinnon* (male) and *kinnari* (female). Also present is the *garuda,* traditional mount of the god Vishnu; Siva's steed, the sacred bull called *nandi;* and *ganesha,* the elephant-headed son of Siva and his consort Parvati.

ARCHITECTURAL DECORATIONS. The various structures at Wat Phra Keo display a virtual textbook of classic Thai decorative techniques and mythological statuary. Entire walls are transformed into shimmering, jewel-like expanses through th use of glass mosaics or carefully fitted pieces of multicolored porcelain; wooden gables and roof supports are richly carved and gilded, and doors and windows are adorned either with intricate mother-of-pearl inlay designs or gold-and-black lacquer paintings. All of them were restored for the 1982 Bangkok bicentennial celebrations, having fallen into a state of disrepair. The multitiered roofs are covered with colored tiles, chedis and stupas with layers of glittering gold leaf, while the interiors of most buildings are decorated with complex mural paintings. The gates leading into the courtyard are flanked by huge statues of *yaksa,* or demons, supposed to ward off evil spirits. They are brightly painted and covered with glass mosaic decorations. Several bronze statues scattered around the buildings represent mythical animals of the Hindu and Buddhist pantheon. Around the basement

> «THIS SACERDOTAL DISNEYLAND IS ENTERED
> THROUGH A GATE SET IN CLOISTERS WHOSE INNER WALLS
> CARRY MURALS DEPICTING THE "RAMAKIEN"».
>
> ALISTAIR SHEARER

THE "RAMAKIEN"

The *Ramakien*, the Thai version of the *Ramayana*, appears in mural paintings, as in the galleries of Wat Phra Keo, in bas-relief carvings, like those at Wat Po, and also in illustrated manuscript books. It provides the stories for the *khon* (classical masked dance) ● *64–5*. Though all the manuscripts recounting the legend from the Ayutthaya period were destroyed when the capital fell to the Burmese in 1767, the story was already an established part of Thai cultural tradition. King Rama I himself rewrote it after the founding of Bangkok, and the second king of the Chakri dynasty also produced a version for the dance.

REPLICA OF ANGKOR WAT

A model of Angkor Wat, the famous center of Khmer culture, was placed in the temple compound by King Rama IV, as a reminder of the time when Cambodia was a vassal state of Thailand. The territory was lost in the late 19th century when the French exerted pressure on King Rama V and redefined the borders of Indo-China.

...here the chedi, the *mondop* and the pantheon are built, ...ere are a number of small Chinese gardens embellished by ...ing statues of animals and heavenly guards.

...URAL PAINTINGS OF THE "RAMAKIEN". On the walls of the ...lleries surrounding Wat Phra Keo are a series of panoramic ...ural paintings that depict the story of the *Ramakien*, the ...hai version of the *Ramayana*, an Indian epic dealing with the ...umph of good over evil. The tale is told in 178 panels, each ...cupying the area between two pillars of the many that ...pport the gallery; poems about the action, composed in the ...ign of King Rama V, are inscribed on marble slabs set into ...e relevant pillar. Though originally painted by order of King ...ama I when the temple was built, ...e murals have been restored many ...nes, most recently for the 1982 ...angkok bicentennial celebrations. ...ese works are almost identical to ...e original 1930 compositions ...ecuted under the direction of ...ra Thewapinimmit, and reflect ...e style of that era with Western ...rspective, the use of shadows, and ...turalistic rendering of the land-...ape, and with characters drawn in ...onventional Thai manner.

STONE BALLASTS
Literally hundreds of
Chinese stone figures
– animals both
realistic and whim-
sical, humans both
small and fearsomely
huge – are scattered
throughout Wat Po;
similar ones can be
seen in other major
Bangkok palaces and
temples. Most came
to Thailand in the
early 19th century as
ballast on ships
returning empty from
the lucrative rice
trade and were placed
in the temple during
King Rama III's
reign, a period that
also saw an increase
in Chinese influence
on architecture and
decorative motifs.
Prominent among the
statues are the tower-
ing door guardians, or
protective demons,
that stand beside each
of the sixteen
monumental gates
leading into the
temple and beside
those that divide the
various compounds.
The latter represent
Europeans, as shown
by their tall, brimmed
hats that the sculp-
tors had perhaps
observed in Chinese
port cities and
assumed all
foreigners
wore.

The oldest and largest temple in Thailand, Wat Phra
Chetuphon, popularly known as Wat Po – derived from its
original name of Wat Bodharam – was founded in the 16th
century during the Ayutthaya period. It was a particular
favorite with the early Chakri kings, most of whom restored

or added buildings to its huge compound. Chetuphon Road,
along which King Rama I supposedly rode on his way to
Thonburi when he was crowned in 1782, separates the
monastic buildings housing some 300 priests from the
enclosure containing the
structures used for religious
ceremonies. In its heyday, this
was the home of more than
500 monks and 750 novices, and
the monks' quarters are still a
veritable city within the city.
Most of the buildings were
reconstructed during the
fifth reign, replacing older
wooden houses, and the
mansions of the most
reverend monks are
often embellished with
precious gilded stucco.

Wat Po's greatest benefactor was King Rama III
(1824–51), who was responsible not only for most of
the buildings the visitor sees today but also for turning
the temple into a kind of open university, filled with
displays of educational material. Twenty small hills
scattered around the compound, for example, conta
geological specimens from all parts of Thailand; a
collection of stone Rishi, or hermits, demonstrates

various yoga positions; and inscriptions and mural paintings deal with such diverse subjects as warfare, medicine, astrology, botany and history. Anyone who was interested in either religious or secular knowledge could study the wealth of information compiled from ancient textbooks and presented

to the public in this most democratic way. It was an unprecedented move in a society where knowledge had always been the privilege of the few. King Rama I, who was the founder of Bangkok and the first restorer of Wat Po, is credited with salvaging 1,200 statues from the ruins of Ayutthaya. The collection contains 689 of the rescued statues. Many others were added to it by later kings. The temple is a veritable gallery of Thai art, practically covering every historical period. Most of the images are displayed along the cloisters and serve to top the chedis containing ashes of the illustrious deceased. In an attempt to preserve these rows of statues, renovation work has since been carried out, and they are now encased in glass.

SCHOOL FOR TRADITIONAL
MEDICINE. One aspect of Wat Po's old educational function that remains very much alive today is the School for Traditional Medicine, in the eastern part of the temple compound. Besides offering courses of instruction in herbal medicines and Thai-style massage, authorized members of the profession offer treatment to the public in the late afternoons; marble engravings on the walls, placed there in the reign of King Rama III, give various rules regarding the subject. Foreigners can take a fifteen-day course in traditional massage, with classes held for two hours daily, while skilled masseurs are usually available at around 120 baht per hour.

Within the monks' quarters on the other side of Chetuphon Road, expert chiropractors attend to local patients using ancient techniques under the watchful eyes of monks who sanction the operation by spitting holy water on the ailing part, while assistants beat furiously at the drums.

TEMPLE ASTROLOGERS. This temple, very popular with local and foreign visitors, also attracts a large number of street vendors, snake charmers, astrologers, palmists and other entertainers to its premises. It is well known for its colony of resident astrologers.

RISHI FIGURES
The stone Rishi, or hermits, in the outer courtyard of Wat Po, were formerly located in a series of sixteen pavilions and moved to their present site during the reign of King Rama V. They demonstrate yoga positions to relieve physical and mental complaints and promote meditative contemplation, a reminder of the time when the temple was a leading center of public education.

TREATISE ON MASSAGE
Small buildings around the cloister that encircles the chedis of the Four Kings display a series of murals, showing the techniques of Thai massage. The subject is further illustrated by statues of hermits in various yoga stances and self-massage techniques.

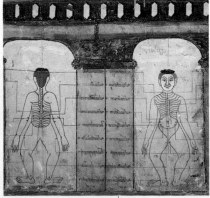

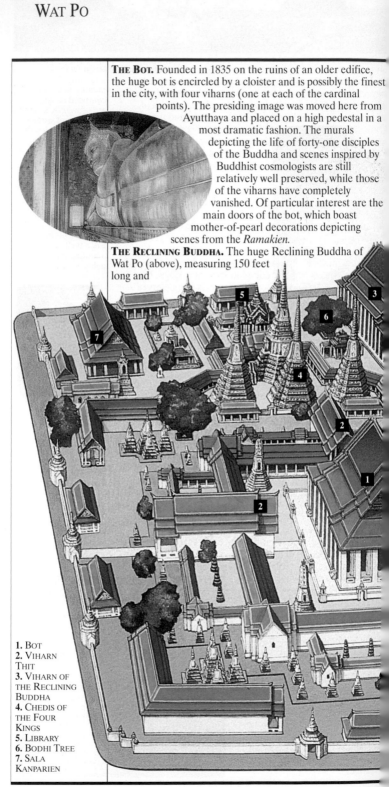

THE BOT. Founded in 1835 on the ruins of an older edifice, the huge bot is encircled by a cloister and is possibly the finest in the city, with four viharns (one at each of the cardinal points). The presiding image was moved here from Ayutthaya and placed on a high pedestal in a most dramatic fashion. The murals depicting the life of forty-one disciples of the Buddha and scenes inspired by Buddhist cosmologists are still relatively well preserved, while those of the viharns have completely vanished. Of particular interest are the main doors of the bot, which boast mother-of-pearl decorations depicting scenes from the *Ramakien*.

THE RECLINING BUDDHA. The huge Reclining Buddha of Wat Po (above), measuring 150 feet long and

1. BOT
2. VIHARN THIT
3. VIHARN OF THE RECLINING BUDDHA
4. CHEDIS OF THE FOUR KINGS
5. LIBRARY
6. BODHI TREE
7. SALA KANPARIEN

«OH! WAT PO IS THE MONASTERY BUILT BY A KING; IT IS NEVER
NEGLECTED AND IT IS RESPLENDENT LIKE HEAVEN...»

SUNTHORN PHU

50 feet high, and covered with layers of gold leaf, represents
the dying Buddha at the moment he entered Nirvana. Its most
impressive artistic feature is the inlaid mother-of-pearl
designs that adorn the soles of its feet, depicting the
legendary signs by which the true Buddha can be recognized.
Only the upper parts remain of the once superb mural
paintings that adorned the interior walls of the building
housing the image, constructed during the reign of King
Rama III.

CHEDIS OF THE FOUR KINGS. Not far from the bot, in a low-
walled enclosure, stand four tall chedis, or stupas, decorated
with porcelain and dedicated to the first four Chakri kings:
the green one, containing a standing Buddha from Ayutthaya,
to Rama I; the white one to Rama II; the yellow one to
Rama III; and the blue one to Rama IV.

THE LIBRARY. Founded by Rama I but restored in the third
reign, the library is one of the most graceful edifices in
Bangkok. The central chamber is topped by an elaborate
crown-like cupola and spire; four extended porticoes create a
Greek-cross plan. The building is decorated with glazed
tiles and polychrome ceramic pieces. John Crawfurd,
who led a British embassy to the court of King Rama
II in 1822, noted the gardens surrounding the
building, one of which had a pond with crocodiles.
Today, the library is set in an elegant Chinese-
style garden.

THE BODHI TREE. Next to the library stands
an ancient Bodhi tree, whose imposing
presence is enhanced by two Chinese
pavilions, where a statue of
Guan Yin (also known as the
Goddess of Mercy), is the
object of devotion. The area
is called the "Garden of
the Transplanted Tree,"
referring to the
tree that grew
from a cutting of
the original
Bodhi tree in
Anura-
dhapura.

"RAMAKIEN" PANELS
Around the base
of the bot are a
series of 152 marble
panels engraved
with scenes from the
Ramakien, the Thai
version of the
Ramayana. The
panels show one of
the main episodes,
the abduction of
Sida and her
eventual recovery
after several battles.
The incompleteness
of the episode and
its abrupt ending
suggest that they
may have been
salvaged from other
temples – perhaps in
Ayutthaya – and
subsequently moved
to Bangkok. There
is, however, no
record of their
origin. The marble
panels were once
used to make stone
rubbings for sale to
tourists; similar
rubbings are now
made from copies of
the carvings
▲ *151.*

2

2

THE SECOND KING
The office of the Second King, who served as vice-ruler, was a peculiarly Thai institution that began in the Ayutthaya period. The position was abolished in the reign of King Rama V, when the heir apparent became known as the Crown Prince.

SANAM LUANG

The large oval field across from the Grand Palace is popularly known as Sanam Luang, "the Royal Field." More formally, it is called the Pramane Ground, the place where royal cremations are held, the last having been that of Queen Rambhai Barni, consort of King Rama VII, in

1985. The Plowing Ceremony to forecast the coming agricultural crop is held here in May, while on the King's Birthday and at New Year Sanam Luang becomes a giant festival, with movies and other amusements. On the eastern side are government ministries, while on the west are Silpakorn University, Wat Mahathat, Thammasat University and the National Museum.

NATIONAL MUSEUM

Bangkok's National Museum – which has over thirty branches throughout the country – is housed partly in the palace of the Second King, a sort of vice-ruler, originally built in the reign of King Rama I. The collection was moved there from the Grand Palace by King Rama V in 1887, and under King Rama VII (1925–34) it was expanded and placed under the Royal Institute of Literature, Archeology and Fine Arts, later the Fine Arts Department. Two modern buildings were

A watercolor sketch of Sanam Luang at the turn of the century, when rickshaws were still in existence.

constructed on either side of the old palace in 1967, while a new gallery on Thai history was opened during Bangkok's bicentennial celebrations (1982).

BUDDHAISAWAN CHAPEL. The Buddhaisawan Chapel was built in 1787 to enshrine an important northern Buddha image called the Phra Buddha Si Hing, and is now within the grounds of the museum. The interior walls are painted with exceptionally fine murals showing scenes from the life of the Buddha, while the building itself is an outstanding example of early Bangkok religious architecture.

TAMNAK DAENG. Tamnak Daeng, or "Red House," was the residence of an elder sister of King Rama I. It was moved from Thonburi by King Rama II to the Grand Palace compound and later, in the fourth reign, to its present location in the museum grounds. Furniture and other items of the early Bangkok period are displayed inside ● 87.

THE MUSEUM COLLECTION. The National Museum's collection covers the whole range of art found in the country, religious and secular, fine and decorative, Thai and otherwise. The Prehistoric Gallery, for instance, includes Neolithic tools and pottery dating as far back as 10,000 BC, in addition to superb painted pots and bronze objects unearthed at various excavations in the northeast. Numerous creations of the pre-Thai Srivijaya, Dvaravati and Khmer kingdoms are also displayed, as well as those of the early Thai settlements of the far north. Thai Buddhist art encompasses images in stone, bronze and terracotta from the Sukhothai, Ayutthaya and Rattanakosin (Bangkok) periods, together with such religious items as illustrated scripture books, manuscript cabinets and votive plaques. Open daily except Mondays and Tuesdays, the museum also contains a large selection of miscellaneous arts, among them Thai and Chinese ceramics, theatrical costumes, textiles, furniture, funeral chariots, palanquins, elephant howdahs, weapons, puppets and assorted objects used in royal households. Guided tours in English are also offered to visitors on certain days of the week by the National Museum Volunteer Group.

PRIZED AMULETS
Amulets, usually in the form of a clay votive plaque bearing the image of the Buddha or of a particularly revered monk, are highly prized by most Thais. Mounted in gold or silver, they are worn on chains around the neck to avert misfortune. Many are sold on the sidewalks near Sanam Luang, particularly around Wat Mahathat.

157

The earliest reminder of Buddha's teachings was a mound of earth, which eventually evolved into the stupa. Later, feeling the need for a more concrete symbol, adherents to the faith began to make images. Various schools of thought arose concerning the exact features and *mudra*, or gestures, of such images, eventually resulting in a wide range of choices as revealed in the different periods of Thai art. This evolution of the image of Buddha can be seen in those displayed in the National Museum.

DVARAVATI
Dvaravati images (7th–11th century), mostly in stone, stucco, or terracotta, are heavy-featured and realistic in appearance, with prominent curls.

LOPBURI
Strongly influenced by Khmer images, those of Lopburi (7th–14th century) have stylized faces with broad mouths that seem to be faintly smiling; later ones are often in royal attire.

SUKHOTHAI SEATED IMAGE
Bronze was the medium preferred by sculptors of 13th–15th-century Sukhothai and the one in which they produced their greatest work. Most images are seated with the hand in the gesture called *bhumisparsa mudra*, or "touching the earth."

CASTING BUDDHA IMAGES

Bronze Buddha images are cast by the "lost wax" process, which involves a clay core in the rough form desired, a covering of wax carved into the shape of the image, and an outer mold of clay. The wax is then melted and drained off and molten bronze poured in to replace it. Casting often takes place in a temple compound, accompanied by a variety of ceremonies. The mural shown on the right, in Wat Bowornivet ▲ *165*, Bangkok, depicts the castings of three famous images, namely the Phra Buddha Chinaraj, Phitsanulok, and two large images now in Wat Bowornivet. The event took place in the late Sukhothai period.

AYUTTHAYA

Ayutthaya images (14th–18th century) display a variety of styles; the most characteristic is richly attired and adorned, reflecting the Ayutthaya association of kingship and religion.

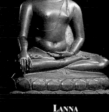

LANNA

The typical northern 13th–20th-century Lanna image has a round face, large curls, a prominent chin, and a thick, solid body; it is often seated on a lotus-blossom base.

RATTANAKOSIN

Rattanakosin or 18th–20th-century Bangkok images are frequently standing and heavily ornamented, the faces narrow and somewhat characterless, and the postures and *mudra* often unfamiliar; after the mid-19th century they display an increased sense of realism.

SUKHOTHAI WALKING IMAGE

The outstanding Sukhothai image is considered by scholars to be the walking Buddha, with exaggerated physical characteristics yet possessing a fluid grace and a powerful spiritual sense.

RATTANAKOSIN

A beautiful ivory image of Buddha, late 19th century.

The stone Bodhisattva Avalokitesvara (left) stands just over 3 feet tall and exhibits Indian influence, which was very important throughout the early to middle centuries of the first millennium. This statue, originally from Chaiya ● *96* ▲ *190*, dates from the 6th–7th century.

A fine example of Sukhothai ceramics, this glazed stoneware figure of a horseman dates from the 14th–15th century.

The stone Vishnu from Takua Pa (left), 7 feet tall, dates from the 8th–9th century and is among the large display of early Hindu statues that make up one of the most interesting sections of the museum's collection.

There are many bronzes of Hindu gods dating from the Sukhothai period. These were once worshiped at the Brahmin temple of Bangkok, having been moved there from the ruins of Sukhothai by King Rama I. Depicted here (left) is a 10-foot-tall image of Shiva.

The art of the early Mon kingdom of Dvaravati can be seen in the large collection of terracottas and stuccos ▲ *187*. Above is a stucco *yaksa* dating from the 9th century and found in Nakhon Pathom. The head (right), dating from slightly earlier, was found at Ku Bua.

Thepanom Sukhothai glazed stone figure, 14th–15th century.

A pair of Sukhothai-period praying deities in terracotta.

The Buddhaisawan Chapel, within the grounds of the National Museum, contains some of the best mural paintings of the Bangkok School, executed during the reign of Rama I. On the right is a detail from a mural showing the descent of Buddha from heaven on a ladder made of *naga* and jewels. On his left is a golden ladder for Indra and on his right a silver ladder for Brahma. These two gods accompanied him back to earth after he preached to his mother and the gods for three months. A gold-lacquered screen from the early 19th century displays a scene from the *Ramakien* (left) ▲ *151*.

The Lanna bronze elephant (right) dates from AD 1575 and was originally used as a support for presenting offerings. The duck-shaped water vessel (below) dates from the 14th–15th century.

OTHER SIGHTS IN SANAM LUANG

WAT MAHATHAT. This temple dates from before the founding of Bangkok, but was extensively restored during the reign of King Rama I and became one of the city's most important monasteries. The future King Rama IV served as one of its abbots. Today, Wat Mahathat (above) houses a college for Buddhist priests and offers meditation classes for foreigners. On weekends, the temple is usually filled with peddlers who display and sell amulets to visitors.

"LAK MUANG." Standing outside the walls of Wat Phra Keo, the *lak muang* (the city's foundation stone pillar) is in the form of a *lingam* (below right) that serves as the abode of Bangkok's guardian spirit and as the spot from which distances in the city are measured. First erected by King Rama I in 1782, it is now sheltered by an ornate pavilion and is visited by large numbers of supplicants who come to ask for almost anything, from matrimonial harmony to a winning ticket in the national lottery. In addition to making offerings of flowers and incense, many also pay for theatrical performances by dancers in traditional costumes.

SILPAKORN UNIVERSITY. Silpakorn (Fine Arts) University is housed partly in an old palace of the first reign. It owes its

A VENERATED PIG
Overlooking a canal near Saranrom Palace is a large statue of a pig, covered with layers of gold leaf offered by supplicants. This was erected in honor of Queen Sowabha Phongsri, the principal Queen of King Rama V, who was born in the year of that animal. It has become an important shrine for people of the area, who believe it has the power to grant various wishes.

«ENTERTAIN NOT THY THOUGHTS WITH WORLDLY THINGS.
DO NO WORK BUT THE WORK OF CHARITY AND TRUTH.»

BUDDHIST PRECEPTS

existence largely to Corrado Ferroci, an Italian sculptor. Ferroci began working for the Thai government in 1924, founded the School of Fine Arts in 1933, and lived in the country under the Thai name of Silpa Bhirasri until his death in 1962. The building fronting Sanam Luang is decorated with a frieze in Art Nouveau style painted by Italian artists.

NATIONAL THEATER. The huge National Theater was erected in the early 1970's. It became the hub of cultural and musical activities: dance troupes and foreign orchestras once performed here. It plays a less important role today, though classical drama performances are still staged occasionally at the theater. Attached to the National Theater is a dance school where young students practice the art of Thai classical dance. On its premises is a temple that was formerly part of the palace of the Second King. It provides an elegant backdrop to the rehearsals put on by the students.

Wat Rajapradit.

MURALS OF 1864
The bot of Wat Rajapradit is decorated with an unusual set of murals painted in 1864, during the reign of King Rama IV. These depict various royal ceremonies held during the twelve months of the year and constitute a rare historical record of early Bangkok since many of those ceremonies are no longer performed
▲ *140*.

WAT RAJAPRADIT ★

A small, serene temple built during King Rama IV's reign, Wat Rajapradit (above right) is located in a compound adjacent to the garden of the former Saranrom Palace, where King Rama IV often said he wished to retire. The main building is sheathed in gray marble from China and raised on a high stone platform, while on both sides of the building are Khmer-style prangs; on the terrace behind the temple is a stupa also covered with gray marble. The doors are adorned with gold-and-black lacquer paintings and the gables and eaves are decorated with fine carvings. Wat Rajapradit has a restful atmosphere not very often found in larger temple compounds, but as the doors are often locked, tourists may only visit the temple on the 1st and the 15th of each lunar month, when the local folk come to pray and present alms to the monks.

A RESTING PLACE
Wat Saket appears in most 19th-century accounts of Bangkok not only because of its Golden Mount but also because it was a resting place for the dead during cholera epidemics. Too numerous for conventional cremation, the bodies were laid out at the temple for vultures to devour. Anna Leonowens, the Englishwoman who was hired by King Rama IV to teach some of his wives and children, wrote: "None but the initiated will approach these grounds after sunset, so universal and profound is the horror the place inspires – a place the most frightful and offensive known to mortal eyes." Paupers and unidentified dead bodies were also brought to Wat Saket for more conventional cremation.

WAT SAKET AND THE GOLDEN MOUNT

"Just outside the city wall is the Golden Mount, a bell-shaped mound faced with brick, but so overgrown by trees that it has the appearance of a natural hillock…From here we look down upon a forest of palms and plane-trees, through which break the red roofs of the houses. Everywhere rising above the trees are graceful spires and the manifold roofs of temples, with their tiles of rich orange or deep purple, great splashes of color against the clear blue sky…" That was a description by P.A. Thomson in 1910 of the view from the Golden Mount. Today a visitor to the mount enjoys a different view altogether. Phu Khao Thong, the Golden Mount, is an artificial hill topped by a large gilded stupa that has long

been the highest elevation in Bangkok and one of
the city's most celebrated landmarks. The stupa
measures 260 feet from its base to the tip of its
spire. A replica of a similar hill in Ayutthaya, this
was a major feat of 19th-century engineering,
begun by King Rama V but not completed until
the following reign. The stupa, reached by a
flight of 300 steps, contains relics of the Buddha
presented to King Rama V by Lord Curzon,
Viceroy of India, in 1897. The Golden Mount
lies within the compound of Wat Saket. Built by
King Rama I, Wat Saket is one of the oldest
temples in Bangkok, though it has often been
restored and few of the original mural paintings
and other decorations remain. One of its
sanctuaries has a large standing Buddha image brought from
Sukhothai by the first Chakri king. The temple contains an
interesting pavilion that was once a temple library and that
was moved to its present location from Ayutthaya. It dates
from the late 17th century and features gilded panels with
Chinese-style motifs and classic lacquered windows. Some of
the windows were exhibited in Paris on the occasion of the
third centenary of Thai-French diplomatic relations.

The window panels of
the library of Wat
Saket portray a series
of foreigners –
merchants, traders
and ambassadors –
who used to frequent
cosmopolitan
Ayutthaya in its
heyday.

CITY WALLS

Like Ayutthaya, Rattanakosin
Island was once surrounded by a
high wall, studded at intervals
with watchtowers. Much of the
wall has been pulled down in the
city's expansion, though a
restored turret remains opposite
Wat Rajanadda.

The city walls fronting
Wat Saket at the turn
of the century.

WAT BOWORNIVET

Built by King Rama III for his brother, who spent the better
part of his life as a monk before ascending the throne as King
Rama IV, this monastery is renowned for the murals of the
bosot, painted for the first time in Thai history in Western
perspective by the monk artist Khrua In Khong ● 106–7. The
temple houses three important large Sukhothai images
● 161 and a Buddha from Borobodur donated by the Dutch
government to King Rama V.

The Lohaprasad
in the compound
of Wat
Rajanadda.

WAT RAJANADDA

With the removal of a movie theater that long
concealed it, the architectural beauties of Wat
Rajanadda are now visible to passers-by. Its
most interesting feature is the Lohaprasad,
started by King Rama III but only completed a
decade ago by the Fine Arts Department. It has
six levels, each housing small ornamental
pavilions, is 110 feet high and overlooks
Ratchadamnoen Klong Avenue. A new pavilion
outside the temple serves as a reception area for
important foreign visitors to Bangkok.

BAMRUNG MUANG ROAD
This road, which leads to the square with the Giant Swing, is almost entirely devoted to shops selling various Buddhist items – images of all sizes, mostly bronze, as well as robes, fans and alms bowls for monks, carved altar tables, little gilded Bodhi trees, ceremonial umbrellas, candles and incense sticks and countless other items used in temple adornment. These are presented by laymen to the temples on a variety of religious occasions.

WAT SUTHAT

Wat Suthat is one of the most important temples in Bangkok. Work on the temple started during the reign of King Rama I, was continued by his successor, and finally completed under King Rama III. The temple's principal attractions are two unusually large buildings, the bot and the viharn, both of which exhibit outstanding classic Thai religious art and architecture.

THE VIHARN ● 89. Noted for its graceful proportions, the viharn is raised on two platforms and surrounded by a cloister; at the corners of the platform are pavilions enshrining Buddha images in various positions. The gables are richly adorned with mythological animals and religious symbols, and the huge doors, carved in three layers, are attributed to King Rama II, who was noted for his artistry. The interior walls and the two rows of supporting columns are covered with fine mural paintings of the early Bangkok period. The principal Buddha image, Phra Buddha Chakyamuni, was moved to Bangkok from Wat Mahathat in Sukhothai and dates from the 14th century. It was cast together with another much revered image called the Prabu Chinaraj, which is now housed in Phitsanulok.

THE BOT ● 88. Constructed between 1839 and 1843 by King Rama III, the bot contains an image known as Phra Trai Lok Chet, in front of which is a group of disciple figures. Well-preserved murals also cover the interior walls of this structure. The door of the low brick wall that surrounds the bot are guarded by statues imported from China, all representing Western sailors and soldiers and reflecting the low opinion both the Thai and the Chinese had of Westerners in those days.

The statues of the Westerners, they were fully convinced, were monstrous enough to ward off the evil spirits lurking outside their houses.

BRAHMIN TEMPLE. Overlooking the square containing the Giant Swing is the Brahmin temple. While of little interest architecturally, it is a reminder of the powerful influence white-robed Brahmin priests once exerted in Thailand, particularly in the royal court. Even today Brahmin rituals play an important part in many ceremonies.

THE GIANT SWING. Across Wat Suthat is the Giant Swing, or

Sao Chin Cha, the Giant Swing.

Sao Chin Cha, once the focus of a colorful Brahmin ceremony honoring the god Siva, when teams of young men swung to great heights in an effort to snatch sacks of money with their teeth, the highest sack being on a 76-foot pole. The ceremonial practice was abolished during the reign of King Rama VII.

WAT RAJABOPIT

Located on a road of the same name, Wat Rajabopit was built in 1870, shortly after King Rama V ascended to the throne, and displays the eclectic approach to architecture that was characteristic of the fifth reign. Its central feature is a graceful gilded stupa, modeled after the famous one in Nakhon Pathom, with a courtyard surrounded by a circular cloister with marble columns and two-tiered roofs, interrupted by the bot and three viharns; the exterior walls of the bot, the lower part of the stupa, and the cloister are covered with glazed Chinese tiles in a subtle blending of colors, while the doors and windows of the bot are decorated with mother-of-pearl inlays depicting the five royal orders. The interior of the bot has a vaulted roof that suggests a Gothic cathedral, and its color scheme of pale blue and gold also has a European flavor that contrasts with the classic Thai surroundings.

MINI CEMETERY
To the west of Wat Rajabopit is an atmospheric little cemetery crowded with tombs in assorted styles of architecture, including Gothic and Khmer. These mostly enshrine members of King Rama V's extensive family, evidence of the high regard in which he held the temple.

WAT KALAYANIMIT · SANTA CRUZ CHURCH · WAT PHRA KEO · WAT PRAYOONWONG · MEMORIAL BRIDGE

⏱ Half a day

A COUP ON THE RIVER
In May 1950, elements of the navy staged a coup on a landing near the Grand Palace. The prime minister of the time was taken at gunpoint to a battle-ship anchored in the middle of the river and held hostage overnight. In the morning, planes from the air force bombed and sank the ship. However, the premier was not aboard: his captors had gallantly told him to swim for it when the bombs began to fall. He reached the shore, rallied his forces and within 36 hours was back in full command of the situation.

Beginning with the confluence of three northern streams snaking 219 miles down to the gulf, the Chao Phraya River ● *108–9* has played a decisive role throughout much of Thailand's history. It waters the broad Central Plains, creating one of the world's most fertile rice-growing areas; at the same time, it provides access to the outside world, making possible the trade that has nurtured three capital cities on its banks – first Ayutthaya, then Thonburi, and last Bangkok – over more than six centuries. The river was the focal point of Bangkok, not only in its early years but also well into the present century. The double and triple rows of floating houses that once lined its banks have vanished, and bridges – seven in the

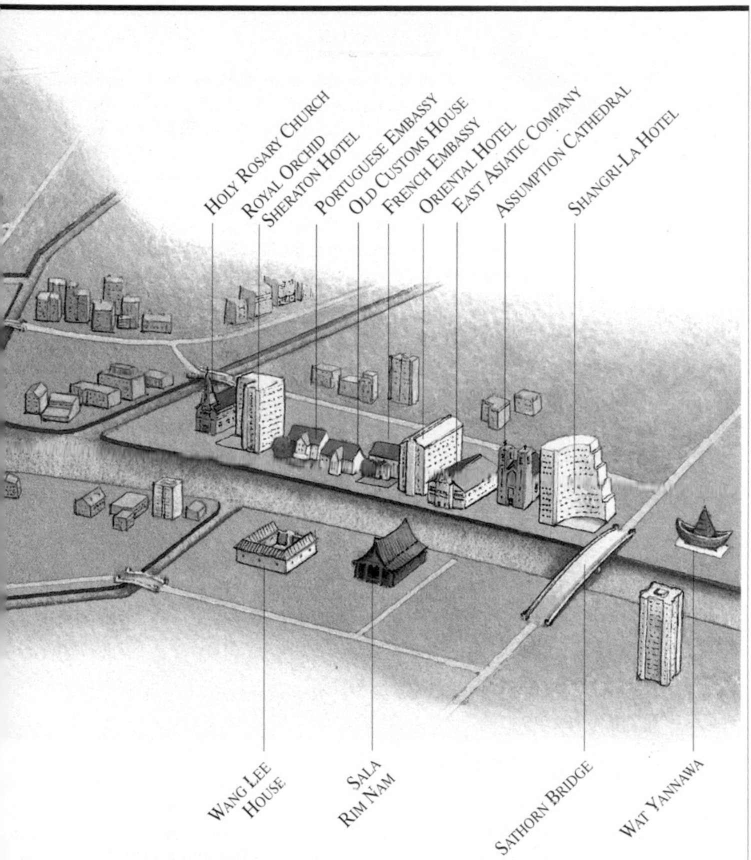

HOLY ROSARY CHURCH
ROYAL ORCHID SHERATON HOTEL
PORTUGUESE EMBASSY
OLD CUSTOMS HOUSE
FRENCH EMBASSY
ORIENTAL HOTEL
EAST ASIATIC COMPANY
ASSUMPTION CATHEDRAL
SHANGRI-LA HOTEL

WANG LEE HOUSE
SALA RIM NAM
SATHORN BRIDGE
WAT YANNAWA

metropolitan area – make communication with Thonburi easier than the old network of canals. Nevertheless, even today, a relatively short cruise along the Chao Phraya reveals a succession of major landmarks, both cultural and commercial: the Grand Palace enclosure and countless important Buddhist temples, the oldest foreign embassies, Catholic churches, the wharfs and godowns of trading companies, wholesale markets for agricultural produce brought to the capital by boat, spacious palaces and houses of old, where the city's élite once resided (and, in some cases, still do). The same trip will also suggest a residential revival along the Chao Phraya in the form of new hotels and towering condominiums rising on both sides amid those nostalgic sights; thanks to the increasingly congested traffic and the difficulty of commuting to distant suburbs, residents are now returning to Bangkok's timeless traditional heart.

CHAO PHRAYA EXPRESS
These ferries operate along the river between 6am and 6pm, with most stops on the Bangkok side.

CROSS-RIVER FERRIES
Operated by the Chao Phraya Express Boat Company, these run between the two riverbanks during the day and until midnight.

WAT ARUN

This 1920's guide-book to Wat Arun shows that the temple has been a popular tourist attraction for many years.

With the possible exception of the Grand Palace, no Chao Phraya attraction is as celebrated as the soaring 343-foot central prang of Wat Arun ● *97*, the Temple of Dawn, on the Thonburi bank. Dating from the Ayutthaya period and considerably restored, the temple served as the royal chapel during the Thonburi reign of King Taksin. The Emerald Buddha ▲ *148* was enshrined here before being brought to its present home at Wat Phra Keo. King Rama II of Bangkok first conceived the idea of raising the great Khmer-style prang, but due to engineering problems, it was

not completed until the following reign. This, as well as the four smaller ones that flank it, are adorned with ceramic tiles and fragments of multicolored porcelain, creating a jewel-like effect in the sunlight. A platform halfway up the tower offers a panoramic view of the river and Bangkok. Traditionally, at the end of the rainy season, the king visits Wat Arun and presents robes to the resident monks in a ceremony, a trip that in the past was made from the Grand Palace using a fleet of carved and gilded royal barges.

THE MEMORIAL BRIDGE
Just before the towering spire of Wat Prayoonwong, the Memorial Bridge was the first to link Bangkok with Thonburi. It was opened by King Rama VII at precisely 8.16 in the morning – the auspicious time chosen by royal astrologers – on April 6, 1932, which was also the 150th anniversary of the capital's founding.

OTHER TEMPLES ALONG THE RIVERSIDE

WAT KALAYANIMIT ★. This imposing edifice, standing where Klong Bangkok Yai enters the Chao Phraya, was built during the reign of Rama III. The *ubosot* shelters a huge bronze Buddha image especially popular with Thai Chinese, who honor the image as Sam Poh Kong in memory of the famous Ming eunuch admiral. The temple grounds contain an impressive collection of Chinese statues brought as ballast by the rice-trade junks. A stone polygonal chedi was also manufactured in China and assembled behind the ubosot. The murals are very well preserved and give a glimpse of life during that period. Next to the monastery a small alleyway leads to a charming little Chinese temple.
WAT PRAYOONWONG. Built during King Rama III's reign, Wat Prayoonwong boasts fine lacquered doors decorated with mother-of-pearl. The temple is also known for its artificial hill surrounded by a pond of turtles that are fed by Buddhist visitors to acquire merit.

WAT RAKHANG KOSITHARAM. Across the river from the Grand Palace landing, this wat was built in the reign of King Rama I. "Rakhang" in Thai means "bell," and part of the name is derived from the numerous bells rung in the temple in the morning and evening. The main building is a particularly beautiful example of early Rattanakosin architecture ● 92–3, with fine Ayutthaya-style stucco decorations around the doors and windows, while the *ho trai* ● 89, a library on a raised platform, contains some well-preserved murals depicting the *Ramakien* epic and the Buddhist cosmology. Of special interest are three traditional Thai-style houses that were occupied by King Rama I before he became the ruler and later moved to the temple compound. The houses, as well as their gold-and-black lacquered windows and ornate entrance-way, were restored during the celebration of Bangkok's bicentennial in 1982.

HO PHRA TRAI PIDOK
When King Rama I donated his former residence to Wat Rakhang to be converted into a library, the buildings were re-arranged, and murals were added. In the early 1980's, these were restored with the help of a well-known Thai painter, Fua Haripitak.

PAK KLONG TALAAD

The sprawling collection of buildings known as Pak Klong Talaad is Bangkok's main wholesale market, which for over a century has served as a central exchange for vegetables, fruit, cut flowers, and other produce brought by boat (right) from the gardens and orchards of Thonburi, as well as others further upriver. The boats come mostly late at night or early in the morning, when the buildings are a hive of colorful activity as traders assemble from all over the city to select produce. In recent years, there has been talk of moving the market because of the increasing use of motor vehicles to bring goods and the consequent traffic jams on land.

THE WANG LEE HOUSE

In between rows of godowns on the Thonburi side of the river, the Wang Lee House is one of the best preserved of the numerous Chinese-style residences that were common in 19th-century Bangkok. Like the others, it was built by a Chinese immigrant who came to profit from the city's growing rice trade and remained to found several other still-thriving businesses. Most of these houses have fallen into disrepair, but the Wang Lee family has maintained its ancestral home in good condition and still uses it for various ceremonies.

THE PICKLED MURDERER
An unusual feature of Sirirat Hospital, on the bank of the river next to the Phra Pink Lao Bridge, is the ten museums that it contains. The most famous is the Museum of the Department of Forensic Medicine, where the focus is on crime. The most celebrated exhibit here is the preserved body of Si-Oui, a Chinese immigrant who murdered seven children before he was captured and executed in the 1950's. Si-Oui suffocated his victims, then ate their internal organs in the belief that it would promote longevity – a theory best disproved by his own fate.

171

View of the Chao Phraya at the end of the 19th century

THE OLD COLONIAL QUARTER

FOREIGN EMBASSIES. All the early foreign embassies – or legations, as they were then called – were located by the river. The earliest was built by the Portuguese, who had also been the first to establish relations with Ayutthaya, and who were granted permission to erect a trading post and consulate in 1820, during the reign of King Rama II; part of the trading office still remains at the back of the property, while the embassy residence, facing the river, was built later. The British came later, on the site now occupied by the General Post Office, followed by the Americans nearby, the French (next to the Oriental Hotel) and others, all with landings from which the diplomats traveled upriver to the Grand Palace on official business. Today, only the Portuguese and French remain at their respective original sites.

COLONIAL INFLUENCE Overlooking the river, both the French Embassy and the Oriental Hotel date from the second half of the 19th century and originally had the louvered shutters and spacious verandas typical of European buildings of the time.

ORIENTAL HOTEL. This building started as a small guest house in 1865, calling itself the Oriental and overlooking the river. The guest house burned down that year, and was replaced with a more substantial establishment, which in turn was acquired by H.N. Andersen, founder of the nearby East Asiatic Company, in 1884. Feeling that Bangkok was ready for a really luxurious hotel, he built a new one, designed by an Italian architect, which opened its "forty commodious and well furnished" rooms in 1887. The Oriental quickly established itself as the place to stay in the Thai capital and accommodated countless distinguished visitors, among them royalty, movie stars and traveling writers such as Somerset Maugham and Noël Coward. Today, the only part of the original structure that remains is the Author's Wing, graced by a pediment that displays a golden rising sun facing the river by which most of its early guests arrived.

«EVERY CURVE OF THE RIVER IS BEAUTIFUL WITH AN
UNEXPECTEDNESS OF ITS OWN.»

ANNA LEONOWENS

EAST ASIATIC COMPANY. Now one of the world's largest trading conglomerates, the East Asiatic Company evolved from a firm founded by H.N. Andersen in 1884, in a group of wooden buildings next to the Oriental Hotel. The present building dates from 1901. Andersen later returned to his native Denmark, where he served as the Thai Consul-General until his death in 1938.

OLD CUSTOMS HOUSE. Built in the 1880's, during the reign of King Rama V, this finely proportioned structure served as the main customs house for Bangkok until the development of the port facilities at Klong Toey, down river. The building has now been taken over by the fire brigade, but will soon be retrofitted and converted to a shopping center. Just behind the building, a narrow lane leads to a small Muslim settlement and cemetery.

CATHOLIC CHURCHES Catholic missionaries began work in Thailand during the Ayutthaya period and one of the buildings of the Church of the Immaculate Conception, near the Krung Thon Bridge, dates from this early time, when visitors stopped off at Bangkok on their way to the capital. Bishop Jean-Baptiste Pallegoix, who taught the future King Rama IV Latin and French, later resided here. Another river landmark is Santa Cruz Church, near the Memorial Bridge, originally built by Portuguese residents after the fall of Ayutthaya and reconstructed by Bishop Pallegoix in 1834; the present cathedral dates from 1913. Also erected by Portuguese Catholics around the same time was the first Holy Rosary Church, beside the Royal Orchid Sheraton Hotel. The present building, though, is of later vintage. The imposing Assumption Cathedral, standing by the Oriental Hotel, is one of Bangkok's largest, and was built in 1910 to replace an older church on the site.

WAT YANNAWA

Built in the early 19th century, Wat Yannawa was particularly popular with Chinese residents who began to settle in that part of Bangkok as the city expanded. Though of no great artistic interest, it contains a notable feature – a building designed in the shape of a Chinese junk, complete with huge eyes to ward off evil spirits and surmounted by two chedis.

This was added to the compound by order of King Rama III, who had observed the increasing number of steam-powered ships calling at the capital and wanted his subjects to remember the older kind of vessel to which they owed so much of their prosperity.

"HUNG HUNTRAA"
Robert Hunter, an English business-man, was granted royal permission to build the first Western-style house on the river in the reign of King Rama II. Known as "Hung Huntraa," it continued to be used as a guest house for notable visitors even after Hunter's departure.

SIAMESE TWINS
Crossing the Chao Praya in 1824, Hunter noticed a strange creature swimming near his boat. It proved to be the famous Siamese twins, Chang and Eng, who, partly with Hunter's support, went on to become celebrated attractions abroad. They eventually settled in America, where they died in 1874.

THE LONG TAIL
The *hong yao*, or "long-tail," boat (below) is perhaps the most often seen (and heard) conveyance along the Thonburi klongs. Reportedly developed in Thailand, it has a propeller on a long pole that can be raised to navigate shallow waterways.

❝The procession of the royal barges, borne along the bosom of the great mother Menam, with all the accessories of splendour that Bangkok could produce, afforded a sight the beauty of which is hardly to be equalled in any part of the gorgeous East.**❞**
Carl Bock

Most of the once-numerous klongs, or canals, of Bangkok have vanished, filled in to widen narrow roads or to create new ones. In Thonburi, however, development has come more slowly, due largely to the lack of bridges across the Chao Phraya until fairly recently, and the klongs retain much of their old atmosphere.

ROYAL BARGE MUSEUM

The Royal Barge Museum, on Klong Bangkok Noi near the point where it enters the river, displays but a few of the spectacular craft that were once used for royal processions along the Chao Phraya. Such processions began in Ayutthaya when, according to one foreign observer, as many as 200 barges were involved, propelled by chanting, uniformed oarsmen "all rowing in synchronized movement and rhythm. The most impressive of the contemporary barges is the gilded Suphanahongsa ● *54* in which the king rides, over 150 feet long and requiring a crew of sixty-four, with a prow in the shape of a mythical, swan-like

THE BROAD DEEP KLONGS ARE THE GREAT STREETS OF THE CITIES AND THE HIGHWAYS OF THE PLAINS.»

ERNEST YOUNG

ird. Another, 149 feet long, is adorned with a many-headed *naga,* or sacred serpent, while other figureheads include orned dragons, *garuda,* and characters from the *Ramakien.* Royal barge processions today are rare, he most recent having been held on he occasion of the King's 0th birthday in 1988.

IFE ALONG THE KLONG ★

To unaccustomed eyes it is surprising to see a decent old oman with a mop of grey hair deftly maneuvering her canoe mid the traffic as she goes methodically about her day's hopping...On houseboats, people lounge about idly; men ostly half-naked wash themselves or their children, and here nd there half-a-dozen urchins scramble about in the water." his description, written by Somerset Maugham in 1923, still remarkably close to what one sees today on a cruise rough the Thonburi klongs. Weathered old wooden houses, me in the steep-roofed traditional style, still crowd the

banks; families still bathe from their doorsteps in the late afternoon, the women preserving their modesty with a well-tied sarong; and vendors in straw hats still paddle small craft laden with various goods.

honburi has long been famous for its mangoes and durians, d, while some of the orchards have been turned into ilding sites, many remain along the waterways. Among the ost popular klongs are Bangkok Yai and Bangkok Noi, ough smaller ones lead off in all directions and offer impses of a fast-disappearing way of life.

AT SUWANNARAM ★

at Suwannaram, located on the southern bank of Klong angkok Noi not far from where it joins the river, is a ell-proportioned temple built on the foundations of an yutthaya-period temple by King Rama I and renovated by ng Rama III. In addition to being a good example of ansitional architecture of the Ayutthaya and Rattanakosin riods, it is noted for the beautiful mural paintings in its nctuary; these works of art are attrib- ed to Luang Vichit Chetsada and Krua onpae, two prominent painters of the rd reign, and have been restored ing modern techniques. On the south ll, behind the principal Buddha age, are vivid scenes from the three rlds of Buddhist cosmology. The trance wall is covered with a huge ral depicting the victory of Buddha er Mara while the side walls are corated with several rows of praying ures facing the altar and scenes of the t ten Jataka tales of the Buddha's evious lives.

KLONG VENDOR
Selling by water is still as much a part of klong life as it was in the distant past. Vendors in small boats offer almost everything needed by waterside residents. Ernest Young in his book *The Kingdom of the Yellow Robe* observed, "There is a water market, but unlike the land market which remains open all day, this one opens and closes before the sun has risen very high. Scores of boats are massed together in one compact crowd. Each boat is sunk to the gunwale with piles of fruit or fish. The occupants barter and bargain with the same incessant deafening noise of shouting, laughing, and swearing that is characteristic of all markets the world over. The women wear flat-topped hats made of leaves, which slope outwards from the crown, and are stuck on their heads by a circular frame-work of cane placed inside."

❝The Chinese here are a model of peaceful intrusion. The several thousands who immigrated into Siam have monopolised trade. Whatever is related to labour in the kingdom is stimulated, organised and soon thriving in their hands. While the Siamese represents sheer idleness, his bustling sycophant counterpart from the Celestial empire is a paragon of greediness and painstaking toil.❞

The Marquis de Beauvoir

LION CARICATURE
The painting above reflects the traditional lion dance, regarded as an essential part of the ceremonies that accompany the official opening of many buildings and also suggesting the importance of Chinese customs in Thai life.

Occupying the site selected by King Rama I for his royal palace in 1782 was a community of Chinese traders. They moved to a new location, just outside the city walls, where they created a teeming district that became Bangkok's Chinatown, long the center of commercial life in the capital.

SAMPHENG LANE

Beginning at Wat Pathum Khongka – an old temple also known as Wat Sampheng, built a century before Bangkok became the capital – and running for seven blocks parallel to Yaowarat Road, Sampheng Lane is a noisy covered alleyway lined with shops selling goods of all kinds: wedding mementoes, buttons, imported textiles, kitchenware, gold chains, beads, toys and clothing, to mention only a few. The road eventually emerges at Pahurat, just across from Klong Ong Ang, a market famous for its numerous shops and stalls selling textiles at prices substantially lower than anywhere else in the city.

YAOWARAT ROAD

Yaowarat ▲ *143* is the main street of Chinatown. The thoroughfare congested and the air heavily polluted but it is nevertheless full of life and fascinating discoveries especially down the narrow lanes leading off each side. It once boasted a large number of opium dens, gambling houses, burlesque shows, and brothels (proclaimed by green lanterns hanging outside); these have mostly disappeared, at least on the surface, but the area still retains a raffish faintly mysterious ambience at night. Paul

> «HALF OF THE POPULATION OF THE MENAM DELTA IS CHINESE
> AND VERY FEW PEOPLE ARE WITHOUT SOME TRACE OF
> THE CHINESE BLOOD IN THEM.»
>
> HOLT S. HALLETT, 1890

Morand, writing at the turn of the century, captured the atmosphere of the area in *Rien que la Terre*: "With the noise of the street, the fanfare of gramophones, the clattering of mahjong, like hail on a tin roof, one is reminded of China, but it is the pawnshops which give the impression reality. Gamblers come to pawn their jewels, their silken robes, their pipes. The more the pipes have been smoked and filled with opium, the more they gain for them. Lotteries, cockfights, fish fights, betting on Shanghai races, ten days' journey from here; all are played. Bets are even placed on the number of pips in a melon! It is reported that naval officers, under arrest and confined to their boats, continue to play at sea, by signal!"

Near the end of Yaowarat Road is an area called Nakorn

Kasem, once known as the "Thieves' Market" because of the existence of its many shops selling antiques and secondhand goods.

CHINATOWN TEMPLES

Chinatown contains a number of temples both large and small, some for Mahayana Buddhists, some for Taoists, and still others for followers of Theravada Buddhism. The leading Mahayana Buddhist temple is Wat Mangkon Kamalawat, on Charoen Krung Road, where enormous candles decorated with Chinese figures are among the altar offerings. Off Plabplachai Road is Wat Kanikaphon, founded by a former brothel owner, where elaborate paper models of luxury items such as automobiles, planes, computers and houses are burned in honor of deceased relatives. This temple is better known as Wat Mae Lao Fang after the brothel owner. Li Thi Miew, a Taoist temple on Plabplachai, has interesting Chinese paintings on the interior walls. Wat Traimit is located close to where Yaowarat Road meets Charoen Krung Road. It contains the Golden Buddha that was found during construction work at a temple near the river in the 1950's. Originally covered in stucco, the gold Buddha was revealed when it was accidentally dropped during moving, shattering the stucco. The solid gold Buddha weighs over 5 tons.

FORTUNE SEEKER
A client eagerly awaits the verdict as a Chinatown fortune-teller consults his almanac. They are consulted on everything from health to the most auspicious dates for marriage or opening a new business.

Vegetarian food offerings at Wat Mangkon Kamalawat.

ITALIAN ARTISTS
While in Europe, King Rama V made contact with many artists and posed in their studios. He later commissioned several Italian artists to work in Bangkok; Cesare Ferro was the first to become a Siamese court painter in 1904. Besides various portraits of the king, Ferro's works also included the wall decorations of the Amphornsathan Throne Hall in the palace. Prince Naris, who was in charge of the public works department, was also keen to promote innovative ideas such as Siamese subjects and Western techniques. He worked closely with a team of craftsmen and painters, notably Carlo Rigoli, on various projects such as Wat Rajathiwat and the Boromphiman Mansion. All the Italian artists gave art lessons to Thai painters and influenced the local art scene. However, the one who left a lasting impression was Corrado Ferroci, who came to Thailand in 1923 and lived there until his death. Ferroci produced a number of royal statues and eventually became a teacher. He founded the institute now known as Silpakorn University, which trains hundreds of young artists.

King Rama V was the first Thai ruler to travel to Europe. The result of such trips was a determination to transform Bangkok into a Western-style capital. The main focus of his effort was the Dusit district, which he linked with the traditional center by Ratchadamnoen (Royal Progress) Avenue and where he proceeded to build a new throne hall and palace, residences for members of the royal family (among them Chitralada Palace, where the present king and queen live), and numerous tree-lined avenues suitable for carriage rides. His successor Rama VI followed up his plans on an even larger scale. Since most of Bangkok's expansion has taken place elsewhere, largely to the east, this district still retains much of its early 19th-century flavor, with many of the old buildings occupied by the military and government offices.

ANANDA SAMAKHOM THRONE HALL. The center of Rama V's Dusit district was the elaborate, Western-style throne hall. Construction began in 1907, directed by a group of Italian architects and engineers, notably Annibale Rigotti, Carlo Allegri, E.G. Gollo and M. Tamagno, and was completed five years later, after the death of the king. Galileo Chini, whose work the king had admired at the Venice Biennale, was commissioned in 1911–13 to decorate the vault with huge frescoes of notable events in Thai history. For a time following the end of the absolute monarchy the building served as the National Parliament. The square in front of the Ananda Samakhom is decorated with a large equestrian statue of Rama V, modeled by Georges Saulo when the king visited Paris. The statue was cast in parts and assembled in

Bangkok, and was unveiled on November 11, 1908, the 40th anniversary of his coronation. Every year, on October 23, the anniversary of King Rama V's death, many people visit the statue and pay homage to his memory.

VIMARN MEK PALACE. This palace is an 81-room structure of golden teak and was originally intended to serve as a residence of King Rama V on the island of Si Chang in the Gulf of Thailand. Due to conflicts with the French over Cambodia, however, he decided to move the structure to Bangkok, and to use it as a residence during the construction of the nearby Dusit Palace. Long neglected after King Rama V's death, it was beautifully restored and furnished with fifth-reign royal treasures by Queen Sirikit as part of the 1982 Bangkok bicentennial celebrations. Queen Sirikit selected the furnishings, which include such curiosities as Thailand's first shower bath as well as historic photographs of the late 19th century.

VIMARN MEK PALACE
This was the first Siamese house to have electricity.

"BIRTHDAY BRIDGES". During the latter part of his reign, King Rama V started an annual tradition of opening a new bridge on the occasion of his birthday. A number of these "birthday bridges" have been lost to progress, but several remain in all their ornate beauty.

WAT BENCHAMABOPIT. Popularly known as the Marble Temple, this wat was built at the turn of the century by King Rama V ● 93. It was designed by his brother, Prince Naris, with the help of Italian architect Hercules Manfredi. The temple is a blend of architectural styles and decoration: gray marble from Italy, for example, was imported to sheathe the bot and pave the surrounding cloisters, while inside there are stained-glass windows as well as a replica of the famous Phra Buddha Chinaraj image. Around the cloister are fifty-three bronze Buddha showing every style of Thai religious art and some from neighboring cultures. Also in the compound is a building in which King Rama V lived as a monk, the interior decorated with murals showing major events of his reign, and an ancient Bodhi tree.

PHYA THAI PALACE
Following King Rama V's death in 1910, Phya Thai Palace served as the residence of Queen Sowabha Phongsri, having previously been occupied by Crown Prince Vajiravudh. The Victorian-style buildings were later a luxury hotel then became the Phra Mongkut Military Hospital.

The three-wheeled vehicle known as a tuk-tuk (right) is a cheap and popular form of transportation in the city.

BANGKOK TRAFFIC
In Bangkok, road expansion has failed to keep pace with that in the number of vehicles, worsening traffic congestion. The speed of traffic flow on main streets has fallen from 8–9 miles per hour in 1984 to 5 miles per hour in 1991, with the prospect that the pace will soon be slower than that of walking. The number of vehicles has more than doubled from 1.07 million in 1984 to 2.5 million in 1991. The road surface increased by only 1 percent between 1984 and 1991, with the result that the area taken up by city streets now accounts for only about 10 percent of the total. This falls far short of the international average of 20–25 percent.

No complete map exists of modern Bangkok – not surprising, really, in view of the speed with which new suburban developments spring up as well as the rapid changes even in older districts. The city's present skyline of towering condominiums, hotels and shopping complexes is actually but a decade or so old, and middle-aged residents can recall a time when now-crowded areas were serene ricefields and "downtown" meant the shops along New Road and Lower Surawong. Today, work, place of residence or particular interests are more likely to determine what one regards as the "center" of Bangkok. Sometimes such places overlap. More often they involve long trips through congested

traffic; thus quite a number of residents have never even seen such older landmarks as Wat Po and the National Museum. I some visitors enjoy strolling about at random, savoring the animated street life that can be found almost anywhere, the majority, for whom time is limited, will probably prefer to plan each day's activities based on the area where their hotel is located.

SILOM ROAD, COMMERCIAL HUB

Silom Road, extending from Rama IV Road to New Road, has become an important commercial area. Many leading banks, advertising agencies, airline offices and handicraft shops are located along it length, as well as several large hotels and popular centers of nightlife such as Patpong and Thaniya Road. Lower Silom is a center o the booming Thai gems and jewelry industry with numerous shops and wholesale outlets. Day and night the sidewalks near the Rama IV Road end are also crowded with vendors offering locally made copies of brand-name clothing and accessories, watches, cassettes and videos.

NIGHTLIFE IN PATPONG. Despite official disapproval, frequent feminist protest, and the looming shadow of AIDS, Bangkok's anything-goes nightlife remains a major attraction for ma visitors. The center of activity is Patpong Road, between Silom and Surawong, and several smaller side streets in the area; Thaniya Road, further up Silor

s a particular favorite with Japanese. The
attractions range from small bars with go-go
dancers, sex shows and massage parlors to
discos, which are as popular with younger
members of Thai society as with tourists.
A smaller but similar concentration can
be found on Soi Cowboy, off Sukhumvit
Soi 23. Though the reputation of Patpong
is mainly due to the development of mass sex
tourism, one should keep in mind that
traditionally in Thailand sex education for males starts with a
visit to a brothel. Despite the natural shyness and puritanism
of the Thais, prostitution remains an accepted part of life.

"As Calcutta smells of death and Bombay of money, Bangkok smells of sex, but this sexual aroma is mingled with the sharper whiffs of death and money."

LUMPINI PARK

Across from the Dusit Thani Hotel, Lumpini (right) is the
only park in central Bangkok. It was
presented to the city by King Rama VI in
the 1920's. Vehicular traffic is banned in
the park, thus enhancing its appeal to
joggers and others who come to exercise in
the early morning and late after-noon.
Many elderly Chinese who are early risers
use the park as a venue for their *tai chi*
exercises and folk-dance sessions.

ERAWAN SHRINE

During the construction of the Erawan Hotel in the 1950's,
work was plagued by a series of mysterious accidents that
included the death of several laborers. The Erawan Shrine,
containing an image of Brahma, was erected near the site in
an effort to stop these mishaps. Large crowds now visit the
shrine and present wooden elephants,
garlands and other offerings in the hope of
having their wishes granted;
many successful supplicants
hire resident dancers to
perform in the courtyard as a
way of showing their gratitude.

Paddle boats await customers at the lake in Lumpini Park.

The ever-busy Erawan Shrine receives various forms of offerings from devotees throughout the day until late evening.

181

MISSING JIM
The disappearance of Jim Thompson, "the Silk King of Thailand," is one of the enduring mysteries of modern Asia. In March 1967, shortly after his 61st birthday, he went with friends for a holiday in the Cameron Highlands, a resort in northern Malaysia. There he went for a walk alone on Easter Sunday afternoon and never returned. Despite an exhaustive search by soldiers and local volunteers – not to mention advice offered by numerous experts in the supernatural – no trace of him was found, nor have any real leads turned up in the more than twenty-five years since. There are plenty of theories, however, ranging from a kidnap that somehow went wrong to any of a variety of misadventures in the surrounding jungle. Interest in the case has been maintained through factual account, several novels, and hundreds of newspaper and magazine articles.

JIM THOMPSON'S HOUSE. Located on Soi Kasemsan 2, off Rama I Road, is the Thai-style house built by Jim Thompson, an American who came to Thailand at the end of World War Two and stayed to revive the Thai silk industry. He

disappeared mysteriously while on holiday in Malaysia in 1967. Actually the house is a group of old teak structures brought from several places and reassembled on the bank of a klong. Thompson filled them with his large collection of art from Thailand and other Asian countries, including paintings, porcelain, statuary and antique furniture. The house is now a museum open to the public daily except Saturdays and Sundays.

SUAN PAKKARD PALACE. The former home of Prince and Princess Chumbhot, Suan Pakkard Palace stands in a large, beautifully landscaped tropical garden on Si Ayutthaya Road. It consists of five traditional Thai houses assembled on the property in the

COLLECTOR'S HOUSE
The components of Jim Thompson's house came from various sources. The largest of the structures came from a village across the canal that runs behind the property; others were found near Ayutthaya. Produced in pre-fabricated sections, they were brought to the site by river barges. Carpenters skilled in traditional methods rebuilt the house and completed it in 1959.

SIAM SOCIETY
The Siam Society was founded by a group of Thais and foreign residents in 1904 for research and investigation in matters appertaining to Siam. Placed under royal patronage during the reign of King Rama VI, it moved to its present location in 1933. The Society has an extensive library of books and other publications on Thailand and the rest of Asia, issues a journal for members, and organizes frequent lectures and exhibitions.

950's as well as the Lacquer Pavilion, an elegant structure ound in Ayutthaya and probably dating from the early Bangkok period. The interior walls of the pavilion are overed with fine gold-and-black lacquer paintings. The art ollection displayed in the houses covers a wide range, from rehistoric bronze jewelry and pottery found in the northeast o furniture and other items that elonged to Prince Chumbhot's amily. The palace is open aily except Sundays.

HE KAMTHIENG HOUSE.
angkok's only real thnological collection fish traps, traditional oves and cooking pots, nplements used by Thai rmers – is displayed in and round the Kamthieng House, in the ompound of the Siam Society on Sukhumwit Soi 21. The assic, northern-style teak house, over 200 years old, came om Chiang Mai and was brought to Bangkok in sections. lso in the society's compound is a fine example of a Central ains house ● 86–7, thus offering visitors an opportunity to ompare the architectural differences between the two styles. oth are open daily except Sundays and Mondays.

GEMS AND JEWELRY
Export of gems and jewelry now ranks as Thailand's fifth-largest earner of foreign exchange. Gems such as sapphires, rubies, zircons, garnets and cat's-eyes are brought into the country from all over the world to be cut and polished by a growing force of skilled workers, while the quality of locally crafted jewelry has acquired an international reputation. A new World Gem and Jewelry Center is scheduled to open soon on Silom Road, where much of the industry is focused.

THE WEEKEND MARKET

From early Saturday morning until Sunday evening, one of the busiest places in Bangkok is the great Weekend Market at Chatuchak Park, just off Phahonyothin Road, across from the northern bus terminal. Almost everything the country produces is on sale somewhere in this huge network of several thousand stalls: fruit trees, garden plants, clothing, antiques, handicrafts, fresh and preserved foods, fruit, furniture, contemporary porcelains, army surplus goods and pets of all kinds. Most of the prices are negotiable, as they are at all Thai markets, and for visitors who mind the heat the early morning hours are the best time to go.

PERMANENT PLANT MARKET. Between the end of the Khamphaengphet Road and the Weekend Market is another market which is open daily and is entirely devoted to plants. Any true garden-lover should devote at least a few hours to strolling along the long row of shops displaying the full range of ornamental trees, shrubs and creepers available to local

enthusiasts, in addition to pots and gardening tools. Of special interest are the shops and sidewalk vendors who offer dazzling displays of flowering orchids at prices that will seem ridiculously low to visitors from more temperate countries.

PRATUNAM MARKET

Pratunam, literally translated, means "water gate," and the market by that name is located near the locks of Klong Saen Sap, at the intersection of Phetchaburi and Rajadamri roads. In addition to all the basic items such as food and household goods, it offers a huge covered area selling cloth and ready-made clothing, attended by seamstresses who are ready to make on-the-spot alterations or even produce a complete outfit. Low prices and an almost limitless choice make this a highly popular place, particularly on weekends, so be prepared for crowds as well as some shrewd bargaining.

SIDEWALK VENDORS. Just about every Bangkok governor, at some point in his term of office, has made a determined effort to clear the city's streets of sidewalk vendors. None has succeeded, for the simple reason that Thais (and most foreign visitors, too) enjoy coming across unexpected bargains as they walk here and there and don't mind whatever hazards the vendors might create. Sidewalk shopping is a city-wide affair, but certain areas are more crowded than others. Upper Silom Road, for

instance, caters more to tourist tastes, and so does the stretch of Sukhumwit Road extending from Soi 11 to Plernchit, no doubt because both areas are convenient to numerous hotels; a street-long bazaar springs up on Patpong after dark. Rajadamri Road from the Rajprasong intersection to Pratunam is another popular gathering place for vendors, as is the short lane leading from New Road to the Oriental Hotel.

SHOPPING CENTERS

Modern shopping centers and department stores are a relatively new phenomenon in Bangkok, but the city has more than made up for lost time in the past two decades. The Plernchit branch of the locally owned Central Department Store is the largest in Southeast Asia and there are numerous others, both Thai and Japanese, in almost every district. The goods are of high quality and, rather surprisingly in view of the luxurious surroundings, the fixed prices are not all that much higher than those at the markets. Popular department stores besides Central Department Store include Robinson's, Sogo, Isetan and Thai Daimaru. Shopping centers are equally ubiquitous and most contain restaurants and fast-food outlets as well as smart boutiques selling ready-to-wear clothing, jewelry, leather goods and other items. Among those frequented by visitors are Amarin Plaza, Peninsula Plaza, Rajadamri Arcade, River City, Mahboon Krong and Siam Center.

THAI SILK
Probably the most sought-after product is Thai silk. The material is believed to have originated from the village folk of northeastern Thailand, who weaved it using primitive handlooms. The silk remained popular until its decline at the end of the 19th century, when Chinese and Japanese silk imports flooded the local market. The silk industry was revived by entrepreneur Jim Thompson after World War Two. The pioneer company he established remains one of the best and biggest silk producers in the country today. The main shop, open 12 hours daily to accommodate the endless flow of customers, is located at the intersection of Surawong and Rama IV roads. There are silk clothes and scarfs as well as the material itself, which can be bought by the yard.

185

THE FLOATING MARKET

Floating markets, consisting of hundreds of vendors congregating by boat, usually in the early morning, at some point on a river or canal, have long fascinated visitors to Bangkok and other parts of Thailand. A few decades ago, the most popular place to view this colorful phenomenon was the canal outside Wat Sai in Thonburi; eventually however this market became overcrowded with tourists.

DAMNERN SADUAK. Today the best of such markets convenient to Bangkok is on Klong Damnern Saduak in Ratchaburi province, a trip most itineraries combine with a visit to Nakhon Pathom. The floating market here takes place somewhat later than at other places – between 8am and 10am – and offers a busy, photogenic scene of boats laden with fruit, vegetables, cooked foods and other produce, sold principally by women wearing the broad straw hats and dressed in the blue cotton clothing favored by rural Thai people. For food lovers there are also many restaurants lined along the banks.

RATCHABURI'S WATER JARS

Ratchaburi province is noted for its production of huge, glazed water jars, often decorated with swirling Chinese dragons and floral motifs, which are sent to many parts of Thailand. A recent industry using similar skills is producing fine reproductions of Chinese blue-and-white porcelains.

NAKHON PATHOM

One of the oldest cultural centers in Thailand, Nakhon Pathom is believed to date from several centuries before the beginning of the Christian era and was an important Mon capital. It was deserted for long stretches at various times in its history, and the present town dates from the middle of the 19th century, when King Rama IV ordered restoration work to be done on its chedi.

PHRA PATHOM CHEDI. Dominating the town of Nakhon Pathom, and visible from many miles away, is the impressive Phra Pathom Chedi which, at 352 feet, is the tallest Buddhist monument in the world and the oldest in Thailand ● 97. It was originally built about a thousand years ago but had fallen into a pile of rubble by the middle of the 19t

RIVER RITUAL
One of the most memorable sights along the canals of Ratchaburi and other provinces is that of Buddhist monks collecting their early-morning alms by boat from waterside houses. Strict rules apply not only to the type of boat used for this ritual but also the seemingly effortless manner in which it is paddled.

DVARAVATI STUCCOES
Nakhon Pathom was an important town of the Dvaravati Mon kingdom (6th–10th century). Excavations at the Chedi Chula Pathom, on the outskirts of the modern town, have led to the discovery of an interesting series of bas-reliefs in stucco. Other terracottas were found at Ku Bua and U Thong. These are now displayed in the museums of Nakhon Pathom, U Thong and Bangkok ▲ *158*. They throw light on the ancient Mon aristocratic life of the elegantly dressed court ladies. Mon society was evidently refined and cosmopolitan, in touch with India, Indonesia and perhaps the Mediterranean.

century, when the future King Rama IV, then a Buddhist monk, came on a pilgrimage. Restoration work, which involved covering the old ruins with an entirely new chedi, began in 1853 but – due to numerous technical difficulties – was not completed until the reign of King Rama V. The base of the chedi is surrounded by a circular cloister, with chapels containing Buddha images from various periods situated at the four cardinal points. A museum houses numerous early religious objects that have been found in the area, among them the Wheel of the Law and terracotta bas-reliefs of the Dvaravati period (7th–11th century). A popular festival is held in the temple grounds each November, when the great chedi is beautifully illuminated.

187

CURING SNAKEBITES
Here is Ernest Young's recipe, from his book, *The Kingdom of the Yellow Robe*, for a mixture that could help cure snakebites in the event of an encounter with poisonous reptiles in the parks or rivers:
a piece of the jaw of a wild hog;
a piece of the jaw of a tame hog;
a piece of the bone of a goose;
a piece of the bone of a peacock;
the tail of a fish; and the head of a venomous snake.

L ush jungles and winding rivers lie but a short distance away from the modern town of Kanchanaburi, which is also haunted by a modern epic of heroism and tragedy.

RIVER RESORTS

In recent years, the Kanchanaburi area – particularly the Kwae Noi and Kwae Yai rivers – has become a popular vacation spot for Bangkok residents in search of lush natural scenery. By boat along one of the rivers, and also by road, you can travel to a number of rural resorts, some built on floating rafts and some substantial structures with all modern conveniences. The Kwae Yai leads to a large, scenic lake formed by the Srinakharin Dam, while the Kwae Noi, the more developed of the two in terms of resorts, winds through Saiyok National Park to another beautiful expanse of water created by the Khao Laem Dam.

ERAWAN NATIONAL PARK

Established in 1975, the 220-square-mile Erawan National Park is protected on the west by Saiyok National Park, on the south by Salak Phra Wildlife Sanctuary, on the east by the Kwae Yai River, and on the north by the Srinakharin National

Park. Its most celebrated feature is the spectacular Erawan Waterfalls, a 4,950-foot cascade that is broken up into seven tiers; according to popular belief, the rock formation above the top level resembles the three-headed elephant Erawan of Hindu mythology. The park provides sanctuary to a considerable variety of wildlife, including eighty species of birds, gibbons, barking deer

> «THE JAPANESE DID NOT CONSIDER HUMAN LIFE OF ANY VALUE
> WHEN VIEWED IN THE LIGHT THAT THE RAILWAY MUST BE PUSHED
> ON REGARDLESS OF COST.»
> C. A. McEACHERN, PRISONER OF WAR

and rhesus monkeys, as well as a profusion of luxuriant plant life; also within its boundaries are two impressive caves, Phrathat and Wang Badang, both adorned with huge stalactites and stalagmites. Bungalows and dormitories are available for visitors who want to stay overnight in the park.

THE DEATH RAILWAY

In June 1942, six months after the start of its triumphant conquest of Southeast Asia, Japan ordered the construction of a railway from Thailand to Burma as a substitute for the long sea route to Rangoon; it was intended to play a major role in the transportation of men and material for the planned invasion of British India. The engineering task was formidable, the track leading through dense malarial rain forest, over rocky mountains, and across swift rivers, finally crossing into Burma at the lofty Three Pagodas Pass. For labor, the Japanese deployed about 61,000 Allied prisoners-of-war captured in Malaya, Singapore and the Dutch East Indies, plus an estimated 270,000 conscripted Asian workers. Slowly, painfully, over the next three years, the almost impossible task was completed, but at a horrifying cost in human life: over 12,000 Allied prisoners and 240,000 Asians died during the ordeal – or 393 men for every mile of the eventually useless Death Railway, as it came to be called by survivors. The bodies of 6,982 victims lie in a tranquil Allied War Cemetery near Kanchanaburi, where the railway began, and a museum displays other grim reminders of what one writer has called a "supreme monument to folly."

The track itself was dismantled by the British after the war but a length still runs along the Kwae Yai River and several of the bridges have been rebuilt. Toward the end of November, an annual fair is held in Kanchanaburi under the auspices of the Tourism Authority of Thailand, featuring a sound and light show at the so-called *Bridge On The River Kwai* (based on the fictitious span made famous by the movie) and displays of prehistoric artifacts found in the region.

THREE PAGODAS PASS
The pass lies on the frontier between Thailand and Burma, and was the historic crossing point for Burmese armies who invaded Ayutthaya. It was also the place where the Death Railway led into Burma, though the tracks were dismantled by the British at the end of the war.

RIVER KWAI
Kanchanaburi gained its fame from the popular film *The Bridge on the River Kwai* – actually filmed in Sri Lanka – which in turn was based on the novel of the same name by Pierre Boulle. Local entrepreneurs cash in on this fame but the story is entirely fictional.

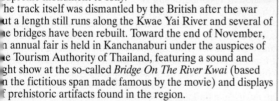

189

PHILANTHROPY
The owner of the
Ancient City looks
upon the project
more as an act of
philanthropy than as
a tourist attraction.
Apart from providing
work for countless
traditional artisans
whose skills are no
longer in wide
demand, he has
preserved many
ancient buildings that
would otherwise have
been neglected or
destroyed.

THE OLD ROAD TO PATTAYA

The old Sukhumwit Road, once the only route to Pattaya and other resorts on the eastern gulf coast, leads through Samut Prakarn Province and passes a number of popular tourist attractions before it joins a newer, more modern highway.
THE ANCIENT CITY. Muang Boran, or the Ancient City, started by an art-loving millionaire in the early 1970's, contains numerous buildings and monuments – some replicas, others genuine – from Thailand's past, on a 200-acre site roughly shaped like the country itself. One enters from the far south, passing such attractions as the Phra Mahathat stupa of Nakhon Si Thammarat and another from the Srivijaya city of Chaiya ● 96, and then moves upward to the north through the splendors of Ayutthaya and Sukhothai. The idea might sound contrived, but it is executed with considerable taste, and expert advice from various authorities – among them a former director of the National Museum – which have been consulted throughout to ensure authenticity of detail. The replicas are one-third the original size, but there are also many original buildings. The village stilt-houses around the

"floating market" and the so-called "Market of Yesteryear" were once Thai houses that have been completely dismantled and moved to the site and then refurbished with original antiques and objects of everyday use. Two northern buildings of significance, a Lanna-style temple from Chiang Rai ● 94 and the Shan-Burmese temple from Ngao, have been salvaged from destruction and carefully restored in the Ancient City.

THE CROCODILE FARM. A popular tourist attraction, the Crocodile Farm is believed to be the largest of its kind in the world, containing more than 30,000 crocodiles, both local and foreign species. The reptiles are bred not only for the amusement of visitors but also as a source of hides to be turned into belts, wallets, handbags, shoes and other items. (A brochure once wittily described the farm as "a happy compromise between wildlife conservation and commercial enterprise.") Starting daily at 9am, there is a show featuring fearless handlers who "tame" some of the larger and more fearsome-looking specimens. There is also a zoo at the farm where other animals are kept.

PATTAYA

The new and faster road to Pattaya passes through Chonburi, a charmless but prosperous provincial capital; Si Racha, noted for a locally made chilli pepper sauce that bears its name; and Bang Saen, a seaside resort popular with Thai families, before reaching the world-famous string of beaches further down the eastern coast. Pattaya began attracting visitors from Bangkok in the 1950's, thanks to the relative ease with which its long stretches of white-sand beach could be reached from the capital. The only form of accommodation in those days consisted of a few simple bungalow complexes, and the first hotel did not open until 1965.

Development began to accelerate at a feverish pace during the Vietnam War, when thousands of American soldiers came here on leave, and by the mid-1970's it had become a major resort, with hotels, restaurants and nightclubs extending the entire length of the main beach. The environmental cost of such rapid expansion has been high and most, if not all, of Pattaya's natural charms are gone; similarly, the free-wheeling nightlife has come in for much criticism in foreign newspapers and magazines. Many visitors enjoy its rowdy, laid-back atmosphere, however, and continue to come in large numbers. Those who prefer a quieter atmosphere and more privacy, at least after nightfall, can go further down the coast to less developed beaches or to offshore islands such as Koh Larn and Koh Sak. There are several good golf courses in the area, as well as shooting ranges and other land-based sports facilities.

CROCODILES
Thailand's rivers, swamps and coastal areas are home to both fresh- and salt-water crocodiles ■ 23. One large fresh-water specimen, nicknamed Ai Dang, was killed in Chantaburi in the 1960's; preserved, it was a popular attraction at fairs all over the country, displayed with a set of false teeth found in its stomach.

TRANSIENT WIVES
❝The Europeans that trade with Siam provide themselves as they will do in Pegou with transient wives and more or less on similar terms and no one would think it shameful to have as many transient husbands but on the contrary to be an honour to have been loved by so many different men.❞
Captain Hamilton, 17th century

❝On the 4th of January, at 8 o'clock in the morning, we arrived in the city of Chantaboon. It is built along the river, six or seven miles away from the mountains. About one third of the population is composed of Christian Annamites. The rest is mostly composed of Chinese merchants, some pagan Annamites as well as Siamese. The latter are all fishermen of Annamese descent. Their ancestors sailed all the way from Cochin-China hoping to fish in the northern waters of the Gulf of Siam. Little by little they settled in Chantaboon.❞ Henri Mouhot

CHANTABURI

Known in old travel accounts as Chantaboon, Chantaburi has been a famous center of gem-mining since the early 15th century. The two main stones found in the area are sapphires and rubies, mostly mined in privately owned pits in the surrounding countryside. Gem trading is concentrated in a few blocks of the downtown area, where nearly all the shops are devoted to the business, particularly on weekends when traders come from Bangkok to make their selections. Chantaburi – the name means "city of the moon" – is also noted for the high quality of its tropical fruits.

KOH CHANG

Koh Chang, the second largest Thai island after Phuket, lies off the coast of Tra Province, near the Cambodian border. Along with fifty other nearby islands, Koh Chang comprises a beautiful marine national park, with numerous beaches and coral reefs. Ferries leave several times daily for the island from Laem Ngob on the mainland.

KOH SAMET

A long, narrow island, Koh Samet lies about 45 minutes by boat off the coast near Rayong. Since 1981, it has been part of a national park that also includes Khao Laem Ya on the mainland, a move that has limited, but by no means removed the tourist facilities overlooking the beautiful beaches on its eastern side.

RAYONG'S GREAT POET
Sunthorn Phu (1786–1856), one of Thailand's greatest poets, was a native of Rayong. He was a particular favorite of King Rama II, with whom he collaborated on a number of works, and wrote the still-popular romantic epic *Phra Apaimani*. A statue has been erected in his memory at Amphur Klaeng, his birthplace.

RAYONG

Rayong, about 133 miles southeast of Bangkok, is a busy fishing port known for the high-quality fish sauce, *nam pla*, which is produced in many small local factories and sold throughout Thailand. Along the coast east of the town are several peaceful resorts. Boats from Rayong can be hired for visits to the various scenic offshore islands.

THE SOUTH

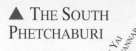

WAT YAI SUWANNARAM — MARKET — WAT KHAMPHAENG LAENG — CITY HALL

A VIEW FROM KHAO WANG
Henri Mouhot, on the view from Khao Wang in 1858: "About 25 miles off stretches from north to south a chain of mountains called Deng...Beyond these rises a number of still higher peaks. On the low ground are forests, palm-trees, and rice-fields, the whole rich and varied in color. Lastly, to the south and east, and beyond another plain, lies the gulf, on whose waters...a few scattered sails are just distinguishable."

Phetchaburi, known as the "City of Diamonds," is an ancient settlement, with Khmer ruins that go back to the late 12th and early 13th centuries. It came under Thai rule during the Sukhothai period and later was an important post on the trade route that led from Mergui on the Andaman Sea to Ayutthaya. Numerous traditional Thai crafts flourished in the town, among them woodcarving, silk-weaving and ornamental work on gold and silver, some of which still survive today. More than most provincial Thai cities, modern Phetchaburi has preserved its old temples, several of which contain important mural paintings, as well as traditional wooden houses in the Central Plains Thai style.

KHAO WANG

Khao Wang, the "Mountain Palace," was built by King Rama IV in the middle of the 19th century as a place where he could escape the pressures of the capital and also spend more time on astronomy, one of his favorite hobbies. Consisting of several European-style buildings, an observatory, and a Buddhist chapel, the palace complex is located on one of the shoulders of a hill just outside Phetchaburi; other buildings are scattered around the hill at lower levels, and a stairway leading to the top is lined

WAT MAHA SAMANARAM
WAT MAHATHAT
SALA YEN
PHIMAN
PHETMAHET HALLS PHRA THINANG
PHRA THINANG SANTHA KAM SATHAN
WAT PHRA KEO
PHRA THINANG PHET PHUM PHAIROT
PHRA THAT CHOM PHET
PHRA THINANG WECHAYAN WICHEN PRASAT

with huge old Plumeria rees that fill the area with their fragrance. Sarah Coffman, an American missionary who visited the palace toward the end of the fourth reign, described the audience hall as "a long, low room, almost completely bare, with a semi-circular throne, consisting of four stone steps, at one end." Two large impressive Siamese paintings – *The Reception of the French Ambassadors at Court* and *Bronze Worshiping Gautama* – decorate the side walls. About a decade after Rama IV's death, another visitor, Carl Bock, found the palace "in a ad state of neglect." However, the palace has been restored by the Fine Arts Department, and its original harms are once more apparent.

🕐 One day

The Buddhist chapel of Khao Wang.

195

Khrua In Khong, one of King Rama IV's favorite painters, responded to the ruler's keen interest in Western culture by including European buildings and landscapes in his murals. At Wat Bowornivet in Bangkok, for example, he incorporated a building similar to that of Mount Vernon, George Washington's home, along with such contemporary subjects as an operation for cataracts.

WAT MAHA SAMANARAM

Located at the foot of the hill near the king's palace, Wat Maha Samanaram was built by King Rama IV. The chapel contains a beautiful Ayutthaya-style Buddha image and is decorated with murals by Khrua In Khong, a famous priest-painter of the fourth reign ● 106 The main scene in the murals depicts the pilgrimage of the Buddhist followers to the Buddha's Footprint at Saraburi.

WAT YAI SUWANNARAM

Dating from the 17th century, Wat Yai Suwannaram is one of Phetchaburi's most beautiful temples. The interior walls of the bot are decorated with some of the oldest surviving mural paintings in Thailand, dating from the late 17th or early 18th century; these show two rows of celestial beings facing the principal Buddha image, a large bronze statue in Ayutthaya style. Within the compound are also several wooden buildings adorned with fine carvings that attest to the high quality of Phetchaburi artisans. The *sala* ● 88–9, in front of the bot, has superbly carved doors, one of which has a gash supposedly made by Burmese invaders; inside are painted panels, one of which shows a rhinoceros, at that time found near the city. Except for this particular *sala* and the bot, the other buildings date from the reign of Rama V, who ardently supported the extensive renovations to the monastery.

WAT MAHATHAT

The most visible feature of Wat Mahathat is its towering central prang, surrounded by a cloister lined with Buddha images. Also noteworthy are the stucco decorations on one of the sanctuaries, which contains a number of Buddha images of the Ayutthaya period as well as several recently restored mural paintings.

> «PHETCHABURI IS A VERY PRETTY PLACE…JUSTLY POPULAR WITH
> EUROPEANS RESIDENT AT BANGKOK AS A SUMMER RESORT FOR A
> CHANGE OF AIR OR A LITTLE BIT OF RUSTICATION.»
>
> FRANK VINCENT

WAT KO KEO SUTHARAM ★

Wat Ko Keo Sutharam, popularly called Wat Ko, lies on the bank of the Phetchaburi River. Inside one of the chapels are some well-preserved murals dating from 1740; one of the figures depicted on the side walls is believed to be that of a Jesuit priest in the robes of a Buddhist monk, possibly recalling an earlier French mission that came through Phetchaburi in the reign of King Narai of Ayutthaya, while another panel shows the conversion of foreigners to Buddhism. The monastic buildings of the temple, raised on posts around a courtyard, have been little altered over the years; one of the buildings contains a small collection of items that have been donated to the monastery.

FOREIGNERS IN WAT KO KEO SUTHARAM
Foreigners first began to appear in temple murals in the latter part of the Ayutthaya period. The earliest were Chinese, Persians and Indians, who came to trade in the capital; later, Europeans were seen, some obviously inspired by the French embassies who came to the court of King Narai in the late 17th century and others by various adventurers of the time.

WAT KHAMPHAENG LAENG

Wat Khamphaeng Laeng is a relatively modern temple that contains within its precincts a very important Khmer ruin dating from the 11th century. Remains of a massive stone wall (*khamphaeng laeng* in Thai), once encircled by moats, and a prang built in laterite can still be seen. The monument is of historical interest as it marks the southernmost point of expansion of the Khmer empire.

KHAO LUANG ★

This famous cave temple, in a hill just outside Phetchaburi, has long been one of the town's major attractions; it reminded Henri Mouhot, who arrived in 1860, of "the beautiful fairy scenes represented at Christmas in the London theaters." Light from a hole at the top of the main chamber dramatically illuminates a display of enormous stalactites along with numerous Buddha images that have been placed in the cave and that are presented with regular offerings. The late morning hours are the best time to view the effective natural lighting. Monkeys rush out from among the bushes to greet visitors to the cave.

197

HUA HIN

Credit for "discovering" the resort possibilities of Hua Hin, a scenic seaside village on the west coast of the gulf, 140 miles from Bangkok, usually goes to Prince Chakrabongse, a brother of King Rama VI, who in 1911 took a visiting group of European royalty there for a hunting holiday. The prince and his Russian wife built a bungalow by the sea, other members of the royal family soon built houses nearby and eventually a king's palace, which was called Klai Klangwan, "far from care." The entire court moved to Hua Hin for several months of the year, thus giving it a fashionable atmosphere still apparent in some of the spacious old bungalows visible from the beach. Completion of the southern railway line in the 1920's made Hua Hin easily accessible to the capital, leading to the Railway Hotel, a golf course, and other holiday homes owned by prominent Bangkok families. Even today, despite the addition of several large hotels and rows of condominiums, Hua Hin retains a sedate atmosphere, especially when compared with Pattaya, its boisterous competitor across the gulf. At Wat Khao Lao, the temple on top of the hill, visitors can enjoy charming views of the town.

FISHING PORT. One of the most colorful sights near Hua Hin town is the fishing port, where the daily catch from the Gulf of Thailand is brought in by fishermen in their trawlers in the early hours of the morning.

RAILWAY HOTEL. A rambling Victorian structure, built in 1923, with broad verandas and a garden of topiary shrubs, the old Railway Hotel fell on hard times when the mass tourist trade shifted to Pattaya in the early 1960's. It has been beautifully restored today by a French company without sacrificing its spacious, airy charm.

GOLF COURSE. The golf course at Hua Hin was the country's first, with "a stock of golf requisites and the loan of clubs" available through the Railway Hotel, according to a 1929 guide book. The 18-hole course overlooking the sea is still one of the most popular in the area, and the fact that it contains a temple and a topiary garden gives it a special Thai flavor.

A STAR PERFORMANCE The Railway Hotel played a prominent role in the award-winning film, *The Killing Fields*, about Cambodia's trials under Khmer Rouge rule. The producers used the picturesque old building in place of the Royal Hotel , where many journalists who covered the war stayed in Phnom Penh.

KHAO SAM ROI YOT
NATIONAL PARK ★

Covering 39 square miles, Khao Sam
Roi Yot – literally, "the mountain of
three hundred peaks" – was established as a park in 1966. Conveniently
situated just a few miles south of Hua
Hin, the park boasts numerous
picturesque limestone peaks, the highest rising to
1,997 feet, as well as caves, and unspoiled beaches fringed by
casuarina trees. It was formerly famous for its marshes,
waterfalls and wading birds. However, recent encroachment

by private shrimp farmers has
seriously affected the state of the
natural habitat. Several scenes in
The Killing Fields were filmed
within the boundaries of the
national park. Bird life is
especially varied in this park,
with more than 275 identified
species, 60 of which – painted
storks, grey herons, egrets and
rare imperial eagles among them
– are found mainly in the marsh
areas. Monkeys and deer are
particularly common. Other
mammals include crab-eating
macaques, Malayan porcupines,
leopard cats and, in the offshore waters, Irrawaddy dolphins.

PHRAYA NAKHON CAVE. The largest cave in the park is Phraya
Nakhon, named after a ruler of Nakhon Si Thammarat
who discovered it two centuries ago when he came
ashore in a violent storm; a pavilion in the cave
was built for a visit by King Rama V in 1896.

PRACHUAB KHIRI KHAN

Prachuab Khiri Khan is approximately 54 miles
south of Hua Hin. Off the main southern
highway, it is a tiny port overlooked by
Khao Chang Krachok ("mirror mountain"),
on top of which sits a temple offering panoramic
views of the sea. There are bungalows to rent and
seafood restaurants down at the beach near the
town.

PINEAPPLES
A common sight
around Hua Hin
and along much of
the southern
peninsula are vast
plantations of
pineapples, which
thrive in the sandy
soil. Today, Thailand
is one of the world's
largest producers
of canned and fresh
pineapples for export,
having long ago
surpassed Hawaii.
Southern pineapples
are especially noted
for their sweetness
and succulence.

FAR FROM CARE
Although Klai
Klangwan, the name
of the royal palace at
Hua Hin, means "far
from care," it hardly
proved so for King
Rama VII. He was
in residence there
when he received
word in June 1932 of
the coup d'état that
ended Thailand's
absolute monarchy.
Though he agreed to
grant a constitution,
he later abdicated in
1935 and died in
England in 1941.

CHUMPHON

Despite the construction of a sizeable seaside hotel some years ago, Chumphon has never really found popularity as a resort. It is noted, however, for its relatively inexpensive supply of edible birds' nests ■ 28–9, gathered from the offshore island of Koh Lanka Chiu. The island can be visited by boat from the port of Paknam Chumphon.

KRA ISTHMUS

Just below Chumphon is the Kra Isthmus, only 15 miles wide and the narrowest point on peninsular Thailand, an area of rocky limestone precipices and breathtaking scenery. For many generations, this spot has been envisioned as the site of a Suez-type canal, which would cut nearly a thousand miles off shipping routes between ports on the Indian Ocean and the Gulf of Thailand. Several plans have been drawn up for such an undertaking – one proposer even suggested the use of nuclea weapons to ease the task – but thus far none has been successful, doubtless to the great relief of Singapore further south.

RANONG

Ranong, located on a river of the same name that empties into the sea across from Victoria Point, the southernmost extremity of Burma, is a quiet provincial capital whose prosperity is mainly based on tin from nearby mines and a fishing fleet that sails far out into the Indian Ocean. The older houses, like those of Phuket and Songkhla further south, are built in the Sino-Portuguese style of Malacca and some of the downtown streets have covered arcades to shelter pedestrians from monsoon rains. The town is noted for a number of hot mineral-water springs, one of which supplies the Jansom Thara Hotel, picturesquely situated at the foot of a mountain just outside the town. Boat trips can be arranged from the port to visit off-shore islands, among them Koh Pa Yam where a company produces cultured pearls. (Entry into Burma, however, is not allowed at this point.) More hot springs – one of which produces 130 gallons of

SRIVIJAYA
The Srivijaya kingdom ▲ 35, which originated in Sumatra, dominated the southern peninsula of Thailand between the 8th and 13th centuries. Though historians disagree over its extent, it was a Hindu culture that also practiced Mahayana Buddhism and produced some of Thailand's finest art in stone and bronze. This bronze Bodhisattva was found by Prince Damrong at Wat Mahathat, Chaiya, together with a number of other excellent pieces, and is now preserved in the National Museum in Bangkok ● 160.

> «AT LOW WATER IMMENSE TRACTS OF MUD AND SAND
> ARE LAID BARE, FOR THE EDIFICATION OF FLOCKS OF
> PELICANS, CORMORANTS AND HERONS.»
>
> H. WARRINGTON SMYTH

ot (158°F) water a minute – as well as tin
nines can be found at Hat Sompin,
bout an hour away from Ranong
y car. Another sight is Nam
ok Ngao, a waterfall on the
ighway southward. It is at
s most impressive after a
eavy rain.

CHAIYA

n ancient town, Chaiya is
elieved by some scholars to
ave been the capital of the
reat Srivijaya kingdom (8th–13th
entury) ● *35*, which ruled most of
eninsular Thailand from its base in Sumatra. The
nly remaining traces of this former glory are the ruins of
everal once-impressive temples. Wat Phra Boromathat is
urrounded by walls and contains a chedi restored by
ing Rama V in 1901, but dating from the 8th century
nd considered the best example of Srivijayan
rchitecture ● *96*, while Wat Keo, which was
iscovered in 1978, has a crumbled brick prang of the
rivijaya period (below left). A small museum displays

antiquities found in the area, mostly within Wat
Phra Boromathat itself, with reproductions of
important pieces that are now displayed in the
National Museum in Bangkok.

WAT SUAN MOK

Wat Suan Mok is a modern temple popular
with Buddhists as a place for retreat and
study. It is renowned for teaching meditation to
foreigners and offers courses in English to
anyone ready to accept its extremely strict and
spartan rules. For others, its most notable
feature is a collection of colorful murals left
by visiting foreigners depicting a somewhat
bewildering variety of subjects, ranging
from Zen to compositions inspired by
Egypt.

SURAT THANI

Surat Thani is an important
southern railway and highway
center as well as a busy seaport.
Although it has a number of
excellent seafood restaurants
serving dishes and offers
attractive views along the water-
front, Surat Thani is of interest
to most travelers today
mainly as an embarkation
point from which ferries
leave for Koh Samui, and
the islands that lie beyond it.

TEN VOWS
A novice monk
takes these ten vows:
"I take the vow
not to destroy life."
"I take the vow
not to steal."
"I take the vow
to abstain from
impurity."
"I take the vow
not to lie."
"I take the vow
not to eat at
forbidden times."
"I take the vow to
abstain from dancing,
singing, music
and stage plays."
"I take the vow
not to use garlands,
scents, unguents,
or ornaments."
"I take the vow
not to use a broad
or high bed."
"I take the vow
not to receive gold
or silver."

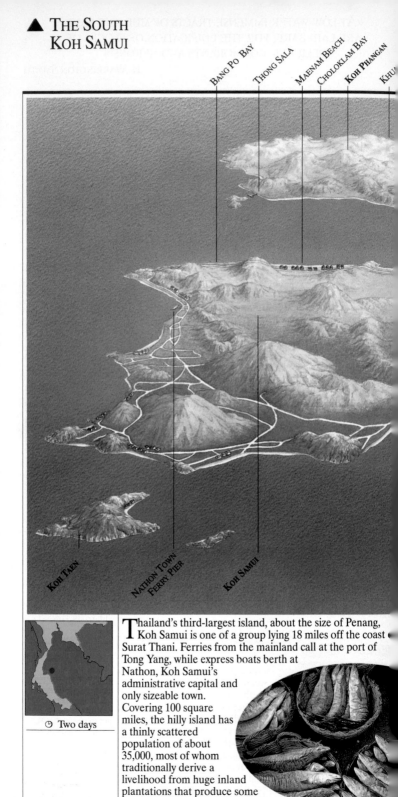

BANG PO BAY

THONG SALA

MAENAM BEACH

CHOLOKLAM BAY

KOH PHANGAN

KHU

KOH TAEN

NATHON TOWN
FERRY PIER

KOH SAMUI

⏱ Two days

Thailand's third-largest island, about the size of Penang, Koh Samui is one of a group lying 18 miles off the coast Surat Thani. Ferries from the mainland call at the port of Tong Yang, while express boats berth at Nathon, Koh Samui's administrative capital and only sizeable town. Covering 100 square miles, the hilly island has a thinly scattered population of about 35,000, most of whom traditionally derive a livelihood from huge inland plantations that produce some of the best coconuts in Thailand.

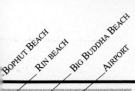

Koh Samui islanders dry squid in the sun.

CHAWENG BEACH
LAMAI BEACH
HIN TA AND HIN YAI

Thousands of coconuts are sent to Bangkok and other parts of the country annually, and there is also a factory producing coconut fiber. Until the late 1970's the physical charms of Koh Samui were a closely guarded secret among a relatively small number of adventurous travelers – mostly budget-minded backpackers in search of accommodation at only a few dollars a night, long, virtually empty beaches, and a generally laid-back atmosphere. All that is now rapidly changing. A regular air service links the island with Bangkok, thus eliminating the time-consuming bus or train journey to Surat Thani for those in a hurry. New, more luxurious tourist facilities are springing up along the beaches, particularly on the east coast, with the result that Koh Samui is beginning to rival nearby Phuket as an international destination. Actually, the two island resorts complement each other in

KOH SAMUI SEASHELLS

Cassis cornuta is very solid and heavy and has a short spine with about seven whorls.

Casum ceramicum is also solid and heavy, with a high spine.

Spondylus regius is a striking thorny oyster with seven elevated ribs bearing pointed spines.

Mitra mitra This is the largest of the mitra family.

...rms of weather, since ...uket's season of heaviest rain ...uly through September) runs ...ncurrently with one of Koh Samui's ...nniest times; the latter island's wettest months are ...ward the end of the year.

BUFFALO FIGHTING. One of the favorite pastimes of ...the islanders used to be buffalo fighting. To ...discourage gambling, the fights that were held every ...weekend are now restricted to festive occasions such ...as the Lunar New Year or the Thai New Year. A long ...ritual is performed before the fight. The brightly ...decorated buffaloes are splashed with holy water and kept ...apart by a curtain that is lifted at the very moment the two ...imals clash against each other. The fight ends when one of ...e buffaloes is pushed out of the arena.

203

BIG BUDDHA
The Big Buddha of Wat Phra Yai towers above the shrine of Koh Fan and is dedicated to the Parinirvana (reclining) Buddha. At the entrance of the temple, a figure of Maitreya, the Buddha of the Future, welcomes monks and visitors before they ascend to the colossal hilltop figure.

WHEELS FOR RENT
In Nathon motorbikes and automobiles are easily available for rent to those who want to tour the island on their own.

NORTHERN BEACHES.

BIG BUDDHA BEACH (HAT PHRA YAI). This beach derives its name from a 40-foot-high image of the meditating Buddha at a monastery on a small islet called Koh Fan, connected by a causeway. The beach boasts a smooth stretch of sand, calm waters and a generally restful atmosphere. A boat ferries passengers daily over to Hat Rin on Koh Phangan.

BOPHUT BEACH. East of Maenam is Ban Bophut, one of Samui's oldest settlements, with wooden shophouses lining the main street. The nearby beach is about a mile long, and the placid water, while not as clear as some others, is ideal for water-skiing. Boats ply the route from the village pier to Koh Phangan and a trip on one of these takes about 40 minutes.

MAENAM BEACH. This beach, near a village of the same name and with easy access to Nathon, is a 2½-mile stretch of white sand on a picturesque bay with a great view of Koh Phangan offshore. Bungalows are available at a wide range of prices and boats can be hired for excursions to other beaches.

BANG PO BAY. This beach is still relatively undeveloped, mainly because the rocks and corals break the surface during the low tide. It is, however, one of the best locations for snorkeling and scuba-diving.

NATHON TOWN

On the west coast of Koh Samui, near the jetty for ferries from Surat Thani, is the small town of Nathon. Apart from the grocery shops and basic essential services such as post and banking that serve the islanders, there are also several bars and souvenir shops catering mainly for tourists.

CHAWENG BEACH

The most developed of Koh Samui's beaches, Chaweng is a 4-mile crescent with white sand and clear water. Tourist facilities and nightlife are concentrated in the central section, which also overlooks the best part of the beach. Unlike other resorts in Thailand, bars, discotheques and restaurants are patronized mainly by foreigners traveling on a shoestring budget. As a result, local nightbirds do not flock here to earn the tourist dollar. Equipment for windsurfing, para-sailing and scuba-diving are available. Water scooters have also invaded the beaches, robbing Koh Samui of its little-island charm.

OVERLAP STONE
This stone is a popular Samui landmark, a huge boulder balanced on a promontory above Lower Lamai Beach, where there are a few bungalows for rent and a refreshment stall. Another mile further up is a point of land that affords impressive views of the island's interior scenery.

LAMAI BEACH

After Chaweng, Lamai is probably the most popular beach, appealing to a younger crowd of budget-conscious visitors. Besides the wide choice of accommodation, there is nightlife with numerous restaurants and discos. Lower Lamai offers good swimming even when the seas elsewhere are too rough.

COCONUT PLANTATIONS

Until the advent of tourism, and to a large extent even today, Koh Samui's economy has been based on the graceful coconut palms that cover most of the interior, even extending to the mountain sides; an average of two million coconuts are transported to Bangkok monthly, a sizeable part of the national production. The sweet juice of young coconuts is a favorite drink, while coconut cream plays a bigger role in the local cuisine than it does elsewhere in the south. Some growers have trained monkeys who scamper nimbly up the lofty trunks, select only those coconuts ready for picking, and drop them to the ground.

HIN TA AND HIN YAI
Hin Ta and Hin Yai, or "Grandfather Stone and Grandmother Stone," are a pair of much-photographed rock formations suggesting genitals at the tip of a headland that separates Central Lamai and Lower Lamai. Hin Ta points toward the sky, while his companion is a wave-splashed cleft about 132 feet away.

WATERFALLS

For those who enjoy waterfalls, the interior of Samui offers a number of scenic opportunities. The two most popular are Hin Lat, which spills over several levels and has a pool good for bathing, and Na Muang, which cascades for over 130 feet down a slab of yellow limestone.

KOH PHANGAN ★

Less developed than Koh Samui – at least for the time being – is Koh Phangan, the largest of its neighboring islands, 9 miles away. The island covers approximately 76 square miles and has a relatively small population of about 8,000, mostly concentrated in the main town of Thong Sala. Tourist accommodation is simple and the atmosphere appeals to the sort of backpack travelers who once flocked to Bali. There are dozens of beautiful, unspoiled beaches, among the most popular being Hat Rin, which has direct boat services to and from Samui; Hat Khuat ("Bottle Beach"), in a secluded cove on the northern coast; and Choloklam Bay, on which there are several stretches of sand. There are daily express boats from Nathon pier to Thong Sala, as well as boats from Bophut Pier and Big Buddha Beach to Hat Rin; all boat services are subject to weather conditions.

KOH TAO

Koh Tao, "Turtle Island," is so called because of its shape. A small island covering only 8½ square miles, it takes two hours to reach by express boat from Thong Sala on Koh Phangan, three to four hours by the regular ferry. Almost untouched by development, the island offers a tranquil ambience. Clear waters and extensive offshore coral reefs make it ideal for scuba diving and snorkeling, and there are a few simple bungalow facilities, the majority on the western and southern coasts of the island.

ANG THONG NATIONAL MARINE PARK ★

Lying 19 miles northwest of Koh Samui, Ang Thong National Marine Park includes some forty islands and is characterized by impressive limestone outcrops and blue lagoons. Koh Tao is one of the larger islands in the group; the others vary greatly in size and many have hidden coves with white-sand beaches. Koh Wua Ta Lap ("Isle of the Sleeping Cow") has bungalow facilities, while Koh Mae ("Mother Island") has a beautiful beach surrounded by towering cliffs. There is a daily boat to the park from Nathon, leaving in the morning and returning in the afternoon.

WATER BABIES
"Little children, long before they can walk, are thrown into the water by their mothers, who fasten under their arms a tin float that always keeps the head above water. The wee brown dots splash and splutter about in the luke-warm current of the river, involuntarily learning the correct action of the limbs in swimming, and gaining an acquaintance with this element that ever afterwards prevents any feeling of fear. In this way many children learn to swim almost as soon as, if not before, they can walk."
Ernest Young

HISTORY

One of the oldest settlements in Thailand, Nakhon Si Thammarat was known to ancient travelers as Ligor and was an important center during both the Srivijaya ▲ 200 and Dvaravati periods, over a thousand years ago. Many notable works of art – both Hindu and Buddhist – have been found in and around the city, testifying to the variety of cultures that influenced its development even before the Thais appeared on the scene. King Ramkhamhaeng of Sukhothai is popularly believed to have visited Nakhon Si Thammarat in the 13th century and to have been so impressed by the teachings of the city's Buddhist monks that he brought a group of them back to the first independent Thai capital.

The resplendent Viharn Luang of Wat Mahathat.

MUSEUM. The Nakhon Si Thammarat branch of the National Museum ▲ 158– 61 is the most important in the country after Bangkok's. Among the items on display is an impressive collection of early Hindu images and some of the earliest Buddhist sculpture. The Hindu figures, found at Takua Pa, include a beautiful Vishnu once wrapped in the roots of a tree. It was decapitated by vandals and when the roots were cut away to move the figure, the missing head was discovered to have been a fake; the original one, now restored to its proper place on the body, was buried beneath the statue.

WAT MAHATHAT. The most revered of Nakhon Si Thammarat's Buddhist monuments is Wat Mahathat, founded during the Srivijaya period (8th–13th century). The temple's dominant feature is a towering 254-foot-high chedi, the spire of which is covered with gold leaf and studded with precious stones. The chedi stands in an immense cloister covered with colored tiles and surrounding it a gallery lined with numerous Buddha images. A standing Sukhothai-style Buddha image is enshrined in one of the temple's two chapels while on the altar of the other there are bas-reliefs that show Westerners among the various figures. Outside the cloister of Wat Mahathat is the Viharn Luang, with columns that lean forward in the Ayutthaya style and a richly decorated ceiling.

NIELLOWARE
One of Nakhon Si Thammarat's outstanding traditional arts is niello, which arrived before the 12th century, probably from India. An amalgam of dark metals is applied to etched portions of silver or gold to create intricate designs covering trays, boxes, vases and other objects. A 15th-century law in Ayutthaya decreed that high-ranking nobles could proclaim their position through the possession of a nielloware pedestal and tray, while in 1687, King Narai is recorded as having sent a nielloware bowl to King Louis XIV of France. Bangkok rulers have also traditionally presented the ware as gifts to foreign heads of state.

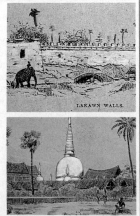

LAKAWN WALLS.

SONGKHLA

Songkhla, once known as Singora, is the only natural port on the lower Gulf of Thailand side of the southern isthmus and as such has long been an important center of trade, founded and largely developed by Chinese. Much of the trade, along with the money it brought, moved some years ago to Haadyai, more conveniently located at a railway junction, with the result that Songkhla has been able to retain some degree of its old atmosphere.

SAMILA BEACH. Koh Samui and Phuket have lured many of the foreign tourists away from the nearby Samila Beach, an attractive strand on the gulf line with casuarina trees and stalls selling freshly cooked seafood, though visitors from Malaysia still come during the hot season. A hill behind the Samila Beach Hotel, surmounted by an ancient chedi, is the highest point in Songkhla and offers scenic views of the sea. Boats can be hired for side trips around an inland sea or Thale Sap, which empties into the gulf, or to nearby Muslim fishing villages.

NANG TALUNG
A form of shadow play called *nang talung*, closely resembling the Indonesian *wayang kulit*, is frequently staged at festivals in the far south. The buffalo-hide figures have movable parts – arms, legs, or chin – and their concealed manipulators accompany their actions with songs and often ribald repartee. ● 68–9.

WAT MACHI MAWAT. This temple boasts a collection of several interesting murals showing life around the port in the late 1800's and early 1900's.

SONGKHLA MUSEUM. A beautiful old Chinese mansion dating from the latter part of the 19th century, once the residence of a provincial governor, has been restored and is now open to the public as a museum (below). Chinese porcelains, statuary and objects from the excavations of nearby Sating Phra are displayed in its spacious rooms.

THALE NOI BIRD SANCTUARY

Just a few miles north of Songkhla is an 11-square-mile region of freshwater and swamp ecosystem known as Thale Noi. Several canals flow through the area, making it accessible to nature-lovers and bird-watchers.

BIRD-WATCHING. Nearly 200 species of birds – including several rare ones such as the lesser adjutant stork, white ibis, spot-billed pelican and gray heron – have been recorded in this nature reserve. Egrets, cormorants, terns and jacanas are also common here. The best period to observe the birds is between January and April. Boats can be hired for a three-hour trip from the nature reserve headquarters to Sala Nang Riam on the other side of the lake. The fishing village offers visitors to Thale Noi a peek at life in this typical southern community.

«IT WAS WITH NO SMALL PLEASURE THAT WE RATTLED DOWN THE
ANCHOR IN SONGKHLA, AND CONTEMPLATED THE BEAUTIFUL HILL-
GIRDLED HARBOR THAT LAY BEFORE US.»

H. WARRINGTON SMYTH, 1898

HAADYAI

Strategically situated at the junction of
major railways and roads, Haadyai has
become one of the most prosperous cities
in the south in recent decades, of little
architectural or cultural distinction but
with a definite boom-town air of
excitement. A considerable part of the
money derived from such major southern
industries as tin, rubber and seafood
processing passes through Haadyai's
bankers and businessmen and to this can
be added a possibly even greater amount
from tourism. Malaysians come in large
numbers – around 600,000 a year,
according to a recent estimate – across
the border just 36 miles away, drawn
partly by lower prices for luxury goods
and partly by an uninhibited nightlife not
available in their own country. Haadyai has more than 5,000
hotel rooms, most of them filled on weekends, plus hundreds
of discos, bars and massage parlors.

FISHING BOATS
The fishing boats
of southern Thailand
have intricate
colorful motifs
similar to those
of the northwestern
coast of peninsular
Malaysia – proof
of the cultural
link existing in
this region. The
decorations are
to please the spirits
and invoke them to
bless the boats and
protect the occupants
from hazards at sea.
When boats are
launched a shaman is
called to perform
an ancient animistic
ritual during which
prayers are recited
and offerings made
to the spirits.

PATTANI AND ANCIENT MUSLIM KINGDOMS

Muslims comprise Thailand's largest religious minority, about
two million in all, mostly Malay living in the southernmost
provinces. Pattani and Pattalung have been in fact prosperous,
independent kingdoms and active
trading posts since the end of the
first millennium. This
prosperity came to an end
when the Siamese invaded
and destroyed Pattani,
bringing the entire area
under the rule of the
Kingdom of Siam. Since then,
there has always been friction
between the Muslims and the Thai government, most evident
during the 1960's and 1970's, when many Muslims fled to the
jungles to join the communists. Today the southern provinces
are relatively quiet but sporadic incidents are sufficient to
dissuade tourists from coming. Although Muslim traditions
are deep-rooted, there is little architectural evidence of the
long history of these ancient Malay
states. Most of the villagers are
simple people, accustomed to a
subsistence livelihood
and spending their
days fishing and
mending nets.

SARASIN BRIDGE

KATU VILLAGE

MONUMENT TO PHUKET'S HEROINES

KOH NAKHA NOI

KOH NAKHA

MAI KHAO BEACH

AIRPORT

BANG TAO BEACH

PAN SEA BAY

SURIN BEACH

PATONG BEACH

KARON NOI BEACH

KARON BEACH

KATA YAI BEACH

KATA NOI BEACH

NAI HAN BEACH

RAWAI BEACH

WAT CHALONG

PHUKET TOWN

SEA GYPSIES VILLAGE

CAPE PHANWA

🕐 Three days

Dazzling white-sand beaches, crystal-clear water, and limestone cliffs rising in fantastic shapes from the sea – these are the magical images most visitors carry back from a visit to Phuket in the Andaman Sea. But the island's modern tourist boom is only the latest development in an eventful history that goes back hundreds of years.

HISTORY

To sailors of the 16th and 17th centuries, Phuket was known as "Junkceylon" or "Jonkcelaon"; only in relatively modern times did Thailand's largest offshore island acquire its present name, derived from the Malay word *bukit,* meaning "hill," referring to its mountainous terrain. The waters around Phuket were notorious hunting grounds for pirates, who hid in countless secret coves along the coast, but traders still came, for the island was rich in one of the ancient world's most prized commodities – tin, easily extracted from seemingly inexhaustible veins close to the surface. There were also other alluring treasures: ambergris, rhinoceros horn, rare corals and edible birds' nests, a delicacy that is much esteemed by Chinese gourmets ■ 28–9. As Thailand's trade with the outside world expanded in the 19th century, tin mining on Phuket enjoyed a boom that brought in thousands of Chinese workers, some of whom later became wealthy mine-owners themselves. The Chinese, indeed, soon comprised the larger part of the island's population while Sino-Thais still controlled its economy. In 1903, the first rubber trees began another major industry. Soon Phuket was the richest province in the country in terms of per capita income, a distinction it continues to enjoy even today. Tourism arrived in the early 1970's, with the opening of the Sarasin Bridge linking Phuket with the mainland. Roads were cut through mountains to the western shore, where the best beaches are located, and within a short time, the island had emerged as one of the leading travel destinations in all of Asia.

PHUKET'S HEROINES
On the road from the airport leading toward Phuket Town stands a memorial to two Phuket heroines. In 1785, the brave pair rallied the residents of Thalang (then the island's main town) to defend it successfully against the Burmese invaders, in reward for which the two ladies were given noble titles by King Rama I of Bangkok.

OLD HOUSES
Adding considerably to the charm of Phuket Town are its surviving old Chinese houses (above), built in the Sino-Portuguese style also found in Malacca. Many of these houses belong to families whose ancestors first came to the island as laborers in the 19th-century tin mines.

MOVIE-MAKERS
The scenic beauties of Phuket and neighboring Phangnga Bay have attracted numerous movie-makers, foreign as well as Thai. Part of the movie *The Man with the Golden Gun* was filmed at Phangnga, while Phuket's interior was used in Brian De Palma's *Casualties of War* and the old District Office appeared as the French embassy in *The Killing Fields.*

PHUKET TOWN TODAY

Phuket Town, the bustling provincial capital, has a population
of around 50,000. A boom in real estate in recent years has
spurred developers to build countless shophouses, hotels and
condominiums, with an inevitable loss of atmosphere, though
many of the elegant old millionaires'
mansions remain, as well as the
stately building that once
housed the District
Office that served as the
French embassy in the
film *The Killing Fields*.
Particularly colorful is
the public market on
Rasada Street, just

across from the main minibus terminus, where all the local
seafood, fruits, vegetables and spices are piled in tempting
abundance amid busy vendors and price-haggling customers.
Close to the center of town is the hill known as Khao Rang,
on top of which are a landscaped "fitness park" and a
restaurant offering splendid views of the town itself, the
harbor and the sea and distant offshore islands.

PHUKET AQUARIUM

Overlooking the sea on Chalong Bay, not very far from
Phuket Town, the aquarium is part of the Marine Biology
Research Center and rears a variety of sea creatures from
local waters. It also serves as a hatchery for the eggs of huge
sea turtles that come ashore to lay between October and
February.

PHUKET PORT

A visit to Phuket's main port, east of the town, reveals the
importance of deep-sea fishing. About 350 industrially
equipped boats fish the waters around the island and all the
way to the Indian Ocean, hauling in about 40,000 tons of
seafood annually. The port scene is most
colorful when the boats return to unload
in the early morning.

«The strongest statement of Chinese culture evident in Phuket is probably the Vegetarian Festival.»

CHINESE TEMPLES

Phuket's Chinese character is reflected in a number of temples. The principal ones are at Kathu, where the Vegetarian Festival originated in the 19th century, and Put Jaw Temple in town, both lavishly adorned with red and gold carvings and images of various gods and goddesses.

VEGETARIAN FESTIVAL. Held annually in October, this is another manifestation of the strong Chinese flavor that pervades the island. The festival was started by immigrants who flocked in large numbers from China and nearby Malaya to work in the tin mines, supposedly in response to a mysterious fever that was afflicting them. It now lasts for ten days and, in addition to abstinence from meat and rituals held at various Chinese temples, features gala processions that attract crowds of visitors as well as local believers. Many of the participants go into deep trances, enabling them to endure a wide range of self-inflicted ordeals, from walking over beds of red-hot charcoal to piercing their cheeks with long metal skewers; such practices are not a part of traditional vegetarian festivals in China and were most probably assimilated over the years from India.

BUDDHIST TEMPLES

Although Phuket has a sizeable number of Muslim residents, about 60 percent of the population are Buddhists, who attend

one or another of the island's twenty-nine temples. The largest and best-known is Wat Chalong, which contains images of two revered monks who helped put down a rebellion of Chinese immigrants in 1876; the images are kept supplied with offerings of flowers and incense. Another important temple is Wat Phra Thong (above), on the airport road, where the main attraction is a large Buddha image supposedly made of gold, half buried in the earth; after its discovery by a farmer, the image was left as it was and the temple built to shelter it.

LAK MUANG. In most old Thai cities, a shrine, or the *lak muang*, was erected at the "central axis," usually around a wood or stone pillar that marked the center of the settlement and provided a home for the spirit who guarded it. In the case of Phuket, the pillar is near the monument to two heroines in the sleepy district of Tha Rua ▲ *211*, where the island's principal community once thrived.

A HEAVY SMOKER
In Phuket, at the end of the last century, a monk who was a heavy smoker became famous. An image was erected in Wat Chalong and ever since has been kept supplied with offerings. These offerings commonly take the form of lighted cigarettes, placed in the mouth. A gentle draft causes the cigarettes to continue to burn. The image of the monk, therefore appears to be smoking.

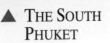

A LOCAL DELICACY
Prawns are skewered
and arranged
between lengths of
bamboo and left to
dry in the sun before
they are eaten.

SOUTHERN CUISINE
Southern food
has a reputation
for being the hottest
in Thailand. As well
as standard dishes
found in most parts
of the country – often
with lashings of extra
chillies – many local
restaurants also
offer Malay-style
fare that reflects
Indian influence
in its use of curry
powder and
turmeric.

PATONG BEACH

Stretching for 2½ miles around a bay, Patong was the first of
Phuket's beaches to be developed and is still the only one to
offer a really varied Bangkok-style
nightlife. Hotels large and
small, restaurants, shops,
bars, even a towering new
condominium, line its
main street, overlooking a
turquoise sea that, so far
at least, remains
remarkably clean. All sorts of
water sports are available, from
windsurfing to para-sailing, and boats
can be hired for trips to less crowded
swimming areas along the coast. The seabed
shelves gently and, with usually calm waters
and the natural grandeur of the
forested backdrop, swimming
and other water activities are
very popular. Visitors
staying elsewhere, on the
other hand, often come to
Patong to enjoy its rich seafood
and after-dark activities.

OTHER BEACHES

All of Phuket's best
beaches are located on
the western side of the
island, facing the Andaman
Sea, and range from strands
several miles long to smaller
crescents. There are thirteen
major ones, starting at Mai
Khao near the airport and

...tending down to Rawai at the southern tip, each with a distinctive character of its own. A narrow road connects the string of beaches and cuts down travel time along the coast considerably.

MAI KHAO AND NAI YANG. The northernmost of Phuket's west-coast beaches, Mai Khao and Nai Yang are still relatively undeveloped and therefore quiet. They stretch for more than 10 miles altogether. The water, however, is not as clear as at other beaches, especially at low tide.

KARON. This stretch actually consists of two beaches, one an idyllic little cove popularly known as Relax Bay and occupied by Le Méridien Hotel, and the other much longer and now lined with a variety of tourist accommodation large and small.

PAN SEA. Scenically, Pan Sea is one of the most enchanting beaches, with very good opportunities for snorkeling and swimming during the dry season. Its principal tourist facility, the Pan Sea Phuket Bay Resort, boasts attractive thatched-roof huts spilling down a hillside.

KATA. Like Karon, Kata is divided into Kata Yai (Big Kata) and Kata Noi (Little Kata). The former, a long stretch of fine beach, is the site of the Club Méditerranée and several smaller facilities; the latter is further south and has a hotel, the Kata Thani, and several bungalow complexes.

SURIN. A picturesque strand with steep hills that rise sharply at the back, this is especially popular with Thai day-trippers on weekends and holidays. The spectacular Thai-style Amanpuri Hotel overlooks one end of the beach.

NAI HAN ★. Site of the Phuket Yacht Club, Nai Han is an otherwise undeveloped beach with white sand, clear water and a scenic view of Phrom Thep at the southern tip of the island.

RAWAI. An attractive strand fringed by coconut palms, Rawai is located on a shallow, silty bay and therefore less popular with swimmers. Boats can be hired here for trips to the offshore islands.

LAEM PHROM THEP. This is an elevation at the far southern tip of Phuket, attracting tourists and many local people because of its panoramic views of the sea and often spectacular sunsets. As a result, traffic jams in the vicinity are a common sight. Among the picturesque islands offshore is Koh Keo, where there are meditation cells for Buddhist monks and a graceful chedi.

SEA GYPSIES
The Sea Gypsies or Chao Ley are probably Phuket's oldest inhabitants. While some still live on board their boats in other parts of the Andaman Sea, most have now settled in Phuket in small villages (such as those in Rawai) close to the sea, their favored element. The Sea Gypsies earn their living by fishing, diving for oysters and other shells, and harvesting edible birds' nests deposited on lofty limestone cliffs and in caves ■ 28–9, ▲ 223, 226.

BEAUTIFUL BEACHES
Kata, Nai Han and Laem Phrom Thep (below) are just three of the beautiful beaches that make up the main tourist attraction on Phuket.

RUBBER TREES

"Beyond the forest the level of the land was higher and there were more rubber plantations – nothing but rubber. Thousands and thousands of acres were planted with the dark, dull green heveas. The trees stood in straight rows, and by the side of each was a stick. On the top of each stick was a porcelain cup upside down. In some places the cup was attached to the tree by a bit of wire below the tin spout

through which the latex flowed when the tree was tapped. Coolies passed barefoot and soundlessly among the trees and turned the cups out into large zinc churns similar to European milk churns."

M.H. Lulofs

SHELLS
The waters around Phuket are a rich source of shells, both rare and common for sale in the numerous shops. Some of the more serious dealers employ divers to search for the rarest specimens at great depths and sell their ...ds to ...ernational ...ectors at high ...s.

RUBBER PLANTATIONS

The first rubber trees, brought from Malaysia, were planted on Phuket in 1903, only a decade after they were first acclimatized to Southeast Asia at Singapore's Botanical Gardens. Thus began the vast plantations that are now scattered over the island, producing around 14,000 tons of dry latex annually. Thanks to these plantations and others on the mainland, Thailand is today a major exporter of rubber.

KHAO PHRA THAEO NATIONAL PARK

Located just off the airport road, Khao Phra Thaeo National Park contains the last remnants of the tropical rain forest that once covered Phuket. Near the entrance to the jungle is Tone Sai Waterfall, an attractive site popular with local day-tripper on weekends but virtually deserted at other times.

OFFSHORE ISLANDS

A number of Phuket's smaller offshore islands can be easily reached by boat on short trips. The most popular with visitor especially snorkelers and scuba divers, is probably Koh Hi, also called Coral Island because of the extensive reefs that surround it, just east of the tip of Phuket. Koh Mai Thong, a little further, has fine beaches on the far side, while up the eastern coast are Koh Nakha Yai and Koh Nakha Noi. The latter has a cultured-pearl farm, where oysters are seeded and carefully tended for two years, the amount of time required for a pearl to form inside. Yet another attractive island is Koh Lawa Yai, located at the southern extremity of Phangnga Bay.

> «THE LAPPING OF THE WAVES IS ALL TOO OFTEN DROWNED OUT BY
> THE RUMBLE OF CONCRETE MIXERS.»
>
> ALISTAIR SHEARER

THE PLEASURES OF PHUKET
Now a leading international resort, Phuket has a wide range of attractions for visitors. Most are still centered around its renowned beaches; para-sailing, surfing, water-skiing, deep-sea fishing and romantic cruises on chartered boats. In addition, though, there are shops selling handicrafts from all parts of Thailand, countless restaurants offering Thai or foreign cuisine, and special attractions such as butterfly farms and orchid nurseries aimed primarily at the tourist trade.

217

MANGROVE
SWAMPS

KOH HONG

LIGHTHOUSE

KOH PHING

KOH MAK

KOH YAO NOI

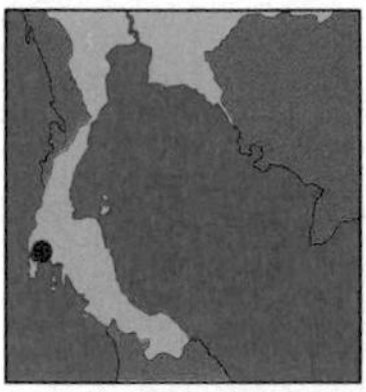

🕙 One day

Millenniums ago, Phangnga Bay was dry land with scattered limestone mountains; the sea invaded as glaciers melted, around 10,000 years before the beginning of the Christian era, leaving only a spectacular profusion of mountain peaks rising from the water to form one of the world's greatest natural attractions. The upheaval also led to the formation of several sea caves, some of which lie below sea level while others rise high above the rocks and remain mostly unexplored even to this day. Thirty-eight miles from Phuket by road, or about three hours by boat, the bay and surrounding areas it were declared a marine national park in 1981. More than forty islands are included, several reaching an altitude of 1,000 feet and shaped like animals, with dramatic sea caves and sheltered, pristine beaches. On the mainland around the bay are canals threading through dense

KOH PANNYI
KOH KHIEN
KOH NOM SAO
PARK HEADQUARTERS
MANGROVE SWAMPS
PHANGNGA BAY RESORT HOTEL
KOH TALU

LIMESTONE BEAUTIES
Much of the attraction of Phangnga's countless caves, both on the mainland and on many of the islands in the bay, lies in their limestone formations. Intricate stalactites and stalagmites and the atmospheric lighting from cave openings produce a theatrical effect.

mangrove swamps and caves. Wildlife in the national park includes dolphins, crab-eating macaques and huge fruit-eating bats (also known as flying foxes) and numerous species of birds, of which the most easily seen are kingfishers, sea eagles and white egrets. Mudskippers, that queer breed of fish that use their flapping fins to move about on land, thrive among the mangroves ■ 22–3. Most visitors come on day trips from Phuket or Krabi, though excellent food and accommodation are provided by the Phangnga Bay Resort Hotel.

219

PHANGNGA NATIONAL PARK

The headquarters of Phangnga National Park are located on Highway 4144, near one of the estuaries leading to the bay. The Phangnga Bay Hotel is nearby and offers the best rooms in the area. This is also a good point from which to explore by boat the park's fascinating mangrove swamps. The trees have strange root systems that protrude from the water and provide shelter for such creatures as mudskippers, fiddler crabs, lizards and numerous colorful birds.

KOH KHIEN

Koh Khien ("Writing Island") has a large cave, on the walls of which are ancient paintings of men and such animals as sharks, dolphins and crocodiles. These paintings are believed to have been the work of people who inhabited the region 3,000–4,000 years ago and are visible from the sea.

KOH PANNYI

GLOSSARY OF
MARINE TERMS
koh = island
khao = mountain
hat = beach
tham = cave
laem = cape
hin = stone
ao = bay
thale = sea

On Koh Pannyi, a picturesque little Muslim fishing village of about 400 people nestles in the shadow of an immense limestone slab that protects it from the

> «THE UNIQUENESS OF PONGA DEPENDS UPON ITS LIMESTONE PEAKS, WHICH STAND IN SHARP POINTS AND STEEP PRECIPICES OUT OF ITS WATERS, SOME MORE THAN 1,500 FEET IN HEIGHT.»
>
> H. WARRINGTON SMYTH

monsoons. The houses are built above the water on stout piles of mangrove wood obtained from the mainland and most of the people earn their living by fishing and making shrimp paste. Additional revenue comes from the many tourists who visit Phangnga Bay to photograph its quaint scenery and enjoy a sumptuous seafood lunch at one of the numerous restaurants.

KOH MAK

A flat round island with coconut palms, a Muslim village and beautiful beaches, Koh Mak makes an ideal picnic spot.

KOH HONG

"Hong" in Thai means "room," and this curiously shaped island – part of a group of the same name – contains an extraordinary enclosed waterway lit by an opening above and accessible to small boats. The chamber offers wonderful opportunities for swimming and photography.

THAM KEO

Tham Keo means "Glass Cave," and a shimmering grotto, hung with dazzling white stalactites, is the principal attraction of this island. Small boats enter the cave, which leads to an adjacent cavern with views of the sea below.

KOH PHING KAN

Consisting of two separate rock formations leaning one against another, Koh Phing Kan is also popularly known as James Bond Island, thanks to the fact that several scenes from the film *The Man with the Golden Gun* were shot there. The island has now become a tourist trap, its natural beauties obscured by boatloads of visitors and others trying to profit from them.

ORIGIN OF PHANGNGA
The name of Phangnga originates from a legend linked to a limestone mountain with dramatic slopes that loom over the provincial capital. Some farmers in remote times had attacked and killed by mistake an elephant god which at once turned into stone. The massive cliff in Phangnga Bay is said to be the petrified form of the pachyderm with its butchered tusks leaning on its flanks.

PHI PHI VILLAGE   YONGKASEM BAY   **KOH PHI PHI DON**   LODALAM BAY   TON SAI BAY   WANG BAY

LANAH BAY

🕐 One day

A bout two hours from either Phuket or Krabi by fast boat, the Phi Phi Islands offer breathtakingly beautiful scenery and a number of good beaches for swimming and snorkeling. The two islands, together with Hat Nop parat in Krabi on the mainland, have been designated by the government as a national park.

KOH PHI PHI DON

The larger of the two islands, Koh Phi Phi Don is also the most developed in terms of tourism. Boats generally unload their passengers at a fishing village on Ton Sai Bay, protected by steep, jungled limestone cliffs on one side and by low hills on the other. Thanks to all the day-trippers, however, plus the numerous restaurants and other tourist facilities, the main beach there has lost much of its former tranquility and serious swimmers go to a series of quieter ones on the west side of the bay, culminating in Hat Yao, or Long Beach. Several other resorts have been built on serene beaches at the northern end of the island on the west coast, while across a narrow strip of

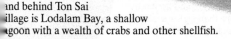

LONG BEACH

VIKING CAVE

KOH PHI PHI LE

MAYA BAY

...nd behind Ton Sai
...illage is Lodalam Bay, a shallow
...goon with a wealth of crabs and other shellfish.

KOH PHI PHI LE ★

...n terms of scenery, the smaller Koh Phi Phi Le is by far the
...nore spectacular, with limestone cliffs that plunge hundreds
...f feet down to the sea and numerous secret coves with small
...rescents of white sand and crystal-clear water; a particularly
...eautiful spot is Maya Bay, surrounded by soaring cliffs and
...arboring three largely unspoiled beaches with good snorkel-
...g to view exotic fish so used to visitors that they can be fed
...y hand. A popular tourist attraction on Phi Phi Le is an
...mmense, cathedral-like cave, festooned with stalactites and
...talagmites, where edible birds' nests are harvested ■ 28–9.
...he cavern is popularly known as Viking Cave because of
...ome ancient rock paintings that do vaguely resemble Viking
...oats, though their origin is unknown.

EDIBLE BIRDS' NESTS. The main ingredient of birds' nest
...oup is produced by a tiny, fork-tailed swift known as
...allocalia esculenta, which favors lofty caves and cliffs. The
...nall cup-shaped nests, about 1½ inches
... diameter, are composed of a gluey
...cretion discharged by the birds in long
...rands that harden after exposure to the
...r. As they are harvested at specified
...mes – by Sea Gypsies ■ 215, who
...arlessly climb tall spindly bamboo
...dders (right), often in total darkness –
...e swiftlets may have to build the nests
... to three times between February and
...ly. The birds' nests can be eaten raw or
...oached in soup, and are an expensive
...elicacy highly regarded for their
...utritional value by Chinese gourmets.

PHI PHI EXCURSIONS
Most excursions to
the Phi Phi Islands
are in large boats,
leaving Phuket
either from Chalong
or Rawai Beach
around 8am and
starting back around
3.30pm. When hiring
smaller fishing craft
be sure to check on
the weather since the
crossing can be rough
during the monsoon
season.

If enthusiastic word-of-mouth reports and increasingly frequent mention in travel literature are any indication, Krabi is definitely the southern Thai destination of the near future. Like Phuket and Koh Samui in the early 1970's, it was accidentally "discovered" by intrepid backpackers and cruising yachts only a few years ago. There are already signs of a more affluent clientèle, appearing in the form of restaurants, shops and bungalow hotels. Krabi's popularity with escapist travelers is not difficult to understand. It has several beautiful beaches with clear water ideal for snorkeling and diving, towering limestone cliffs, a prehistoric shell cemetery, atmospheric caves, mangrove forests ■ 22–3, rubber plantations, a national park (Khao Phanom Bencha) full of interesting wildlife, and access by boat to more than eighty scenic offshore islands. Krabi has yet to encounter – though it is only a matter of time – the sort of rapid, uncontrolled development that has disfigured so many beaches on Phuket and other southern island resorts, and if the efforts of newly aware Thai environmentalists are successful, Krabi has more than a fair chance of escaping this unhappy fate.

OIL PALMS
Extensive oil palm plantations can be seen on the mainland around Krabi, forming an important local industry. The palms, which yield an oil used in both cooking and food processing, originated in Africa and were first acclimatized to Southeast Asia by the Dutch during their rule of Indonesia.

BEACHES ★

Krabi's beaches, though less numerous than those of Phuket, are relatively unspoiled and exceptionally beautiful. The most easily accessible beach from Krabi town is Hat Nang, on a wide, shallow bay, where there are several small resorts and such amenities as a telephone service; the town can be reached either by road or, more quickly, by the local long-tail boat up the mangrove-lined river. About a mile further on is Nopparat Thara Beach, a casuarina-lined strand

hat is part of the national park including the Phi Phi Islands. ar more spectacular in terms of scenery, however, are several thers that are only accessible by boat around the sheer mestone cliffs of Laem Nang. The rst is Re Lai, framed by mammoth ocks on the north and south, with an xtensive coral reef at the southern nd of the sandy beach. Around nother headland and past the lofty, icturesque island of Koh Nang is a long, palm-fringed strand that many visitors regard as the most beautiful in the entire region; between the beach and Koh Nang is a coral reef excellent for snorkeling and diving.

CAVES

The limestone mountains around Krabi contain a large variety of splendid caves, several of them popular tourist attractions. Sua (Tiger) Cave, down a jungle trail about 2 miles from Krabi town, is a noted Buddhist monastery for meditation. Along Highway leading to Ao Luk, is a small cavern called Tham Sadet, hile two unspoiled caves, Tham Lot and Tham Phi ua To, can be reached by boat from Tao Than illage in Ao Luk. The so-called Princess ave in the cliffside of Cape Phra ang contains a shrine where hermen leave offerings before ing out to sea.

FFSHORE ISLANDS

oats can be hired for trips to the i Phi Islands from both Ao ang Beach and Krabi town, but ere are many closer offshore ands that are good for imming and diving. Koh Poda, 30 minutes by long-tail boat om Ao Nang, has a large coral reef teeming with colorful h. Further out, but even more alluring, is the Koh Dam

group of two large islands and a number of smaller ones. A good beach, shaded by casuarina trees, surrounds Koh Dam Hok, which also has a few simple bungalows and a restaurant, while Koh Dam Khwan boasts a superb expanse of reef that extends from the island to a group of rocky islets off the north end.

VANISHING TURTLES
Visitors to the park at night may be able to spot huge black turtles, which some-times come ashore for a breath of air. However, any slight distraction may cause the creatures to return to the water and – since they are already quite breathless after surfacing – possibly be drowned. The turtles can lay as many as 150 eggs in 20-inch-deep sandpits. After a period of 50–60 days of incubation, the hatchlings break out of the eggs and waddle their way to the sea, guided only by the glittering reflection of moon-light. The hatchlings are easily distracted by artificial light such as camera flashes or lamps, which will cause them to lose their way. Accidental capture and the slaughter of turtles for their meat and skin have led to the rapid decline of this endangered marine species.

KOH SIMILAN NATIONAL PARK ★

Approximately 60 miles northwest of Phuket in the Andama Sea, the Similan group covers 51 square miles and consists o nine small islands, the name being derived from the Malay word *sembilan*, meaning "nine." Designated a national park 1982, the islands have long been uninhabited except for Sea Gypsies ■ *28* ▲ *215* who come to fish the rich coral reefs surrounding them. Tour groups have been coming in large numbers, attracted by the unspoiled beaches and the remarkable variety of underwater life, especially off Koh Miang. The Similans have over two hundred species of hard coral, hundreds of colorful fish and other sea creatures such as huge sea fans and barrel sponges, manta rays and whale sharks. Sea turtles come to lay their eggs on some of the beaches ■ *30*, and wildlife on land ■ *18–19* includes macaques, langurs, bats and about thirty species of birds.

TARUTAO NATIONAL PARK

Established as Thailand's first national marine park in 1974, Tarutao consists of fifty-one mountainous islan in the Indian Ocean near Malaysia. The largest of the group is Koh Tarutao, about 16 miles off the mainland and 3 miles from the Malaysian island of Langkawi, while the mos beautiful is Koh Adang, which has fine beaches, clear water and coral reefs. Dolphins, sea turtles, and rare whales and dugongs are occasionally spotted in the area. Gover ment bungalows and tents are available on both Koh Adang and Koh Tarutao. The best time to visit the park is between December and March, when the sea is usually caln

THE NORTHEAST

The northeast – or Isan as it is called by most Thais – makes up a third of the country's total area, contains seven of its most populous provinces, and offers both varied scenery and numerous ancient sites of great interest. Nevertheless, it remains the least known of Thailand's major regions among tourists for a variety of reasons. One was its long isolation. Though a railway linked Bangkok with Nakhon Ratchasima (Korat), the region's commercial center in 1900, it was not extended to the large city of Ubon Ratchathani until 1926 and reached Nongkhai on the Mekong River only in 1955. Even as late as the 1950's, there were few all-weather roads in the region, and northeastern Thais did not receive a personal visit from their ruler until the mid-1950's, when the present king and queen made a pioneering tour of the area. Another probable reason was social prejudice. The northeast has long been Thailand's chronic "problem" region, afflicted with drought and hampered by infertile soil, its people often driven to seek a livelihood in Bangkok as taxi drivers, laborers or domestic servants. To other Thais, Isan hardly seemed a place to spend a pleasant holiday, nor were foreigners much encouraged to do so. Many of these obstacles have now been overcome. Sharing borders with Laos and Cambodia, the northeast suddenly assumed a strategic importance during the Indo-Chinese war and an excellent network of highways was built, while government concern has brought greater prosperity to its cities. Moreover, thanks to the region's increased accessibility, more outsiders are beginning to discover the region's natural and archeological attractions.

NAKHON RATCHASIMA GATE
Nakhon Ratchasima is the most populous town in the northeast of Thailand.

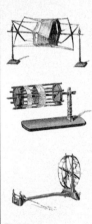

TOOLS OF THE TRADE
Traditional silk spinning wheel and implements (above).

"MUDMEE"
Mudmee is a kind of handwoven silk material (*ikat*) in which the threads are dyed before weaving. Popularized by Queen Sirikit, *mudmee* is now fashionable among Thai women.

THAI SILK PRODUCTION

Silk is undoubtedly the most famous of northeastern handicrafts. Even in the early decades of the present century, when production declined in other regions due to competition from foreign textiles, the family loom remained a part of most Isan village households and thus kept the skill alive. The booming industry of today depends to a large extent on silk from the northeast, particularly in the area around Nakhon Ratchasima; at nearby Pakthongchai, for example, the Jim Thompson Company ▲ *182–3* has the largest handwoven silk

facility in the world. Other notable weaving centers are Surin and Roi Et.

BAN CHIANG

In the early 1960's, during the construction of a road, some extraordinary fragments of painted pottery were unearthed near a small hamlet called Ban Chiang in Udon Thani Province. Subsequent excavations led to the discovery of a major prehistoric culture going back to 4000 BC and numbering among its achievements not only the painted pots but also the art of bronze metallurgy, at a period far earlier than any scholars had previously believed. A museum at Ban Chiang displays some of the remarkable items that have made the name world famous among archeologists and one of the excavations has also been preserved to show the different levels at which they were found. The discoveries at Ban Chiang are still very much a controversial subject; on the other hand, the site has undeniably shaken the traditional view of Southeast Asia as a "cultural backwater" that received its influences entirely from outside sources like China and India ● 34.

ARCHEOLOGICAL REMAINS
This vase was found at a dig in Ban Chiang, and is now on display in a Bangkok museum. Genuine pieces should not be confused with "discoveries" that are in fact manufactured in neighboring villages.

ELEPHANT ROUNDUP

Each year in November the provincial capital of Surin holds a gala elephant roundup in which up to 150 of the huge animals take part, demonstrating their ability to haul logs and serve as mounts in warfare ● 52–3. The Tourism Authority of Thailand organizes special tours from Bangkok by train or bus for this popular event.

BEASTS OF BURDEN
Apart from spectacles promoted by Thailand's tourist authority, elephants are mostly used to work in the ricefields.

NAKHON RATCHASIMA

PRASAT PHANOM WAN

PHIMAI

PRASAT PHANOM RUNG

PRASAT MUANG

BURI P

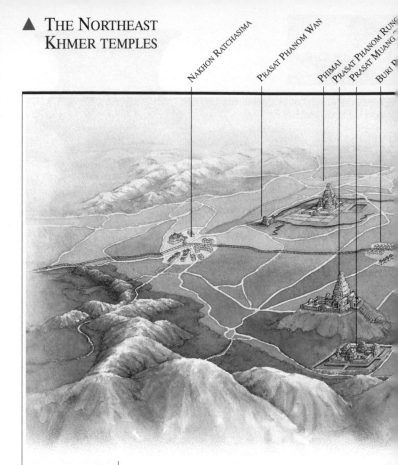

⏱ Four days

The Prasat Phanom Wan, viewed from the outside.

THE KHMER LEGACY

For almost 400 years, from the 9th century onward, much of the northeast was dominated by the Khmer civilization, whic was centered around the famous temples of Angkor, in Cambodia. Khmer power extended much further at its peak during the 11th and 12th centuries, covering much of the Chao Phraya River valley and reaching down into the southern peninsula; not until the 13th century did it begin to wane and eventually give way to the rising Thais. The growth of the Khmer empire ● 35 began with the reign of King Jayavarman II (AD 802–50), who removed the capital to Angkor, but the great period of building in Thailand came under King Suriyavarman I (AD 1002–50), whose father had seized the throne of Lopburi from a Mon king an who himself captured the Cambodian throne at Angkc Northeastern Thailand lay i the path of Khmer expansio and was thus regarded as a natural part of the empire, while the central region was an outlying province. Severa monuments were built durir this period in Nakhon Ratchasima, Surin and Buri

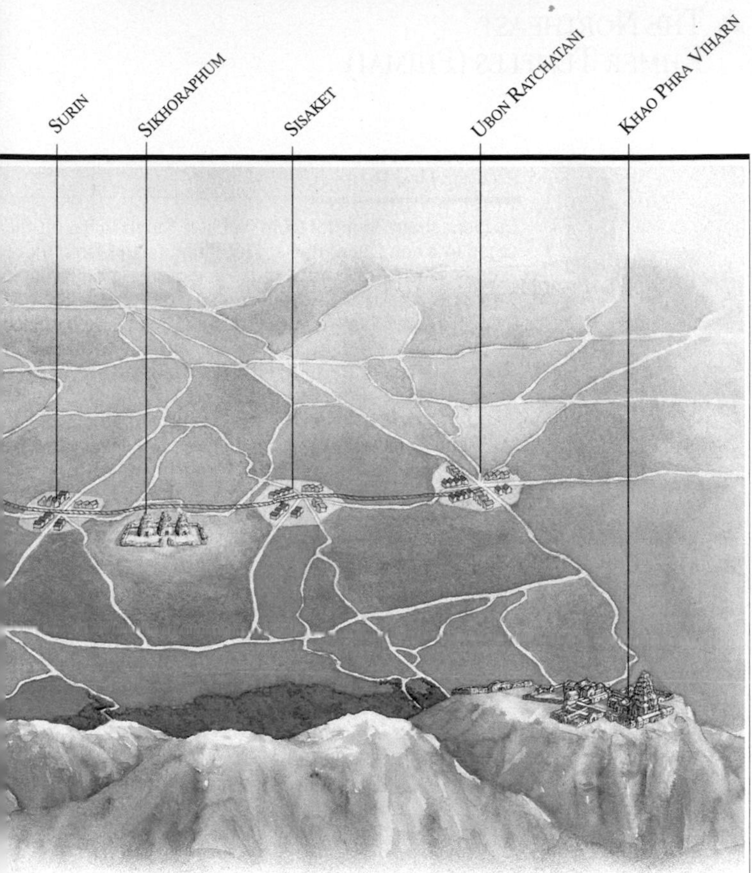

...am provinces, splendid earthly abodes in stone and brick,
...nd lateritc for Hindu deities; temples with rounded prangs
...at represented the thirty-three levels of heaven, the
...ighest being occupied by the god Indra. Suriyavarman II
...AD 1113–50), who built Angkor Wat, was also responsible for
...ortheastern edifices, among them Phimai in Nakhon
...atchasima. By the late 12th century, Mahayana Buddhism
...ad replaced Hinduism and the last great Khmer builder-
...ing, Jayavarman VII (AD 1181–1218), adapted many of the
...lder structures, including Phimai, to suit the new religion.
...fter his death, the empire collapsed, leaving several temples
...ill unfinished ● 35.

PRASAT PHANOM WAN
The interior of the
11th-century Prasat
Phanom Wan, with
several Buddha
images still venerated
by local people.

PRASAT PHANOM WAN

...uilt in the early 11th century
...uring the reign of Suriya-
...arman I, Prasat Phanom Wan,
...ear Nakhon Ratchasima, is a
...indu temple later converted
...or Buddhist use. A central
...rang dominates its rectangular
...ourtyard, surrounded by four
...der ones. There also is a fine
...one lintel above the north
...ntrance to the main sanctuary,
...nich contains a number of
...uddha images.

JAYAVARMAN VII
(AD 1181–1218),
the last of the great
Khmer builder-kings,
adapted many Hindu
temples in northeast
Thailand built by
earlier kings. Jaya-
varman VII is
considered the last
great Khmer ruler of
the Angkor period.
In less than 15 years,
the borders of the
kingdom were
extended further to
the south and to the
north into neigh-
boring Malaya,
Burma, Annam and
Champa. Under his
rule Mahayana
Buddhism was
declared the state
religion, thus
replacing Hinduism.

PRASAT HIN PHIMAI

Located about 30 miles from Nakhon Ratchasima, off the
road to Khon Kaen, Prasat Hin Phimai dates from the
end of the 11th century and is one of the finest examples
of early Angkorian art, which was later modified to suit
the needs of Mahayana Buddhism. The temple has been
restored by the Thai Fine Arts Department in
cooperation with Bernard Groslier, who had previously
been in charge of the restoration work at Angkor.

THE TEMPLE COMPLEX. The complex of buildings
stands in a large quadrangle that once also included a
town and was surrounded by a fortified wall. The
complex was originally an artificial island, surrounded
by the Mun River, two other natural waterways, and a
man-made canal, the last trace of which has now
disappeared.

GATEWAYS. The imposing southern gate, known as Pratu Chai
or Victory Gate, is a pavilion-like structure with walls of pink
sandstone. It faces in the direction of Angkor, with which
Phimai was linked by a straight road; traces remain of three
other gateways at the other cardinal points.

ROYAL RESIDENCES. Among the notable structures within the
walls are a group of royal residences added by Jayavarman
VII; a laterite prang called Meru Baromathat (supposedly
where the cremation of King Baromathat took place) that
once enshrined a statue of Jayavarman VII, now in Bangkok's
National Museum; the remains of a pink sandstone prang
known as the Hin Daeng; and a central sanctuary, topped by
lotus-bud finial.

THE CENTRAL SANCTUARY. The sanctuary predates the
construction of Angkor and was modified when Phimai was
converted into a Buddhist structure in the 12th or 13th
century. It is the best-preserved part of the complex.

t stands on a square base and has four entrances, each guarded by five-headed *naga*, or sacred serpents; the main door, a major projection, is to the south. The lintels inside are particularly fine, and are richly carved with scenes from the Buddha's life and with Tantric deities that rank among the finest in Khmer art.

General floor plan of Prasat Hin Phimai (above) and east (side) elevation of the Inner Courtyard (top and left).

Khmer temples were built according to symbolic criteria: the moat represented the cosmic ocean, the surrounding walls the mountains, and the sanctuary tower Mount Meru, the mythological axis of the world, according to Hindu cosmology.

FEMALE DEITY
This small sandstone figure, found at Phanom Rung and now relocated at the National Museum of Bangkok, is believed to be Uma, Siva's consort, but since none of her attributes are preserved, her identification is uncertain. She wears a pleated sarong with a twist at the waist and a belt, indicating that she can be attributed to the Baphuon style (AD 1010–80).

Prasat Phanom Rung ★

Scenically situated on a small hill in Buri Ram Province and facing the Dongrek Mountains that mark the frontier with Cambodia, Prasat Phanom Rung was built over a long period of time. Three of its brick prangs date from the early 10th century, while the main sanctuary was started in the 11th century but was never completed. The temple has since been restored by the Fine Arts Department with the help of several French experts, and with the same techniques as those used at Phimai. An impressive avenue built by Jayavarman VII, 600 feet long and 36 feet wide, leads to the main building atop a series of terraces, the lowest of which has a balustrade of *naga* (sacred serpents). Situated on an east-west axis, the main sanctuary consists of a prang on a square base with antechambers at the four compass points, the main entrance facing east. Beautifully carved lintels adorn the doorways, and there are friezes of very fine quality on the walls and columns.

Prasat Muang Tham ★

About 3 miles from Prasat Phanom Rung is Prasat Muang Tham (below right). Construction of the temple began in the second half of the 10th century and was completed by Jayavarman V. Consisting of an outer and an inner courtyard surrounded by a laterite wall, Prasat Muang Tham is notable for the well-preserved bas-reliefs on small prangs at the four corners of the outer courtyard and for a large variety of beautifully carved lintels, doorway decorations and stone mullions, all rich in Hindu deities. To the north of the temple is one of the reservoirs built during the period to provide a constant source of water.

STOLEN LINTEL
In the early 1960's, one of Prasat Phanom Rung's most beautiful lintels vanished, only to reappear some 25 years later in the collection of Boston Museum in the United States. After protracted negotiations, the museum agreed to return the piece, which has now been restored to its proper place over one of the temple doorways.

Khao Phra Viharn ★

The imposing sanctuary of Khao Phra Viharn perches on a spur of the Dongrek mountain range, 1,800 feet above sea level. After a long dispute between Thailand and Cambodia over the ownership of the temple, international law in 1962 adjudged it to lie in Cambodian territory, even

though it is quite easily accessible from the Thai side of the border. Khao Phra Viharn is expected to reopen soon to visitors, after being closed for nearly three decades. Built partly during the reign of Suriyavarman I in the early 11th century, then continued later by other Khmer rulers, the complex was built on four different levels, each connected by stairways and each containing the remains of numerous buildings as well as tanks for water storage. Walls and doorways are decorated with a profusion of carvings. However, from the architectural point of view, the structures at the summit are more impressive than those below.

PRASAT HIN SIKHORAPHUM

Prasat Hin Sikhoraphum (right), in Surin Province, dates from the late 11th century and is built in the Angkor Wat style. It consists of a central brick prang and four smaller prangs at the corners of a laterite platform; the lintels and pillars of the entrance to the main prang are intricately carved with guardians, *apsara* (female divinities) and scenes from Hindu mythology.

OTHER KHMER RUINS

Besides major Khmer ruins, such as those mentioned in these and preceding pages, the northeast has thirty other smaller sites. Among the most interesting are Prasat Hin Non Ku in Nakhon Ratchasima Province and Prasat Thamuen Thom in Surin, both in the Baphuon style of the late 10th and 11th centuries; Prasat Ban Phluang in Surin, on the road from Angkor to Phimai; and Prang Ku in Chaiya-phum, which boasts several carved lintels.

" There is no doubt that the Khmer art created in Thailand contains foreign elements beyond the style which evolved in the metropolitan area. However, the local differences are but variations upon a theme; the guiding analytic principle is that such provincial Khmer art was made with the standard technology and within the esthetic context of Khmer civilization."
Piriya Krairiksh

CHIANG KHONG

NAM NAO NATIONAL PARK

ERAWAN CAVE

VIENTIANE AIRPORT

NONGKHAI

UDON THANI

KHON K

⏱ One week

MEKONG MOSAIC
Two scenes (right) of daily life by the Mekong in the 19th century and fishing boats (below) at the confluence of the Mekong and Mun rivers.

The world's twelfth-longest river, the great Mekong originates on the Tibetan plateau and winds its way across 2,500 miles, through six countries, before it empties into the South China Sea. It serves as the border between Thailand and Laos for more than 500 miles in both the north and the east before flowing on through Cambodia and Vietnam. The most fertile areas of the northeast lie along the banks of the Mekong, where the rich alluvial silt from the river nourishes mulberry and tobacco plantations, vegetable gardens and orchards. Its waters provide a steady supply of fish as well, including a gigantic variety of catfish called *pla buk* in Thai, which can weigh up to one ton. For nearly 20 years after the end of the Indo-Chinese War, the Laotian side of the Mekong was closed to most tourists. Recently, however, relations between Thailand and its neighbor have improved and traffic across the river is steadily increasing, bringing greater prosperity to such old Thai ports of entry as Nakhon Phanom and Nongkhai.

FROM NONGKHAI TO KHONG CHAM

A weathered road runs along the Mekong from Nongkhai, a bustling port that serves as the gateway to the Laotian capita of Vientiane, to Mukdahan, across from Suwannakhet. Among the attractions that lie along this scenic route are the Phu Wua Wildlife Sanctuary, across from the Laotian town of Pakse, the riverside provincial capital of Nakhon Phanom, and That Phanom with its famous chedi. A small national park at Mukdahan contains some unusual rock formations and Buddhist sites. At Mukdahan, the main highway moves away from the river and leads to Ubon Ratchathani, where each year in July, on the eve of the three-month Buddhist Lent period, there is a procession of enormous carved candles and figures carried on boats through the city streets. A boat can be hired here for the short trip along the Mun River to Khong Cham, a picturesque confluence of waterways at the point where the Mekong curves and heads toward Cambodia and Vietnam on its journey to the sea.

WAT PHRA THAT PHANOM. Overlooking the Mekong, Wat Phra That Phanom is the most famous of all northeastern Buddhist temples. Its central chedi, originally built in the 8th century and containing a sacred relic, was modeled after the well-known That Luang in Vientiane. When the spire collapsed during a monsoon storm in 1975, it was regarded as a dire omen and was immediately reconstructed; the present one was inaugurated four years later by the Thai king.

THE MEKONG'S OTHER NAMES
The Mekong probably has as many names as the countries it passes through. Also called Lancang Jiang in the province of Yunnan, the river first flows into Burma at an altitude of 8,250 feet and continues through Thailand and into Laos (Kingdom of a Thousand Elephants). The river then meanders towards Thailand and Laos again, then into Cambodia and Vietnam, assuming the names Han Giang, Co Chien, Cua Dai and Bassal respectively.

237

FOREST TYPES
In Khao Yai National Park some of the last remaining rain forests can still be observed ■ 18–19. Most of the forests of the dry northeast, however, are deciduous, including teak trees and deciduous dipterocarps, so called because of their two-winged seeds. Found in both types of forest are more than 70 species of bamboo. The acidic soil of the northeast also supports pine trees at an altitude of between 1,980 feet and 4,620 feet. The Phu Kradung National Park is famous for its pine trees. Flowering trees thrive in the dry northeast and, after long spells of drought, spectacular blooms appear. Khao Yai's pride are the thousands of species of orchid ■ 20–21 that cling to the trees in the wetter parts of the forest.

The northeast was once a densely forested region, teeming with wildlife. Logging, together with the demands of an expanding population, has denuded vast areas and its former natural wealth can be found mainly in those designated national parks.

KHAO YAI

Covering 869 square miles in four provinces – Nakhon Ratchasima, Saraburi, Nakhon Nayok and Prachinburi – Khao Yai was established in 1962 as the first of Thailand's national parks. It is also the most popular, thanks to its ease of accessibility from Bangkok, 120 miles away. Largely because of the number of visitors (700,000 in 1990), the government has recently decided to close a motor lodge and golf course run by the Tourism Authority of Thailand, as well as other bungalow facilities, although visitors with special permission will still be allowed to camp overnight in the park. There are picturesque trails through lush forests and a rich variety of wildlife ■ 16–19, including a sizeable number of elephants, clouded leopards, gibbons, mouse deer, Malayan sun bears, and such birds as the great hornbill, the Siamese fireback pheasant, the silver pheasant and the brown needle-tail, allegedly the fastest bird in the world.

NAM NAO

Established as Thailand's fifth national park in 1972, Nam Nao covers 387 square miles of rolling hills and pine forests in Chaiyaphum and Petchabun. It was once a stronghold of communist insurgents but has been made safe for visitors

since the early 1980's. Thanks to the adjacent Phu Khieo Wildlife Sanctuary, the park is unusually rich in animal life ■ 16–19, including elephants, Asiatic black bears and clouded leopards. In 1979 rhinoceros tracks were found in the park. Over 200 species of birds have been confirmed. A popular attraction in the park is Yai Nam Nao Cave, home to hundreds of thousands of bats.

KAENG TANA

Located near Ubon Ratchathani, where the rivers Mekong and Mun meet, the Kaeng Tana National Park covers a sprawling 32-square-mile expanse of land. Although not ranked as one of the popular ones in Thailand's northeast, the scenic park boasts features such as giant sandstone slabs, a cave and a waterfall with rapids.

PHU KRADUNG ★

Phu Kradung is a bell-shaped mountain in Loei Province, crowned with a 24-square-mile plateau of exceptional natural beauty. The climb to the top involves a 5-mile trek, sometimes up steep areas, but there are benches and shelters along the way. Plant life on the cool plateau includes many temperate-zone specimens such as rhododendrons, pines and oaks, and among the existing wildlife are elephants, sambar deer, gibbons and 130 bird species. The park is closed from June to August to allow for environmental recovery from the damage caused by visitors.

239

«TODAY, NO LARGE MAMMALS SURVIVE
OUTSIDE THE BOUNDARIES OF NATIONAL PARKS.»
NATIONAL RESEARCH INSTITUTE OF THAILAND, 198?

ENDANGERED SPECIES

The national parks of the northeast provide sanctuary for several once-common animals that are now regarded as endangered species. Around 200 wild elephants, for example, live within the boundaries of Khao Yai, the largest population of any park in the country. Some of Thailand's estimated 250 remaining tigers have also found their habitat there. Thailand has recently signed the international CITES treaty, and increasing attention and resources are dedicated to the country's natural heritage.

LEOPARDS. Though rare today, leopards and clouded leopards may still be sighted in Khao Yai and Nam Nao. Prized for their skin, these beasts have been the target of persistent poachers who flout wildlife preservation laws.

BEARS. The Malayan sun bear is a smallish jungle bear that eats mostly fallen fruit, fish and carrion. It has the misfortune of being highly regarded as a medicinal ingredient by certain groups like the Koreans, who come on special tours just to eat grilled bear meat. The Asiatic black bear, still existing at Khao Yai and Nam Nao, is a much bigger animal, distinguished by its long hair and a wide V-mark from the upper breast to the shoulders.

THE KOUPREY. A recent discovery by Western zoologists, the kouprey is a bovine distinguished by huge lyre-shaped horns and a long dewlap drooping from the neck. Once commonly found along the Dangrek range near the Cambodian border, the beast was slaughtered for meat during the Cambodian conflict and is probably now an extinct species.

THE GAUR. This is a huge ox up to 10 feet long and 6 feet tall at the shoulder. Black with scimitar-like horns and white legs they inhabit open forests in herds of six to 20, although one will see only their tracks. Nocturnal browsers, they feed in open spaces and are the prey of tigers, leopards and humans, who have reduced their numbers to under 500 and put them on the endangered species list.

FURS
Up to the early 1980's, tiger and leopard skins were openly sold at souvenir shops in Bangkok. Today, they are sold secretly in small border villages.

EXTINCT SPECIES
During the 19th century, Thailand exported about 8,000 rhinoceros horns a year to China, where they were much prized for their supposed medicinal qualities, including that of high male potency. The number of rhinoceros was so drastically reduced that by 1977 it was estimated that not more than ten Sumatran rhinos and perhaps only a few of the Javanese species remained in the country. Today, none are left; rhinoceros-horn powder, however, is still sold at exorbitant prices in the markets of Bangkok's Chinatown.

THE CENTRAL PLAINS

▲ THE CENTRAL PLAINS
AYUTTHAYA

WAT PHRA SI SANPHET

VIHARA PHRA MONGKOK BOPIT

WAT NA PHRA MERU

NATIONAL MUSE...

WAT PH... B...

WAT CHAI WATTANARAM

WAT PHUKAOTHONG

TREASURES OF GOLD
In a crypt beneath Wat Raja Burana's central prang King Boromaraja II once hid a collection of gold objects in memory of his two dead brothers. They are now housed at the National Museum at Ayutthaya.

HISTORY

Founded in 1350 by King Ramathibodi I, Ayutthaya grew from a small town with fortified mud walls on an artificial island on the Chao Phraya River into one of the largest, most cosmopolitan cities in Southeast Asia. With only one interruption, when it fell to the Burmese in the mid-16th century, it was the center of Thai power for more than 400 years, its rule extending over the entire Central Plains as well as many areas of the far east and south. The 33 rulers of Ayutthaya adopted the Khmer concept of divine kingship, complete with Brahminic rituals, and built spectacular palaces as well as great Buddhist monuments; most of the major remains visitors see today were constructed in the city's first 150 years. The peak of opulence, however, came in the 17th century, when ships from all over the world sailed up the Chao Phraya to trade and Ayutthaya had a population of more than a million, among them Indians, Chinese, Japanese and assorted Europeans; during the reign of King Narai (1657–88), two French embassies came from the court of Louis XIV and a

WAT RAJA BURANA

WAT PHRA MAHATHAT

MARKET

CHANTARAKASEM PALACE

WAT PHANAN CHOENG

RAILWAY STATION

WAT YAI CHAI MONGKOL

⏱ One day

Thai embassy was sent to Paris. Ayutthayan power began to decline after the death of Narai, and a series of wars ensued with Burma, Thailand's traditional enemy. In 767, after a 15-month siege, the city fell to an invading army that wasted little time in burning almost every building. Under the leadership of the future King Taksin, the Thais allied and managed to expel the enemy in a remarkably short time. Ayutthaya was too thoroughly destroyed for re-occupation and the capital was moved further downriver, first to Thonburi and later to Bangkok.

THE RUINS OF AYUTTHAYA

WAT RAJA BURANA. The best known of Ayutthaya's monuments, Wat Raja Burana was constructed in 1424 by King Boromaraja II, on the site where two princes had killed one another in a duel on elephant-back. The king first built two chedis and later a far more imposing temple surrounded by a wall, with monumental gateways, a towering prang on a stepped platform and numerous smaller prangs and chedis ● 97.

Thailand's oldest paintings decorate the vault of the crypt of Wat Raja Burana.

A drawing of the ruins of Wat Phra Si Sanphet in Henri Mouhot's diary.

ISLAND CAPITAL
Ayutthaya, like Bangkok later, was conceived as an island fortress, formed by digging a canal at a point where the Lopburi River curved sharply. Later shunts were dug linking the city with the Chao Phraya and Pasak rivers and these in time became the main courses of the two rivers. Canals also provided avenues of communication within the walled city as well as out into the surrounding countryside. Huge water gates blocked the access to the city when necessary.

WAT PHRA SI SANPHET. Dating from 1491, Wat Phra Si Sanphet (left) was located inside the compound of the king's palace – the foundations of which are still visible – and served as the royal chapel, as Wat Phra Keo does in Bangkok. The three main chedis, although poorly restored, contain the ashes of three Ayutthaya kings, and the extent of the temple's ruins attests to its former splendor.

VIHARN PHRA MONGKOL BOPIT. Near Wat Phra Si Sanphet, this modern building houses huge seated Buddha image, dating from the 15th century and originally intended to stand in the open air. The image was restored several times and is the object of considerable veneration among Buddhist visitors to Ayutthaya.

WAT PHRA MAHATHAT is believed to be one of Ayutthaya's oldest temples, possibly built by King Boromaraja I (1370–88). Its central prang, of which only the base remains today, once rose to a height of 165 feet. Traces of the original stucco decorations can still be seen on some of the surrounding chedis.

WAT PHRA RAM. Though founded in 1369, the ruins of Wat Phra Ram (right) date mostly from its restoration in the 15th century. Its main feature is a well-proportioned prang that stands on a stepped terrace adorned with chedis. Some of the prang's stucco decorations, including walking and standing Buddhas, still remain.

WAT MAHEYONG. This temple is unique as its main feature is chedi supported by a base with stucco elephants, similar in style to those seen in Sukhothai and Si Satchanalai.

NATIONAL MUSEUM

A branch of the National Museum, also known as Chao Sam Phraya Museum, is located on Rojana Road and is open daily except Mondays and Tuesdays. On display in the museum is a remarkable collection of Buddhist art, mostly Ayutthayan, as well as the treasure found in Wat Raja Burana, which, besides the famed gold objects, comprises a collection of small well-preserved Buddha images of exquisite workmanship. Worthy of mention also are a set of painted banners with religious subjects and a lacquered book cabinet decorated with a representation of the Buddhist cosmos.

> «THE CITY OF AYUTTHAYA, AT THE PERIOD OF OUR VISIT,
> CONSISTED OF SOME SIX FISHERMAN'S HUTS AND
> A BETELNUT VENDOR'S STALL.»
>
> FREDERICK A. NEALE

TEMPLES ALONG THE RIVERSIDE

WAT CHAI WATTANARAM. Built in 1630 by King Prasat Thong, Wat Chai Wattanaram (left) was conceived as a replica of an Angkorian temple, with a huge prang surrounded by smaller ones, symbolizing Mount Meru, the abode of the heavenly gods. Now restored, the temple has lost much of its former charm.

WAT YAI CHAI MONGKOL. A lofty chedi dominates Wat Yai Chai Mongkol (right) on the opposite side of the river. It was given its name by King Naresuan to commemorate a battle fought against the Crown Prince of Burma in 1592. Naresuan's victory brought independence to Ayutthaya after 15 years as a Burmese vassal. In the complex is also a huge image of a reclining Buddha in brick and stucco ● 97.

WAT NA PHRA MERU. Located across the river north of the palace, this temple ● 91 has been restored a number of times but still has a finely proportioned bot and a viharn. The latter contains a large Dvaravati stone Buddha seated in European style, his hands on his knees, which some scholars think originated in Nakhon Pathom.

WAT PHANAN CHOENG. Overlooking the river on the opposite bank from the main city, Wat Phanan Choeng was founded shortly before the establishment of Ayutthaya as the capital. Its main building enshrines a huge, seated Buddha image, 57 feet tall, the object of particular devotion to Thais of Chinese origin. The temple is a popular stopover for riverboat cruises along the Chao Phraya.

ELEPHANT CORRAL

Off the road from Ayutthaya to Ang Thong is the Elephant Corral. Repaired by King Rama I of Bangkok and restored by several of his successors, it was once the place where wild elephants were rounded up, sorted, and eventually trained for work and use in warfare.

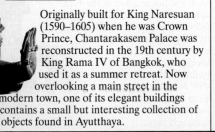

CHANTARAKASEM PALACE
AND MUSEUM

Originally built for King Naresuan (1590–1605) when he was Crown Prince, Chantarakasem Palace was reconstructed in the 19th century by King Rama IV of Bangkok, who used it as a summer retreat. Now overlooking a main street in the modern town, one of its elegant buildings contains a small but interesting collection of objects found in Ayutthaya.

ELEPHANT SHOWS
Although the Elephant Corral was not used for its original purpose after the destruction of Ayutthaya, later Bangkok kings staged spectacular roundups there as a form of entertainment for distinguished visitors from abroad. One of the last great shows was recorded by photographer Robert Lenz in 1890.

Leading off the river in this area are numerous klongs, or canals, all dug centuries ago to facilitate communications. Cruising along these, one can catch glimpses of a lifestyle that has largely vanished in most other parts of the country: elegant wooden houses in the Central Plains style, raised above the ground on tall posts; huge hump-backed barges loaded with rice, being towed to the markets and warehouses of Bangkok; vendor boats supplying waterside houses with various necessities; the spires of Buddhist temples rising above feathery bamboo groves; and stretching away on either side, all the way to the horizon, the vast ricefields ■ *24–5* that have traditionally nourished and enriched the kingdom.

RICE FARMING. The majority of rural Thais are rice farmers, following an ancient cycle that begins with plowing the fields in April or May just before the rains; the young seedlings are then planted and carefully tended until harvest time, usually in late November or early December.

TRADITIONAL HOUSE PRODUCTION. In Ang Thong Province, a short drive from Ayutthaya, many skilled craftsmen earn their livelihood by prefabricating the components of traditional Thai-style houses: paneled walls, gables, roof beams, and the characteristic curving bargeboards. These are then transported elsewhere, mainly to Bangkok, and assembled on a framework of pillars in private compounds ● *86*.

BANG PA-IN

A few miles down the Chao Phraya River from Ayutthaya is the Bang Pa-In Summer Palace. The site was first used by the royal court as a retreat from the hot weather in the 17th century but fell into ruin after the fall of Ayutthaya; it was restored by King Rama IV in the mid-19th century, though most of the buildings that exist today date from the reign of King Rama V, who regularly spent his summers there.

KLONGS

❝ The numberless canals that thread their way across the plains in every possible direction, have turned the lower portion of Siam into a veritable labyrinth of winding waterways. The klongs differ in age, appearance and size, as do the roads of more densely populated countries.❞

Ernest Young

THE THAI HOUSE

The classic Central Plains house is raised off the ground on stout pillars, with a veranda in front where most family activities take place. The walls lean slightly inward and the roofs are steep; traditionally, it has bargeboards that curve gracefully at the end, adding to the general effect of lightness and airiness ● *86*.

Typically of the fifth reign, the structures represent a variety of architectural styles, set in a large park around ponds and waterways. The only one of the royal residences open to the public is the Chinese-style Vehat Chamroon Palace, constructed entirely of materials imported from China. In addition, there is an Italian-style palace, a circular pavilion with steps leading down to a pool, the graceful Thai-style Aisawan Tippaya Asna pavilion in the middle of a lake, and, across one of the waterways, a Buddhist chapel in neo-Gothic style with stained-glass windows. Scattered around the extensive gardens are European statues as well as monuments erected by King Rama V in memory of members of his family, one of them to a much-loved Queen who was drowned in a boating accident.

RICE BARGES
For many centuries, the Chao Phraya has been the main highway for transporting rice and other produce to Bangkok and the outside world, usually in long processions of huge teakwood barges pulled by tugboats. Filled with heavy rice sacks, the round-bottomed barges appear to be almost submerged in the water.

WAT PHAI RONG RUA

Located on the river near Bang Pa-In, Wat Phai Rong Rua is worth visiting mainly as a curiosity, since its grounds are filled with large, rather garish statues depicting scenes from Buddhist hell and the grim fate that awaits those unlucky enough to go there.

BANG SAI

Bang Sai, also near Bang Pa-In, is a small riverside village established in 1982 by Queen Sirikit as a place where farmers are given the opportunity to learn the traditional crafts and thus acquire a supplementary source of income. There are regular demonstrations of basket making, cloth weaving, and leatherworking. A souvenir shop markets the finished products.

WAT PHAI LOM

Located on the riverbank below Bang Pa-In is Wat Phai Lom, famous as a bird sanctuary. Each December, thousands of are open-billed storks fly over the temple from Bangladesh and head for their nests among the treetops to raise their young before departing in June.

The Aisawan Tippaya Asna pavilion at Bang Pa-In.

Once known as Louvo, Lopburi served as an important city during the Dvaravati period and also as an outpost of the Khmer empire. King Narai of Ayutthaya (1656–88) began using it as a summer retreat and eventually spent so much of his time there that it became virtually a second capital.

KING NARAI'S PALACE. Known as Phra Narai Raja-nivet, this palace was built by King Narai between 1665 and 1677 and was the scene of most of the important events during his reign. High crenellated walls with imposing gateways surround the large compound, which in turn was divided into separate areas for government offices, ceremonial buildings and the king's private residence. French architects assisted in the design of part of the palace, particularly the Dusit Sawan Thanya Maha Prasat, where the king regularly received foreign ambassadors. Here King Narai spent the winter months going out in search of wild elephants, often hoping to find an auspicious white one; walked through gardens described by Simon de la Loubère as "delightful," filled with

The fortifications of Lopburi were built with the help of the French engineer Monsieur de la Marre, who came to Siam with the mission of the Chevalier de Chaumont.

plants and cool fountains; discussed affairs of state with his chief minister, the shrewd Greek adventurer Constantine Phaulkon; and, in a hall said to have been ablaze with mirrors brought from France, met with the envoys of Louis XIV. It was here too, in the spring of 1688, that he fell ill and subsequently died. The palace was restored and used again as a residence by King Rama IV in the 19th century. The buildings from the latter period are now used to display the finds from excavations of prehistoric sites in the Central Plains as well as numerous memorabilia from King Rama IV's reign, including giant shadow puppets and various items of furniture. A collection of Lopburi-style Buddha images is displayed in the throne hall.

> «LOUVO STANDS MOST PLEASANTLY AND IN A MOST WHOLESOME AIR; THE COMPASS OF IT IS VERY LARGE AND IT IS BECOME VERY POPULOUS SINCE THE KING HATH BEEN PLEASED TO LIVE THERE.»
>
> FATHER GUY TACHARD

PHAULKON'S RESIDENCE. "One of the most amazing of the adventurers who have made the east the scene of their exploits" is how Somerset Maugham described Constantine Phaulkon, and many other writers and historians have agreed. Born in 1647 on the island of Cephalonia, then under Greek rule, he came to Asia as a cabin boy on an English merchant ship and after a series of adventures turned up at King Narai's court in Ayutthaya. A natural talent for politics, together with a gift for languages and what must have been considerable charm, led him to the highest echelons of power; by 1685, he was in charge of Ayutthaya's foreign trade and was one of the king's closest confidants, with the royal title of Chao Phraya Vichayen. The remains of Phaulkon's Lopburi residence – he had another, much grander one in Ayutthaya – stand in a compound with those of a Catholic church and a house built for members of a French embassy that came in 1685, all in a blend of European and Thai styles. Though the French mission was regarded as a success, it increased opposition to Phaulkon among conservative elements at court. When King Narai fell mortally ill in 1688, one of them, Phra Petchara, took the opportunity to stage a revolt; Phaulkon was arrested, tortured for several days, and finally beheaded near a lake outside Lopburi.

FRENCH EMBASSIES
When King Narai reigned, two French embassies from the court of King Louis XIV were received by him in Ayutthaya (1685) and Lopburi, (1687); a Thai embassy bearing royal gifts returned with the first group and was received by the French king at Versailles in 1686. The French were encouraged by reports from Jesuit missionaries, who believed that Narai might be converted to Christianity; the king, however, was more interested in countering increased pressure from the Dutch and the British. After Narai's death, his conservative successor expelled nearly all foreigners from Ayutthaya
● *61, 100–101, 118.*

WAT PHRA SAM YOT. Built in the 13th century and located in the center of old Lopburi, Wat Phra Sam Yot (left) is a Khmer temple with three laterite prangs; two of the prangs contain partially ruined Buddha images. The laterite blocks were once covered with elaborate stucco decorations, of which only a few traces now remain.

WAT PHRA SI RATANA MAHATHAT. Lopburi's most important religious structure, Wat Phra Si Ratana Mahathat (right) dates from the period of Khmer rule but was restored and enlarged by King Narai. It contains a large laterite prang as well as a brick viharn, added by King Narai, which reflects foreign influences in its pointed arch windows.

PHRA PHUTTHABAT

Phra Phutthabat, more commonly known as the Temple of Buddha's Footprint, is a much-revered shrine about 17 miles from the town of Saraburi. The sacred footprint – measuring 5 feet long – was discovered during the Ayutthaya period, but the buildings that enshrine it today were built by King Rama I of Bangkok and his successors. Many hermits still live in caves in the surrounding hills.

Khamphaeng Phet, on the left bank of the Ping River, was one of the most important centers of the Sukhothai kingdom, although its principal monuments were built somewhat later than those of the other satellite city of Si Satchanalai. It was in Khamphaeng Phet that the last ruler of Sukhothai submitted to King Boramathat of Ayutthaya in 1378.

INSIDE THE "DIAMOND WALL"

A WESTERN VISITOR
In 1882, traveler Carl Bock spent a night in Khamphaeng Phet on his way to the far north. He dined with the governor of the province, an occasion he described as follows: "The menu was a good one, and the dinner was served in a style that would have done credit to a first-class hotel... Soon after I returned from the hospitable table of the governor, I was disturbed by the noise of drums and gongs, accompanied by the desultory discharge of firearms in all directions. Hastily getting up, I crossed over to a temple which stood opposite to my *sala*, where I found the priests assembled in full force, surrounded by an excited multitude of natives gazing at the great dragon swallowing the moon, and endeavoring by dreadful clamor to avert the calamity. In other words there was an eclipse of the moon."

Khamphaeng Phet ("Diamond Wall") was surrounded by massive ramparts of earth topped with laterite. The two principal temples are Wat Phra Keo (top and above left), which has two large seated Buddha images, and Wat Phra That, which has a chedi surrounded by columns. Also of interest is the *lak muang*, the city's foundation stone pillar.

OUTSIDE THE WALLS OF KHAMPHAENG PHET

The finest of Khamphaeng Phet's ruins lie outside the city walls, where the surroundings were more conducive to prayer and meditation. Wat Phra Non enshrines the remains of a reclining Buddha, while Wat Phra Si Iriyabot (above and left) has images of the Buddha in four attitudes – standing, walking, seated and reclining. Wat Chang Rob, "Temple Surrounded by Elephants," is notable for the remains of a large chedi surrounded by imposing elephant buttresses made of laterite covered with stucco, a decorative motif that originated from Sri Lanka.

TWO FORTS. Standing at the southern and northern corners of Khamphaeng Phet's walls are the remains of two forts, known as Phom Chao Indra and Phom Phet. The latter, which has been excavated, is well preserved and suggests the impressive scale of ancient fortification

One of Sukhothai's many chedis, photographed in 1910.

SUKHOTHAI

Sukhothai was the northernmost citadel of the Khmer empire and had flourished for centuries before the Thais began emigrating from the north in increasing numbers. During the first half of the 13th century, when Khmer influence was waning, a Thai chieftain later known as King Intradit united various groups, overthrew their Khmer overlord, and founded the kingdom of Sukhothai, the Pali version of which means "Dawn of Happiness." Sukhothai's power lasted less than two centuries before it became a vassal of Ayutthaya in 1378, but it enjoyed a brilliant flowering in both politics and culture. Under its third and most famous ruler, King Ramkhamhaeng (1279–98), direct or indirect rule was extended over much of present-day Thailand, and a Thai alphabet was devised. Most impressive of all were the remarkable achievements in art and architecture. Drawing from a variety of cultures – not only Khmer but also Mon, Indian and Sinhalese – Sukhothai artisans created superb temples, Buddha images and ceramics that were also distinctively Thai and are generally regarded as the finest examples of the country's cultural heritage ● *36*.

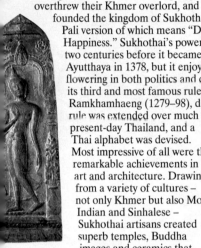

The Sitting Buddha at Wat Si Chum ▲ *255*.

RESTORATION OF SUKHOTHAI

Declared a national historical park by the Thai government, Sukhothai has also received international attention in the form of aid from UNESCO. Over the past decade, many of the ancient capital's principal monuments have been carefully restored and villagers who had settled in the ruins were moved elsewhere. The original layout of the city was revealed and enhanced by dredging the moats and ponds, which had filled with silt over the centuries.

LOY KRATHONG
According to legend, the beautiful Loy Krathong festival held at the end of the rainy season to honor the water spirits originated at Sukhothai. The festival has been revived under the auspices of the Tourism Authority with a gala event that includes spectacular illuminations, colorful parades and thousands of lotus-shaped floats set adrift on ponds and waterways ● *73*.

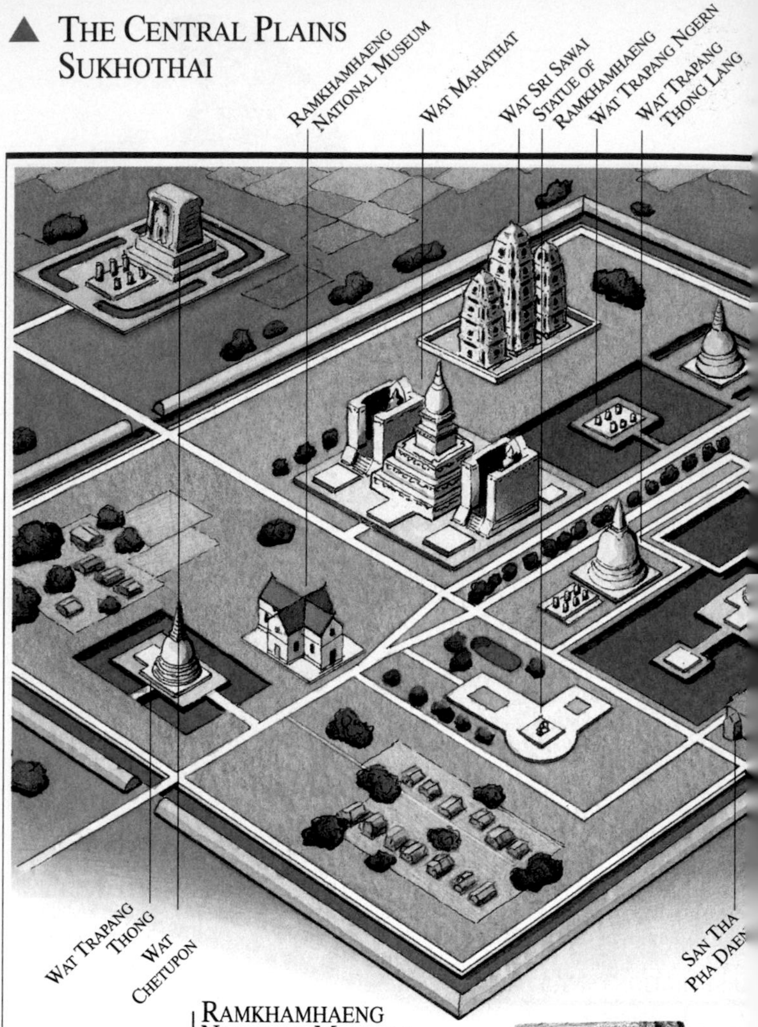

RAMKHAMHAENG NATIONAL MUSEUM
WAT MAHATHAT
WAT SRI SAWAI
STATUE OF RAMKHAMHAENG
WAT TRAPANG NGERN
WAT TRAPANG THONG LANG
WAT TRAPANG THONG
WAT CHETUPON
SAN THA PHA DAEN

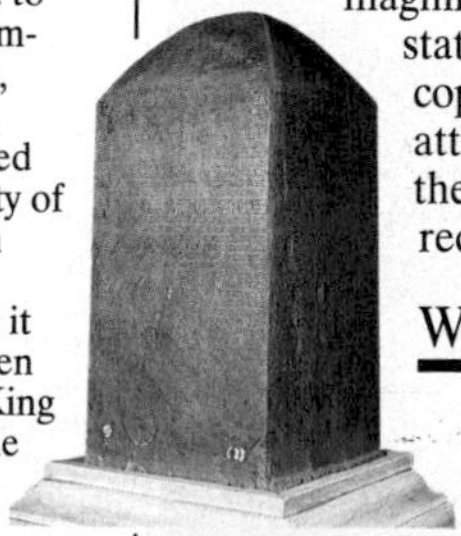

RAMKHAMHAENG INSCRIPTION
"This Sukhothai is good. In the water there are fish. In the fields there is rice." Every Thai schoolchild learns these lines taken from a stone inscription dealing with life in the ancient capital, usually dated 1292 and attributed to King Ramkhamhaeng. Of late, some scholars have questioned the authenticity of the inscription and even suggested that it might have been produced by King Rama IV in the mid-19th century.

RAMKHAMHAENG NATIONAL MUSEUM

The Ramkhamhaeng National Museum of Sukhothai, one of the richest in Thailand, is the best introduction to a visit to the ruins of the ancient capital. Located in a garden to the east of Wat Mahathat, the museum houses a large collection of Sukhothai Buddha images (among them a magnificent bronze Walking Buddha), Khmer statues, stucco decorations, ceramics, and a copy of the famous 1292 stone inscription attributed to King Ramkhamhaeng. In front of the museum, the Fine Arts Department has reconstructed an open Sukhothai-style viharn.

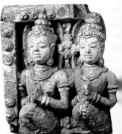

WAT MAHATHAT

Sukhothai's main Buddhist monastery, Wat Mahathat was adjacent to the former royal palace and covers a square measuring

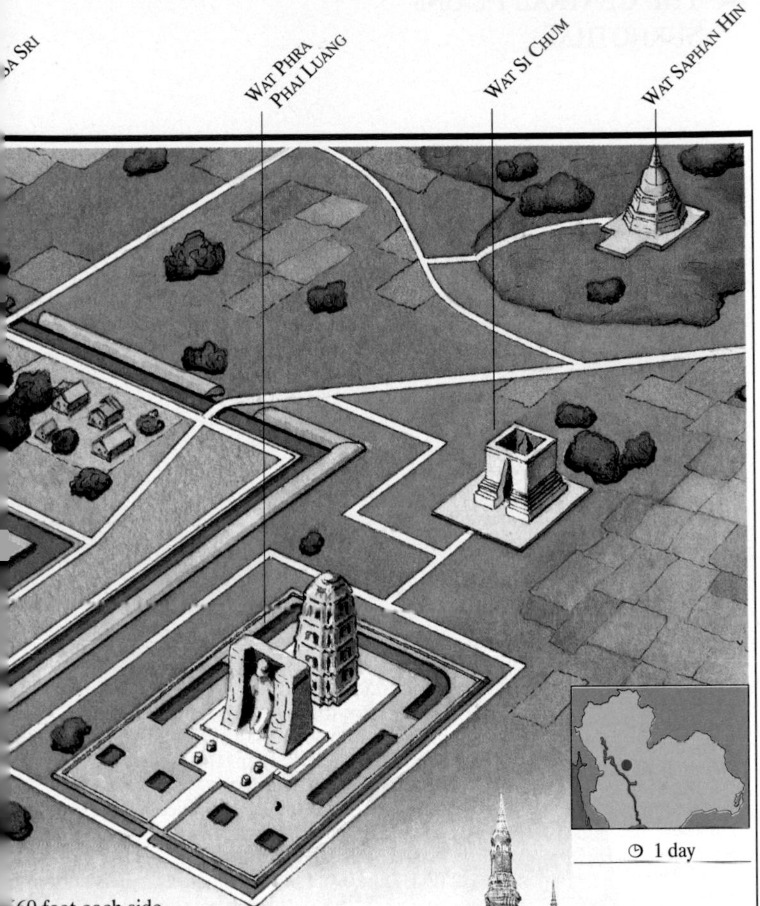

⏱ 1 day

60 feet each side.
Construction of the temple, started by King
Intradit, Sukhothai's founder, continued
under several other rulers before its
completion by King Li Thai in 1345. 
THE LOTUS CHEDI. The dominant
structure is a central chedi, covering
an old Khmer tower, with a lotus-
bud finial, a distinctive feature of Sukhothai architecture. A
fine stucco frieze showing Buddhist disciples adorns the base
of the main chedi.
OTHER BUILDINGS. On two sides are towering standing
Buddha images enclosed in a *mondop* (open image-
house). There are also nearly 200 other chedis and the
remains of 10 viharns, among other structures, all axially

aligned with the rising and setting
sun. Noteworthy is a stepped
chedi that resembles the one
in Polonnaruwa, and which
acts as an important link
between Sri Lankan and
Thai art. Its unusual shape
was replicated in several northern Thai
temples, the most famous of which is at Wat
Ku Kut, Lamphun ▲ 275. Sukhothai was a
center of influence for Sinhalese culture,
which spread to the northern mountains in
Thailand ● 90, 116.

SUKHOTHAI BUDDHA
The Sukhothai
Buddha
image
(below),
particularly
when cast in bronze, is
regarded as the most
beautiful in all Thai
art ▲ 158–9. Depicted
in seated, standing,
reclining and
walking attitudes,
the images are
not meant to be
realistic. Rather,
they
emphasize
the
Buddha's
super-
natural
qualities.

253

OTHER TEMPLES WITHIN THE WALLS

WAT SRI SAWAI. A Khmer-style temple south-west of Wat Mahathat, Wat Sri Sawai (left) was probably dedicated to the Hindu god Siva in pre-Thai times before it became a Buddhist shrine. Three well-restored prangs adorned with some of their original stucco decorations stand behind the remains of the principal sanctuary, which was added in the 15th century.

SUKHOTHAI KINGS
Between 1238 and 1488, Sukhothai was ruled by nine kings, the last three of whom served mainly under the control of Ayutthaya. The most famous was King Ramkhamhaeng, under whom the kingdom achieved its greatest power, though the scholarly King Li Thai (1347–74) is remembered as the author of the *Tribhumikatha* (the Three Worlds of Buddhism), the oldest Thai literary work.
● *36*.

WAT SA SRI. Picturesquely sited on an island in a pond northwest of Wat Mahathat, Wat Sa Sri (right) shows the refinement of Sukhothai architecture. Roofless columns rise from the base of the main sanctuary, which also contains a large stucco Buddha image; behind are two elegant chedis, one of them in rounded Sinhalese style.

WAT TRAPANG THONG LANG. This temple has some remarkable stucco decorations (left) on the outer walls of a square chapel. Perhaps the most famous is the southern panel, which shows the descent of the Buddha from heaven surrounded by celestial attendants and which is regarded as one of the masterpieces of Sukhothai art.

WAT TRAPANG THONG. Situated on an island set in a peaceful pond, this temple (below) is marked by a bell-shaped chedi. The viharn has been reconstructed and the temple reconsecrated.

WAT TRAPANG NGERN. Located just behind Wat Mahathat, this temple comprises a number of buildings sited around a big pond. The main feature is an elegant lotus-bud chedi. Many visitors enjoy walking across the wooden bridge to the islet that once housed a viharn.

LOTUS CAPITAL
The lotus capital is one of Sukhothai's unique contributions to religious architecture. Though possibly inspired by finials from the Mon period at Pagan in Burma, it is original enough in design to be called Thai
● *90–91*.

SAN THA PHA DAENG. East of Wat Sa Sri, inside the city walls, San Tha Pha Daeng is a Khmer laterite sanctuary consisting of a square cell and an antechamber. It is believed to be the the oldest building in the Sukhothai area, dating from the first half of the 12th century.

WAT CHETUPON

Located south of Sukhothai's city walls, Wat Chetupon is notable for an interesting, partially ruined chedi with images of the Buddha in the four ritual attitudes in stucco bas-relief; the tall standing Buddha is particularly fine. A wall of gray stone surrounds the compound.

WAT SAPHAN HIN

Situated west of the city on a small hill, Wat Saphan Hin derives its name (Stone Bridge) from the stone stairway leading up to it. Within the columns that remain of the viharn is a 41-foot-tall standing Buddha built against a thick brick wall that provides support for the huge image. In the groves and on the surrounding hills there are ruins of monasteries once inhabited by forest-dwelling ascetic monks.

WAT SI CHUM

This temple, southwest of the walled city, is one of the most impressive religious monuments in the area ● 90. It is dominated by a huge structure, 50 feet tall, enclosing a seated Buddha of stucco-covered brick almost the same height and 37 feet wide at the lap; the image is referred to as Phra Achana in the 1292 stone inscription attributed to King Ramkhamhaeng. Within the wall is an enclosed stairway, the ceiling of which is lined with engraved slabs of stone. The reason for the construction of the stairway, which leads to the top of the structure, is not known. Some have suggested that it may be linked with a legend that the image could speak to supplicants below.

STONE SLABS OF SI CHUM
Perhaps the earliest examples of graphic expression found at Sukhothai are the incised drawings above the stairway of Wat Si Chum.

Each of the 100 engravings depicts a self-contained scene from the Jataka tales, moralistic stories dealing with the Buddha's previous lives. The slabs may have been made for Wat Mahathat and later moved to Wat Si Chum for safekeeping.

WAT PHRA PHAI LUANG

North of Sukhothai's walls and partially surrounded by ponds are the extensive ruins of Wat Phra Phai Luang (below), which rivaled Wat Mahathat in size and importance. Originally, three concentric moats surrounded the main religious complex, consisting of a group of buildings. The complex, besides the religious symbolism related to the representation of the Primordial Ocean, undoubtedly served a practical purpose, similar to the one in Angkor. It is thus evident that the original layout of the city of Sukhothai was set out by the Khmers according to their religious beliefs. The temple originally had three Khmer-style prangs, only one of which remained when it was converted into a Buddhist temple by the Thais. On the same terrace are the remains of a viharn and a chedi, decorated with Buddha images in stucco. A nearby structure enshrines the Buddha in walking, standing, sitting and reclining attitudes.

WAT KHAO SUWAN KIRI   ROAD TO POTTERY KILNS   WAT KHAO PHANOM PLOENG   WAT CHANG LOM   WAT CHEDI CHET THAEW   WAT SUAN KEOW UTAYAN NOI

⏱ Half a day

BAN KO NOI
EXCAVATIONS
Anyone interested in
ceramics should visit
an ancient kiln site
at Ban Ko Noi, a few
miles north of
Si Satchanalai.
Here a Thai-
Australian project
headed by Don Hein
has uncovered more
than 200 kilns and
evidence of more,
many of them
predating those of
Sukhothai by four
centuries.

About 40 miles north of
Sukhothai, on the west bank of the
Yom River, Si Satchanalai was a satellite city
usually governed by a son of the
Sukhothai ruler. Though smaller
than the capital, it was similar
in plan and has a more
picturesque location
overlooking the river and
rural scenery; the two cities
were linked by the Phra Ruang
Highway. A number of impressive
Buddhist temples were built in Si Satchanalai, some as
beautiful as those at Sukhothai, and a nearby district to the
north became famous for kilns that produced superb ceramic
known as Sawankhalok, the name given to the area during th
early Ayutthaya period.

WAT CHANG LOM. Located in the center of the old city, Wat
Chang Lom was built in the late 13th century. Its main featur
is a large bell-shaped chedi that enshrines relics placed there
by King Ramkhamhaeng; around the base of the chedi are
several elephant buttresses, hence the name "Temple
Surrounded by Elephants."

WAT CHEDI CHET THAEW. Covering a large area, this temple
consists of a sanctuary and seven rows of chedis,
which probably contain the ashes of Si Satchanalai
rulers. Adorning one of the chedis is an impressive
stucco image of a seated Buddha protected by the
hood of a *naga*, or sacred serpent ● 96.

WAT KHAO PHANOM PLOENG. Wat Khao Phanom
Ploeng, "Temple of the Mountain of Fire," is
located on a hill within the city, accessible by a ste
flight of steps. The laterite columns of the temple remain,
along with a restored seated Buddha image and a tall chedi.

CHALIENG
VILLAGE

WAT PHRA SI
RATANA MAHATHAT

SUSPENSION
BRIDGE

The hilltop site affords sweeping views
of the old city and the countryside.

KILNS

The popular legend that the art of making ceramics came
to Sukhothai through Chinese potters brought back from a
mission during the reign of King Ramkhamhaeng has been
disproven. Nevertheless, ceramics were certainly a thriving
export of the kingdom since the early 14th century. The first
cask-shaped kilns were built in Sukhothai itself, outside the
city wall, but around 1350 the craft moved to three main sites
near Si Satchanalai, where superior clay was available. Water
jars, bowls, jarlets, covered boxes and numerous other items
were produced in bulk, mostly for export to the Philippines,
Indonesia and Borneo; the glazes were equally varied, ranging
from dark brown to sea-green celadon.

FISH MOTIF
One of the
characteristic motifs
on bowls and dishes
produced during the
Sukhothai period is
that of a gracefully
curving fish, drawn in
profile. Sometimes
surrounded by flower
and leaf patterns, the
fish has an appealing
light-hearted quality.
appealing to the eyes.

WAT PHRA SI RATANA MAHATHAT ★

Located just a mile from Si Satchanalai, in the village of
Chalieng, Wat Phra Si Ratana Mahathat is one of the most
remarkable Sukhothai-style temples, believed to
date from the 13th century but restored and altered
during the Ayutthaya period. The temple complex is
aligned on an east-west axis and consists of several
ruined buildings, a large Sinhalese-style chedi, and a
magnificent prang showing Khmer influence.
Among the images are a large seated Buddha and a
standing Buddha partially imbedded in the ground;
the walls of a sanctuary near the prang are decorated with very fine stucco reliefs that include a
beautiful walking Buddha.

A bout 35 miles away, Phitsanulok is often used as a meeting base for visitors to Sukhothai. It is an almost entirely new provincial capital, as much of the old town burned down in the 1970's.

PHRA BUDDHA CHINARAJ
Such is the fame of Wat Mahathat's Phra Buddha Chinaraj that many replicas have been made for other temples in the country. The most noted was enshrined by King Rama V at Wat Benchama-bopit (the Marble Temple), the last royal monastery to be built in Bangkok at the beginning of the present century ● 93.

FLOATING HOUSES

Along the Nan River that flows through Phitsanulok, there can still be seen many of the floating houses and shops that were once characteristic of all Thai towns on waterways, including Bangkok. Some of the floating houses have been converted by their enterprising owners into restaurants where visitors can enjoy their meals and watch life go by on the river ● 86.

WAT MAHATHAT

Wat Mahathat, more formally known as Wat Phra Si Ratana Mahathat, is the most important temple in Phitsanulok and well known throughout the country; thanks to its large compound, it escaped serious damage from the fire that destroyed many buildings nearby. Its dominant feature is a gilded, Khmer-style prang, built during the Ayutthaya period, and the doors of the main sanctuary are beautifully decorated with inlaid mother-of-pearl designs. Surrounding the prang is a cloister that also contains the main sanctuary flanked by two chapels. The principal Buddha image, a majestic seated bronze figure known as Phra Buddha Chinaraj and dating from the late Sukhothai period, is one of the most revered in Thailand. On either side of the altar where the majestic bronze image sits are numerous other Buddhas, while the wall behind is beautifully decorated with paintings of gilded angels and floral motifs.

THE NORTH

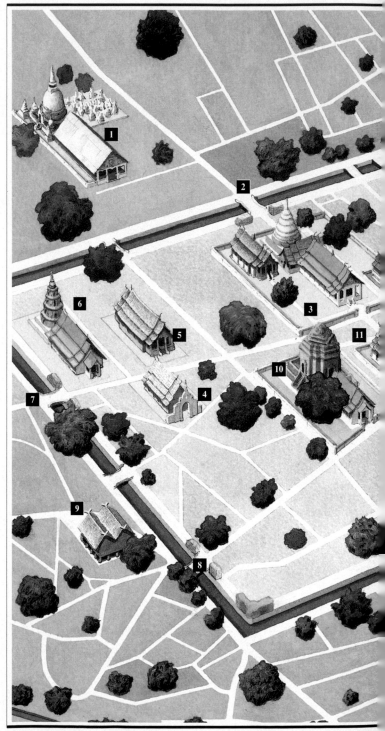

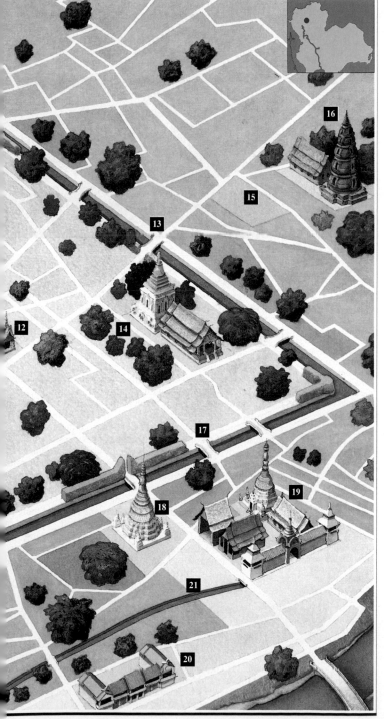

"The city of Zimmé, which lies 430 yards to the west of the river, is divided into two parts, the one embracing the other, like a letter L, on the south and east sides. The inner city faces the cardinal points, and is walled and moated all round. The inner city contains the palace of the head king, the residences of many of the nobility and wealthy men, and numerous religious buildings. In the outer city, which is peopled chiefly by the descendants of captives, the houses are packed closer together than in the inner one, the gardens are smaller, the religious buildings are fewer, and the population is more dense. The roads in both cities are laid out at right angles to each other; no rubbish is allowed to be placed outside the gardens of the houses, which are palisaded; water is led into the town from a stream flowing from Loi Soo Tayp (Doi Suthep); the floors of the houses are all raised six or eight feet from the ground; and the whole place has an air of trim neatness about it.**"**
Holt S. Hallett,
*A Thousand Miles
on an Elephant,*
1890.

Appealing in both culture and scenery, the Chiang Mai valley is one of the most popular Thai destinations. It may no longer be the remote Shangri-La described by early visitors – who had to journey for weeks by river and elephant to reach it – but it still possesses a beguiling blend of ancient ruins, local crafts and continuing traditions.

HISTORY

Once the cultural, religious and political center of a northern kingdom known as Lanna Thai, Chiang Mai (once known as Zimmé) was founded in 1297 by King Mengrai, who had previously established the city of Chiang Rai and also conquered the old Mon capital of Haripunchai (Lamphun today) ● *38–9.* A northern legend says Mengrai had the assistance of two allies, King Ramkhamhaeng of Sukhothai and King Ngam Muang of Phayao, and that the site was selected because an auspicious assembly of rare animals had been seen there: two white sambar deer, two white barking deer, and a white mouse with a family of five. Over 90,000 laborers were supposedly involved in the construction of the city. By the time of Mengrai's death in 1317, he had set up a well-organized kingdom that extended from the northern frontiers of Sukhothai to the southern provinces of China, as well as a dynasty which would rule the north for another 200 years. The original walled city of Chiang Mai, containing the royal palace, noble houses and several important temples, was modified often by subsequent rulers. Chiang Mai's golden age came in the reign of King Tilokaraja (1441–87), during which a major Buddhist conference was held there in 1455 and numerous splendid temples were built. A period of instability followed, marked by wars with Ayutthaya and Burma. By 1558 Chiang Mai had fallen to the King of Pegu, and most of Lanna Thai remained under Burmese control for the next two centuries. King Taksin of Thonburi ● *39,* who expelled the Burmese after the fall of Ayutthaya recaptured Chiang Mai in 1776 but shortly afterward the impoverished city was abandoned for 20 years, its population being moved to Lampang. It was revived by King Rama I in 1796, with a son of the Prince of Lampang as ruler, and remained semi-autonomous until the late 19th century. The last Prince of Chiang Mai died in 1939, by which time the city was merely a provincial capital under control of the central government.

«THE WOODWORK OF THE TEMPLES IS BEAUTIFULLY CARVED
AND GILDED, AND RICHLY INLAID WITH GLASS AND TINSEL
OF VARIOUS COLOURS.»

HOLT S. HALLETT

THAI TEMPLE DÉCOR
Anyone who spends even a short time exploring Thailand's religious buildings ● *94–7* is struck by the Thai penchant for elaborate decoration. Nowhere has this fondness been more abundantly realized than in Chiang Mai, where it is supported by a wide variety of traditional skills that have been handed down through generations and that remain vividly alive today. Most temples, and private homes as well, are adorned by a profusion of splendid wood-carvings, large and small, on gables, lintels, doorways, windows, columns and roof eaves, often further embellished by bright gilding and colored-glass mosaics. In addition there are murals depicting both religious and secular subjects, intricate designs in gold-and-black lacquer, stucco decorations, and numerous figures of mythological creatures, from fierce guardian *naga,* or sacred serpents, to serene divinities. Techniques brought by Burmese artisans, such as gilded metal filigree and embossed lacquer panels, add to the overall sense of richness that distinguishes even lesser-known temples in the northern city. Relatively few are allowed to fall into disrepair; the desire to earn merit through donations and other forms of assistance ensures that most undergo frequent renovations, thus maintaining their splendid appearance.

THE OLD AND THE NEW
Chiang Mai in the 1940's (above), and the city today (right). If some of the main streets have lost their charm due to modern construction, many smaller ones still to recall a more leisurely past, with picturesque temples and bungalows set in shady compounds among fruit trees.

🕐 Five days

NAWARAT BRIDGE
The first bridge built across the Ping River in Chiang Mai was the Nawarat, which leads into Tapae Road. Originally a covered structure made of wood, it was replaced by the present one in the 1950's. Five other bridges now span the river in the city area.

CHIANG MAI TODAY

Modern Chiang Mai, with a population of around only 150,000, is Thailand's third-largest city, after Bangkok and Khon Kaen. Its center, just east of the reconstructed Tapae Gate, is Tapae Road, especially around Charoen Prathet and Chang Klan roads, where many hotels, guest houses, and shops are located. The most fashionable residential area – as well as the site of several new hotels and Chiang Mai University – is along Huay Kaeo Road leading to Doi Suthep, the low mountain that overlooks the city. While progress has come in the form of unsightly high-rise buildings, traffic congestion and air pollution, numerous Buddhist temples and shady side streets offer ample opportunities to discover the city's fabled charms.

NIGHT BAZAAR. Originating as a cluster of stalls on Chang Klan Road and conveniently located near several hotels, the night bazaar now consists of a permanent structure but also has many sidewalk vendors who offer a variety of things for sale every evening from sundown until about 11pm. Most of the local specialties are here: woodcrafts, lacquerware, silverware, antiques, sausages, fruits, fancy clothes and garments.

WALLS AND MOATS. The original layout of Chiang Mai was altered by several of King Mengrai's successors. The walls and moat that can be seen today, for example, date only from the early 19th century; and the Ping River, which was once a considerable distance away, has changed its course and now flows through the middle of town.

THE PING RIVER. Flowing through Chiang Mai, the Ping River is one of the four major northern waterways, and stretches for over 350 miles. Until the construction of the Bhumibol Dam across the Ping near the town of Tak in 1964, it was possible to go most of the way by boat from Chiang Mai to Nakhon Sawan and then on the Chao Phraya to Bangkok. The Bhumibol Dam is one of Thailand's largest and generates electricity for Bangkok and many of the country's provinces.

FESTIVALS

Chiang Mai not only celebrates more festivals than anywhere else in Thailand but does so with an enthusiasm that attracts tourists and native visitors from all over the country. Dates of the festivals may vary from year to year since some celebrations are based on the lunar calendar, so it is best to check beforehand when planning a trip. The Chiang Mai Flower Festival, replete with colorful parades of blossom-covered floats, takes place in February, while Songkran ● 73, the traditional Thai New Year, is celebrated for a full three days beginning April 13 and blends solemn religious ceremonies with riotous throwing of water on passers-by. Late October or November brings Loy Krathong ● 49, 73, the magical water festival, when by the light of a full moon thousands of little lotus-shaped boats are set adrift on the Ping River and all sorts of activities take place on land. The year ends with the Winter Fair, three days of shows, sports and competitions, and a popular beauty pageant to select Miss Chiang Mai. In addition to these major functions, innumerable smaller ones that are equally high-spirited are held in surrounding towns. In January, for instance, the little umbrella village of Bor Sang, which is approximately 3 miles from San Khamphaeng, stages a festive fair along its main street, while in August the annual harvest of longan – a highly prized lychee-like fruit known in Thai as *lamyai* – is celebrated by the people of Lamphun. The paper umbrellas made in Bor Sang are waxed and painted in vivid colors with flowers and scenes from folk tales. Beauty contests are an essential element of any northern Thai festival, large or small, resulting sometimes in such singularly colorful events as the selection of a Miss Garlic.

A restored section of the walls near Suan Prung Gate (top) and the banks of the Ping River (above).

The traditional way of entertaining guests in Chiang Mai is with a *khantoke* dinner – *khan* meaning "bowl" and *toke* being a low round table made of lacquer or rattan. Guests sit on the floor around the table and help themselves to various dishes, generally eaten with glutinous rice, a specialty of the northern region.

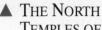

An aerial view of Wat Phra Singh in about 1930.

WAT PHRA SINGH

One of Chiang Mai's most important sanctuaries, Wat Phra Singh was founded in 1345 by King Pha Yu of the Mengrai Dynasty to enshrine the ashes of his father, King Kham Fu. The lofty main viharn, however, was built in 1925 and has recently been restored. Of greater interest is the older Viharn Laikam on the left, perhaps the finest building that survives in Chiang Mai, built in late Lanna style in 1806 or 1811 ● *94, 98*. This structure houses the famous Phra Buddha Singh, an early Lanna bronze image brought from Chiang Rai in 1400; the head of the original image was stolen in 1922 and the present one is a replica. The walls of the viharn are decorated with some fine murals painted in the late 19th century. Also notable in the compound is a wooden bot with beautiful stucco decorations and a graceful, elevated library adorned with carved wood and glass mosaics.

WAT PHRA SINGH PAINTINGS
The late-19th-century mural paintings at Wat Phra Singh, believed to be the work of a local artist named Jek Seng, are the best-preserved in Chiang Mai. In addition to scenes from Jataka stories, they vividly depict everyday northern life a century ago, from children's games to interior decoration ● *104–5.*

OTHER TEMPLES WITHIN THE WALLS

WAT CHEDI LUANG. Located on Phra Pokklao Road, Wat Chedi Luang is noted for its enormous ruined chedi. The structure was originally built in 1401, enlarged and raised to a height of 300 feet by King Tilokaraja, and destroyed by an earthquake in 1545. What remains has remnants of beautiful stucco figures flanking the steps and a seated Buddha in a niche. Also in the compound, to the left of the entrance, is an ancient gum tree, below which a small building

shelters Chiang Mai's City Pillar; according to local legend, King Mengrai, founder of the city, was killed by a bolt of lightning near this spot in 1317.

WAT PAN TAO. Near Wat Chedi Luang on Phra Pokklao Road, Wat Pan Tao has one of the most beautiful Lanna-style viharns, with walls made wholly of wood panels and a roof resting entirely on wooden columns. The doors and windows of the viharn are decorated with exceptionally fine gilded stucco work.

MENGRAI SHRINE. Located across from Wat Pan Tao, at the corner of the Ratchadamnoen intersection, the Mengrai Shrine honors the founder of Chiang Mai and the dynasty that ruled the Lanna kingdom for 600 years. Local devotees regularly bring offerings to the shrine.

WAT PUAK HONG. Not far from Suan Prung Gate, on a lane off Samlan Road, Wat Puak Hong has an unusual chedi in the form of a round, stepped pyramid dating from the 16th or 17th century. Decorated niches on the chedi shelter images of meditating Buddhas.

WAT CHIANG MAN. Located on Ratchaphanikai Road, in the northeastern corner of the old city, Wat Chiang Man is believed to be the first temple built by King Mengrai ● *38* ▲ *262* on the spot where he camped when Chiang Mai was being constructed. Most of its buildings, however, are of more recent date, the chedi itself probably being a 15th-century reconstruction of the first one ● *98*.

A 19th-century wooden bot contains an interesting collection of bronze images, while two more recent viharns enshrine a number of revered images, among them the tiny crystal Phra Buddha Setang Khamanai, which probably dates from the 7th century and is believed to have the power to bring rain.

TEMPLES ALONG TAPAE ROAD

WAT SAEN FANG. Just off Tapae Road, at the intersection with Kamphaengdin Road, a lane flanked with *naga* (sacred serpents) leads to Wat Saen Fang. Burmese influence is strong in its tall chedi, adorned with golden parasols, a large building where the monks reside, and a recently restored viharn resplendent in fresh red and gold paint.

PUAK HONG, THE "WHITE SWAN"
The seven-story chedi was built in the 16th and 17th centuries.

The shape of the chedi of Wat Puak Hong is probably inspired by that of Chinese pagodas. Although unusual, it is not the only one in the north; a similar one can be seen at Wat Rampoeng, just outside Chiang Mai.

MENGRAI IMAGE
Though a modern temple made entirely of cement, Wat Mengrai, off Ratchamanka Road, Lane 6, is of interest because of its ornate stuccoed entrance gate and a Buddha image cast during King Mengrai's reign and believed to resemble the first ruler.

267

WAT BUPPARAM Facing Wat Saen Fang on Tapae Road, Wat Bupparam is a blend of Burmese and Lanna styles. The facade of the main viharn, for example, has Burmese-style arches under a Lanna roof, while another small wooden viharn with stucco decorations is classic Lanna and enshrines three large Buddha images ▲ *161*.

WAT MAHARAM. This temple contains a chedi and a viharn in Burmese style while the bot is Lanna. Of particular interest are the witty caricatured figurines of mythological beasts that stand on the wall facing the road.

NEW YEAR FLAGS
During the celebration of Songkran, the traditional Thai New Year ● *73*, held in mid-April, devout Buddhists build small piles of sand in temple grounds to represent chedis. On each they place a little flag of colored paper as an auspicious adornment.

WAT BUA KROK LUANG

Across the Ping River, on a side lane off the road to San Khamphaeng, Wat Bua Krok Luang has a viharn containing the second most important mural paintings in Chiang Mai, after those in Wat Phra Sing. These were painted more than a century ago and show the life of the Buddha and scenes from the Jataka tales.

WAT UMONG

PAPER LANTERNS
During the festival of Loy Krathong ● *73*, houses and temples in Chiang Mai are decorated with colorful paper lanterns. These lanterns are hung outside the doors, framed by arches of banana leaves and branches of the tree.

Wat Umong, at the end of a long, winding lane off Suthep Road, contains underground cells for meditation and is one Chiang Mai's oldest monasteries. Of the original stucco decorations, only a few fragments of *naga* and the guardian giants known as *yaksa* remain. The chedi, which rises above the old meditation cells, is a recently built monument, thoug the cells themselves contain faint traces of the oldest surviving paintings in early Lanna style, dating from the 15th century. The new monastery in the compound is popular with Western Buddhists, who are welcome to join in the retreat and meditation.

WAT CHED YOD

Also known as Wat Potharam Maha Viharn, Wat Ched Yod is located outside the city walls on the highway near the Chiang Mai branch of the National Museum. Its principal feature is a chedi unlike any other in the north, composed of seven chedis on a laterite base with a barrel-vaulted chamber inside. The shape was possibly inspired by the Indian Mahabodhi temple of Bodhgaya or by

Mon replicas in Burma. Most northerners are convinced of the former source and claim that it was built by King Tilokaraja in 1455 for a major Buddhist gathering. The fine stucco decorations on the walls represent 70 celestial deities.

WAT KUTAO

Wat Kutao's unusual chedi is probably the main reason for visiting the temple, which is not very far from the National Stadium. Showing Chinese influence ● 92, it consists of a series of hemispheres superimposed in descending order of size. Wat Kutao was supposedly built in 1613 to hold the ashes of a Burmese ruler of Chiang Mai.

WAT SUAN DOK

About half a mile west of Suan Dok Gate is Wat Suan Dok, the "Flower Garden Temple," which was built on the site of a royal garden. The temple's huge, bell-shaped chedi, similar to those in Sukhothai, was erected at the end of the 14th century by King Ku Na in honor of a well-known monk named Maha Tera Sumana. The latter had come from Sri Lanka to teach in Chiang Mai and supposedly lived in the garden. Near the chedi is a complex of tombs and other structures containing the remains of Chiang Mai's royal family. Wat Suan Dok is the scene of a major religious ceremony during Songkran ● 73, which is the traditional Thai New Year's celebration in mid-April.

BURMESE INFLUENCE
Many temples in Chiang Mai reflect traces of Burmese influence. This is due to the immigrant carpenters and craftsmen from Burma who, in the late 19th century, came to work for British timber firms and also took part in temple construction. The use of Burmese clothing in murals reflects a tradition of idealizing heroes and other noble characters by using the attire of rulers, who were Burmese at the time ● 98.

A ROYAL CEMETERY
Behind Wat Suan Dok are the funeral chedis of the royal family of Chiang Mai.

The themes of traditional Thai woodcarving were more often than not religious. In the early 1980's a ban on the

export of religious Thai items was enforced. Wood-carvers turned to Burma as a source of inspiration, since Burmese religious items were not included in the official ban.

Partly because of skills handed down from generation to generation and partly because of its long relative isolation from the changing fashions of Bangkok, Chiang Mai has preserved its strong crafts tradition, with skills that have remained unchanged for centuries. These constitute an important aspect of its attraction for modern visitors as well as a profitable export industry for many local producers.

WOODCARVING

Considering the extensive forests of teak and other hardwoods that once covered the northern mountains, it is not surprising that woodcarving ranks high among the local skills, as can be clearly seen in the splendid gables, panels and roof supports that decorate almost every temple in the region. Though wood is scarcer today, craftsmen still produce a wide range of furniture, animal figures, trays and other wooden items. The largest concentration of dealers is at Bantawai, off the highway to Mae Hong Son.

POTTERY

Local potters make a handsome array of lightly glazed earthenware water jars and pots used in most households according to northern tradition, jars of cool water were placed outside gates for the relief of thirsty strangers who passed by. Celadon pottery production – which moved to the northern town of San Khamphaeng after the collapse of Sukhothai and eventually died out there – has also been revived by several local companies whose handsome tableware, vases and lamp bases are being exported and sold throughout the world.

LACQUERWARE

Lacquerware, which probably came to Thailand from Burma, is made by applying successive coats of translucent colored lacquer to a wood or bamboo base, then embellishing it with designs. The most popular decorations are gold-and-black lacquer paintings, either figures or traditional motifs. Many household objects, from simple bowls to large cabinets, are made by this ancient process, which can be observed at the cottage factories in the Chiang

CELADON WARE
Pale blue-green celadon is one of Chiang Mai's most popular crafts. The Mengrai Kilns, started by a former British consul who settled in the city, produce fine replicas of old designs, both Thai and Chinese, which are now being exported and sold in leading shops all over the world.

Mai area, especially on the road to San Khamphaeng.

UMBRELLAS

The small village of Bor Sang ▲ 265, on the San Khamphaeng Road, is almost entirely devoted to the production of umbrellas. These are made of handmade paper stretched over a frame of bamboo, then lightly lacquered to make them relatively waterproof and adorned with colorful flower patterns by artists. The umbrellas come in varying sizes, from tiny to huge, and are popular as souvenirs or as sunshades on patios and terraces.

TEXTILES

Northern weavers are noted for the quality of their silks and cottons, as well as for their skill at embroidering them with bands of brocade and woven designs. These are traditionally produced in sarong-length pieces for women, the silk being reserved for special occasions and the cotton for everyday wear; a cotton sarong for men, called a *phakoma* ● 56, comes in plaid patterns. The villages of San Khamphaeng and Pasang, near Chiang Mai, are noted for their weaving, and a wide selection is also available at the night bazaar.

SILVERWARE

Even though silver is not mined in Thailand, silverware has long been a Chiang Mai specialty, particularly bowls with intricate *repoussée* designs that are used in numerous ceremonies. The main community of silversmiths is based at Wualai Road, near Chiang Mai Gate, where one of the characteristic sounds is the constant clangor of hammer on metal. In addition to the classic bowls, more contemporary items like trays, teapots and tableware are also produced. In former days, the silver was generally obtained by melting down old coins from British India and Burma. Some of the hill tribes still produce their distinctive silver jewelry by this method, but the Chiang Mai artisans now import their silver from abroad. The price of a silver item is based not so much on the workmanship as on the quality of the metal.

BETEL BOXES
A set of beautifully crafted betel-nut boxes was an accessory found in every aristocratic household and many ordinary ones as well, consisting of a lacquerware tray and assorted containers used in the once-universal ritual of betel chewing.

DOI SUTHEP

Overlooking Chiang Mai is the 5,283-foot mountain called Doi Suthep, which is part of the twin-peaked Doi Suthep–Doi Pui National Park. There was no proper road up the mountain until the mid-1930's, when a monk named Phra Khruba Srivijaya initiated the construction of one, mainly with volunteer labor, to help pilgrims who wanted to visit the famous Wat Phra That Doi Suthep near the summit. The winding road offers spectacular views of the city below and considerably lower temperatures even in the hottest months. The National Park headquarters are just beyond the temple car park.

GOLDEN CHEDI
The famous golden chedi of Wat Phra That Doi Suthep, 79 feet high and 39 feet across at its base, is covered with engraved gold plates; on the platform around it are four ornamental umbrellas, brightly gilded and adorned with beautiful filigree decorations, while the walls of the surrounding cloister are painted with murals from the life of the Buddha.

WAT PHRA THAT DOI SUTHEP. According to legend, holy relics discovered during the reign of King Ku Na (1355–85) were placed in a howdah on the back of a white elephant, which carried them to Wat Suan Dok. The elephant was then set free to wander at will and it climbed Doi Suthep to the site of Wat Phra That, where it dropped dead. The present complex dates from the 16th century and was expanded or restored several times later.

A flight of 290 steps, bordered by a *naga* balustrade, leads up from the parking area to the temple, which has beautifully decorated buildings and a Lanna-style chedi covered with engraved gold plates, flanked by four ornamental umbrellas.

PHUPING PALACE. Built in 1972, Phuping Palace is located about 2½ miles beyond Wat Phra That Doi Suthep and serves as the royal family's northern residence. The buildings are closed to the public, but when no members of the family are present the extensive gardens are open. January is the best month to see of the numerous temperate-zone plants and trees in flower.

CHIANG MAI ZOOLOGICAL PARK

The Chiang Mai Zoological Park, near the foot of Doi Suthep, began as the private collection of Harold Young, an American working in Chiang Mai, and was taken over by the government in 1965 after his death. It has more than 500 animals in an attractively landscaped setting.

SAN KHAMPHAENG

The 8-mile road from Chiang Mai to the village of San Khamphaeng is lined for most of its length with shops selling and producing various handicrafts and also passes the Bor Sang umbrella village ▲ 271. San Khamphaeng itself is famous for its handwoven silks and cottons, sold at many shops along the main street.

> «FINE FRUIT TREES, AND BEAUTIFUL BAMBOO CLUMPS
> IN THE GARDENS BORDERING THE ROAD,
> FORM A MAGNIFICENT AND SHADY AVENUE.»
>
> HOLT S. HALLETT

HANDICRAFT VILLAGES

Several interesting villages devoted to handicraft production lie on or just off the Chiang Mai-Chom Thong highway. In Muang Kung the people make pottery for household use, while villagers at Hang Dong specialize at weaving bamboo into attractive baskets ● 74–5. In the once-sleepy village of Bantawai, there are hundreds of woodcarvers, as well as modern facilities for packing and shipping their products all over the world.

DOI INTHANON NATIONAL PARK

Covering an area of 193 square miles, this scenic park can be visited on day trips from Chiang Mai. The park includes the 8,465-foot Doi Inthanon, Thailand's highest mountain. At the top is a chedi containing the ashes of the last ruler of Chiang Mai. Pilgrims wishing to pay homage originally had to go up on foot or on ponies. During the 1970's, despite the protests of conservationists, the army built a 28-mile road to the summit, opening it to a greater number of visitors. However, the park still has many unspoiled trails, superb waterfalls (such as the Mae Ya falls in the southern part), beautiful mountain butterflies and 383 species of birds.

WOODCRAFT
"Woodcarving is a favorite occupation, in which some technical artistic skill is displayed, and the native chiefs and some of the princes constantly employ men to make ornaments. Carved scroll work for doors, posts, household articles, is in much request."

Carl Bock

WAT SI CHOM THONG

Less than a mile beyond the turn-off to Doi Inthanon is Wat Si Chom Thong. It contains a Lanna-style chedi ● 98 dating from the 15th century and sheathed in brass plates, as well as a more recent Burmese-style chedi. The viharn, built in 1516 and restored in 1817, is beautifully decorated with intricate woodcarvings.

CATTLE MARKET
About a mile beyond the village of San Pa Thong on the Chiang Mai-Chom Thong highway, a colorful *kadwua*, or cattle market, is held on Saturday mornings, perhaps the largest of its kind in the north. Besides cattle and buffaloes, a wide range of other items are on sale, from exotic foods to herbal medicines.

WAT PHRA THAT HARIPUNCHAI
The compound was originally built to face the river, with the entrance at the back of the temple. There is a mixture of styles, as is often the case in Thailand.

A new expressway can now be used for the trip to Lamphun, 16 miles south of Chiang Mai, although the old road is still the more attractive of the two; some people, indeed, regard it as the most beautiful in the north, lined as it is with stately trees growing to 66 feet tall and meeting at the top to form a cool canopy. On the way, it passes large plantations of *lamyai*, a fruit much prized in the north, and the basket-weaving village of Saraphi.

HISTORY

SERENITY
The tranquil terracotta face (right) is on display in the museum opposite Wat Phra That Haripunchai.

Lamphun, now a quiet town on the Kwang River, was once an important cultural center. Founded in AD 660, it was the capital of the Mon kingdom of Haripunchai and remained independent until it was incorporated into the Lanna kingdom by King Mengrai in 1281. The walls and moat that can be seen today date only from the early 19th century, but a number of fine temples attest to the city's ancient glory ● *38–9.*

WAT PHRA THAT HARIPUNCHAI

WORLD'S LARGEST GONG
One of the most popular attractions in Wat Phra That Haripunchai is an enormous bronze gong. Cast in 1860, this is supposedly the largest gong in the world ● *63.*

One of the major temples in the north, both historically and architecturally, Wat Phra That Haripunchai, facing the Kwan River, was founded in 1044 by King Athitayaraj of Haripunchai on the site of a former royal palace. A modern viharn, built in 1925 to replace the original, houses the Phra Chao Thongthip, a Chiang Saen-style bronze Buddha image; to the right of the viharn is an enormous bronze gong, while to the le is a Lanna-style repository for religious scriptures built in the early 19th century. The most prominent feature of the temple complex – and the most sacred part – is a 165-foot-tall Lanna-style chedi built in 1467, sheathed in copper and adorned with a gold umbrella. Slightly behind this monument is the Suwanna Chedi, a stepped-pyramid form of chedi, datin from 1418 and a replica of one in Wa

Chamadevi, also in Lamphun.
Elsewhere in the compound are
a viharn enshrining a standing
Buddha known as Phra Chao
Tan Jai and a pavilion
containing four Buddha
footprints, one inside another.

MUSEUMS. Some of the many
Buddha images presented to
Wat Phra That Haripunchai
have been been placed in a
small museum within the temple
grounds. Opposite Wat Phra That Haripunchai is a small
branch of the National Museum. It contains a fine collection
of bronze Buddha images, together with stucco and terracotta
figures of the early Haripunchai period found during
archeological excavations in the area.

WAT CHAMADEVI

Also known as Wat Ku Kut, Wat Chamadevi
contains Lamphun's oldest monuments: two
brick chedis decorated with stucco figures
of the Buddha. According to the noted
authority Jean Boisselier, these ruins date
from 1218 and are among the last surviving
examples of Dvaravati-period (7th–11th
century) architecture. The larger chedi, Sat
Mahal Pasada, is in the form of a stepped
pyramid 69 feet high and 51 feet wide and was
possibly inspired by a similar monument at
Polonnaruwa in Sri Lanka; it served as the model for
similar structures elsewhere in the region. The other small
chedi is octagonal and dates from the same period.

VIANG KUNGAM

Viang Kungam, which can be visited on an excursion to
Lamphun, is a recently unearthed old city built by King

Mengrai shortly before he founded Chiang
Mai. He lived there for six years before he
decided the site was inconvenient and moved
across the river to a new one. Among the
temples in the area, Wat Chedi Liem has a
tall chedi – it is similar to the one at Wat
Chamadevi – which was restored at the turn
of this century with the addition of Burmese-
style decorations. Wat Chan Kham has a
spirit house where the soul of King
Mengrai himself is believed to reside.

MCKEAN INSTITUTE

Not far from Wiang Kungam, on a small island in the
Ping River, is the McKean Institute, where leprosy
patients are treated. It was founded in 1908 by
Dr James W. McKean, a Presbyterian missionary, and
has become internationally recognized for its approach
to the once-dreaded disease.

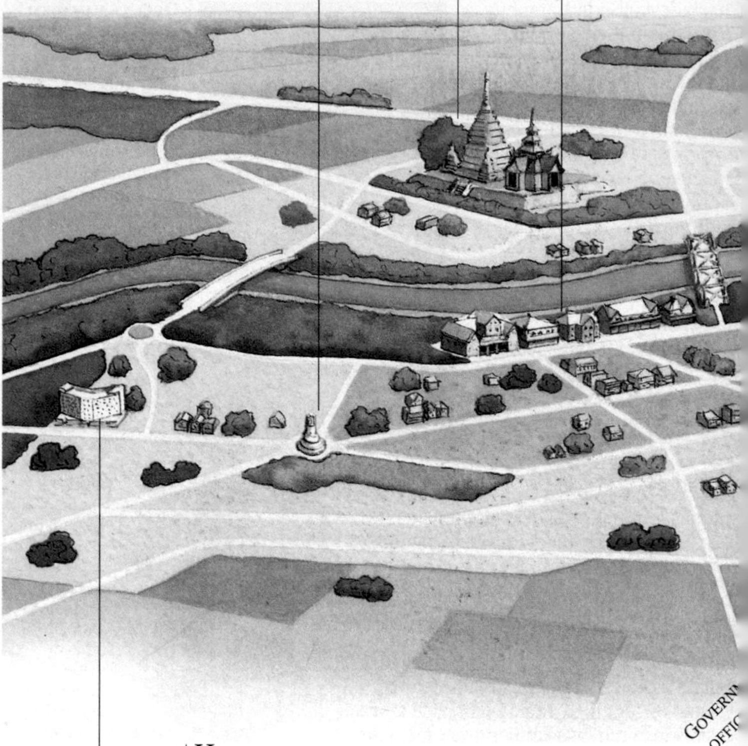

CLOCKTOWER

WAT PONGSANUK TOI

OLD HOUSES

GOVERN
OFFIC

TIP CHANG
HOTEL

HISTORY

Located in the valley of the Wang River, a tributary of the Ping, Lampang is the second-largest town in northern Thailand. Its long history goes back to the 7th century, when it was supposedly founded by a son of the Haripunchai queen Chamadevi ▲ 275, who had established a Mon kingdom in the north. Originally known as Kelang Nakhon, it had four outlying fortified satellite settlements, of which only Wat Phra That Lampang Luang still exists ● 94. Lampang theoretically became part of the Lanna kingdom under Mengrai, though in many ways it was ruled autonomously; like Chiang Mai, it was occupied by the Burmese for three centuries. The specific location of Kelang Nakhon is unknown, but the town that thrived in the Lanna period was on the opposite bank of the river from the main part of today's city. At the beginning of the 20th century, Lampang was a center of the northern teak industry, with a population of more than 20,000 and some 4,000 working elephants; it was also visited yearly by ten caravans from the Shan states of Burma, bringing goods that

The distinctive style of Lanna temples ▲ 94–5 is captured in this old engraving based on a sketch by Carl Bock, who visited the town in the early 1880's.

Lampang women during a local festival.

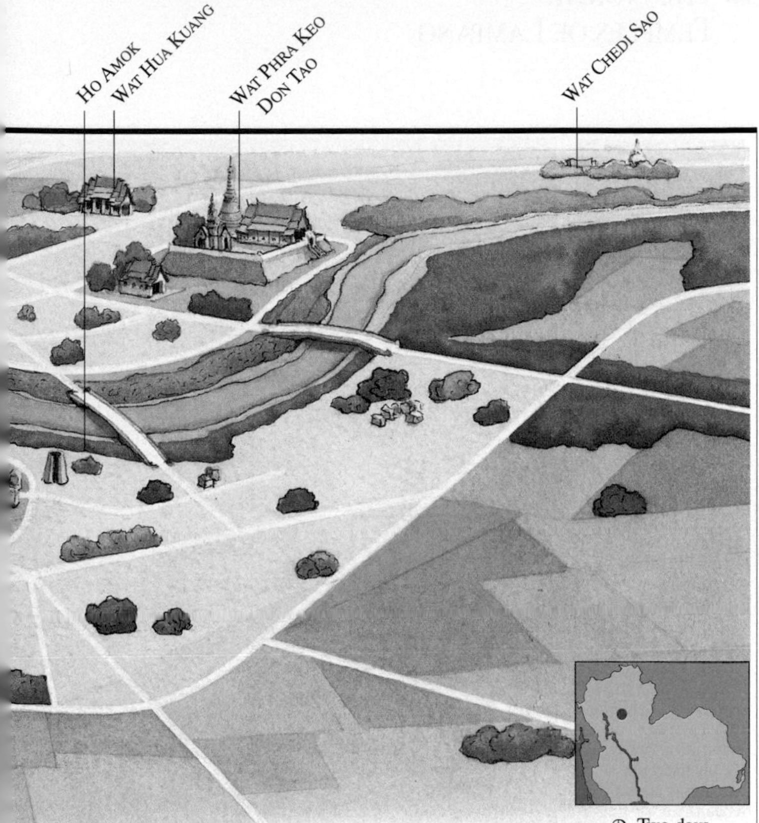

HO AMOK
WAT HUA KUANG
WAT PHRA KEO DON TAO
WAT CHEDI SAO

⏱ Two days

anged from lacquerware to opium. Despite
he less appealing cement constructions of
ecent years, this era is still reflected in a
umber of fine old teak mansions in the
rea of the old market along the river.

TALAT KAO

Lampang's old market, known as the *talat
kao*, was located along the river and still
preserves much of its former charm. The
shophouses display a mixture of Chinese,
Burmese and Western influences, and many
are adorned with
Victorian fretwork
imported by
Burmese
carpenters.

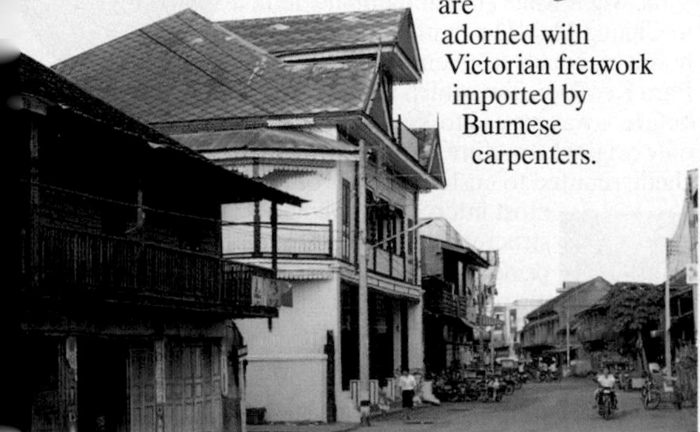

**HORSE-
DRAWN
CARTS**
The symbol of
Lampang, at least to
Thai visitors, is the
horse-drawn cart.
Such carts were
originally imported
from England in the
early years of the
present century and,
while they are no
longer as common as
they once were,
enough remain to
give the town a
leisurely ambience
and offer a pleasant
way to explore it.

277

MOSAIC CEILING
"The only note of incongruity," wrote Reginald Le May in 1926, "was a series of small gilt angel figures (of the Raphael type), pendent from the ceiling. How easily and only too well they learn from the West!" Such figures of cupids as well as horses and soldiers of Victorian inspiration had been widely used by Mandalay artists since the early days of the British occupation of Burma.

WIANG LUANG LAKON
Each year, usually in February, a festive parade called *Wiang Luang Lakon* is staged in Lampang. This celebrates the splendors of Queen Chamadevi's 7th-century court, with hundreds of participants in colorful period dress.

WAT PHRA KEO DON TAO

The most important temple in Lampang, Wat Phra Keo Don Tao supposedly once enshrined the famous Emerald Buddha, which is now housed at Wat Phra Keo in Bangkok ▲ *148, 170*. This image, according to legend, was being brought from its place of discovery in Chiang Rai to Chiang Mai in 1436 when the elephant bearing it stopped in Lampang and refused to proceed; it therefore remained in the town until 1468, when King Tilokaraja finally took it to Chiang Mai. The name of the temple, however, comes from another image, the Phra Keo Don Tao, which was housed there before it was moved to Wat Phra That Lampang Luang. The only original structure remaining in the temple is a 165-foot chedi, reputed to enshrine a hair of the Buddha, while the most interesting building is a Burmese-style structure built in 1909 as a donation by a Thai prince. The latter has a three-tier roof, elaborate mirror mosaics and superb woodcarvings. The principal viharn, Phra Chao Thong Tip, was constructed in 1930 by the venerated northern monk Khruba Srivijaya and contains a fine Buddha image. A small museum in the temple

«THIS COUNTRY OF LANNA...MAKES THE STRANGER FEEL THAT, IF HE MUST BE EXILED FROM HIS NATIVE SHORES, HE COULD NOT FIND A LAND OF GREATER CHARM AND SYMPATHY TO SPEND HIS DAYS.»

REGINALD LE MAY

compound displays a collection of Lanna-style furniture.

WAT SUCHADA. Adjacent to Wat Phra Keo Don Tao, Wat Suchada is regarded as part of the same monastery. Built by residents of Chiang Saen who were forcibly resettled after their hometown was destroyed at the beginning of the 19th century, it has a chedi and two viharns in late Lanna style; the main viharn houses a large brick and stucco Buddha and has some beautiful lacquer decorations.

OTHER OLD LANNA TEMPLES

WAT SENG MUANG MA ★. Also one of the Chiang Saen temples, Wat Seng Muang Ma is located on Thamma Oo Road. It contains a small but well-proportioned chedi, as well as a viharn that enshrines a large Buddha image and has some interesting paintings on wood panels dating from the turn of the century (above).

WAT HUA KUANG. Like Wat Suchada, this was built by resettled Chiang Saen people and has an interesting old viharn in late Lanna style, as well as Chiang Saen images and manuscripts on the art of casting bronze that the displaced people brought with them.

WAT PONGSANUK TAI ★. Located on Pongsanuk Road in Viang Neua, the area occupied by the old Lanna town of Lampang, Wat Pongsanuk Tai is regarded by many as the most charming temple in the town. Within a tree-filled new monastery is an old one, almost intact, in Lanna style on a high platform that can be reached by flights of steps on each side. A Lanna chedi ● 95, 98 is covered with copper sheets and also on the platform is a splendid open-sided structure with a tiered roof and a mondop (right) in old Lanna style and a newer viharn containing a reclining Buddha image. All the buildings are gracefully proportioned and elegantly decorated.

U YA SUDHA ★. "The Grotto of Grandmother Sudha" is the local name of the gatehouse of a now-destroyed monastery on Wiang Neua Road. Decorated with deities in stucco, it dates from the 15th century and is one of the oldest examples of Lanna art.

HO AMOK. The Octagonal Tower is one of the few parts of Lampang's ancient fortifications that remain today. Located in the modern part of the new town, on the west bank of the Wang river, it served as a lookout and is today a venue of a grand shamanistic ceremony in honor of the spirits of the town.

▲ The North
Temples of Lampang

WAT PRATU PONG ★ Not far from the Ho Amok and near a remaining part of the old city wall is Wat Pratu Pong, which, although slightly restored, is still one of the best examples of classic northern style. The gable is decorated with a fine woodcarving of a mythological creature with a serpent emerging from its mouth, while the doors of the temple are also exquisitely carved.

BURMESE TEMPLES

After the Burmese Occupation, many Burmese came to the north in the late 19th century to work in the timber trade and some became prosperous resident businessmen. The latter built or restored numerous temples ▲ *289*, which partly accounts for the strong Burmese element in northern architecture ● *94–5, 98*.

WAT PHA FANG Located opposite the office of Thai International Airways on Airport Road, Wat Pha Fang is one of several temples in Lampang that show a strong Burmese influence, even though it has been recently restored. Its chedi, for example, is typically Burmese, while each of the chapels surrounding the temple contains an image in Mandalay style. The bot, which i located near the chedi, is more elaborately decorated than the viharn.

WAT CHEDI SAO. Located a few miles to the left off the road to Jae Hom, Wat Chedi Sao – "Temple of the Twenty Chedis" in northern Thai – is a charming country monastery. The whitewashed chedis after which the temple is named are built in a blend of Thai and Burmese styles, and the compound also contains a remarkable collection of fanciful statues added by imaginative abbots in recent

EARLY TOURISTS IN LAMPANG
Unfortunately destroyed by fire early in 1991, Wat Sri Chum, one of Lampang's Burmese-style temples, contained some fine lacquered wall paintings. Among the subjects depicted were foreigners, shown traveling by automobile through the forest to visit the temple and pausing at a local refreshment stand.

Some of the twenty chedis of Wat Chedi Sao.

years. These include the twelve animals associated cyclically with various years in the Chinese calendar as well as figures from Buddhist legends. The principal image in the viharn is a Lanna Buddha made of brick and stucco.

TEMPLES OF LAMPANG LUANG

Located just about 12 miles from Lampang in the Kokha district, Lampang Luang was once a *wiang* (citadel) established during the early Haripunchai period. Protected by three earthen ramparts separated by moats, the site was part of a group of satellite fortresses associated with the ancient city of Kelang Nakorn.

WAT LAI HIN ★. The first temple in the Kokha district, Wat Lai Hin ● *98*, is located on high ground overlooking a stream and ricefields. The main viharn, in old Lanna style, has elaborate stucco decorations on the gable and fine lacquerwork inside, both possibly 200 years old, while the gatehouse dates probably from the 15th or 16th century.

WAT PONG YANG KOK ★. Just past Wat Phra That Lampang Luang on the road to Hang Chat, Wat Pong Yang Kok has a beautiful open wooden viharn in the old Lanna style. Inside are some famous lacquer decorations featuring a motif of the bodhi tree repeated throughout.

WAT PHRA THAT LAMPANG LUANG ★

THE PHRA KEO DON TAO
A small jasper image believed to have magical powers, the Phra Keo Don Tao, now housed at Wat Phrathat Lampang Luang, was much coveted by northern rulers of the 15th century. It was eventually placed in Wat Phra Keo at Bangkok's Grand Palace compound.

Many an enchanted traveler in northern Thailand has called Wat Phra That Lampang Luang the most beautiful temple in the country. Offering a spectacular display of Lanna religious architecture ● *94–5* and decorative skills, the temple was founded in early Haripunchai times, part of a group of satellite fortresses, and contains a 165-foot chedi believed to contain genuine relics of the Buddha. This and all the most important buildings are located within a porticoed enclosure, situated on top of a hillock; the main entrance is a monumental gatehouse adorned with superb stucco-work. Lions and *naga* (sacred serpents), also in stucco, guard the steps. The main viharn to the gatehouse is an open-sided structure built in 1496 and restored several times. The painting on the wooden panels below the roof eaves date from the late 19th century, but the building was actually reconstructed by Phra Khruba Srivijaya in the 1930's. It enshrines a gilded *ku* ● *94* (pagoda-like structure inside the temple) containing the presiding Buddha image (right). Also in the enclosure are a bot, a *mondop* and three viharns. The Viharn Nam Tam, in particular, is worthy of attention, as it is probably the oldest surviving Lanna building, beautifully restored to its original form. Sixteenth-century paintings were revealed during the restoration.

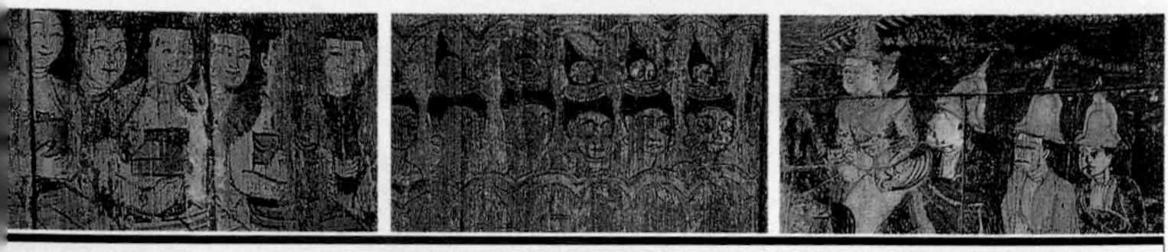

Lampang Luang is the main surviving example of a fortified settlement, which was built around a citadel, or *wiang*. This type of stronghold was once very common in northern Thailand, and is quite similar to those found in Europe in the Middle Ages. The ancient settlement was used for military purposes until the 18th century, when it was occupied by the Burmese. In 1736, Lampang Luang became the scene of a famous duel between the Burmese general and the Thai hero, Tip Chang, who had cleverly sneaked inside the walls through a drain to confront the enemy. Today the farming community is still clustered around the temple, which was built on high ground, though its fortifications have been dismantled. Traces of three parallel earthen ramparts – separated by two moats filled with water – can still be seen in various parts of the village.

MAIN STRUCTURES OF WAT PHRA THAT LAMPANG LUANG
1. Phra That – a chedi containing relics of the Buddha
2. Principal viharn
3. Viharn – built in 1802
4. Viharn (contemporary)
5. Viharn Nam Tam (early 16th century)
6. Viharn – reconstructed in 1967
7. Bot – built in 1924
8. *Mondop* – housing Buddha's footprint
9. Ceremonial gate-house leading to the porticoed enclosure
10. Stairways flanked by *naga*
11. Bodhi tree

Wat Phumin (above) is undoubtedly the most famous wat in Nan.

Nan can be reached from Chiang Mai by road in around four hours or by air in 45 minutes. The road trip is worthwhile since it offers an opportunity to enjoy some pleasant rural scenery – forested hills and lush, fertile valleys – and also to visit some interesting attractions, such as Phrae and Phae Muang Phi, along the way.

PHRAE

Coal mining and, until recently, logging have traditionally been the sources of Phrae's prosperity, still evident in some fine old wooden mansions and a thriving local furniture industry. Burmese influences can be seen in Wat Chom Sawan, while the most famous temple is Wat Phra That Cho Hae, atop a teak-covered hill just outside the town.

PHAE MUANG PHI

Phae Muang Phi, the "Ghost City," is located off Highway 10 on the way to Nan. This is actually not a town but a shallow depression where soil erosion has resulted in a number of strange rock-like formations that do indeed resemble the deserted dwellings of some mysterious race.

NAN TOWN ★

As late as the first decade of the present century, Nan was the capital of a semi-autonomous principality, founded in 1368. In its early period, until around 1450, the city had a close relationship with Sukhothai, and subsequently came under the indirect control of the Lanna kingdom. It was ruled by the Burmese from 1558 to 1788, when it pledged allegiance to Bangkok, but the local ruling dynasty retained considerable authority until the central government finally assumed full

HILL TRIBES
The Phi Thong Luang, "Spirits of the Yellow Leaves," who live in the Nan area, are among the most elusive of the hill tribe groups, still following a virtually prehistoric lifestyle ● *33*. Only in the 1960's was their existence confirmed by an expedition that came across some of them in their jungle hiding place. In the Nan Valley are also several hundreds of Khamus, an Austro-Asiatic tribe that inhabited the region before the arrival of the Thais.

control in 1931. Spread out along the west bank of the Nan River, the modern town has a prosperous air suggested and many shops selling luxury goods.

TEMPLES

WAT PHUMIN. This temple is the leading landmark of Nan, established in 1596 by a ruler named Phra Chao Chetabutra Phromin and extensively renovated in 1867. The cruciform viharn has steps leading up to splendidly carved doors on each of the four sides, while the interior is dominated by four large Buddha images facing the cardinal points ● *95*. Of special interest are the murals that adorn the walls, probably painted at the turn of the

century by Tai Lue artists. These mainly depict the Khatta Kumara and Nimi Jataka tales and contain a wealth of detailed visual information about the dress, tattoos and hairstyles of the period.

WAT PHRA THAT CHAE HAENG. Located southeast of the town on the opposite bank of the Nan River, Wat Phra That Chae Haeng is notable for the enormous *naga* (serpent) stairway that leads to the entrance. Inside the courtyard is a 180-foot-high golden chedi with four smaller chedis, while the viharn is a beautiful structure showing Laotian influence.

WAT CHANG KHAM VORA VIHARN. This temple, directly opposite the local branch of the National Museum, dates from 1406 but has been restored several times; it once contained five Buddha images commissioned in 1426 by a Nan ruler, only one of which – a 5-foot walking Buddha in solid gold – is kept at the temple in the monks' residence.

WAT PHRAYA PHU. This houses two of the other images, both made of bronze in the Sukhothai style. Wat Suan Tan, on the western side of town, enshrines the important Buddha image known as Phra Chan Thong Chip, a fine example of Sukhothai style, while Wat Satharos on the northern outskirts has an unusual chedi mounted on a high square base.

WAT DON JADEE

WAT PHRA THAT DOI KONG MU

WAT HUA WIANG

MARKET

WAT PANG LOR

ON THE WAY TO MAE HONG SON

The first metalled road from Chiang Mai to Mae Hong Son was opened in 1965 and has been extensively improved in recent years. It winds through some of Thailand's most beautiful scenery – misty mountains and forests of pine trees planted to replace those cut down by the hill tribes – with the view at its most spectacular as the road descends steeply into the valley of the Pai River where Mae Hong Son is located.

OB LUANG GORGE. A narrow defile with steep walls, the Ob Luang Gorge is one of Thailand's most celebrated beauty spots. Nearby is a nature park, where trails lead 650 feet down to the bottom of the gorge.

MAE SARIANG. A small town 62 miles from Ho on the road from Chiang Mai to Mae Hong

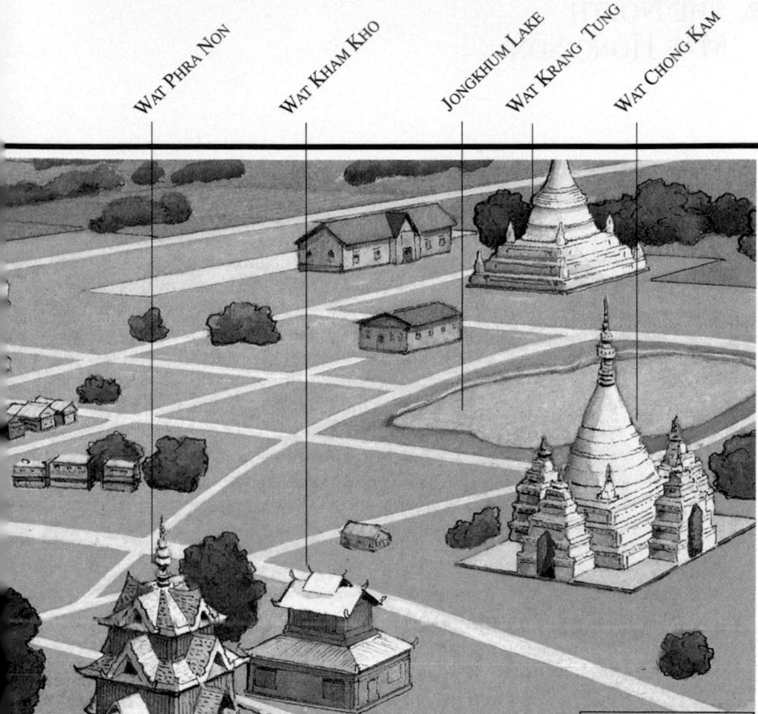

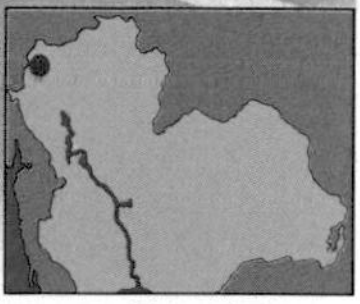

🕐 Four days

Son, Mae Sariang has wooden shophouses and a rickety bridge that spans the Yuam River and leads to the mountain range bordering Burma. Two local temples are worth visiting for their Burmese-style architecture ● 98. Wat Utthayarom, which dates from 1896, has three chedis, one of which has nine spires, while nearby Wat Boonruang is much more elaborately decorated and has the monks' quarters in a longhouse raised on stilts. A dirt track leads south from Mae Sariang along the Burmese border all the way to Tak, but as it is known to be unsafe, the route is seldom used by foreigners.

HISTORY

Though constituted as a city by the ruler of Chiang Mai in 1874 and as a province under the Ministry of Interior in 1893, Mae Hong Son is regarded as the back of beyond by most people in Thailand. It remained isolated from the rest of Thailand until 1965 when the metalled road was opened. Mae Hong Son is in fact so remote that it was a favored place of exile for government officials charged with serious offenses against the State. Today, however, a regular domestic air service links the city with Chiang Mai, thus opening up the valley to tourism.

SHANS
Shans, who belong to the same ethnic group as the Thais, began visiting the Mae Hong Son valley from northern Burma centuries ago, and worked seasonally in the forests. By the mid-19th century increasing numbers were settling permanently, and one group built an elephant-trapping corral on the site that eventually became Mae Hong Son. The Shans still constitute nearly 50 percent of the province's population.

287

MAE HONG SON TODAY ★

Nestled amid forested, mist-shrouded mountains, Mae Hong Son still has a tranquil feeling of remoteness, a leisurely ambience that comes as a welcome contrast to the bustle of most other modern northern towns. The liveliest time of day is between 6am and 8am, when a busy market springs up behind the Mae Tee Hotel, with stalls selling food, clothing and household goods, and colorful hill tribe people mingle with the local populace. Otherwise the chief charm of Mae Hong Son is strolling about scenic Jongkhum Lake, visiting various temples in the area, and enjoying its cool climate during the winter months.

WAT PHRA THAT DOI KONG MU ★

Doi Kong Mu is the name of the small hill that dominates Mae Hong Son, often covered with mist in the morning. A road leads to Wat Phra That Doi Kong Mu at the summit, where there are a number of Buddha images and two chedis – one built in 1860, the other in 1874. The mist

Wat Chong Kam and Wat Chong Klang are situated beside a small lake (above).

SHAN ORDINATION CEREMONY
Each year in early April the Shans of Mae Hong Son observe a colorful ritual known as Poi Sang Long. This marks the initiation of young boys into the monkhood ● 47 and involves a gala procession in which the novices are carried to the monastery with dances performed by participants dressed in animal costumes.

clears in the afternoon, giving visitors spectacular panoramic views of the valley and the surrounding mountains; the wonderful experience is enhanced by the tinkle of bells from the tops of the chedis, which are quite dramatically illuminated after dark.

LOY KRATHONG. The water festival ● 73 is celebrated in Burmese fashion in Mae Hong Son. Instead of being set adrift on rivers and ponds, as in the rest of the country, the lotus-shaped *krathong* are attached to paper lanterns and released into the air from the top of Doi Kong Mu overlooking the town.

OTHER TEMPLES

WAT HUA WIANG. Located near the morning market, Wat Hua Wiang is a dilapidated wooden temple that houses an exceptionally fine brass seated Buddha, a replica of the one in Mandalay. Sections of the image were cast in Burma, then transported overland and by river and assembled in Mae Hong Son.

WAT KHAM KHO. Across the road from Wat Phra Non, Wat Kham Kho was built in 1890; the covered walkway from the main gate and the viharn have elegant filigree work on the eaves. The viharn contains five principal Buddha images, the central one being Burmese in style. In front of the altar there is a beautiful 80-year-old peacock throne inlaid with colored glass.

WAT PHRA NON. Located at the foot of Doi Kong Mu is Wat Phra Non, a rebuilt temple that houses two large Buddha images made of plaster over brick. One, 40 feet long, is in the reclining position, and the other is seated; both have realistic, painted faces in the Burmese style. Just behind this temple are two huge stone lion statues carved in Burmese style. They guard the entrance to the old deserted footpath up Doi Kong Mu. A few steps further on is a row of six chedis built on an elevated platform – all that remains of Wat Muay Toh.

WAT CHONG KAM AND WAT CHONG KLANG ★. These are two Burmese-style temples in the same compound, picturesquely sited beside a small lake and surrounded by a palm grove. Of special interest is a collection of 33 wooden figures. These figures are kept in a small barred room just inside the entrance to the viharn of Wat Chong Klang. Representing figures from the Vessantara Jataka – one of a collection of stories dealing with the Buddha's previous lives – these were brought from Burma in 1857. Near Wat Chong Kam is Luang Pho To, which enshrines a revered 16-foot-tall brick and plaster Buddha image.

Wat Hua Wiang is the town's most important wat. Its wooden roofs are tiered.

Detailed filigree work is a feature of Shan temples.

289

One of the most scenic drives in the Chiang Mai area is through the Mae Sa Valley, a recently developed area that begins with a left turn at Mae Rim, about 7 miles out of Chiang Mai on the road to Fang. Several resorts have appeared in the valley over the past few years, with terraces on the mountain slopes and neat, landscaped gardens of mostly temperate-zone plants. There are also rustic cottages that attract city-dwellers longing for a change of scene and a taste of country life without the usual discomforts. The winding road eventually slopes down to the Chiang Mai–Chom Thong Highway. The scenery, however, is most attractive along this least developed section.

"The road to Tatong lay through a somewhat open forest, with a high mountain-chain, running north and south, rising abruptly to the left. The trees were literally covered with orchids, which were just past their prime, the dry season being the time for flowering. Many other varieties of flowers, of most gorgeous colours and often of gigantic size, flourished in the open patches between the trees. I do not remember to have seen anywhere such a profusion of flowers as when travelling through Lao and in this particular district they seemed more abundant than ever."
Carl Bock

ORCHID FARMS

There are several orchid nurseries in the Mae Sa Valley, all open to visitors for a nominal entrance fee. In addition to dazzling displays of blooming plants ● *20–1*, both native and hybrid, most of the nurseries also have demonstrations of orchid propagation and shops selling such souvenirs as orchid blossoms coated with gold.
FA MUI ORCHID. One of the most beautiful of northern Thailand's indigenous orchids is *Vanda coerulea*, known in Thai as Fa Mui, the natural color of which is a heavenly blue that comes in a variety of subtle shades. This is prized by foreign orchid growers for hybridization and was used to produce the famous *Vanda rothschildiana* (right) ● *20*.

ELEPHANT-TRAINING CAMP

One of the most popular tourist stops along the Mae Sa Valley road is an elephant-training camp near the Mae Sa Waterfall. The animals and their trainers give a performance

at around 9am every day. Elephant rides through the jungle to the Mae Sa Valley Resort can also be arranged.

CHIANG DAO CAVES

Doi Chiang Dao, at 7,540 feet Thailand's third-highest mountain, is 45 miles from Chiang Mai. Nestling at the foot of the mountain are the Chiang Dao Caves, accessible through a narrow entrance at the top of a covered stairway. They consist of several chambers (above), the first of which receives some light from an opening above and is the most impressive. Shan Buddhists have long venerated the caves and have placed a number of large Buddha images there. Further in, more steps flanked by a long *naga* lead down to a large reclining Buddha carved out of the limestone and a life-sized statue of one of the Buddha's disciples.

FANG

Founded by King Mengrai ● *38* in 1268 and once a prosperous, independent city, Fang was destroyed by the Burmese at the beginning of the 19th century and deserted until 1880. The present town is mainly of interest because of its proximity to Burma and the colorful tribal people who come to its market to sell their goods.

TO CHIANG RAI BY BOAT

Tha Thon is a small village on the bank of the Kok River, about 14 miles north of Fang. From a landing near Wat Tha Ton, long-tail boats leave at 12.30pm daily for a three-hour trip down the river to Chiang Rai, which offers exciting rapids and exceptionally beautiful natural scenery. A three-day trip can be made by bamboo raft. Booking for the trip should be made 10 days in advance.

PHI POB PEOPLE
Legend has it that the little town of Chiang Dao was once inhabited by people possessed by *phi pob*, spirits ● *51* who ate the entrails of their victims. Like lepers, such people were sent to live in remote communities far away from others.

FARMHOUSES
The Fang valley, is peppered with picturesque farming communities made up of simple native huts with thatched roofs, reflecting a timeless way of life in striking contrast to the bustling, modern ways of larger northern towns and cities.

HILL TRIBE TREKS
Treks into the northern mountains to enjoy the scenery and visit remote and exotic hill tribe villages became an important part of Chiang Mai's appeal about 15 years ago, especially with adventurous travelers. That area eventually became "overtrekked," at least among more dedicated enthusiasts, and the main center of operations has now shifted to Chiang Rai. Consequently, dozens of agencies have opened in the city offering everything from a two-day mini-excursion to one that lasts a week or more, with a wide range of prices and amenities available. Look for an agency that meets your particular requirements, keeping in mind a few basic considerations. The best time for trekking is the cool, dry season from November through the end of February; March through May

can be hot and hazy, while during the rainy season the mountain trails are often muddy and slippery. Most of the villages provide a place to sleep, and food is generally part of the trek package, but bring along snacks to supplement the limited variety of food available there.

Though relatively little remains of its past, Chiang Rai has an ancient history, having been founded by King Mengrai in 1262 ● *38*, on a site protected by the Kok River and by three small hills. Its strategic location near the border made it an important trading center but also ensured that it would suffer during the frequent wars between Thailand and Burma for a long period during the 19th century it was more or less abandoned, with only a few hundred families remaining within the old city walls. Prosperity returned slowly – as late as 1970, it had a population of only around 10,000 and has had a strong visible effect only in recent years.

CHIANG RAI TODAY. Modern Chiang Rai has little to offer in the way of physical beauty or exotic atmosphere, being for the most part a typical Thai provincial capital full of nondescript rows of cement shops and drab, dusty streets. Nevertheless, it has enjoyed a considerable boom over the past decade, thanks to its proximity to the fabled Golden Triangle and its convenience as a base for trekking expeditions into the nearby hills. New hotels, including a large one on an island in the Kok River, have risen almost everywhere, along with restaurants and shops catering to foreign tourists and numerous agencies that organize visits to tribal villages.

CHIANG RAI TEMPLES. Wat Phra Singh, on Singhakai Road, once enshrined the revered image known as Phra Buddha Si Hing, now at the temple of the same name in Chiang Mai; a replica is kept at the Chiang Rai temple. Wat Phra Keo, on Ruang Nakorn Road, contains an early bronze Chiang Saen image and a reconstructed chedi, where in 1436 the famous Emerald Buddha was discovered. Wat Ngam Muang has an ancient chedi with the remains of King Mengrai. Wat Doi Tong is on a hill that commands a fine view of the Kok River.

CITY WALLS. In the late 1980's, the municipality of Chiang Rai became aware that the city's claims to an ancient and glorious past are not supported by an adequate amount of archeological and architectural evidence, and tourist attractions are somewhat wanting in the town. It was then decided to build them and sponsors, historians and artists were called in to help to restore the glory of the city.

The first objective was the city walls. The original walls were pulled down in 1920 on the advice of Dr Briggs, an American missionary physician who argued that they were not only useless but were also a permanent source of all kinds of illnesses because they obstructed the flow of fresh air. Initially, it had been hoped that a complete city gate and a good part of the walls could be rebuilt, but no evidence whatsoever was found to help with the reconstruction except an engraving showing an elephant passing through a gate against the rays of the rising sun. The elephant was quickly taken as a yardstick, and assuming that its height may have been at least 8 feet, a stretch of cement wall covered with bricks was quickly built. It measured 330 feet long and 16 feet high, with an opening in the middle (no evidence upon which to reconstruct the gate was found). This "antiquity" now stands proudly in front of a shopping center.

CITY PILLAR. The second achievement was the construction of a city pillar, which Chiang Rai never had. This was erected on a hilltop – Doi Chomthong – on the outskirts of the town where a telephone exchange was about to be built. Pittaya Boonag, a lecturer from the Faculty of Architecture at the University of Chiang Mai, was called in to design a city pillar according to Thai cosmology, and he ended up with a complex of 108 granite pillars surrounding "the navel of the Universe," a larger column of phallic shape 5.5 feet high. The design represents major features of the universe as illustrated in various Thai murals in Bangkok, and therefore completely alien to the Lanna culture of old Chiang Rai. The complex was inaugurated on January 31, 1989 (six days after the date on the commemorative inscription), but has gone unnoticed since.

OPIUM
Source of heroin, opium is prepared from the juice of *Papaver somniferum*, one of the more than 250 species of poppy, which requires very specific climatic and geographical conditions for commercial cultivation. The plant grows best at altitudes of 3,000 to 7,000 feet and prefers a relatively dry climate; crop production can vary 300 percent from year to year depending on the weather. When the petals fall, the seed pod is sliced to release the juice, which is milk-white at first but dries to a gummy brown substance that can be stored for years without losing its potency ▲ *294–5*.

OPIUM EATER
"The vapors of opium fill up her empty head, Reclining her bust on the silky cushions; She follows in the ether the fanciful reverie, That phantasy unravels to her eyes."
Anonymous

293

The mountains of Thailand's far north, along the borders of Burma and Laos, are home to a number of tribal groups, each with its own distinctive culture and traditions. Only one tribe, the Karens, has lived in the region since ancient times; others began migrating in the 19th century into what was then rugged hills, left unpopulated by the Thais, who are lowland farmers. Some have come only in relatively recent years, driven by the wars in Indo-China and the unrest in northern Burma. The total tribal population is estimated at about half a million, divided into two general ethnic groups. The Hmongs and the Miens belong to the Sino-Tibetan group, while the Karens, Akhas, Lisus and Lahus are members of the Tibeto-Burmese group.

HILL TRIBE SETTLEMENTS

The tribes ● 33 do not possess definite territories but live interspersed in a number of settlements, each at a preferred altitude. Traditionally all the tribes are semi-nomadic. They will settle on the hills, clear the land by fire, and cultivate it for a few years until the soil is impoverished.
They will then move on to another hill site. Slash-and-burn cultivation has caused considerable damage and efforts are being made to resettle them at lower altitudes where the land can be irrigated. However, tribesmen find difficulty adapting to the heat in the valleys and to new developments in rural life.

OPIUM CULTIVATION

With the exception of the Karens, the hill tribes are mainly opium cultivators. The practice of opium cultivation was originally forced upon the Hmongs by the French government in Indo-China, which was secretly selling

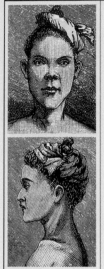

THE FIRST HILL TRIBES
The Lahus were the first hill tribes to migrate to northern Thailand in the last quarter of the 19th century. The Akhas were the last to arrive and their first village was erected in 1905. The largest migration took place in the 1960's and 1970's, and by 1983 the total population was 416,000.

«WHEREVER YOU GO…MAY YOUR FEET NOT STUMBLE,
YOUR ARMS NOT FALTER; MAY YOUR WORDS PROVE TRUE, YOUR
HOPES BE FULFILLED…AND ALL YOU UNDERTAKE FLOURISH.»

TRIBAL BLESSING

Old postcards from the early 20th century depicting typical Akha attire (left) and Karen dress.

opium to the Marseilles gangsters to finance the war against the communists. When the Hmongs migrated, they spread opium cultivation and trade in the region. Subsequently the Americans through the CIA encouraged opium cultivation to win the support of the Hmongs in the secret war against the Pathet Laos. Only when public opinion became concerned about drugs did the Western powers try to stop opium cultivation, forcing Third World countries to ban what had become a major source of income and a powerful political tool. While the military elites of many Indo-Chinese countries are still actively involved in the opium trade and drugs keep reaching the West, the big losers are the hill tribes, who see their only source of income under constant threat. Once addicted to opium, most tribesmen now turn to heroin, and cases are reported of children below school age who are already addicted. An interesting scheme to eradicate opium cultivation has been initiated by the King of Thailand, who has sought to introduce new commercial crops to replace the opium poppy as well as to bring better medical treatment and social welfare to the tribal groups. Among the crops introduced successfully thus far are coffee, vegetables, strawberries, peaches, lychees and apples. As a result of such efforts, opium production has dropped drastically in the country, many hill tribe children are receiving a basic education in settled villages, and their elders are more often seen mingling with the majority Thais in lowland towns and cities.

THE KARENS

Numbering about 250,000, the Karens are the largest hill tribe group. They are skilled farmers and have become sedentary, living on irrigated land. Karen women are noted for their skill in weaving cotton, commonly red or orange, which they embroider and decorate with seeds.

"Hill tribes" is not an ideal term for these diver[se] peoples of Thailand. Though they each possess [a] strong ethnic identity, their communities are dispersed throughout northern Thailand, with n[o] unifying "tribal" organization. These groups do[n't] share some characteristics that justify the name[s] hill tribe, differentiating them from the other ethnic groups of northern Thailand. One of the[se] characteristics is a rich material culture. The M[ien] or Yao peoples are among the most "Chinese" of the hill tribes, probably originating from southern China about 2,000 years ago[.] There are large numbers of Mien in China, Laos and Vietnam. They first migrated to Thailand from Laos in the mid-19th centu[ry.] They use Chinese script, their social organization is patriarchal, and their religion shows a strong Chinese influence. They share with other groups great skill in textile-making, specializing in cro[ss-] stitch embroidery work.

MIEN TEXTILES
Homespun cotton cloth, dyed a deep indigo is the basic material for most Mien textiles. Today that cloth is purchased from Thai weavers of the lowlands. The patterns were originally embroidered with naturally dyed homespun silk, the embroidery stitches running in parallel with the warp or weft. Today Mien embroiderers buy threads, in new colors, and prefer the cross-stitch, in which the embroidered thread runs diagonally across the warp and weft. The turban, waistcloth and pants of a traditional woman's outfit are embroidered; the tunic with its red fur collar is not as fully adorned.

APPLIQUÉ

The appliqué technique allows women to adorn their textiles with shapes which are more organic than motifs on embroidered cloths. Though still symmetrical, the shapes are made of complex lobes and tendrils. The appliqué example shown above is from a saddlecloth, white braiding highlighting the appliqué shapes.

SILVER

Silver is a crucial part of hill tribe costume. These ornaments, to be suspended from a silver neck ring, are also decorated with cloisonné enamel.

RELIGIOUS PAINTINGS

Mien religion draws its visual expression from archaic forms of Chinese folk religion. These paintings depict figures in a large hierarchical pantheon of gods and spirits.

CESTOR FIGURES

e Mien traditionally practice forms of cestor worship that owe much to Chinese al. Ancestors' names are recorded in a cial book, and recited when offerings are de. Ancestor figures such as this one nbolize the generalized presence of the cestors, who are informed of births and ddings, and who provide protection to ir descendants.

Hmong women are particularly skilled in the production of textiles. Their traditional version of the backstrap loom is unique, equipped with foot treadles for shifting the warp threads. They are the only group in mainland Southeast Asia to use the batik resist-dyeing technique, producing designs in blue and white monochrome. These designs are often enhanced with a layer of embroidery. To a modern eye, the Hmongs' mastery of geometric designs is especially pleasing. Special clothes are worn by young women at New Year, but the Hmongs traditionally reserve their full repertoire of textile expression for ornate funerary costumes, as in this woman's set.

CHILDREN'S JACKETS
The Chinese-style asymmetrical front fastening is highlighted with fine embroidery in this child's jacket. The abstract embroidery motifs are particularly attractive and even the smallest clothes are richly adorned.

SPIRIT LOCKS
This silver ornament, one of many kinds favored by Hmong men and women, is said to represent a lock, binding the soul to the body. It hangs from a neck ring. The incised patterning seems to be derived from the embroidery patterns used in women's collars.

> «A TINY NEEDLE, STRANDS OF BRIGHT THREAD, AND THE GENIUS OF A HMONG WOMAN – THESE ARE THE INGREDIENTS OF SOME OF THE MOST EXQUISITE NEEDLEWORK TO BE FOUND ANYWHERE.»
>
> PAUL AND ELAINE LEWIS

ERARY ELEGANCE
al clothes are made by
ife for her husband
erself. Made from
mp cloth, apart from
he pants or skirt,
there are three or
more upper richly
embroidered
garments.

COLLARS
These collar pieces (right), made by the women of the White Hmong subgroup, demonstrate a range of embroidery and appliqué techniques. Measuring around 5 y 6 inches, they hang from a flap down the back.

299

The Lahu, Akha and Lisu peoples are distinguishd from the other hill tribes by their languages, all in the Yi subgroup of the Tibeto-Burmese family. These hill tribes migrated to Thailand from the Shan states of Burma and from Yunnan, China in this century. Though all the peoples of the Golden Triangle use silver ornaments, arguably the most dramatic use of the precious metal is by these three Tibeto-Burmese speaking groups. Silver is plentiful in Yunnan and the upper Irrawaddy in Burma, and has been used in mainland Southeast Asia for centuries. But it became even more popular in the region thanks to the influence of the Europeans, who brought in relatively cheap New World silver to trade for Asian goods. Today, silver is still used for exchange and as a currency. Aluminum is now replacing silver for some uses.

BANGLES
Many of these dramatic twisted wire bracelets are made by Chinese silversmiths. They are hollow and some feature engraved designs. They are worn predominantly by the Akha people.

AKHA HEADGEAR
Adorned with silver coins and hollow silver balls, beads and buttons, Akha head-dresses show one of the most striking uses of silver by a hill tribe group. This piece (right), with a large trapezoidal silver plate at the back, is in the Loimi-Akha style, favored by recent migrants from Burma. It is worn by young girls on festive occasions.

PENDANTS
The fish is a favorite motif in the pendants worn by many hill tribe groups. Such pendants like the one shown above, can be worn around the neck in the front or hanging from a solid neck ring at the back, over a jacket. Elongated bell-shaped beads and a set of stylized grooming implements such as tweezer and ear cleaners, hangs below this fish.

NECK RINGS

Plain flat silver neck rings are particularly favored by Akha women. Often they serve as a kind of a base for the many silver ornaments that may be dangled from them, in front or at the back. They are often covered by the ornaments that hang from the headdress. The omega shape, with the scrolls at each end, is a popular form in much Southeast Asian jewelry, though this is a particularly vigorous expression of the basic form. These rings are flat, but others may be hollow, with a similar shape but rounded in profile. Neck rings like these are often copied in aluminium, to deter robbers.

PIPES

Apart from opium, the hill tribes also use the more respectable tobacco. The two pipes pictured here are solid silver, the bottom one exhibiting some cloisonné decoration as well. They could have been used by any of the three groups considered here, or indeed by the Miens or Hmongs as well.

CONTAINERS

Small silver containers like these are usually made by the Shan peoples who live mostly in Burma, and traded to the hill tribes. Used for betel nut paraphernalia and tobacco, they are collected as status objects, particularly by the Akhas.

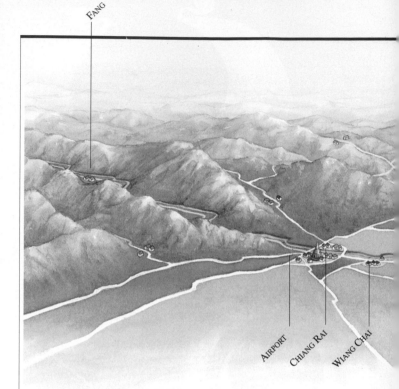

FANG

AIRPORT CHIANG RAI WIANG CHAI

🕓 Two days

Wat Phra That
Chom Kitti.

HISTORY

The origins of Chiang Saen ● *38, 39* are obscure. However, most historians agree that a town of considerable influence probably existed earlier on the site before the city of Chiang Saen was founded in 1328 by Phra Chao Saen Pu, a grandson of King Mengrai ● *38*. Chiang Saen became associated with Chiang Mai and was ruled by Lanna kings until 1558, when it was invaded by the Burmese, who remained in control for more than two centuries. In 1804, forces loyal to King Rama I seized the city and burned it after which the city was abandoned. Chao Inta, an offspring of the Prince of Lamphun, brought back the descendants of its former population and rebuilt the town 70 years later.

CHIANG SAEN SIGHTS

Chiang Saen's former importance is underlined by the fact that the Fine Arts Department lists 66 ruined monuments within its once-fortified walls and 75 outside. Among these is Wat Pa Sak, the city's oldest chedi, built in 1295 and adorned with fine stucco decorations; the structure displays a number of influences, in particular that of the early

The labels on the illustration at top:

MAE CHANAI · MAE SAI · WAT PA SAK · WAT PHRA THAT CHOM KITTI · MEKONG RIVER · CHIANG KHONG

KOK RIVER · CHIANG SAEN MUSEUM · CHIANG SAEN

Haripunchai period. About half a mile away, atop a hill accessible by 350 ancient steps, is Wat Phra That Chom Kitti, which contains an 82-foot-high chedi on a rectangular base. At Wat Chedi Luang, an octagonal chedi rises 190 feet, supposedly constructed in 1331 and rebuilt in 1515. Nearby is the Chiang Saen Museum, which displays several Chiang Saen bronze images as well as objects unearthed during excavations at Wat Chedi Luang. Along the road leading to the old town are several other ruined chedis, most notable among them being Wat Mung Muang and Wat Phra Buat.

THE GOLDEN TRIANGLE

The so-called Golden Triangle – a term coined by journalists and since then often used by novelists – is the area where Thailand's borders meet those of Burma and Laos. Its fame, or, more accurately, notoriety, stems from the fact that over 50 percent of the world's opium supply is produced there; converted into heroin by secret refineries, it eventually finds its way to the streets of major Western cities, bringing "gold" to a number of dealers

"Chiang Saen is a mysterious old city, surrounded by a high thick, strong wall with palisades on top of the brick, and deep trenches dug outside. …The whole city is now so overgrown with plantations of teak, and thick sedentary growth, that one cannot see more than 20 yards ahead.**"**

MAE SAI
Situated at the pinnacle of the Golden Triangle, the atmosphere in this frontier town is more Burmese than Thai.

THE LOST ARMY
When the communists took over mainland China in 1949, the 93rd Army of the Kuomintang operating in Yunnan was cut off from the forces of Chiang Kai-shek, which were then retreating to Taiwan. The army settled on the Thai border, and to sustain itself became involved in opium cultivation and smuggling. The Kuomintang forces made Doi Mae Salong their stronghold for more than 20 years. Their presence was tolerated by the Thai government as it was felt that they were useful to keep communist infiltration at bay. The Kuomintang forces have since surrendered and the government has accepted them as Thai citizens.

AKHA VILLAGES
The Akha do not cultivate opium poppies; their villages are generally built at altitudes that are too low for these plants to flourish.

who act as middlemen but not to the tribal people who actually grow the poppies. Thailand's share of the market has dropped dramatically in recent years, thanks to a royalty-sponsored program to introduce new, more profitable crops for the tribes; but sizeable quantities are still coming from beyond its borders. Although geographically inaccurate, a spot designated as the center of the triangle is located near Chiang Saen where the Kok River joins the Mekong, complete with a noticeboard and a picnic pavilion.

MAE SAI

Thailand's northernmost town, Mae Sai is located on the Mae Sai River, which forms the border with Burma. While foreigners are not allowed to cross the bridge linking the two countries, there are numerous shops and stalls on the Thai side of the border, some selling herbal medicines but most offering tourist souvenirs brought from Chiang Mai.
DOI MAE SALONG ★. A popular excursion from Mae Sai, this mountain is inhabited by the Akhas and the Miens. Most of the villages along the road set up street bazaars, which of course attract tourists. At the end of the road is the village of Santi Kiri, inhabited by the families of the former Kuomintang army. The village is now developing into a hill station with several hotels and guest houses, but the town still looks very much like a typical Chinese settlement. Most of the products in the market are imported over the mountains from China. Many families here are Chinese Muslims, originating from Yunnan.

RIVER TRIP TO CHIANG KHONG

From Chiang Saen visitors can hire a boat down the Mekong River to the small town of Chiang Khong. The trip takes about two hours and offers some scenic views, particularly of the less developed Laotian side. With Thai-Laotian relations improving, Chiang Khong may once more become an important point for crossing the river.

PRACTICAL
INFORMATION

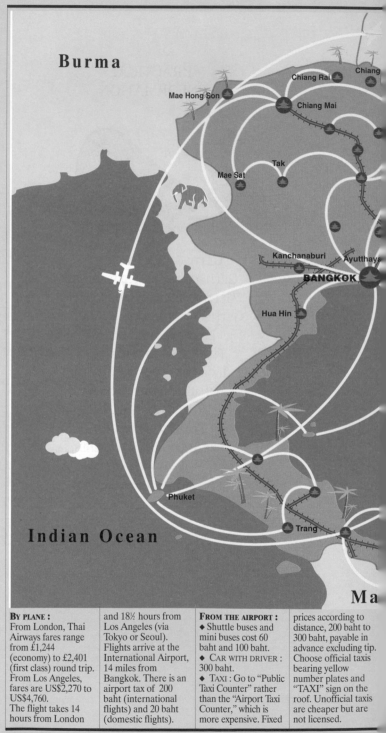

Burma

Chiang Rai
Chiang
Mae Hong Son
Chiang Mai
Tak
Mae Sat
Kanchanaburi
Ayutthaya
BANGKOK
Hua Hin
Phuket
Trang
Indian Ocean
M a

BY PLANE :
From London, Thai Airways fares range from £1,244 (economy) to £2,401 (first class) round trip. From Los Angeles, fares are US$2,270 to US$4,760.
The flight takes 14 hours from London and 18½ hours from Los Angeles (via Tokyo or Seoul). Flights arrive at the International Airport, 14 miles from Bangkok. There is an airport tax of 200 baht (international flights) and 20 baht (domestic flights).

FROM THE AIRPORT :
◆ Shuttle buses and mini buses cost 60 baht and 100 baht.
◆ CAR WITH DRIVER : 300 baht.
◆ TAXI : Go to "Public Taxi Counter" rather than the "Airport Taxi Counter," which is more expensive. Fixed prices according to distance, 200 baht to 300 baht, payable in advance excluding tip. Choose official taxis bearing yellow number plates and "TAXI" sign on the roof. Unofficial taxis are cheaper but are not licensed.

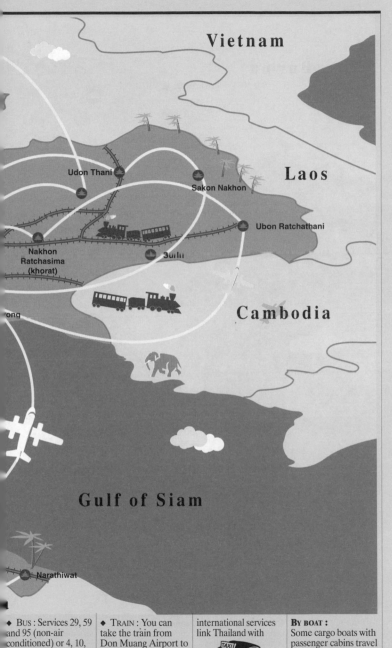

Vietnam

Laos

Udon Thani

Sakon Nakhon

Ubon Ratchathani

Nakhon
Ratchasima
(khorat)

Surin

Cambodia

ong

Gulf of Siam

Narathiwat

♦ Bus : Services 29, 59 and 95 (non-air conditioned) or 4, 10, 13 and 29 (air-conditioned, 100 baht). A list of the buses and the hotels they call at is available from the Tourism Authority of Thailand (TAT) at the airport.

♦ Train : You can take the train from Don Muang Airport to Bangkok (45 minutes), costing 10 baht to 100 baht, depending on class of train.
By train :
There is an extensive train network within Thailand and

international services link Thailand with

Singapore and Malaysia.

By boat :
Some cargo boats with passenger cabins travel between Thailand, the United States and Europe. Cruise liners stop at Pattaya, while some charter boats depart from ports on the coast of the Malaysian peninsula.

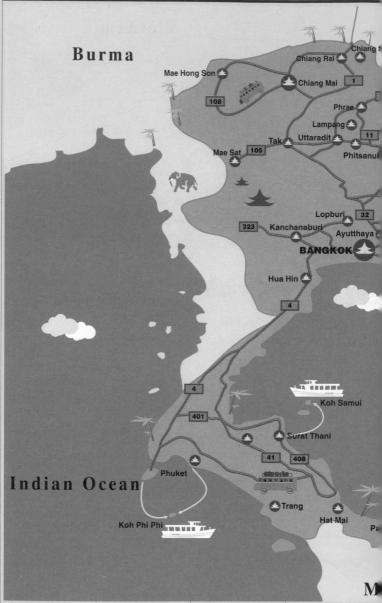

Burma

Mae Hong Son

Chiang Rai
Chiang

Chiang Mai

108

1

Phrae

Lampang

11

Tak   Uttaradit

Mae Sat   105

Phitsanul

Lopburi   32

323   Kanchanaburi

Ayutthaya

BANGKOK

Hua Hin

4

Indian Ocean

4

Koh Samui

401

Surat Thani

41   408

Phuket

Trang

Koh Phi Phi

Hat Mai

P

M

BY CAR :
This is undoubtedly the most pleasant way of exploring a region, especially the North. Car rental, with or without driver, is very common in Thailand. You must have an international driving license. Cars can be rented from companies such as Avis or Hertz. Rates include insurance but the deposit is usually very high.

BY BUS :
An efficient means of transport. The national Thai bus company has regular connections to all cities and towns in the country, covering

over 100 routes. Private bus companies operate air-conditioned tour buses, which are more comfortable but also more expensive.

BY TRAIN:
Thai trains are comfortable and safe, even if they are packed, and fares are

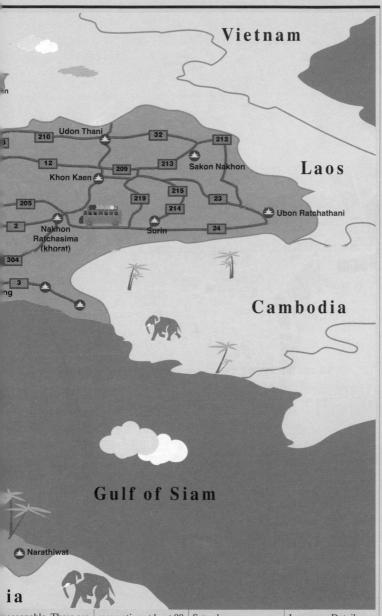

Vietnam

Laos

Cambodia

Gulf of Siam

210 Udon Thani 32 212

12 209 213 Sakon Nakhon

Khon Kaen

205 219 215

2 Nakhon 214 23

Ratchasima Surin 24

(khorat) Ubon Ratchathani

304

3

Narathiwat

ia

easonable. There are
three kinds of train
international
express, express and
tandard), and four
lasses. Choose
express over standard
trains, which often
top to let other
rains by. To be sure
of a seat make a

reservation at least 90
days in advance. Train
timetables can be
obtained from the
main station in
Bangkok
(tel. 223 70 10 or
223 70 20). There is
normally one fixed
rate for one-day
journeys, on

Saturdays,
Wednesdays and
holidays, and a Rail
Pass costing 1,000
baht or 2,000 baht
will allow you to
travel 2nd and 3rd
class for 20 days;
apply to the Advance
Booking Office in
Bangkok Hua

Lampong. Details are
easily obtainable from
most large stations.

BY BOAT:
Express boats ply the
Chao Phraya from
6 am to 6.30pm and
ferries make river
crossings between
6am and midnight.

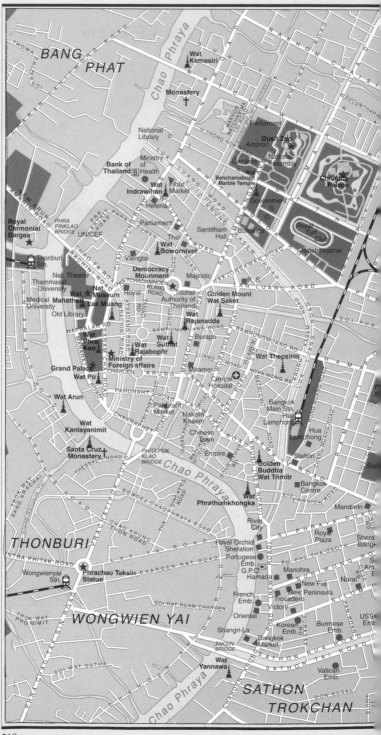

BY BOAT. "Long-tail" and motor boats are available if you want to slice along the klongs (board at the Hotel Oriental or under Memorial Bridge; fixed price about 15 baht). You can also take an omnibus launch from Chao Phraya River Express; they run every day from 6 am to 6 pm. For the modest sum of 1 or 2 baht, passing boats will take you down the Thonburi from under any of the five bridges.

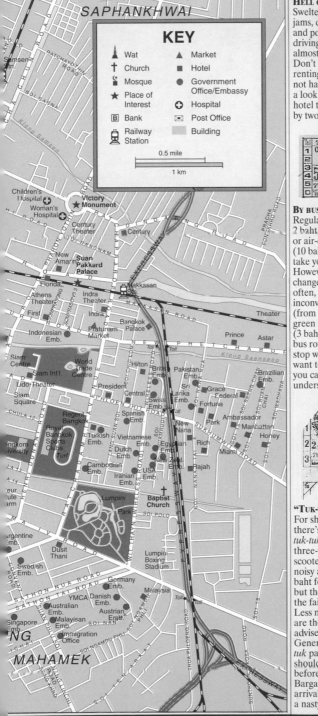

KEY

卍	Wat	▲	Market
✝	Church	■	Hotel
☪	Mosque	●	Government Office/Embassy
★	Place of Interest	✛	Hospital
Ⓑ	Bank	⌧	Post Office
🚉	Railway Station		Building

0.5 mile

1 km

HELL ON EARTH

Sweltering traffic jams, deluges of rain, and pollution make driving in Bangkok almost impossible. Don't even think of renting a car. Taxis do not have meters. Take a look at the tariffs of hotel taxis and divide by two.

BY BUS

Regular (blue – 2 baht, red 3 baht), or air-conditioned (10 baht) buses will take you everywhere. However, you have to change buses quite often, which can be inconvenient. *Songteo* (from 3 to 5 baht) and green minibuses (3 baht) follow the bus routes. They will stop wherever you want to – that is, if you can make yourself understood.

"TUK-TUK"

For short distances, there's the famous *tuk-tuk*, a sort of three-wheeled motor scooter-cum-taxi, noisy and cheap (25 baht for a short ride) but they are not for the faint-hearted. Less nerve-wracking are the taxi-bikes (not advised at night). General rules for *tuk-tuk* passengers: fares should be negotiated before setting out. Bargaining upon arrival could result in a nasty confrontation!

OUTSIDE BANGKOK
Although Chiang Mai
is Thailand's second
city ▲ 260–71, it
remains a simple
provincial town and is
primarily departure
point for visitors
setting out to explore
the North. In spite of
the influx of tourists,
the town is still
extremely peaceful
and best explored on
foot. To get about the
streets you can also
rent a bicycle at 100
baht a day or a
moped at 300 baht a
day. You must
produce some form of
identification and
make a deposit in
addition to the rental
when registering.
Although motorized
tuk-tuks have
appeared recently,
Chiang Mai's *samlo*
are still powered by
bicycles. The road
leading to Doi Suthep
▲ 272 is long and
steep. To get there,
you can rent a car or
catch a taxi, or take
one of the many
songteo that criss-
cross the town. These
are canvas-covered
vans with a twin seat
in back. For long
trips, negotiate the
price in advance. To
avoid making a return
trip without a fare,
the enterprising
driver will suggest
waiting for you and
charge you for it.

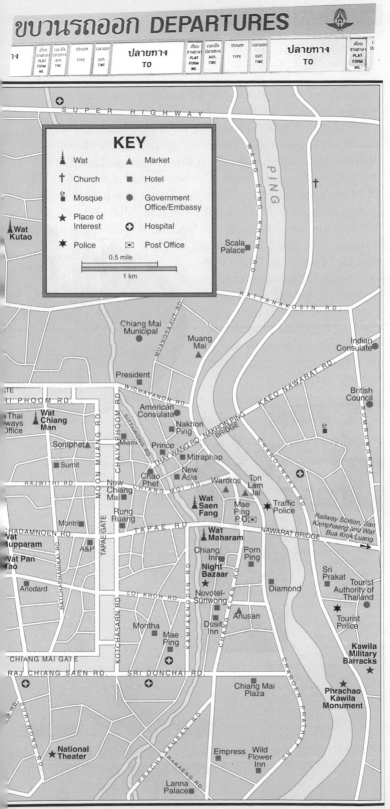

	เวลาถึง	ประเภท	เวลาออก	ปลายทาง	เที่ยว	เวลาถึง	ประเภท	เวลาออก	ปลายทาง	เที่ยว
	ช่องชานชาลา PLAT FORM NO.	TYPE	DEP. TIME	TO	ช่องชานชาลา PLAT FORM NO.	ARR. TIME	ประเภท PLAT FORM NO.	DEP. TIME	TO	ช่อ

KEY

- 🛕 Wat
- ✝ Church
- ☪ Mosque
- ★ Place of Interest
- ✹ Police
- ▲ Market
- ■ Hotel
- ● Government Office/Embassy
- ✛ Hospital
- ⌧ Post Office

0.5 mile
1 km

SUPER HIGHWAY

WANG SING KHAM RD.

PING

Wat Kutao

Scala Palace

RATTANAKOSIN RD.

Chiang Mai Municipal

Muang Mai

Indian Consulate

President

WICHAYANON RD.

KAEO NAWARAT RD.

British Council

SI PHOOM RD.

Thai ways Office

Wat Chiang Man

American Consulate

Nakhon Ping

NAKHON PING BRIDGE

BUMRUNGRAJ RD.

Somphet

Miami

Prince

THAI WANG RD.

NAKHON PING

Sumit

SUTHEP RD.

CHAIYAPHOOM RD.

Mitraphap

New Asia

Waroros

CHAROENRAT RD.

RAJWITHI RD.

Chao Phet

CHIANG MOI RD.

Ton Lam Jai

New Chiang Mai

MOON MUANG RD.

Wat Saen Fang

Mae Ping P.O.⌧

Traffic Police

Railway Station, San Kamphaeng and Wat Bua Krok Luang →

Montri

Rung Ruang

TAPAE GATE

TAPAE RD.

Wat Maharam

NAWARAT BRIDGE

HADAMNOEN RD.

Wat Supparam

A&P

BATCHAPHANIKAT RD.

Chiang Inn

Porn Ping

Sri Prakat

Tourist Authority of Thailand

Wat Pan Tao

Night Bazaar

KAMPAENGDIN RD.

Anodard

LOI KROH RD.

Novotel-Suriwong

Diamond

Tourist Police

Montha

Mae Ping

KOTCHASARN RD.

Dusit Inn

Anusan

Kawila Military Barracks

CHIANG MAI GATE

RAJ CHIANG SAEN RD.

SRI DONCHAI RD.

Chiang Mai Plaza

Phrachao Kawila Monument

SURIWONG RD.

CHAROEN PRATHET RD.

National Theater

PRACHASAMPAN RD.

PRACHARAKAENG RD.

Empress

Wild Flower Inn

Lanna Palace

313

A tropical country situated in the heart of Southeast Asia, halfway between India and China, Thailand covers some 198,400 square miles. The country is divided into four regions: the mountainous north; the fertile central plains; the semi-arid northeastern plateau; and the southern peninsula, with its myriad beaches and islands. The population is about 55 million, of whom 6 million live in Bangkok. Other important ethnic groups beside the Thais include: Chinese, Malays, Laotians, Khmers, Indians and Burmese. Buddhism is the national religion and is practiced by 95 percent of all Thais. Close to 80 percent of the population relies on agriculture, fishing or forest exploitation. Rice is the main cultivated crop and the number-one export, followed by maize, jute, manioc, rubber, teak and coconut milk.

CUSTOMS

Remember to take your shoes off when you enter a temple or private dwelling. Buddhist monks must be shown respect: women are not allowed into their quarters nor permitted to pass anything to them hand to hand. Almost every garden contains a miniature house where the spirit of that place lives. The human inhabitants come to leave food, fresh flowers and incense sticks there.

HAWKERS

The hawkers set up along the pavement offer a wide range of *khanom* (sweetmeats), which they prepare. They use very simple equipment (charcoal burner and miniature pots and pans). But watch out! Thai food is very spicy. A typical meal consists of four or five dishes served with rice (beef, chicken, shrimp, fish soup, etc.), followed by a dessert of fruit. Thais love sweets and coconut milk form the basis of most desserts. You can get an introduction to Thai food by joining a cooking class at the Oriental Hotel or the UFM Food Center at 593 Sukhumwit 33/1.

คลินิกบ้านคุณหมอ
CLINIC ✚

โค้ก

ถนนท้ายวัง
THANON THAI WANG

← ทางไปสุขา ←
TOILET

โฟนพ้อยต์
FONEPOINT

ROAD CONGESTION

Today about 90 percent of vehicles are registered in Bangkok and the average speed in town has fallen to 5 mph. The thousands of backfiring, three-wheel motorbikes, *tuk-tuk*, are the only remaining fast and economical means of transport, if, that is, you know how to negotiate a price for the ride.

STREET SIGNS

Along the *thanon* (avenues or major roads) and the *soi* (minor roads), the blue road signs are in Thai and English.

You can't drink the tap water in Bangkok, and it's not even recommended that you brush your teeth in it, so stick to mineral water.

SHOPPING

Arts and crafts can be bought all over Thailand, but Chiang Mai offers the greatest choice. There you will be tempted by fabrics, jewels, statuettes, dolls in traditional costumes, musical instruments, masks, painted parasols and silks. The latter are handwoven and sold by the yard, plain or in monochrome colors. Thai silk is renowned as being the best in the world. Bangkok is also a paradise for antique collectors: porcelain, Chinese furniture, sculpture, carpets and the like. Many vendors undertake buying trips throughout the world, or almost. The major stores open at 10am and close from 6.30pm onwards.

EXOTIC FRUIT
On the street, the fresh-fruit stalls are a delight. They sell some of the tastiest fruit in all of Southeast Asia: mangoes, rambutans, papayas, lychees, durians…

MARKETS
At the famous Weekend Market in Bangkok, you will find anything and everything, and bargaining is always possible and, in fact, highly recommended.

CONSUMER GOODS AND SERVICES

BUS 6 BAHT	CULTURAL SHOW 350–750 BAHT	HOTEL ROOM 500–4 000 BAHT
		FRUIT 5 BAHT A BUNCH
		MEAL 3–400 BAHT
TAXI 150 BAHT	ENTRY TO MUSEUM… 10–100 BAHT	BEER 35–50 BAHT

Thailand has a first-rate hotel system, ranging from 5-star establishments to very simple pensions. Fluctuating exchange rates preclude quoting exact prices here. In Bangkok, most hotels are located near the tourist districts. Rooms are usually air-conditioned, with a double room plus breakfast costing a minimum US$25 in Bangkok and US$18 outside the capital.

BANKS

All banks are open throughout the country from 8.30am to 3.30pm, Mondays to Fridays, except public holidays.

POST

The main post office in New Road in Bangkok is open from 7.30am to 4.30pm, Monday to Friday, and from 9am to 12 noon, weekends and public holidays. Outside the capital, post offices close at 4pm There is a central *poste restante* service at the main post office in Bangkok (1 baht per letter), and most hotels have excellent postal facilities.

MONEY

The Thai monetary unit is the baht, divided into 100 satang. There are two copper coins (20 satang and 50 satang), three silver coins (1 baht, 2 baht and 5 baht), and a 10-baht piece, which is silver around the edge and copper in the middle. Notes come in 10, 20, 50, 100 and 500 baht denominations.

EXCHANGE RATE

The baht is linked to the US dollar. Travelers' checks (in US$ and other currencies) are accepted at all banks and official moneychangers. The exchange rate for cash is best in Bangkok, but travelers' check rates are fixed.

1 baht

10 baht

5 baht

NEWSPAPERS

The three main English-language dailies are the *Bangkok Post*, *The Nation* and *Bangkok World*. The *International Herald Tribune* can also be found, as can other major international newspapers, in some hotels and larger bookshops. The Tourism Authority of Thailand also produces a free, English-language weekly called *Where*. It is distributed to hotels.

TELEGRAMS

Numerous post offices offer telegram, telex and fax services. You can also send telexes and faxes from the major hotels.

Phone card.

TELEPHONE

You can telephone from hotels or private booths, but is is easier and less expensive to use the Overseas Telephone Service at post offices. To make a national call, simply dial the regional code; for international calls, dial 100, followed by the number.

TELEPHONE CODES

Ayutthaya	035	Mae Hong Son	053
Bangkok	02	Nakhon Ratchasima	044
Chiang Mai	053	Nakhon Si Thammarat	075
Chiang Rai	053	Pattaya	038
Hua Hin	032	Phangnga	076
Kanchanaburi	034	Phitsanulok	055
Koh Phi Phi	076	Phuket	076
Koh Samui	077	Sukhothai	055
Krabi	075	Surat Thani	077

THE COST OF A THREE-MINUTE CALL

BANGKOK	7am to 6pm	6pm to 10pm	10pm to 7am		
	18 baht	9 baht	6 baht		WITHIN THAILAND
	6 baht	3 baht	2 baht		AROUND BANGKOK

BANGKOK	7am to 9pm	9am to midnight	Midnight to 5am	Operator assisted	
	70 baht	56 baht	49 baht	63 baht	EUROPE
	50 baht	40 baht	35 baht	50 baht	JAPAN

Constantly in search of some *sanuk* (fun), the Thais seize every opportunity to organize celebrations and these become major attractions for tourists and holiday-seekers. The Thai calendar is punctuated with numerous holidays, sporting events, and religious ceremonies. Some of the holidays are also linked to the lunar calendar, which is why the Tourism Authority of Thailand publishes annually a revised list of festivals celebrated throughout the country. Although Thailand officially follows the Western calendar, it still counts the years according to the Buddhist era, which started in 543 BC.

HOLIDAYS AND FESTIVALS

	JANUARY	FEBRUARY	MARCH	APRIL	MAY	JUNE	JULY	AUGUST	SEPTEMBER	OCTOBER	NOVEMBER	DECEMBER
MAGHA PUJA		•										
FLOWER FESTIVAL		•										
PATTAYA FESTIVAL				•								
SONGKRAN FESTIVAL				13-15								
LABOR DAY					•							
ROCKET FESTIVAL					•							
VISAKHA PUJA					•							
HER MAJESTY THE QUEEN'S BIRTHDAY								12				
OK PHANSA AND THOT KATHIN										•		
CANOE RACES										•		
LOI KRATHONG											•	
ELEPHANT RALLY IN SURIN											•	
BRIDGE ON THE RIVER KWAI WEEK											•	
HIS MAJESTY THE KING'S BIRTHDAY												5

MAGHA PUJA (February full moon): During this festival Thais perform deeds that earn them merit – making offerings to Buddhist monks, freeing caged birds, etc. Thousands of devotees bearing candles and flowers come along to attend temple sermons and follow the rituals conducted by priests.

SONGKRAN (April 13–15): Thai New Year. Mainly a celebration of water and purification. Especially joyful at Chiang Mai, where the locals splash each other with water on the streets.

ROCKET FESTIVAL (second week in May): Held in Yasothon (Northeast), before the monsoon. Giant rockets are made and launched to encourage an abundant harvest for the farmers.

QUEEN'S BIRTHDAY (August 12): Celebrations includes the illumination of major national monuments.

OK PHANSA AND THOT KATHIN (October): End of the Buddhist fasting period and start of Kathin. The faithful offer robes, alms and other essentials to Buddhist monks.

CANOE RACES (October): The most famous take place at Nan, 490 miles north of Bangkok.

LOI KRATHONG (November): The most beautiful celebration of the year. Thais release small, lotus-shaped rafts onto streams and rivers. The rafts carry flowers, joss sticks and lit candles in honor of the water spirits and symbolizing the purification of sins committed during the previous year.

BANGKOK, CHIANG MAI, PHUKET : AVERAGE TEMPERATURES

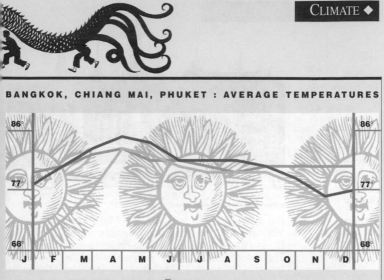

THE SEASONS

Thailand is a tropical country with only three seasons: summer (March to May); the rainy but also very sunny period (June to October); and the cool season (November to February). The average temperature throughout the year is 80°F. In Bangkok, the temperature ranges from 60°F in December to almost 100°F in April and May.

RAINFALL IN BANGKOK, CHIANG MAI AND PHUKET (BANDON)

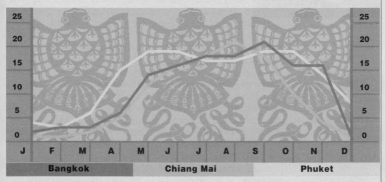

Bangkok   Chiang Mai   Phuket

THE MONSOON

The monsoon season brings five months of unpredictable weather: some days you are caught by sudden storms, followed on others by brilliant sunshine. In the North, between November and February, temperatures can fall to 46°F overnight, so you will have to wear warm clothes during the cool season.

HUMIDITY LEVEL FOR BANGKOK, CHIANG MAI AND PHUKET

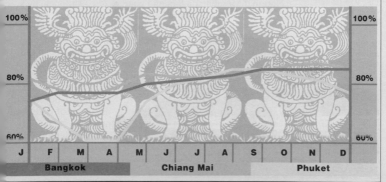

Bangkok   Chiang Mai   Phuket

319

NOSTALGIC BANGKOK

THE SACRED WALL COMPOUND
Wat Phra Keo ▲ 148, within the walls of the Grand Palace, is open from 8.30am to noon and from 1pm to 4pm. The staff take a lunch break, but you don't have to leave the premises. Decorum is advised in the matter of dress: you can always hire a long skirt or trousers on the spot.

JIM THOMPSON'S HOUSE
Open to the public Monday to Friday from 9am to 4.30pm, it houses the superb collection of Thai and Burmese art collected by the American Thai silk magnate between 1950 and 1960 ▲ 182.

DAY 1. Why not start with the klongs? Take your time visiting Wat Arun ▲ 170 and the Royal Barge Museum ▲ 174. Then cross to the east bank of the Chao Phraya to look around Jim Thompson's house ▲ 182 or the Suan Pakkad Palace ▲ 182 (it is possible to combine both visits on the same day if the traffic is flowing smoothly). Depending on your mood, you can have a snack lunch in one of the small restaurants in Pratunam or you can try *ho muk pla* (steamed fish) in an old renovated spice warehouse in the Spice Market. Then you can choose between tea in the Authors' Lounge of the Oriental Hotel or classical ballet at the National Theater (performances begin at 5.30pm) ▲ 163. To end the first day in style, dine at the Bussaracum, the restaurant attached to a school specializing in royal Thai cuisine.

DAY 2. Get up early to go to the Damnern Saduak floating market ▲ 186 (a 2-hour trip), which is only held during the morning. Another option is a romantic cruise to the ancient capital of Ayutthaya ▲ 242 (return by road) with lunch at a small floating restaurant near the Pridi Damrong bridge, which leads to the city. After a tiring morning trip, the afternoon could be spent browsing in the antique shops in New Road and the River City Centre. In the evening, relax and enjoy a cocktail on the terrace of the Oriental Hotel, overlooking the Chao Phraya, before dinner at the Sala Rimnan restaurant in the hotel, or at the Salathip, the restaurant in the Shangri-La Hotel, with its sumptuous decor of teak and silk, overlooking the river.

DAY 3. The Marble Temple (Wat Benchamabopit ▲ 179) is a peaceful and elegant place to visit, as is the Vimarn Mek Palace ▲ 179, the former house of Rama V, which has been converted into a small museum, which richly illustrates daily life at court. Another option is to spend the morning in the National Museum, on Sanam Luang ▲ 156. For lunch, make your way toward the river (there are pleasant restaurants along both sides of the Krung Thon bridge) or go to Ratchadamnoen Road. Spend the afternoon wandering around within the 20-acre walled compound of Wat Po ▲ 152, a real monastic city, with its school of traditional massage. In the evening, sample *tom yam koung*, a spicy shrimp soup flavored with lemon grass.

THONBURI
There are two ways of exploring the klongs: take a water-bus (from the foot of the Memorial Bridge) on a regular route or rent an individual *hangyao*.

FRENETIC BANGKOK

DAY 1. Early birds can go to Lumpini Park ▲ *181* to see Chinese performing *tai-chi* exercises. To join in, simply choose a group and copy the movements of the leader. Take a morning stroll near the temples and you will see the Buddhist monks pass their bowls around ● *46*. The Grand Palace opens at 8.30am: arrive early for your first sight of the exuberance of Rattanakosin architecture ▲ *92–3*. The National Museum ▲ *156–61* is not far away and you can choose to look around just a few rooms: palanquins, arms, costumes… From there, in a cloud of smoke, a *tuk-tuk* will take you to the heart of Chinatown, through the small crowded streets of the "thieves' market" ▲ *176*. After browsing round the stalls in this congested labyrinth swarming with vendors and customers, take a break in one of the restaurants in the area or sit on a bench, between two stalls, and in Thai style quickly drink a bowl of *saen lek nam*, a rice noodle soup sprinkled with ground chilli. To get away from the crowd, you can go admire the panorama from the top of the Golden Mount ▲ *164*, where the gilt chedi houses a relic of the Buddha. Another *tuk-tuk* will take you finally to the giant shopping centers so popular with young Thais ▲ *185*, Mahboon Krong (Phyathai Road) for example. Dine at Tum Nak Thai, the largest open-air restaurant in the world, where the waiters get around on roller skates.

DAY 2. Visit the Pak Nam crocodile farm (19 miles from Bangkok) ▲ *191* where crocodile-taming shows are held. For an original gastronomic experience, try crocodile meat in sauce in the restaurant at the complex. On your return in the afternoon, wander around Pratunam market ▲ *184* and say your prayers at the Erawan Shrine, with its semi-permanent classical Thai dance performances ▲ *181*. If you feel like shopping, take a look at the marvels of Thai handicraft at Narayanaphand (275/2 Larn Luang) or the clothing and luggage in the shopping gallery at the Indra Hotel (Rajprarob Road). End the day with dinner at the Sea Food Market, where you can choose from a wide range of fish, shellfish and seafood before handing them to the chef who prepares them to your taste right in front of you. You may also opt for the tense atmosphere of a Thai boxing match in one of the big stadiums in Bangkok, Lumpini or Rajdamnoen.

DAY 3. There is nothing like an excursion on the klongs to wake you up in the morning: your pilot will be only too pleased to give a demonstration of speed. After a brief stop at Wat Arun ▲ *170*, you can then explore the network of Thonburi canals. On your return trip to Bangkok, have lunch at Silom Village, where a number of beautiful boutiques display Thai goods. At Wat Traimit ▲ *177*, near the Odeon cinema (in Chinatown), you will come across a golden Buddha weighing a full 5 tons. When the night markets begin to light up in the streets, leave your hotel room and go have a drink at Bobby's Arms (Patpong 2) or at the famous go-go bar, the King's Castle, before facing the swirling lasers of a giant disco (Nasa Spacedrome) or going on to Superstar (Patpong 1) to listen to Thai rock music.

ROYAL CRUISE
Sail along the river of the kings from Bangkok to Ayutthaya on board the *Mekhala*, an old rice barge fitted out as a cruise liner. At

night, the *Mekhala* moors alongside the pontoon of a temple in the countryside. The cabins are fitted out in polished teak and a candlelit dinner is served. For information, consult a travel agent.

THE SILK ROUTE
In Silom Road, be tempted by the silk on offer at Anita's, Choisy's or Jim Thompson Silk Co.

THE SUAN PAKKARD PALACE

THE FLOATING MARKET
Bangkok owes its name "the Venice of the Orient" to its network of canals and floating markets. There are flower-

sellers and traders selling exotic fruits in abundance. But the authorities are tending more and more to fill in the klongs and convert them into streets. Traditional floating markets can hardly be found anymore except on the outskirts of town.

POTTERY
Pottery in Thailand is a tradition that goes back for centuries. During the mid-1960's, in Ban Chiang, in the northeast of the province of Udon Thani, pottery fragments led to the discovery of a civilization 3,000 years old, which cultivated rice, reared animals and practiced weaving. Some pottery is now exhibited at the Suan Pakkad Palace.

DAY 1. If you are staying in one of the hotels of Bangkok along the banks of the Chao Phraya, such as the Oriental, the Menam, the Royal Garden Riverside, the Shangri-La or the Royal Orchid Sheraton, take a water-taxi to reach the old town. Spend your first morning in Bangkok visiting the Grand Palace ▲ 144, Wat Po ▲ 152 and the National Museum ▲ 156-61. In the afternoon, take a water-taxi to the Royal Barge Museum at the mouth of the Bangkok Noi klong, then take a trip on the Thonburi klongs.

DAY 2. In the morning, visit Wat Benchamabopit (better known as the Marble Temple) and Jim Thompson's house ▲ 182. Buy some antiques at the River City Shopping Centre, precious stones and jewelry along Silom Road and handicrafts at Silom Village (286/1 Silom Road). For dinner with a Thai dancing show, go to Sala Rim Nam, opposite the Oriental Hotel, on the other side of the river.

DAY 3. Go to Damnern Saduak ▲ 186, in the province of Ratchaburi, two hours by road to the south of Bangkok. A lively and colorful floating market is held every morning from 8am to 10am. From there, proceed to Nakhon Pathom ▲ 186 to visit the Phra Pathom Chedi, the tallest Buddhist pagoda in the world. You could have lunch in one of the restaurants in the Rose Garden, in Samphran, on the main road back to Bangkok. The Rose Garden puts on displays of traditional dancing, Thai boxing and elephant training every afternoon from 3pm.

DAY 4. Take a plane to Chiang Mai ▲ 260–71. The flight takes about one hour. Spend your day exploring the main Buddhist temples in the town: Wat Phra Singh, Wat Chedi Luang, Wat Pan Tao and Wat Chiang Man. After dinner, go to the night market (6 pm to 11 pm) located in the center of Chiang Mai, on Chang Klan Road, where a wide variety of handicrafts can be found: wooden sculptures, lacquerware, fabrics, jewelry as well as embroidery stitched by the northern tribes.

DAY 5. In the morning, go by bus to Doi Suthep ▲ 272, the hill overlooking Chiang Mai. Wat Phra That Doi Suthep occupies the summit of the hill and the view from the Wat over the valley is superb. Outside Royal Family holiday periods, you can visit the gardens of Phuping Palace, behind the temple. In the afternoon, go back up the Mae Sa Valley, to the north. On your route, you will find orchid farms, an elephant-training center, many rest areas in the midst of vast gardens, and restaurants.

DAY 6. Take a day to explore Lampang ▲ 276–81 and its environs, to the south of Chiang Mai. Stroll around its old market and take a drive along the river in a horse-drawn carriage. Visit Wat Phra Keo Don Tao, where Thai and Burmese architectural influences intermingle.

After lunching in one of the restaurants on the banks of the river, move on to Wat Phra That Lampang Luang, located 12.5 miles to the south, which is one of the most beautiful temples in Thailand.

DAY 7. Take a direct flight (2 hours) from Chiang Mai to Phuket ▲ *210–17*, in the south of Thailand. The many beaches on the west coast of the island, separated by limestone cliffs, offer a wide variety of scenery. Patong has plenty of shops and a lively nightlife; Pan Sea, Kata and Nai Han ▲ *215* are much quieter.

DAY 8.. To explore Phangnga Bay ▲ *218–9* rent a boat in Phuket. This way, you can explore the islands of limestone rock rising straight out of the sea, some with small sandy beaches. For lunch, stop at Koh Pannyi, where you can enjoy fish and shellfish at the little Muslim village. Then you can make your way to the south of the bay to the far-out Phi Phi islands. Phi Phi Don has many beauty spots, suitable for bathing and diving, and has a superb view of Phi Phi Le. The latter island is a tourist attraction, and is known for its haunting caves, in which colonies of swifts build their nests.

DAY 9. The island has other interesting features: the town of Phuket ▲ *212*, the capital and business center of the province, has a market on Rasada Street and the main fishing port in the bay. For lunch in Phuket Town, choose a restaurant at the top of Khao Rung hill, where the view is superb. In the south of the island, on the small bay of Chalong ▲ *212*, visit the aquarium of the Marine Biology Research Center. Not far away is Wat Chalong, the largest Buddhist temple on the island. Khao Phra National Park is located 12½ miles to the north of Phuket Town.

DAY 10. After returning to Bangkok by air, take a look around one of the city's markets ▲ *184*: the big Weekend Market, where absolutely everything made in Thailand can be found, is held in Chatuchak Park; Pratunam market specializes in ready-to-wear clothing; and Sampeng market, in the heart of Chinatown, offers a wide choice of cooking utensils and household goods, as well as traditional medicines and gold jewelry.

THE ORCHID
This flower is treated with reverence in Thailand because of its beneficial powers. It plays a major role in the preparation of offerings that Thais place at temples. Often, garlands made up of jasmin, roses and orchids are offered for sale in the form of a good-luck-charm necklace.

A richly decorated door on one of the Chinese houses in Phuket. The variety of motifs and inlaid work shows various European, Chinese and Thai influences.

THE OLD CITIES OF SIAM ROUTE

WAT CHETUPON
This Sukhothai temple is famous for the standing Buddha that decorates its *mondop* ▲ *254*.

THE CAPITALS OF SIAM. At the Tha Thien landing stage, in Bangkok, take a boat that slowly makes its way up the Chao Phraya River as far as AYUTTHAYA, the lake city of 33 kings ▲ *242*, (53 miles north). Spend the night at the comfortable U-Thong Inn, which offers a magnificent panoramic view of the town. LOPBURI ▲ *248*, the next stop, is only 43 miles away. You can rent a *samlo* or tuk-tuk (a three-wheel taxi) to go on

a tour of the town. Beware of the monkeys, which will probably pester you as you make your way around the ruins. The next day, cross Thailand's rice-producing region by train – a slow but relaxing journey – to reach PHITSANULOK ▲ *258* (137 miles to the north). It is a good idea to stop over in SUKHOTHAI ▲ *252* (31 miles northeast of Phitsanulok). Spend the night at the Chinnawat, a fairly simple but well located hotel, before branching out to visit the other two major sites of the region: Kamphaeng Phet (50 miles southwest) and Si Satchanalai (36 miles north). The ancient city of KAMPHAENG PHET ▲ *250* merits a lengthy stop. The ruins cover 41 square miles, so you will need time to cover them all. Take in the bronze and porcelain collections that are to be found in the National Museum and arrange to visit Wat Chang Rop, with its 68 caryatid elephants, in the cooler hours of the day. Spending the night there is no problem (the town has several comfortable hotels). Then return to Sukhothai and visit SI SATCHANALAI ▲ *256*, the second city, now abandoned, in the kingdom of Sukhothai, on the banks of the Yom. You could add a touch of spice to your visit by renting an elephant in Ban Pa Kluay (mahouts are included).

WAT PHRA SI RATANA MAHATHAT
This Chalieng temple ▲ *257* (below) is a classic example of the Sukhothai style .

WAT CHEDI CHET THAEW
This temple at Si Satchanalai ▲ *256* (bottom) is named for the seven rows of chedi which are said to contain the ashes of the viceroys of Sukhothai.

THE ANCIENT KINGDOMS OF LANNA. Leave the ancient capitals of Siam to their melancholy solitude and head for the brilliant and secluded kingdoms of Lanna. Unlike the rice-growing plains that stretch away to the sea, the north was for a long time a closed world. LAMPANG ▲ *276*, as you might expect, still has the charming air of a bygone age, with its old-world carriages and glorious temples, such as Wat Phra Keo Don Tao ▲ *278*. LAMPANG LUANG ▲ *282–3* (12.5 miles to the south) exemplifies the 16th-century-period Lanna style of architecture ● *94* in all its splendor. LAMPHUN ▲ *274* already feels like a suburb of Chiang Mai, which lies just 16 miles away. Do not miss Wat Phra That Haripunchai, one of the oldest temples in northern Thailand. Built in 1044 by the Mon king Athitayaraj, it houses an enormous gong,

supposedly the biggest in the world. CHIANG MAI ▲ *260* is the last stop on the old cities of Siam route. The northern capital cannot be appreciated in a hurry. Whether by trishaw or bicycle, try to move at a leisurely pace from one temple to the next. After that, and on a more adventurous note, you may decide to visit the heart of the Golden Triangle ▲ *302* or the jungles of Myanmar (Burma).

THE GROWTH OF THE KHMER EMPIRE

The road from Bangkok to NAKHON RATCHASIMA ▲ *230* (165 miles to the east of the capital) is dull, so take the train or hire a car. Nakhon Ratchasima (formerly known as Korat) is the doorway to the chedis (Prasat Hin) of the Khmer Empire. This town is convenient as a base for exploring the various archeological sites in this area. Visit the serene PRASAT PHANOM WAN ▲ *231*, which lies about 10 miles to the northeast of Nakhon Ratchasima, then take in the scope and majesty of the region's main attraction, PHIMAI ▲ *232*, which is referred to as "the Angkor Wat of Thailand." This beautiful temple was originally erected at the beginning of the 12th century. It has now been painstakingly restored. Take time to explore the site and to fit in a visit to its branch of the National Museum, fitted out in rustic style. A full day is needed to visit the two temples of Phanom Rung and Muang Tham (62 miles east of Nakhon Ratchasima). PRASAT PHANOM RUNG ▲ *234*, is dated at between the 10th and 13th centuries. It is exceptionally beautiful, and ascending its majestic staircase guarded by stone *naga* is an unforgettably moving experience. From the terrace of the temple, you will have a clear view of the setting sun if you time your visit appropriately. The following day, visit PRASAT MUANG THAM ▲ *234*, just a few miles away, which can offer interesting bas-reliefs and lintels. Start early and you may also have time to reach BAN PHLUANG ▲ *235*, quite close to the Cambodian border, where there is a small, carefully-restored Khmer temple. You could spend the night at SURIN ▲ *229*. In SIKHORAPHUM (19 miles from Surin), Wat Ra Ngeng is also worth a visit ▲ *235*. Continue on into the province of SISAKET ▲ *234* and take Route 221, which will take you as far as the Cambodian border (about 62 miles away). On a spur in the Dongrek mountain range you will find PRASAT KHAO PHRA VIHARN ▲ *234*, one of the most important Khmer sites. This temple actually stands on Cambodian territory, but it was recently reopened to visitors arriving from Thailand. You can easily spend several hours there, exploring the extensive ruins and taking in the beauty of the surrounding countryside. From Prasat Khao Phra Viharn, it is an easy ride to UBON RATCHATHANI ▲ *234*, which is the last Thai town before the Laotian border, from where you can organize the rest of your trip. An extended tour through Isan and along the banks of the majestic Mekong River are two possibilities to consider.

PRASAT PHANOM RUNG
Constructed at the top of an extinct volcano and consecrated to the Hindu god Siva, this "stone castle" would have been one of the important stopping places on the Angkor-Phimai route.

The main sanctuary of Prasat Hin Phimai.

HENRI MOUHOT ON PHANOM WAN
❝When you reach the summit, you would think you were in the middle of the ruins of Angkor Wat: the same architecture; the same art, the same taste which governed the construction of both sites. Here, as there, are the immense blocks, polished like marble, joined together as if they had been cemented... Bars, roofs, the whole building is a Khmer work of art and not an imitation, dating back to the illustrious reigns which left traces of their grandeur at various points throughout the empire.❞

UMBRELLAS
The umbrellas of Bor
Sang consist of a
wooden frame and
bamboo ribs over
which cotton, silk or
brown paper made
with bark from local
mulberry trees is
stretched.

CHIANG MAI AND THE NORTH

THE HANDICRAFT ROUTE. The road linking Chiang Mai with San Kamphaeng is lined with an uninterrupted succession of boutiques and specialist workshops ▲ 270. In BAN MUANG KUNG (in Hang Dong) the type of earthenware jars used by villagers for storing water has been produced for centuries. In BAN THARAM (on the Mae Hong Son road), you can watch the delicate and complex workmanship involved in producing lacquerware. Silks and cottons from SAN KHAMPHAENG or PASANG (to the south of Chiang Mai ▲ 271) also feature among the craft traditions of the region, as does pottery, which is a specialty of LAMPANG ▲ 276, where several hundred workshops have been set up. CHIANG RAI ▲ 292, well known for the gold and silver work of the tribes from the Golden Triangle ▲ 302, is also the center of a flourishing business in precious and semi-precious stones (diamonds, rubies and sapphires). On the borders of this creative northern region, SUKHOTHAI ▲ 252 and BAN HAT SIO produce garments of hand-woven silk.

BEAUTY QUEENS. Dinner *khantoke*-style is a unique experience: seated on the floor, you will enjoy *saukrok* (sausages) and *pikkaoyang* (chicken wings), accompanied by glutinous rice, served on a small low table made of rattan or lacquered wood. The north is famous for its festivities: agricultural fairs and religious ceremonies are just as much occasions to pick beauty queens as to bring out decorated floats and honor the temples and priests. Note these festivals: Flowers in Chiang Mai, Umbrellas in Bor Sang ▲ 265 (February), Lychees in Chiang Rai (May), Longans in Lamphun (August), Luang Wiang Lakhon in Lampang ▲ 278 (February), Songkran in Chiang Mai ▲ 265 (April), and Poi Sang Long in Mae Hong Son ▲ 288 (April).

THE EAST AND NORTHEAST

SILK AND SAPPHIRES. Isan also has its riches: silk and gems. Follow the precious-stones road as far as Chantaburi ▲ 192, which is surrounded by sapphire mines. By following the course of the Mun toward Nakhon Ratchasima ▲ 228 (Korat), you will pass the quarries from which the clay for the potteries of DAN KWIAN is extracted. PAK THON CHAI ▲ 228 (16 miles to the south of Nakhon Ratchasima) is a center for silk weaving but the real silk capital is still KHON KAEN, on the road to Laos. The incomparable *mudmee* silk is manufactured in the village of CHONABOT (34 miles before Khon Khaen). There you can observe all the various stages of the production process, from the raising of the silkworms and the mulberry trees to the final weaving. In SISAKET, bamboo articles of exceptionally fine quality are produced, as is sheet bronze in UBON

RATCHATHANI, particularly in the small village of PA AO. Like SURIN, ROI ET ▲ 228, CHAYAPHUM and SAKHON NAKHON, KALASIN owes its reputation to the outstanding quality of the silk woven in its workshops. UDON THANI and the neighboring village of NA KHA produce traditional cotton fabrics and copies of Ban Chiang pottery ▲ 229. Finally, it is from the village of SAN SI THAN that the famous triangular *mon khit* cushions come.

PLA BUK FISHING AND THE FESTIVAL OF ELEPHANTS. *Puk siao*, the friendship ceremony that consists of tying a symbolic piece of string around the wrist of a host, is practiced in honor of a visitor or when festivals are held. The Mekong also has its traditions on the Thai and the Laotian side. *Pla buk* fishing ▲ 236 (giant catfish) is one aspect of this river culture. If you are in CHIANG KHONG, in the north of Isan in April-May, you will be able to watch the fishing rites. The exuberant festivals of the northeast are unique: the Festival of the Tamarind in Mukdahan (January), of Rockets ● 72 in Yasothon (May), of Phi Ta Khon in Loei (June), of Wax Figures ● 73 in Ubon Ratchathani (July), of Illuminated Boats in Nakhon Phanom (October), of Elephants in Surin ▲ 228 (November), and of Kites in Buriram (December).

THE SOUTH

BASKETRY AND INLAID ENAMEL WORK.
NAKHON SI THAMMARAT ▲ 207 is still the home of an original craft tradition encouraged by Queen Sikirit. The art of basketry *yan lipao* (bags, and purses made out of liana which grows in this region) is one notable aspect of this tradition; others are shadow puppets cut out of buffalo hide and of enameled silverware (below). In a more modest way, NARATHIWAT manufactures mats of remarkable quality and SONGKHLA ▲ 208 produces traditional clothing. From the kilns of BAN SAKOM comes domestic stoneware such as pots, jugs and basins.

LION DANCES AND BUFFALO RACES. If Muslim traditions (such as the observance of Ramadan and pilgrimages to Mecca) increase the closer one gets to Malaysia, the south by contrast is a region marked by Chinese traditions, as seen for example in the lion and dragon parade in Narathiwat (February), the vegetarian festivals in Trang and Phuket ▲ 213 (September-October), during which ascetics put on amazing exhibitions, and the feast of the goddess Chao Mae Lim Ko Nieo in Pattani ▲ 209 (February-March). Animals inspire or feature in certain festivities: the release of reared turtles in Phuket at New Year (April), love-cooing competitions in Yala (March) and buffalo races in Chonburi (October). Other festivals take as their theme the sea (the fishing competition in Krabi in November), or fruit (the mangosteen fair in Nakhon Si Thammarat in July), or the arts (the *manora* dance competition ● 66 in Pattalung in June).

ANTIQUES
Be careful: the export of ancient and religious artifacts (particularly images of the Buddha) is strictly controlled. Obtaining a license may take up to a month.

ORNAMENTAL FRETWORK
The woodworkers of Ban Tawai, to the south of Chiang Mai, and in other regions of Thailand as well, are incredibly skilled and amazingly produce intricate work. Lovers of antiques will be interested in sculptured panels from ox-carts which, before the arrival of tractors and cars, were used in the countryside for transporting people, beasts and merchandise. Panels from Chiang Mai, sometimes painted in brilliant colors, are often decorated with elephant motifs. Old or reproduction fretwork lamps can also be found and, more rarely, sugar cane presses and coconut graters.

Erawan National Park.

KOH SAMET
When the turtles come to lay their eggs, the island is closed to tourists. It is wise to check in advance with the local authorities or the Tourism Authority of Thailand.

NATURE RESERVES

Take advantage of your stay in Thailand for some rest and relaxation in natural surroundings. There are 58 parks to choose from, managed by the National Parks Division (Pahol Yothin Road in Bangkok), most of which have reception facilities. For a breath of fresh air well away from civilization, choose a mountain park such as PHU KRADUNG ▲ *239* (382 miles northeast of Bangkok) or the 31 miles of marked paths of KHAO YAI ▲ *238* (120 miles from Bangkok), the oldest nature reserve in the country, with an 18-hole golf course and a hotel that is the complete opposite to a hikers lodge. But Thailand also has the sea and national marine parks, islands and archipelagos circled by coral reefs. In the gulf of Siam, KOH SAMET ▲ *192* is easily accessible from Rayong and has accommodation. More spectacular, ANG THONG PARK ▲ *206*, in the Samui archipelago, with its 37 uninhabited islands, provides a real opportunity to get away from it all. You can take a day trip (from Samui or Ban Don on the mainland) or stay in the tiny lodge at Wua Ta Lap. On the Andaman Sea side, the KOH SIMILAN AND KOH TARUTAO PARKS ▲ *226* can be explored by boat. Individual or group tours from Phuket can be organized.

THE RIVER KWAI

Tradition dictates: you must go to KANCHANABURI ▲ *189* by train, from Hualampong station in Bangkok (about 76 miles). On weekends and holidays, a train follows a tourist route through NAKHON PATHOM ▲ *186* (the tallest chedi in the world), Kanchanaburi and Nam Tok. The last section of this "death railway" ▲ *189*, which passes over a wooden viaduct, is impressive. However, do not stay long in Kanchanaburi which, apart from its famous bridge and its war museums, has nothing special to offer. You can get around on foot, by motor-bike, by jeep or, more economically, by *songteo*. It is much more exciting to canoe or raft along the two River Kwae (the Noi and the Yai) with their forests of giant bamboo, wild orchids and waterfalls...

ANG THONG NATIONAL PARK
Among the 37 islands in the marine park, the beauty of Koh Mae island ▲ 206 merits a trip: in a natural depression at the center of the island, is a large jade-green lake, linked to the sea by an underground river.

Raft excursions can last several days; you stop when you feel like having a swim and the level of comfort varies according to the category chosen. For a total "escape," spend at least one night at a boatel such as the River Kwae Village. Along the east coast, do not miss PATTHAYA ▲ *191* (93 miles from Bangkok), Thailand's most famous beach resort. It is a large town nowadays but the beach has remained surprisingly clean in spite of the number of tourists. Many people prefer BANG SEN, which is more family-oriented and closer to Bangkok (65 miles), or RAYONG ▲ *192*, although it is less easily accessible and farther away (133 miles). Do not miss KOH SAMET ▲ *192*, the pride of Rayong, 30 minutes by boat from Ban Phe. If you opt for the southern route, your first stop will be in CHA AM (112 miles from Bangkok) or

HUA HIN ▲ *198* (140 miles) – both resorts well equipped with hotels. Hua Hin is the favorite beach resort of the Royal Family. Beyond Hua Hin, and as far as Surat Thani, there is a long stretch of beaches, many of which are still quite deserted: PRACHUAB ▲ *199* (180 miles), with its strange "mountain mirror" and CHUMPHON ▲ *200* (292 miles), with its circle of uninhabited islands. SONGKHLA ▲ *208* (596 miles), a seaside and lagoon resort, has a charming old-world atmosphere.

THE ISLANDS IN THE SOUTH CHINA SEA

For a sudden and dramatic change of scene, catch a plane from Bangkok to Samui ▲ *202* (422 miles away). For a more gentle contrast, go by sea; boats make the 2-hour journey from the mainland to the island. The trip can be organized from the airport or station at SURAT THANI ▲ *201*. Samui offers white sand, coconut palms and a turquoise sea. KOH PHANGAN ▲ *206*, the neighboring island, is more rustic in character. You can get there in 40 minutes from Nathon or Bophut (ports in Samui) and rent an idyllically simple bungalow. To get away from it all, go to Koh Tao ▲ *206* (about 31 miles further north), a divers' paradise, which can also be reached by boat to Chumphon (regular 6-hour crossings).

THE ANDAMAN SEA

The best way to get to PHUKET ▲ *210* (420 miles from Bangkok) is by air. The island is a world in itself, and from it you can branch out and visit the surrounding islands. The possibilities are endless. If your time is limited, visit PHANGNGA BAY ▲ *218*, which is surrounded by strange rock formations rising straight out of the jade-colored sea. Excursions can be organized from all the hotels (it is best to go by boat and return by road). Equally spectacular are the PHI PHI ISLANDS ▲ *222*, one with dark caves full of birds' nests and the other luxuriant, with two beaches divided by a coconut grove. Though the trip can be made in a single day, you can also stay in one of the charming hotels in this little paradise.

THE CAVES OF THAM LOT. To explore the bay of Phangnga: take the *Reef Explorer*, a glass-bottomed boat that enables you to see the coral without getting wet, or rent a real Chinese junk (3,000 baht per day) or small boat (500 baht to 1,000 baht per day), means you can stop whenever you fancy and dive into the clear waters.

HEAW SUWAT WATERFALL, KHAO YAI NATIONAL PARK Night trips to watch the wildlife in the forests of Khao Yai National Park ▲ *238* can be organized. However, avoid the monsoon season when everything is drenched and leeches abound. Information is available locally or from travel agents.

◆ **ao**: bay.
Apsara: female divinity.
Avalokitesvara: compassionate *bodhisattva* in Mahayana Buddhism.

◆ **bai-sri**: traditional Thai flower arrangement.
ban: village.
baray: Khmer artificial lake surrounded by earth levees and fed by diverted river water. Their prime function was originally to irrigate ricefields, but they also symbolized the primordial ocean that, in Buddhist cosmology, surrounds the earth.
bodhisattvas: enlightened human or celestial beings who voluntarily delayed *Nirvana* to devote themselves to the salvation of all human beings on earth.
Bodhi tree: the tree under which the Buddha reached the state of enlightenment.
bot (or *ubosot*): main building in a temple complex where novice monks are ordained.
Brahma: The creator god and, with Siva and Vishnu, one of the three main Hindu deities. He is always depicted with four heads, each facing one of the four directions of the universe.
Brahmanism: original form of Hinduism.
bun bang fai: northeastern village festival at which homemade skyrockets are fired into the air.

◆ **chakhay**: guitar-like instrument usually played in a large orchestra.
chakra: in Hinduism, a solar wheel and weapon given by Vishnu. To Buddhists it symbolizes the completeness of the law (*dharma chakra*).
Chakri: name of the present Thai dynasty, founded in 1737 by Rama I. *Chakri* is also an honorific title that can be conferred on a high-ranking civilian or a religious or military leader. It means "he who carries the *chakra* or Wheel of the Law".
chedi (or *stupa*): monument where relics of the Buddha and ashes of prominent people are enshrined.
ching lek (or *ching yai*): set of small cymbals.
chula: star-shaped male kite.

◆ **dharma**: Buddhist teaching or law.
Dharmacakra: The Wheel of Law.

◆ **Erawan**: three-headed elephant, mythical mount of Brahma.

◆ **Farang**: term derived from *farangse*, a phonetic translation of *français* (French), the first Europeans received by the Siamese Court. By extension, *farang* today refers to any Westerner.
floating house: Thai shophouse on a river.

◆ **Gajasingha**: mythical beast with the head of an elephant and the body of a lion.
Ganesha: Siva and Pavarti's son; elephant god of wisdom. In Thailand, considered the protector of artists and students.
garuda: half human half bird, the legendary steed of the Hindu god Vishnu; appears as royal insignia among the wall decorations in the Grand Palace compound
Guanyin: goddess of mercy, one of the main Mahayana bodhisattvas,

◆ **hat**: beach.
hin: stone.
Hinayana (*Lesser Vehicle*): a form of Buddhism that originated in Sri Lanka and incorporates elements of Hinduism and local beliefs. Predominates in Thailand, Burma, Laos and Cambodia.
ho trai: library built in the middle of a pond or on a raised platform to keep away termites.
hong: mythological swan-like creature.
hong yao: long-tail boat, a common form of river transport along the klongs of Thonburi.
howdah: palanquin mounted on an elephant saddle.
huai: waterfall
hun: small carved marionettes for enacting classical tales.
hun krabok: rod puppets, similar to Punch and Judy puppets.
hun lek: small marionettes modeled on characters from Chinese legends.

◆ **jad paan** (or *poom*): flower arrangement in the shape of a bowl.
Jataka: collection of stories dealing with Buddha's previous lives.
jongkrabane: women's garment in which a length of cloth is wrapped around the waist then pulled through the legs and secured at the back.

◆ **Kadwua**: local village cattle market near Chiang Mai.
kalae: v-shaped protrusion (like a pair of buffalo horns) at end of rooftop, common on northern Thai houses.
kao: mountain.
khanom: sweet.
khanom krok: popular delicacy made from a mixture of thick coconut milk, rice flour, eggs and sugar, and cooked in a special clay mold.
khantoke: traditional dinner where guests and hosts sit on the floor round a low table and help themselves to a variety of dishes, usually eaten with glutinous rice.
khao niaow: glutinous rice.
khoi: book, with pages folded in concertina-fashion, containing illustrations on subjects such as religion, anatomy, warfare and elephants. Old Thai manuscripts were written on khoi paper, made from the bark of local trees.
khon: traditional masked dance drama performed at the royal court.
khong wong lek and **khong wong yai**: circular series of small or large gongs suspended on rattan frame
kinnon and **kinnari**: mythological male and female bird-human creatures
klawng yao: huge drum played at festivals.
klong: canal.
klong tad thapon: double-ended drum.
koh: island.
krabung: rice basket.
krathong: colorful miniature boat of paper, flowers and candles, with either a banana-leaf or styrofoam as its base; an array of krathong can be seen on waterways during the Loy Krathong festival. Krung Thep (City of Angels): abbreviated version of the name given to Bangkok by Rama I in the 18th century; for full name see page 141.
ku: gilded brick structure housing the Buddha image inside a temple.

◆ **laem**: cape.
lakhon: theatrical performance, derivation of the khon performed in public.
lamyai: lychee-like fruit grown in the north, mainly in Lamphun
likay: popular satirical pantomime.
lingam: sacred standing stone in the form of a phallus symbolizing the Hindu god Siva.
look choop: ornamental fruit mixture made from mung bean paste and sugar.
Loy Krathong: probably the loveliest of Thai festivals, held

in late October/early November in honor of the water spirits with, the launch of several small *krathong*.

◆ **mah** (or *timah*): water basket.

malai: garland.

Mahayana (*Greater Vehicle*): northern Buddhism practiced in China, Korea and Japan, stressing the importance of mercy.

Maitrey: a future Buddha in Mahayana Buddhism.

mandala: esoteric meditation pattern in the form of a labyrinth representing cosmic order, and tracing the various stages in the Buddha's life. The best-known mandala is the Borobadur temple in Java.

mandapa: cube-like roofless structure that houses an object of worship, such as a Buddha image or a sacred footprint.

Manora a lakhon: romantic drama of Javanese origin.

mondop: cube-like building housing an object of worship, such as a Buddha image

mudmee: handwoven silk fabric popular among Thai women.

Mara: in Buddhism an evil spirit that represents all forms of earthly temptation.

menam: river.

mor hom: cotton shirt worn by Thai farmers

mudra: hand gesture in Buddhist iconography.

◆ **naga**: serpent

nak: novice about to enter monkhood

nakhon: town.

nam pla: condiment, sauce made from fermented fish.

nandi: Siva's sacred bull.

nang: shadow play. Nang yai and nang talung are variations of nang.

ngao: roof gable of Khmer origin.

Nirvana: absolute truth, "extinction of passions," end of the cycle of rebirth and,

thus, liberation from suffering.

◆ **Parinirvana**: "complete extinction," as when the Buddha was about to attain Nirvana

pannung: men's garment, counterpart of the jongkrabane

pasin: women's sarong (wrap-around garment) of northern Thailand

pha lai-yang: silk or cotton fabric with Thai motifs.

phakoma: multi-purpose cotton piece used as a sarong, headband or wash cloth.

phi: guardian spirit, which, many Thais believe, must be placated through offerings.

phi pob: legendary spirits that eat the entrails of their victims

phipat: small musical ensemble.

Phra: honorific title meaning "sacred".

phrachedi: old term for a *chedi*.

pinai: oboe-like musical instrument that sounds like a bagpipe.

pla buk: catfish.

prang: Thai temple tower; older form of religious monument adapted from Hindu architecture.

prasat: Khmer temple tower and, by extension, temple at Khmer sites. The term *prasat hin*, "stone castle," is also frequently used.

prik: Thai for chilli.

pukpao: diamond-shaped "female" kite

◆ **Ramakien**: Thai version of the Indian epic *Ramayana*.

ranad: Thai musical instrument that works like a xylophone.

Rattanakosin: 18th-century name of Bangkok (for full name see page 141)

rishi: generic term for prophets and poets to whom the Vedic hymns were first revealed.

rua chai: gunboats steered by 60-strong

team of oarsmen into battle during the Ayutthaya period.

rua duang and **rua saeng**: small attendant boats in a royal barge procession of the 19th century.

◆ **Sabai**: long piece of cloth about one foot wide, usually worn diagonally above the waist and draped over the shoulder.

sai: elongated trap for small fish and prawns.

sala: open pavilion mainly for rest and relaxation.

sala kanprien: meeting hall.

sangha: Buddhist clergy.

sanuk: fun, leisure pursuit.

sarb: 3-foot-long fish trap of the northeastern region.

sarong: term of Indonesian origin meaning a fabric used as clothing, wrapped around the body.

saw sam sai: fiddle consisting of a coconut shell, an ivory neck and three silk strings.

sing: guardian lion (statue).

soi: lane.

Songkran: two-day celebration in mid-April of the solar New Year, a blend of ritual and riotous festival with parades, beauty contests and buckets of water thrown in fun at passers-by.

spirit house: miniature house where the *phi* is believed to dwell; usually supported on a pole outside the residence.

sutra: sacred texts containing sermons attributed to the Buddha.

◆ **taiji** (or *tai chi*): Oriental form of martial art, mainly for relaxation and light exercise, practiced among the older generation.

takraw: hardcourt game using a light rattan ball volleyed between two teams, three players a side, on opposite sides of the net.

talat: market.

Tamnak Daeng (*Red House*): a royal house with decorative features built by Rama II, now in the compound of the National Museum in Bangkok.

tantima: mythological bird.

Thai boxing: sport where any part of the body other than the head can be used against the opponent in the ring; apparently the foot is the most effective offensive weapon in this sport.

thale: sea.

tham: cave.

Theravada: southern Buddhism, the only surviving school of the Hinayana (Lesser Vehicle) system, which originated in Sri Lanka.

Thod kathin: ceremony in which groups of Buddhist devotees visit monasteries and offer alms to resident monks.

thong sampao: literally the hull of a ship; a concave curved base feature of the *viharn* or *bot* of the Ayutthaya period.

Tonsure Ceremony: a complex ritual held in the Grand Palace to mark the coming-of-age of children in the Inner Palace.

tuk-tuk: three- and four-wheeled open-end taxis plying city streets.

◆ **Vedas**: the four sacred books of Hinduism, revealed by Brahma.

viharn (or *vihara*): assembly hall for sermons, originally a meditation hall.

◆ **wai**: traditional Thai greeting.

wang luang lakon: festival in Lampang celebrating the 7th-century reign of Queen Chamadevi; colorful parade of participants in period costumes.

wat: temple.

wiang: citadel.

◆ **yaksa**: demon.

Note: Thai is a tonal language and is spoken syllable by syllable. The five tones are :
unaccented monotone,
\ : *low,*
^ : *falling,*
/ : *high,*
v : *rising.*
The accents used here do not relate to conventional European accents.

Greetings
Hello: (man) *sà wàt dii khráp,* (woman): *Sà wàt dii khâ.*
How are you? (man): *khun sa baï dì roĕu khráp?,* (woman): *khun sa baï dì roĕu khâ?*
Fine, thank you!: (man): *sa baï dì, khòp khun khráp,* (woman): *sa baï dì, khòp khun khâ.*
Thank you very much: *khòp khun mâk.*

General
Excuse me: *khŏw thôde*
That's OK: *maî pen raï.*
Yes: *tchaï.*
No: *paï tchaï .*
I don't speak Thai, (man) *phŏm phoûd pha sǎ thaï maî daï,* (woman): *dì-chǎn phoǔd pha sǎ thaï maî daï.*
I speak a little Thai, (man): *phŏm phoûd pha sǎ thai nít nói,* (woman): *dì-chǎn phoǔd pha sǎ thaï nít nói.*
What's that called in Thai?: *nî khŏw khaŏw rîak araï pha sǎ thaï ?*
I don't feel well, (man): *phŏm maî sà baï,* (woman): *dì-chǎn maî sà baï.*
What is your name ? *khun tchôeu à-raï ?*
My name is..., (man): *phŏm tchôeu...,* (woman): *dì-chǎn tchôeu...*
Where do you live?: *khun yoù thî nǎi ?*
I am English/ American/Australian: (man) *phǒm pen khone Ankrit/ Amerikan/Australian- sèt,* (woman): *dí-chǎn pen khone Ankrit/Amerikan/Austr- alian-sèt.*

I don't understand: *maî kaôw djaï.*
Do you understand me ? *kâo djaï mǎi ?*
May I telephone?: *kor chaï tho rá sàp dai mǎ ï ?*
Where are the toilets?: *hông nám yoù thî nǎi ?*
I need a doctor: *tông kan môw ma reów.*

Getting around
Where: *thî nǎi.*
When: *meûaraï.*
To go: *paï.*
I want to go...: *yàak dja paï...*
To come: *maa.*
Airport: *sǎnǎm bine.*
Hotel: *rong raime.*
Hospital: *rongpháyabane.*
Post office: *praïsànǐ.*
Embassy: *sàthǎn thoûde.*
Bus station: *sàthani rótmai.*
Railway station: *sàthani rótfaï.*
Market: *ta-làt.*
Floating market: *talàtnám.*
Restaurant: *ráne à-hǎ nne.*
Police station: *sàthani tamruat.*
Street: *thà nǒne.*
Lane: *soï.*
Bridge: *sà phǎne.*
To stop: *yoùt.*
To turn: *líaów.*
To the left: *saï.*
To the right: *kwǎ.*
Straight on: *trong paï*
To go by boat: *Paï rouea*
To go to the temple : *paï wát.*
Beach: *haàt.*
Island: *kò.*
Mountain: *phoù khaǒw, doï.*

Shopping
To go shopping: *paï soĕu khŏng.*
Too expenisve: *pherng mâk koeun paï.*
Larger, bigger: *yǎï kwà.*
Smaller: *nǒï kwà, laík kwà.*
This one: *ahne ní.*
That one: *ahne nône.*
How much is it?: *thaôw raï ?*
Do you have a differnt color?: *khun mi sǐ hoeùn mǎï ?*
Color: *Sǐ.*

Food
To eat: *ráprathan,* slang: *kin.*

I would like to eat: *than.*
I don't want any: *maî than, mâî aow.*
To eat rice: *kin khaôw.*
Thirsty: *hiǒu nám.*
Hungry: *heo kao*
Food: *a-hǎne.*
Is it good ?: *a-rǒï mǎï?*
Salty: *khaim.*
Salt: *kloeua.*
Side dishes: *kàb khâow.*
With chilli: *phaít.*
Without chilli: *maî phaít.*
Hot: *rónne.*
Cold: *yen.*
Mild, sweet: *wǔan.*
Beef: *noeúa.*
Pork: *mǒu.*
Chicken: *kai.*
Duck: *pait.*
Fish: *pla.*
Crab: *pou.*
Shrimp: *koûng.*
Lemon and shrimp soup: *thòme yam koûng.*
Cuttlefish: *pla moeùk.*
Egg: *khàï.*
Spicy soup: *thome yam.*
Noodles: *pà mì.*
Rice (fine) noodles: *sen láik.*
Fried rice: *khaôw phàt.*
Fried noodles: *phàt thaï.*
Water: *nám.*
Coffee: *kafaidam.*
Iced coffee: *o-liéng.*
Sugar: *nám than.*
Bread: *kànôm pàn.*
Beer: *biya.*
Orange juice: *nám sôm.*
Alcohol: *laôw.*
Banana: *khoûeï.*
Pineapple: *sapparót.*
Orange: *sôm.*
Papaya: *máláko.*
Rambutans: *ngnów.*
Mango: *má mǔang.*
To smoke cigarettes: *soùp bouli.*
To drink: *doeùm.*
Sour: *priaów.*
Tea: *nám tcha.*
French loaf: *ta kiàp.*
The bill/check please : (man): *Gep taang khráp,* (woman): *Gep taang khǎ.*

Counting
Zero: *sǒun*
One: *nùng*
Two: *sǒng*
Three: *sǎm*
Four: *sì*
Five: *hâ*
Six: *hòk*

Seven: *djèt*
Eight: *pèt*
Nine: *kaǒw*
Ten: *sìp*
Eleven: *sìp aìt*
Twelve: *sìp sǒng*
Twenty: *yî sìp*
Thirty: *sǎm sìp*
Forty: *sì sìp*
Fifty: *hâ sìp*
Sixty: *hòk sìp*
Seventy: *djèt sìp*
Eighty: *pèt sìp*
Ninety: *kaôw sìp*
One hundred: *rói, nùng rói*
Two hundred: *sǒng rói*
One thousand: *phane*
Ten thousand: *moeùan*
One million: *láne*
How many children?: *dèk kì khone ?*

Days of the week
Monday: *wane djan*
Tuesday: *wane ang kane*
Wednesday: *wane phoút*
Thursday: *wan pároeuhàt*
Friday: *wan soúk*
Saturday: *wane saǒw*
Sunday: *wane ha thít*
Today: *wane ní*
Yesterday: *moeùa wane ní*
Tomorrow: *phroung ní*
Week: *sàpda*
Month: *dœuene*

Family
To greet: *waï*
Brothers/sisters,
- elder: *phî,*
- younger: *nóng*
Woman: *phoû yǐng*
Man: *phoû tchaï*
Mother: *maî*
Father: *phǒ*
Daughter: *loûk saǒw*
Son: *loûk tchaï*
Age: *a-yoú*
How old are you?: *khun a-you thaôwraï ?*
I am...: *dì-chǎn/phǒm a-you...: pi*

On the street
House: *bâne.*
City: *nakhorn*
Town: *mou bâne*
Garden: *suǎn*
Temple: *wát*
Canal: *klong*
River: *maî nám*
Country: *muang*
Royal: *luǎng*
Tree: *tôn maí*
Flower: *dòck maî*
Lotus: *bua*
Telephone: *khǒ*

USEFUL ADDRESSES

☀	VIEW
C	CITY CENTER
⊡··	OUTLYING
⊕	LUXURY RESTAURANT
◑	TYPICAL RESTAURANT
○	BUDGET RESTAURANT
🏛	LUXURY HOTEL
♠	MODERATE HOTEL
⌂	BUDGET HOTEL
🅿	CAR PARK
🚗	SUPERVISED GARAGE
▭	TELEVISION
⌂	QUIET
⌿	SWIMMING POOL
▭	CREDIT CARDS
⚘	REDUCTION FOR CHILDREN
♫	MUSIC
📯	LIVE BAND

	AIR-CONDITIONED	T.V. IN ROOM	PARKING	QUIET	VIEW	RESTAURANT	24-HR ROOM SERVICE	NO. OF ROOMS	RATE
BANGKOK									
ASIA HOTEL								600	♦♦♦
ERAWAN GRAND HYATT								400	♦♦♦
FLORIDA								110	♦
IMPALA								197	♦♦
KHAO SAN PALACE HOTEL								40	♦
MANOHRA								220	♦♦♦
MERIDIEN PRESIDENT								400	♦♦♦
MONTIEN BANGKOK								500	♦♦♦
NANA								334	♦♦
NARAI								500	♦♦♦
ORIENTAL								393	♦♦♦
PARK HOTEL								139	♦♦♦
REX								131	♦♦
ROSE								105	♦
ROYAL HOTEL								200	♦♦
ROYAL ORCHID SHERATON								773	♦♦♦
SHANGRI-LA								900	♦♦♦
SIAM INTERCONTINENTAL								389	♦♦♦
SUKHOTHAI								190	♦♦♦
THAI HOTEL								100	♦
THE REGENT								400	♦♦♦
VIENGTAI								240	♦
YMCA								58	♦
KANCHANABURI									
BAMBOO GUEST HOUSE									♦
RIVER KWAE VILLAGE								100	♦♦
SAM'S PLACE								27	♦
PATTAYA									
DIANA INN								140	♦♦
ORCHID LODGE								226	♦♦♦
PATTAYA 11 HOTEL								64	♦
ROYAL CLIFF BEACH HOTEL								270	♦♦♦
ROYAL GARDEN RESORT								300	♦♦♦
WELKOM INN								20	♦
HUA HIN									
BAN BOOSARIN								10	♦♦
JED PEE NONG								20	♦♦
SIRIN								25	♦♦
SOFITEL CENTRAL								216	♦♦♦
SURAT THANI									
SERI HOTEL								30	♦
WANG THAI HOTEL								230	♦♦
KOH SAMUI									
BOAT HOUSE HOTEL								186	♦♦♦
CHATKAEO RESORT								-	♦♦
CORAL BAY RESORT								42	♦♦
CORAL COVE RESORT								-	♦
IMPERIAL TONGSAI BAY HOTEL								73	♦♦♦
NARA GARDEN								-	♦♦
PEACE BUNGALOW								-	♦
PRINCESS VILLAGE								-	♦♦♦
SEASIDE PALACE HOTEL								30	♦
SONGKHLA									
NARAI									♦
SAMILA								150	♦♦♦
PHUKET									
CASUARINA BUNGALOWS								42	♦♦
CLUB MÉDITERRANÉE								300	♦♦♦
CORAL BEACH HOTEL								200	♦♦♦
KATA THANI								202	♦♦♦

♦ < 1,000 baht in Bangkok and
   < 500 baht out of town
♦♦ 1,000 to 2,000 baht in Bangkok and
    from 500 to 1,000 baht out of town
♦♦♦ > 2,500 baht in Bangkok and
     > 1,500 baht out of town

	AIR-CONDITIONED	T.V. IN ROOM	PARKING	QUIET	VIEW	RESTAURANT	24-HR ROOM SERVICE	NO. OF ROOMS	RATE
LE JARDIN								-	♦♦
ON ON HOTEL								43	♦
PANSEA PHUKET BAY								110	♦♦♦
PEARL HOTEL								250	♦♦♦
PEARL VILLAGE								80	♦♦♦
PHUKET YACHT CLUB								120	♦♦♦
SANDY INN								12	♦♦
THAVORN HOTEL								67	♦♦
PHANGNGA									
PHANGNGA BAY RESORT								100	♦♦♦
PHI PHI ISLANDS									
KRABI PEE PEE RESORT								70	♦
PEE PEE INTERNATIONAL RESORT								186	♦♦♦
PEE PEE ISLAND VILLAGE								-	♦♦
KRABI									
PHRA NANG BAY VILLAGE								-	♦
PHRA NANG INN								50	♦♦
NAKHON RATCHASIMA									
SIRI								60	♦
SRI PATANA								100	♦♦
THAI POKAPHAN								27	♦
AYUTTHAYA									
BJ GUEST HOUSE								19	♦
SRI SAMAI								-	♦♦
U-THONG INN								-	♦♦
SUKHOTHAI									
CHINAWAT								40	♦
SUKHOTAI HOTEL								50	♦
PHITSANULOK									
PAYLIN								242	♦♦♦
PHITSANULOK YOUTH HOSTEL								30	♦
RAJAPRUK								125	♦♦
THEP NAKHORN								150	♦♦
CHIANG MAI									
ANODARD HOTEL								150	♦
CHIANG INN								170	♦♦♦
CHIANG MAI ORCHID								267	♦♦♦
CHIANG MAI YOUTH HOSTEL								15	♦
GALARE GUEST HOUSE								35	♦♦
LE P'TIT PARADIS								13	♦
NEW CHIANG MAI HOTEL								43	♦
ONCE UPON A TIME								12	♦♦
PHA THAI GUEST HOUSE								15	♦
ROYAL PRINCESS								198	♦♦♦
TIMES SQUARE GUEST HOUSE								10	♦
CHIANG RAI									
CHAT HOUSE								15	♦
DUSIT ISLAND RESORT								270	♦♦♦
GOLDEN TRIANGLE INN								40	♦♦
WANGCOME HOTEL								243	♦♦♦
MAE HONG SON									
BAIYOKE CHALET								40	♦♦
MAE HONG SON GUEST HOUSE								12	♦
PEN PORN HOUSE								10	♦
PIYA COMPLEX								12	♦
TARA MAE HONG SON								104	♦♦♦
CHIANG SAEN									
CHIANG SAEN GUEST HOUSE								-	♦
GIN'S GUEST HOUSE									♦
GOLDEN TRIANGLE RESORT								70	♦♦♦
JS GUEST HOUSE								-	♦

Legend:
- ◆   < 100 baht
- ◆◆   100 baht to 400 baht
- ◆◆◆   > 400 baht

	VIEW	OPEN-AIR	AIR-CONDITIONED	CLIENTÈLE	SPECIALTIES	CREDIT CARDS	PRICE
BANGKOK							
Ambassador Food Center		●		TL	NCW		◆
Bussaracum			●	L	N	●	◆◆◆
Cabbages and Condoms			●	T	NW	●	◆◆
Café des Artistes			●	TL	NW		◆◆
C. D. S. Coffee Shop			●	TL	NW	●	◆
Charuvan Duck Shop			●	L	N		◆
D'jit Pochana			●	T	N	●	◆◆
Harlequin			●	TL	W	●	◆◆◆
Hello Restaurant			●	T	NW		◆
Laikhram			●	T	N	●	◆◆
Le Dalat			●	T	O	●	◆◆◆
Lemon grass		●		TL	N		◆◆
Mandalay			●	T	O		◆◆◆
New Rincome Restaurant			●	TL	C		◆◆
Noodle Garden				L	NC		◆
Pan Pan Capri			●	T	W	●	◆◆
Sala Rim Nam	●		●	T	N	●	◆◆◆
Seafood Market & Restaurant		●	●	T	NW		◆◆◆
Sorn Daeng					NW		◆◆
Thai Room			●	T	N		◆◆
Tum Nak Thai			●	T	NW		◆◆
Vijit			●	L	N		◆◆
Whole Earth			●	TL	N		◆◆
Yok Yor Restaurant	●	●		T	NCW		◆◆◆
YWCA Restaurant			●	Y	N	●	◆◆
HUA HIN							
Saeng Thai	●			TL	F	●	◆◆
Sunshine Sukeyaki & BBQ				TL	NF		◆◆
KOH SAMUI							
A Bird in the Hand					W		◆◆
Le Bateau				T	NW		◆◆
Thai Cat		●		C	NW		◆

Specialties	Clientèle
N : National	T : Tourists
C : Chinese	L : Locals
W : Western	Y : Young
O : Other	C : Celebrities

	VIEW	OPEN-AIR	AIR-CONDITIONED	CLIENTELE	SPECIALTIES	CREDIT CARDS	PRICE
PHUKET							
BAAN RIM PA	■		■	T	NF	■	♦♦♦
LE JARDIN		■	■	TL	NO		♦♦
MAE PORN			■		NF		♦
SUNSET	■	■		T	NF		♦♦
THUNGKA KAFAE	■				F	■	♦♦
NAKHON RATCHASIMA							
BAAN KAEW RESTAURANT			■	L	N	■	♦♦
JULDIS KHAO YAI RESORT			■	T	NW		♦♦♦
AYUTTHAYA							
PAE KRUNG KAO	■		■	T	NF	■	♦♦
PHITSANULOK							
RIMNAN	■			TL	N	■	♦♦
CHIANG MAI							
AARON RAI RESTAURANT		■		L	NC		♦
COQ AU RICO - CHEZ JOHN			■	TL	W		♦♦♦
DARET'S		■		T	N		♦
HONG TAUW INN			■	L	N	■	♦♦
JULIE GUEST HOUSE	■			T	NW		♦
LA VILLA		■	■	T	NW		♦♦
LE JARDIN			■	TL	NW		♦
LE P'TIT PARADIS			■	L	NW	■	♦♦
OLD CHIANG MAI CULTURAL CENTER		■		TL	NO	■	♦♦♦
ONCE UPON A TIME	■	■		TL	NW	■	♦♦
CHIANG RAI							
GOLDEN TRIANGLE INN			■	T	N	■	♦♦
HAWNARIGA		■		L	NCO		♦♦
MAE HONG SON							
FERN RESTAURANT				L	N	■	♦♦
KHAI MUK				T	NC		♦♦
CHIANG SAEN							
RIM KHONG	■			T	N	■	♦
SALATHAI RESTAURANT	■			L	N		♦

GENERAL

ENTRY FORMALITIES

Foreigners entering Thailand must hold a passport valid for 6 months. A visa, obtainable at the Thai embassy, is required for stays exceeding 14 days. Present your passport, two photographs, and a return ticket. Visa applications take 48 hours to process.

HEALTH

No vaccination is required but innoculation against typhoid, tetanus and hepatitis B, along with malaria prophylaxis is recommended, especially if you intend trekking in the jungle and national parks. To be safe, take out travel insurance as well.

TOURIST INFORMATION OFFICES

TOURISM AUTHORITY OF THAILAND (TAT)
LONDON
49 Albermarle Street
London WIX 3FE
United Kingdom
Tel. (071) 499 7679
Fax (071) 629 5519.
LOS ANGELES
3440 Wilshire Boulevard
Suite 1100, Los
Angeles, CA 90010,
USA
Tel. (213) 382 2353
Fax (213) 389 7544.
NEW YORK
5 World Trade Center
Suite 3443,
New York,
N.Y. 10048,
USA
Tel (212) 432 0433
Fax (212) 912 0920

SYDNEY
12th floor,
Royal Exchange
Building,
56 Pitt Street,
Sydney 2000,
Australia
Tel. (02) 247 7549
Fax (02) 251 2465.

PARIS
90 Champs-Elysées,
75008 Paris,
France
Tel. (01) 45 62 86 56
Fax (01) 45 63 78 88.

There are branches of TAT throughout Thailand. They are efficient but the staff do not always speak English. They are generally open daily, 8.30am–4.30pm. Closed Sat. afternoons.

HOTELS

Numerous hotels in Thailand negotiate preferential rates with travel agents in Bangkok and abroad. This procedure means savings of up to 50 percent off the normal rates. However, allow for seasonal variations. During the high season (September to June) reservations are essential. In the low season, you can easily get good rates.

BANGKOK

PRACTICALITIES

ZIP CODE
10400

EMBASSIES
AUSTRALIA
37 Sathon Tai Road
Tel. 2872680
Open 8.15am–12 noon.
CANADA
11th–12th floor,
Boonmitr Building,
138 Silom Road
Tel. 2341561.
Open 8am–11am
JAPAN
1674/4 New
Phetchaburi Road
Visa Section, Asoke
Tower,
Sukhumvit 21
Tel. 2526151.
Open 8.30am–12 noon.
UNITED KINGDOM
1031 Phloenchit Road
Tel. 2530191
Open 8–11am, Fri.

8am–12 noon.
UNITED STATES OF
AMERICA
95 Witthayu Road
Tel. 2525040.
Open 7–10am.

Offices open Mon. to Fri.

TOURISM AUTHORITY OF THAILAND (TAT)
The TAT office at Ratchadamnoen Nok Road is currently being renovated and offers only pamphlets. The new address is 372 Bamrung Muang Road,
Bangkok 10100
Tel. (02) 2260060
or (02) 2260072
Fax (02) 2246221.
Open 8.30am–4.30pm.
Closed weekends.

HOSPITALS
BANGKOK GENERAL
HOSPITAL
2 Soi Soonvijai (Soi 7)
New Phetchaburi Road
Tel. 3180066.
Open 24 hours.

BRITISH DISPENSARY
CLINIC
109 Sukhumvit Road,
(entrance between sois
5 and 7)
Tel. 2528056.
Open 9am–3.30pm.
Closed Sat. afternoon
and Sun.

SIRIRAJ HOSPITAL
Phrannok Road,
Thonburi
Tel. 4114230.
Open 24 hours.

POLICE
Crime Squad, 509
Worachak Road
Tel. 2216206.
Open 6am–12 midnight.
Opening hours may vary with each department.

POSTAL SERVICES
1160 Charoen Krung
Road
Tel. 2349530.
Open 8.30am–6pm,
Sat. 8.30am–4pm.
Closed Sun. and public
holidays.

BANKS
BANGKOK BANK
333 Silom Road
Tel. 2343333
Fax 236 5913.
BANK OF AMERICA
2/2 Wireless Road

Tel. 25163 33
Fax 253 1905.
BANK OF THAILAND
273 Sam Sen Road
Tel. 2823322
Fax 2800449.
HONGKONG AND
SHANGHAI BANKING
CORPORATION
64 Hong Kong Bank
Building,
Silom Road
Tel. 2331904
Fax 2367687.
STANDARD CHARTERED
BANK
946 Rama IV Road,
Lumpini
Tel. 234021
Fax 2369422.
WORLD BANK
5th Floor,
Udom Vidhya Building,
956 Rama IV Road
Tel. 2355300
Fax 2366467.
Banks open 8.30am–3.30pm Mon. to Fri.

BOOKSTORES
DK BOOKSTORE
Alliance Française,
29 Sathorn Tai Road
Tel. 2871926.
Open 9am–7pm.
Closed Sun.

MARKETS
CHATUCHAK PARK
WEEKEND MARKET
Phahonyothin Road,
(International Airport
Road)
Open officially
9am–6pm, Sat. and
Sun.
Enormous market offering a wide range of consumer goods and others: vegetables and fruits, spices, handicrafts, antiques, souvenirs, household items, clothings, plants, pets...
PATPONG NIGHT MARKET
Patpong Road
Open 7pm–12 midnight.
Shop for T-shirts, watches and souvenirs, in a street otherwise known for attractions of another kind...
PRATUNAM MARKET
Corner of Phetchaburi
and Ratchaprarop
Roads.
12 noon until late in the
evening. Closed Sun.
Another huge market, partly housed in building. Food, spices, clothing, fabrics, household items, gadgets...

TRANSPORT

TRAVEL AGENCIES
ANCIENT CITY COMPANY
Ratchadamnoen Road
Tel. 22410 57.
Organized tours.
EXCELSIOR TRAVEL
76/1 Napasap Yaek 1
Sukhumvit 36
Tel. 2591460,
2593009
Fax 3812767.
Open 9am–12 noon,
1–6pm.
Closed Sat. afternoon
and Sun.
J. P. TRAVEL
6 Sukhumvit Road,
Soi 4
Tel. 2529644
Fax 2552223.
Open 9am–7pm.
Closed Sunday.
*Organizes tours all over
Thailand, as well as to
the neighboring
countries of Vietnam,
Cambodia and Laos.*

AIRLINES
BANGKOK AIRWAYS
140 Pacific Place
Building,
Sukhumvit Road
Tel. 2534014
Fax 2534005.
Open 8am–12 noon,
1–5pm.
THAI AIRWAYS
485/2-3 Silom Road
Tel. 2343100
or 2343110.
Open 8am–12 noon,
1–5 pm.
Closed weekends.

AIRPORTS
DON MUANG DOMESTIC
AIRPORT (DOMESTIC
FLIGHTS)
Tel. 5352081.
*Flight information on tel.
5239010-12-13.*
DON MUANG
INTERNATIONAL AIRPORT
Vibhavadi Rangsit
Tel. 5352081
or 5351111.
*Departure information
on tel. 5351254 or
5351386.
Arrival information on
tel. 5351301, or
5351310.*

RAIL
HUA LAMPONG RAILWAY
STATION
Rama IV Road
Tel. 2237020
or 2237020,
*Information counter
opens 5am–10pm.
Departures for the
North, Northeast and*
*several destinations to
the South (enquire at
the information counter.
Reservations should be
made as early as
possible.*

BUSES
BUSES FOR THE OLD
CITIES
Bureau Mercedes,
near the Democracy
Monument
*Daily departures
7.45am–12.45pm.
Alternative route:
Bus No. 38 from the
Eastern Bus Station,
Fare 50 baht.*
EAST BUS STATION
(EKAMAI)
Sukhumvit Road
Soi 63
Tel. 3912504
or 3922521.
Open 6am–11pm.
*Departures for Pattaya
every 20 minutes. Fare
51 baht, one-way.*
NORTH AND NORTHEAST
BUS STATION
(THALAT MO CHIT)
Phaholyothin Road,
opposite Chatuchak
Park
Tel. 2710101
or 2794484-7.
*Departures for
Chiang Mai at 30-
minute intervals,
9am–9pm. Fare 47
baht, one-way.*
SOUTH BUS STATION
(KHONSONG SAI TAI)
Charansanitwongse
Road,
Thonburi
Tel. 4114978–9
or 4110112.

*Air-conditioned buses
for destinations in the
South and West.
Departures for Hua Hin
every 30 minutes,
9.30am–9pm. Fare 82
baht, one-way.*
Pinklao-Nakorn Chaisri
Highway
Tel. 4351196
or 4351194.
*Air-conditioned buses
for destinations in the
South and West.
Departures for
Kanchanaburi at 20-
minute intervals,
5am–7.30pm.*

CAR RENTAL
*The TAT office has a list
of car rental agencies in
Thailand.*

AVIS
2/12 Wireless Road
Tel. 2555300
Fax 2533734.
Open 7.30am–7pm.

HERTZ
1620, New Phetchaburi
Road
Tel. 2517575
Fax 2545320.
Open 8am–12 noon,
1–5pm.

CULTURE

NATIONAL ART
GALLERY
Chao Fa Road,
opposite National
Theater
Tel. 2812221.
Open 9am–noon,
1–4pm.
Closed Mon., Tues. and

◆ WAT ARUN ◆

Take an afternoon or evening cruise on the
Chao Phraya and discover Wat Arun, one of
the most famous temples in Bangkok.

public holidays.
*Exhibition of classic and
contemporary Thai
paintings. Admission 20
baht.*

GRAND PALACE
AND WAT PHRA KEO
Naphralan Road
Tel. 2228181.
Open 8.30am–12 noon,
1–3.30pm.
*Not to be missed.
Guided tours in all
languages. Suitable
dress required (pants
can be rented opposite
the entrance).
Admission 100 baht.*

PASTEUR INSTITUTE
AND SERPENTARIUM
Corner of Henri Dunant
and Rama IV Roads
Tel. 2520161.
Open 8.30am–4.30pm.
Closed Sat. afternoon
and Sun.
*Demonstration of
venom extraction at
11am and 2pm.
Admission 40 baht.*

JIM THOMPSON'S
HOUSE
Soi Kasemsan 2,
Rama I Road
Tel. 2150122.
Open 9am–4.30pm.
Closed Sun.
*Experienced voluntary
guides accompany tours
in various languages.
Admission 100 baht.
Profits are donated to
the charities for the
visually handicapped.*

KHAM THIENG HOUSE
Siam Society,
131 Soi Asoke,
Sukhumvit 21.
Open 9am–12 noon.
Tues. and Sat. 1–5pm.
Closed Mon., Wed. and
public holidays.
*Houses the library of
the Siam Society, where
you can consult
numerous works on the
history of Thailand.
Admission 30 baht.*

ROYAL BARGE
MUSEUM
Klong Bangkok Noi,
on the Chao Phraya,
near Phra Pin Klao
Bridge
Tel. 4240004.
Open 8.30am–4.30pm.
*To get there, take a
ferry to the Bangkok Noi
jetty, then walk to the
bridge. A walkway leads
to the barges.*

Alternatively, you can take a water taxi. Admission 10 baht.

NATIONAL MUSEUM
Opposite the Grand Palace, on the far side of Sanam Luang
Tel. 2241333.
Open 9am–12 noon, 1–4pm.
Closed Mon., Tues. and public holidays.
Free informative guided tours at 9am, including one in English on Thai culture (Tues.), Buddhism (Wed.) and Thai art (Thurs.). Admission 20 baht.

SUAN PAKKARD PALACE
On the corner of Si Ayutthaya and Phaya Thai Roads
Tel. 2454934.
Open 9am–4pm.
Closed Sun.
Admission 50 baht.

VIMARN MEK PALACE
Behind the Parliament Building, access is via Par Rajavithi Road
Tel. 2811569.
Open 9.30am–3.30pm.
Closed weekends.
Admission 50 baht (free entry for holders of an admission ticket to the Grand Palace). Free guided tours.

LUMPINI STADIUM
Rama IV Road, near Sathorn Tai Road
Tel. 2514303.
Open 6–11pm.
Thai boxing matches on Tues., Wed., and Fri. at 6pm, Sat. at 4pm. Seats 150–500 baht.

RATCHADAMNOEN STADIUM
Ratchadamnoen Nok Road, near Tourism Authority of Thailand (TAT) office
Tel. 2814205.
Thai boxing matches every Mon., Wed., Thurs. and Sun. at 6pm. Seats 150–500 baht.

NATIONAL THEATER
Na Phrathat Road, next to National Museum
Tel. 2214885.
Quality performances include classical Thai dances, masked dramas, shadow puppet plays. See the daily

newspapers for current schedule of programs.

WAT ARUN (TEMPLE OF THE DAWN)
West bank of the Chao Phraya.
Open from sunrise to sunset.
Access via Arun Amarin Road or by taking a boat from Tha Tien jetty (next to Wat Po), from Wat Phra Keo (on Naphralan Road) or by renting a hong yao (long-tail boat). Admission 10 baht.

WAT BENCHAMABOPIT (MARBLE TEMPLE)
Corner of Si Ayutthaya and Nakhon Pathom Roads
Tel. 2812501.
Open from sunrise to sunset.
Admission 10 baht.

WAT BOWORNIVET
Phra Sumen Road.
Open 8.30am–5pm.
Bus nos. 15, 49, 50, 76.

WAT KALAYANIMIT
Entrance to Bangkok Noi Klong.
Open 9am to 5pm.

WAT MAHATHAT (TEMPLE OF THE GREAT RELIC)
Between Phrathat Road and Silpakorn and Thammasat universities.
Open 9am–5pm.
Those visitors who are interested in learning Buddhist meditation can obtain guidance or receive instruction from the monks in section five.

WAT PO (TEMPLE OF THE RECLINING BUDDHA)
Chetuphon Street, opposite Grand Palace
Tel. 2220933.
Open 8am–12 noon, 1–5pm.
The largest temple in Bangkok and one of the the best massage schools in the country. Also offers traditional Thai massage to the general public. Admission payable.

WAT RAJABOPIT (EARTHENWARE TEMPLE)
Atsadang Road, near the offices of the

Ministry of the Interior.
Open 9am–5pm.

WAT RAJANADDA
Mahachai Road, opposite Golden Mount.
Temple famous for its amulet market.

WAT SAKET (GOLDEN MOUNT TEMPLE)
Next to Bang Lampu Klong Bridge
Bus nos. 8, 15, 37, 47, 49, 52 and 55.
Admission to the temple is free but visitors pay 5 baht to climb the hill to view Buddha relics. Holds a major candlelight festival procession in November.

WAT SUTHAT (GREAT SWING TEMPLE)
Bamrung Muang Road.
Open 9am–5pm.

WAT SUWANNARAM
South bank of Bangkok Noi Klong.
Open 9am–5pm.

WAT TRAIMIT (TEMPLE OF THE GOLDEN BUDDHA)
Traimit Road, end of Yaowarat Road.
Open 9am–5pm.
Admission 10 baht.

DUSIT ZOO
Between Radjawithi Road and Si Ayutthaya Road
Tel. 2810000.
Open 8 am–6pm.
The largest zoo in Southeast Asia. Good food available at very reasonable prices. Admission 10 baht.

BANGKOK ENVIRONS

CHEDI PHRA PATHOM
Nakhon Pathom, 37 miles west of Bangkok.
Open 9am–12 noon, 1–4pm. Closed Mon. and Wed.
Bus leaves from South station (Charansanitwongse Road). Visit also the museum opposite the botanical gardens.

OLD CITY (MUANG BORAN)
Old road from Pattaya (19 miles south of

Bangkok), in Samut Prakan Province.
Open 8.30am–5pm.
Admission 50 baht.

CROCODILE FARM
Old road from Pattaya, about 1.2 miles from the Old City, Samut Prakan Province.
Tel. 3870020.
Open 8am–6pm.
Visit weekdays and catch the crocodiles between 5pm and 6pm.

RESTAURANTS

AMBASSADOR FOOD CENTER
Ambassador Hotel Complex, Sukhumvit 11 (before the Ambassador Hotel).
Open 11am–10pm.
Numerous stands offering Thai, Chinese and other specialties. Good value for money. Operates on system of coupons bought at the entrance. Unused coupons are refunded.
○

BUSSARACUM
Trinity Complex, 425 Soi Pipat 2, Silom Road
Tel. 2342600.
Open 11am–2pm, 5–10.30pm.
Branch: 35 Soi Pipat (near Convent Road), tel. 2358915 or 2354519.
The ultimate in dishes created for the royal family. Excellent service. Reservations necessary.
⏸ 🍽 ℗

CABBAGES AND CONDOMS
10 Sukhumvit, 12 Phrakanong
Tel. 2527349.

ROYAL ORCHID SHERATON
VIJIT
SORN DAENG
MANOHRA
ROSE
NEW RINCOME RESTAURANT
BUSSARACUM
NARAI
ORIENTAL
CENTRAL DEPARTMENT STORE
SHANGRI-LA
HARLEQUIN
SALA RIM NAM

Open 11am–2pm, 6–10pm.
Owned by the Thai Family Planning Association. Renowned restaurant whose earnings go to charity. Original décor with male contraception theme.
100–400 baht
◐ ▭

CAFÉ DES ARTISTES
Alliance Française, Sathorn Tai Road
Tel. 2132122.
Open 7am–7pm.
Closed Sun.
Simple French cooking. Frequented by students from the French School. Diners can get useful information on Bangkok and source for contacts/ guides at this friendly establishment.
◐

CENTRAL DEPARTMENT STORE COFFEE SHOP
Central Department Store, 4th level, 2150 Silom Road (corner of Soi 30)
Tel. 2336930.
Open 10am–7.30pm.
Thai cooking. Usually crowded at lunch. Clean, modern surroundings and satisfactory service. Another branch at Phloenchit Road.
120–250 baht
○ ▭

CHARUVAN DUCK SHOP
70–2 Silom Road, near Soi 4.

Simple good dishes. About 20 baht per dish. Guests may enjoy air-conditioned comfort for another 5 baht, or be contented with fans.
○

D'JIT POCHANA
1082 Phaholyothin Road, Lardprao
Tel. 2795000.
Open 10am–10.30pm.
Excellent traditional cooking combined with good service. Very popular with tourists.
◐ ▭

HARLEQUIN
118 Sathorn Nua
Tel. 2343259.
Open 11am–2pm, 5pm–1am.
International cuisine with pleasant service and satisfactory quality.
250–1,000 baht
◍ ▭ ℙ

HELLO RESTAURANT
63–5, Khao San Road, Banglampoo Area.
Large European clientèle, mainly because of the numerous guest houses nearby (Hello is itself one). Appetising snacks.
○

LAIKHRAM
11/1 Sukhumvit 49, near Samitivej Hospital
Tel. 3925864.
Open 10am–9pm.
Offers excellent Thai cuisine.
100–50 baht
◐ ▭

LE DALAT
Patpong Building, 2nd level, Patpong 1 Surawong Road
Tel. 2340290.
Open 11am–2pm, 6–10pm. Closed Sun.
Another branch at: 47/1 Sukhumvit Road, Soi 23
Tel. 2584192.
Same business hours.
Most famous Vietnamese restaurant in Bangkok. Good food and pleasant surroundings.
◍ ▭

LEMON GRASS
5/1 Sukhumvit Road, Soi 24
Tel. 2588637.
Open 11am–2pm, 6–11pm.
Thai nouvelle cuisine. Small restaurant with pleasant atmosphere, especially at tables near the garden. Attentive and discreet service.
◐ ▭

MANDALAY
23/17 Soi Ruam Rudee
Tel. 2552893.
Open 6–10.30pm.
The only Burmese restaurant in Bangkok. Good food and service, but on the expensive side.
◍ ▭

NEW RINCOME RESTAURANT
144/19–22 Silom Road, opposite Thai Dhanu Bank
Tel. 2352781.
Open 6–10pm.

Very lively Chinese restaurant. Sumptuous dishes served by pleasant and knowledgeable staff.
160 baht
◐ ▭

NOODLE GARDEN
Robinson Department Store, 2 Silom Road
Tel. 2350414.
Open 10am–12 midnight.
Fast food, specializing in noodles and Thai dishes. Quick and inexpensive.
○ ▭

PAN PAN CAPRI
45 Soi Lang Suan, Phloenchit Road
Tel. 2527104.
Another branch at: 6–6/1 Soi 33, Sukhumvit Road
Tel. 2589304.
Open 11am–11pm.
Italian cuisine. Pizzas, pasta and homemade Italian ice cream.
◐ ▭

SALA RIM NAM
Hotel Oriental, 48 Oriental Avenue
Tel. 4376211.
Open 7–9.30pm.
Traditional Thai cuisine in an exceptional setting beside the Chao Phraya River. Guests eat in the traditional Thai manner, sitting on floor cushions. Classical Sukhothai dance performances are staged in the evening. Reservations are required.

341

Arrive at about 7pm.
750 baht
⦾ ▭ ゞ

SEAFOOD MARKET AND RESTAURANT
388 Sukhumvit Road
(corner of Soi 16)
Tel. 2580218.
Open 11am–3pm,
6pm–12 midnight.
Another branch at:
New Phetchaburi Road
(corner of Soi 39),
Less expensive and
quieter.
*The market is a
spectacle in itself. You
buy what you want
(infinite choice) and pay
at the cashier. You then
pay for the cooking of
the dish and the service.
From 450 baht*
⦾ ▭ 🅿

SORN DAENG
Ratchadamnoen Klang
Road
Tel. 2243088.
Open 10am–10pm.
*Thai and Western
cuisine, simple and
inexpensive. Pleasant
restaurant, well located.
100–250 baht*
❶

THAI ROOM
Patpong 2
Tel. 2337920.
Open 8am to 12
midnight
*Convenient eatery
when in Patpong. Quite
good food at very
reasonable prices. Thai,
Chinese, Italian,
Mexican and American
dishes.
120–250 baht*
❶ ▭ 👤

TUM NAK THAÏ
131 Ratchapisek Road
Tel. 2773828.
*Proud to be included in
the* Guinness Book of
Records, *this is the
largest restaurant in the
world. The waiters
move around deftly on
roller skates. An
institution. Traditional
dance performances at
8pm. Thai and Western
cuisine.
180–500 baht*
❶ ▭ 🅿

VIJIT
77/2 Ratchadamnoen
Klang Road
Tel. 2816472.
Open 11am–11pm.
Thai, Japanese and

Western cuisine. This
well-located
establishment is very
popular and deservedly
so. Music from 5pm.
Also prepares takeouts.
150–250 baht
❶ ▭

WHOLE EARTH
93/3 Soi Lang Suan,
Phloenchit Road
Tel. 2525574.
Open 11.30am–2pm,
5.30pm–12 midnight.
*The best-known
vegetarian restaurant
in Bangkok. Peaceful,
intimate ambience
guaranteed. Traditional
soothing guitar music
in the evenings; you
can eat near the stage,
seated on cushions.
150–300 baht*
❶ ▭

YOK YOR
3 Witsut Kasat Pier
Tel. 2811829
or 2827385.
Open 10am–11pm.
*Floating restaurant on
the Chao Phraya.
Leaves from the
Rama IX bridge every
evening at about 8pm.
40 baht per person for
the cruise, excluding
dining charges. Thai,
Japanese, Chinese and
Western cuisine.
30 baht*
⦾ ▭ ゞ

YWCA RESTAURANT
13 South Sathorn Road
Tel. 2864258.
Open 8am–10pm.

*Quiet and very pleasant
restaurant inside the
YMCA courtyard. Good
Thai and German
cuisine (reputedly the
best sauerkraut in
Bangkok). Reservations
required at the
weekend.
140–250 baht*
❶ ▭ 🅿

HOTELS

ASIA HOTEL
296 Phyathai Road
Tel. 2150808
Fax 2154360.
*Luxurious, well-located
grand hotel.
Unimposing façade but
pleasant interior
decoration and
comfortable rooms.
Breakfast 175 baht.
2,100–3,700 baht*
🏛 🄲 🛏 🔲 🛆 🚗
▭ 👤

**BANGKOK
YOUTH HOSTEL**
25/2 Phitsanulok Road,
See Soa Theves, Dusit
Tel. 2820950
Fax 2816831.
*Average. Quiet and
pleasant. IYH card
required. Rooms with
fans or air-conditioned.
Dormitories.
300 baht*
🛏 🄲 🛏

**ERAWAN
GRAND HYATT**
494 Rajdamri Road
Tel. 2541234
Fax 2535856.
One of the oldest hotels

*in Bangkok, acquired by
the Hyatt Restaurant.
Breakfast 320 baht.
4,500–5,600 baht*
🏛 🄲 🛏 🔲 🛆 🚗
▭ 👤

EURO INN
249 Soi 31
Sukhumvit Road
Tel. 259940
Fax 2599490.
*Well located. Coffee
shop offers wide
variety of food and
buffet lunch.
1,450–1,600 baht*
🏛 🄲 ⦾ 🔲 🛆 🚗
▭

FIRST HOTEL
2 Phetchaburi Road
Tel. 2550111
or 2553055.
Fax 2550121
*Well located, Thai
hospitality with warm
and friendly service.
2,220–6,600 baht*
🏛 🄲 ⦾ 🔲 🛆 🚗
▭

FLORIDA
43, Phyathai Sq
Tel. 2470103
Fax 2477419.
*Old but clean
establishment. Neat
rooms. Good value for
money.
Breakfast 77 baht.
1,000 baht*
🛏 🄲 🔲 🛆 🚗 ▭

IMPALA
9 Sukhumvit
Soi 24
Tel. 2590053
Fax 2588747.
*Out of town. Pleasant
atmosphere, rather
small but comfortable
and attractive rooms.
Breakfast 160 baht.
2,600–5,400 baht*
🏛 🛏 🛏 🔲 🛆 🚗
▭ 👤

**KHAO SAN PALACE
HOTEL**
139 Khao San Road
Tel. 2820578.
*Well located. Small
rooms with fans or air-
conditioning. Poorly lit
but very clean.
Breakfast 100 baht.
350–450 baht*
🛏 🛏

LEK GUEST HOUSE
125–127, Khao San
Road, Banglampoo
Tel. 2 81 27 75.
*Rooms without shower
or air-conditioning, but*

clean enough. Lots of other similar hotels in Khao San Road, among them the Merry V and the Grand Guest House.
Breakfast 50 baht.
80–120 baht
⌂

MANOHRA
412 Surawongse Road
Tel. 2345070
Fax 2377662.
Well located, pleasant atmosphere. Charming, small rooms, clean and comfortable.
Breakfast 17 baht.
2,825–5,000 baht

MERIDIEN PRESIDENT
135/26 Gaysorn Road
Tel. 2530444
Fax 2537565.
Central location (popular with airline crews). Small but attractive rooms.
Breakfast 296 baht.
3,600–4,200 baht

MONTIEN BANGKOK
54 Surawongse Road
Tel. 2337060
or 2365219
Fax 2365218.
Well located. Good atmosphere. Spacious, welcoming rooms. Restaurant.
Breakfast 275 baht.
3,800–4,500 baht

NANA
4 Nana Tai Sukhumvit Road
Tel. 2520121
Fax 2551769.
Central and popular for one-night or one-hour stands... Rooms are small but clean. Nightclub, tour agency.
Breakfast 100 baht.
900–1,500 baht

NARAI
222 Silom Road
Tel. 2370100
Fax 2367161.
Well located. Attentive service. Attractive rooms. Ask for one at the front with the view.
Breakfast 220 baht.
2,900–5,000 baht

◆ ORIENTAL HOTEL ◆

The majestic lobby of the oldest and most prestigious hotel in Bangkok, where Joseph Conrad, Graham Greene and other famous people have stayed.

NITH CHAROEN
183 Khao San Road
Banglampoo
Tel. 2819872.
Well located, pleasant atmosphere. Small, neat rooms, air-conditioned. Breakfast 50 baht.
300–450 baht

ORIENTAL
48 Oriental Avenue
Tel. 2360400
Fax 2361937.
Supposedly "the most beautiful hotel in the world" (and the most prestigious in Bangkok). Notable for its gardens, its superb view over the Chao Phraya, and unrivaled comfort and service. Renovated. Departure point for night river cruises.
Breakfast 377 baht.
7,500–9,200 baht

PARK HOTEL
Sukhumvit 7
Tel. 2 55 43 00
Fax 2554309.
Well located. Affordable luxury. Pleasant surroundings and staff.
Breakfast 177 baht.
2,200–3,000 baht

REY
762/1 Sukhumvit 32–4
Tel. 2590106
Fax 2586635.
Out of town but quiet

and well maintained. Spacious, pleasant and clean rooms.
Breakfast 90 baht.
1,100 baht

ROSE
118 Surawongse Road
Tel. 2337695
Fax 2346381.
Well located. Good value for money. Suites at reasonable prices. TV extra 100 baht.
Breakfast 80 baht.
900 baht

ROYAL HOTEL
2 Ratchadamnoen Road
Tel. 2229111
Fax 2242083.
Well located, with most of the advantages of a luxury hotel. Spacious rooms. Restaurants and piano bar.
Breakfast 120 baht.
1,300 baht

ROYAL ORCHID SHERATON
2 Captain Bush Lane
Tel. 2345599
Fax 2368320.
Huge hotel with spacious and very comfortable rooms. Pleasant view over the Chao Phraya River and of the city. Also offers tennis, squash and a nightclub.
Breakfast 333 baht.
6,100–6,500 baht

SHANGRI-LA
89 Soi Wat Suan Plu
New Road, Bangrak
Tel. 2367777
Fax 2368579.
Classic luxury beside the Chao Phraya. Pleasant rooms. Tennis, squash, jacuzzi, massage, gym.
Breakfast 290 baht.
5,000–6,300 baht

SIAM INTERCONTINENTAL
967 Rama I Road, PO Box 2052
Tel. 2530355
or 2545474
Fax 2532275.
Truly charming hotel. Its magnificent gardens make you forget you are in the middle of bustling Bangkok. Copious and delicious noon buffet.
Breakfast 270 baht.
4,200–5,400 baht

SUKHOTHAI
13/3 Sathorn Tai Road
Tel. 2870222
Fax 2874980.
Magnificent and modern, decorated in Sukhothai style, including lotus-shaped basins of expensive Thai materials. High-quality restaurants with impeccable service.
Breakfast 300 baht.
5,000–6,400 baht

SWISS PARK
155/23–4 Soi 11
Sukhumvit Road
Tel. 2540228
or 2529191
Fax 2540378.
Well-located business hotel. Room facilities include personal safe and hair dryer.
2,900–5,200 baht

THAI HOTEL
78 Prachatipatai Road
Tel. 2822831
Fax 2801299.
Small neat rooms.Only accepts American

Express and Diners Club cards.
Breakfast 120 baht.
1,000 baht to1,300 baht

THE REGENT
155 Ratchadamri Road
Tel. 2516127
Fax 2539195.
Beautiful, first-class hotel.
Breakfast 295 baht.
1,800–6,500 baht

VIENGTAI
42 Tanee Road
Banglumpoo
Tel. 2805392
Fax 2818153.
Well-located establishment. Pleasant rooms. Restaurants, travel agency, hair salon. Often full.
Breakfast 77 baht.
900 baht

YMCA
13 Sathorn Tai Road
Tel. 2861936
Fax 2873016.
Impeccable cleanliness. Small rooms, some with a splendid view of the Sukhothai gardens. Huge swimming pool. Travel agency. Restaurant.
680–900 baht

NIGHTLIFE

FRENCH KISS
Patpong II
Tel. 2 34 99 93
Open 10pm–3am.
French-run bar in the very lively Patpong quarter. Grab a quick bite and seek tips or advice on happenings in the other entertainment outlets around the area.
♫

KING'S CASTLE
Patpong I
Open 10pm–3am.
Well-known go-go bar, said to have the prettiest girls in the Patpong district.
♫

NASA
999 Ramkhamhaeng Road
Tel. 3143368.
Huge nightclub with futuristic decor.

Occasionally organizes concerts. Attracts a young and sophisticated clientèle.
Admission 200 baht.
♫

ROUND MIDNIGHT PUB AND RESTAURANT
106/2 Soi Lang Suan.
Regular jazz concerts. One of the numerous bars along busy Soi Lang Suan.

SAXOPHONE PUB & RESTAURANT
3/8 Victory Monument
Phyathai Road
Open 11pm–1am.
Jazz and blues band every evening.

KANCHANABURI
PRACTICALITIES

ZIP CODE
71000

TOURIST INFORMATION OFFICE
Saengchuto Road,
Amphoe Muang
Tel. 511200.
Open 8.30am–4.30pm.

HOSPITAL
PAHOLPOLPAYUHASENA HOSPITAL
Saengchuto Road
Tel. 511233.

TOURIST POLICE
Tel. 512795
6am–12 midnight.

ATM
THAI FARMERS BANK
160/80–2 Saengchuto Road, Baan Noue Village
Tel. 5112 03.
Open 8.30am–4.30pm.
Closed weekends.

TRANSPORT

TRAVEL AGENCIES
BT TRAVEL
Saengchuto Road,
Baan Noue Village
Tel. 511967.
Open 7am–5pm.

RAILWAY STATION
Saengchuto Road
Tel. 5112 85.
Departs from Bangkok 8am and 2.30pm.
25 baht.

BOATS
THA KRADAN JETTY
Departure point for day excursions to Nagarina National Park.

PAK SAENG JETTY
Tambon Tha Seo.
Departure point for excursions to Lawa cave and the Sai Yok falls (about 60 miles northwest). Seven-hour journey.

CULTURE

JEATH WAR MUSEUM
Wisuttharangsi Road,
near Wat Chaichumphon
Open 8am–4pm.
Replica of barracks of PoWs who built the

"Death Railway" and other exhibits recalling the terrible living conditions experienced by these inmates.
Admission 20 baht.

ERAWAN NATIONAL PARK
Take bus no. 8170 to Kanchanaburi. Departures every 50 minutes from 8am–4pm. Last bus returns at 4pm.

HOTELS

BAMBOO GUEST HOUSE
3–5 Soi Vietnam
Patthana Road,
Thamakarm Village
Tel. 512532.
A pleasant location in view of its proximity to the bridge.
Breakfast 50 baht.
50–400 baht

RIVER KWAE VILLAGE
Baan Phu Ta Kien,
Sai Yok District
Tel. 34591055
Fax 38391054.
Reservations in Bangkok tel. 2517522.
Very well-known hotel far to the north of Kanchanaburi (upriver from Nam Tok). Accommodation in floating bungalows.
Breakfast 90 baht.
780–1,300 baht

SAM'S PLACE
Song Kwai Road,
Tel. 513971
Fax 34512813.
Floating hotel with very pleasant bungalows. Welcoming restaurant and interesting cruise on the River Kwai.
Breakfast 40 baht.
70–300 baht

PATTAYA
PRACTICALITIES

ZIP CODE
20260

TOURIST INFORMATION OFFICE
382/1 Beach Road
Tel. 428750
Fax 429113.
Open 8.30am–4.30pm.

HOSPITAL

PATTAYA INTERNATIONAL HOSPITAL
Pattaya Soi 4, Beach Road
Tel. 425725.
Open 24 hours.

TOURIST POLICE

382/1 Beach Road
Tel. 42 931
6am–12 midnight.

POSTAL SERVICES

Soi Chaiyait
Beach Road
Tel. 429341.
Open 8.30am–3.30pm.
Sat. and Sun. 9am to 12 noon.

ATM

THAI FARMERS BANK
22 South Pattaya
Tel. 42 9294
Open 8.30am–3.30pm.
Closed on weekends.
Cash dispensed until 9pm.

TRANSPORT

AIRLINES

THAI AIRWAYS
Royal Cliff Beach Hotel
Pattaya, Chonburi
Tel. 429286.
Open 8am–5pm.
Closed weekends.

CAR AND BIKE RENTAL

AVIS
Dusit Resort Hotel
Tel. 42 99 01
or 42 99 03.
Open 24 hours.
Other branches at Royal Cliff Beach Resort and Royal Garden Resort. Shuttle service from Bangkok Dusit Thani to Pattaya.

PATTAYA VEHICLE RENTAL SERVICE
205/29 Moo 10
Pattaya 2nd Road
Tel 428085.

SUNSHINE SERVICE
217/1 Pattaya 2nd Road
Tel. 429247.
Motorbike rental. Bikes can also be rented at the Diana Inn and along Beach Road. Make sure insurance is included in the rental and remember… ride carefully.

BOAT

SANGKAEO EXPRESS BOAT
463 Sunset Avenue
Tel. 428085.
Open 8am–9pm.

SEAT PATTAYA
175, Beach Road,
South Pattaya
Tel. 428108.
Open 8am–12 noon,
1–5pm.
Closed Wed.

SPORTS

BILLIARDS AND BOWLING

PATTAYA BOWL
Pattaya Second Road
Tel. 429466.
Open 10am–12 midnight.
International standard bowling alley with air-conditioning. There are several other alleys in Pattaya.
Around 30–40 baht.

GOLF

**BANG PHRA ·
GOLF COURSE**
45, Moo 6 Tambon Bang
Phra. Amphoo Si Racha
Tel. 311321.
From Pattaya, a half-hour ride by car to one of the most attractive golf courses in Thailand.
Around 650 baht.

SIAM COUNTRY CLUB
50 Tambon Pong,
Amphoe Bang Lamung
Tel. 428002.
Reputable private 18-hole golf course (par 72). Conveniently sited about 20 minutes' ride from town. Guests may book a round through their hotel.
Around 800 baht.

DEEP-SEA FISHING

DEUTSCHES HAUS
Beach Road
corner of Soi 4
Tel. 425725.
Deep-sea fishing parties (up to a maximum of 25 persons). Around 500–600 baht, depending on whether you want to fish or just spectat. Fishing tackle and bait are available for a fee. Contact Dieter Floeth.

PATTAYA'S GAME FISHING CLUB
Jenny's Bar,
Soi Pattayaland
Tel. 429645.
Two fishing trips weekly. To take part, join the club. Around 500 baht. Contact Martin.

DIVING

DAVE'S DIVERS DEN
437/11–12 Soi Yodsak
Tel. 423486.
Good contact for diving enthusiasts. Minimum 2000 baht for basic training and diving trip.

THE SCUBA PROFESSIONALS
Dusit Resort Hotel,
240 Beach Road
Tel. 429901.
Deep-sea diving school with a good reputation. Minimum 2,000 baht.

ARCHERY

NONG NOOCH VILLAGE
Route 3, 11 miles south
of Pattaya
Open 10am–6pm.
Admission 30 baht.

RIFLE AND PISTOL SHOOTING

TIFFANY'S
464 Pattaya 2nd Road
Tel. 429642.
Open 9am–9pm.
Nineteen well-equipped ranges for rifles (22 mm) and pistols (38, 22 and 9 mm).
120 baht.

HOTELS

DIANA INN
216/6–9 Pattaya 2nd
Road, enter by Sois 11
and 12
Tel. 429675
Fax 424566.
Renovated in 1992. Rooms of varying degrees of comfort but all very pleasant and clean. No elevator. Breakfast 75 baht.
450–600 baht
🏨 🆑 ⌂ ▯ ⌱ 🚙 ▭

ORCHID LODGE
240 Moo 5,
Beach Road
Tel. 428161
Fax 428165.
Like the Nipa Lodge, it is part of the Siam Group. Comfortable rooms, splendid garden. Breakfast 260 baht.
1,500–2,000 baht
🏛 ⌂ ▯ ⌱ 🚙 ▭ 🏃

QUEEN PATTAYA HOTEL
365/Mu 4, Central
Pattaya Road
Tel. 428234, 429915
Fax 422798.
Beach resort hotel with

friendly service, hair salon. Five minutes' walk to Pattaya town.
400–1,200 baht
🏨 🆑 ◑ ⌂ ▯ ⌱
🚙 ▭

PATTAYA 11 HOTEL
Soi 11 Beach Road
Tel. 429239
Fax 429650.
Looking onto the sea. Small clean rooms. Very good value for money.
Breakfast 45 baht.
150–400 baht
⌂ 🆑 ⌱ ▭

ROYAL CLIFF BEACH HOTEL
353 Moo 12, Cliff Road
Tel. 421421
Fax 428511.
Reservations in
Bangkok:
Tel. 2801737.
Probably the smartest hotel in Pattaya. Unrivaled comfort and magnificent view. Breakfast 260 baht.
3,885–5,400 baht
🏛 ⌂ ▯ ⌱ 🏊 ▯ ⌱
🚙 ▭ 🏃

ROYAL GARDEN RESORT
218 Beach Road
Tel. 428126
Fax 429926.
Beautiful surroundings, and luxurious rooms. Very pleasant lobby. Breakfast 260 baht.
1,900–2,600 baht
🏨 🆑 🏊 ▯ ⌱
🚙 ▭ 🏃

WELKOM INN
Beach Road Soi 3,
PO Box 43
Tel. 422589
Fax 422558.
Very pleasant Flemish proprietor. Small, clean rooms. Those upstairs are most attractive. Breakfast 55 baht.
200–350 baht
⌂ 🆑 ⌂ ⌱ ▭

NIGHTLIFE

TIFFANY'S SHOW
464 Pattaya 2nd Road
Tel. 429642
Open 7am–12 midnight.
Famous and spectacular transvestite revue. Stages three shows per day, at 7pm, 8.30pm and 10pm. There is an additional show at 11.30pm on Saturday.

PHETCHABURI

KHAO WANG
To the west of town.
A tram takes you to the top of the hill where the view is magnificent (5 baht).
Admission 20 baht.

HUA HIN

PRACTICALITIES

ZIP CODE
77110

TOURIST INFORMATION OFFICE
Cha Am,
500/61 Phetkasem Road
Tel. 4710 05.

HOSPITAL
HUA HIN HOSPITAL
Phetkasem Road
(2 miles from town)
Tel. 511743.

TOURIST POLICE
Damneonkasem Road
Tel. 511063.
24 hours.

POSTAL SERVICES
Damneonkasem Road
Tel. 511063
Open 8.30am–3.30pm.
Sat. 9am–12 noon.
Closed Sun.

TRANSPORT

TRAVEL AGENCIES
HUA HIN PRAN TOUR
1st level,
Siriphetchkasem
Building, Srasong Road
Tickets for air-conditioned bus to Bangkok. Departures on the hour 4am–8pm.

WESTERN TOURS
11 Damneonkasem Road
Tel. 5125 60.
Open 8am–7pm.
Ticket reservations and confirmations, taxi, excursions.

RAILWAY STATION
Damneonkasem Road
Tel. 511073.
Departs for Bangkok at 6.20am, 2.30pm and 8.30pm. 192 baht.

BUS
SUPHAPCHON
RESTAURANT
2 miles north of town
Tel. 512150.
Buses for the south.

Reservations recommended (at the southern terminus or in Bangkok) because the buses only stop at Hua Hin by special request. You can call from the restaurant for 30 baht.

BUS TERMINUS
Srasong Road
Tel. 512543.
From 5pm to 9pm, then from midnight to 4.30pm, stopping alternately at the station or opposite Chartchai Market. Departures for Bangkok at 30-minute intervals.
82 baht.

CAR AND BIKE RENTAL
AVIS
Dusit Resort and Polo Club
Tel. 5200008.
Another office at:
Royal Garden Resort,
Tel. 511881.
Damneonkasem Road opposite the bazaar.
From 100 baht per day for a motor bike to 50 baht per day for a bicycle.

SPORTS

ROYAL HUA HIN GOLF COURSE
Tel. 32511099.
Open 6am–6pm.
The oldest golf course in Thailand, with the added luxury of panoramic sea views. A golfer's paradise.

◆ HUA HIN STATION ◆

The first Thai health resort (1911) and a holiday venue for the Court, Hua Hin could be reached by train in the 1920's. The station has retained its elegant royal reception room.

RESTAURANTS

SAENG THAI
Near the port.
Open 11am–10pm.
The oldest fish and seafood restaurant in town. Excellent.
100–350 baht
◐ ▭ ⌇

SUNSHINE SUKEYAKI & BBQ
Srasong Road
Open 10am–10pm.
Very pleasant restaurant serving Barbequed meat, seafood and fish. Karaoke sessions take place on some evenings.
120–180 baht
◐ ℙ

HOTELS

BAN BOOSARIN
8/8 Poonsuk Road
Tel. 512076.
Clean and well-maintained family hotel. Large rooms. Pleasant staff.
Breakfast 50 baht.
700 baht
◐ ☗ ⌂ ▭ ♀

JED PEE NONG
13/7 Damneonkasem Road
Tel. 512381
Fax 512381.
Bungalows around a swimming pool. Small but clean rooms. If the price doesn't deter, opt for a deluxe room. Restaurant.

Breakfast 60 baht.
600–800 baht
○ ☗ ⌂ ▭ ⌇ 🚗

SIRIN
Damnoenkasem Road
Tel. 5111 50.
Charming, comfortable hotel situated close to the sea. A drawback is that the hotel's, swimming pool is a mile away. However, there is also a pleasant covered terrace restaurant which serves Thai cuisine.

Breakfast 80 baht.
790–1,300 baht
◐ ☗ ⌂ ▭ ⌇ 🚗
▭ ♀

SOFITEL CENTRAL (EX-RAILWAY)
1, Damnoenkasem Road
Tel. 5120 21
Fax 511014.
Famous hotel in magnificent surroundings. Small but charming rooms in colonial style with breathtaking sea views.
Breakfast 271 baht.
2,400–4,700 baht
◍ ⌂ ▭ ⌇ 🚗 ▭
♀

SURAT THANII

PRACTICALITIES

ZIP CODE
84000

TOURIST INFORMATION OFFICE
5 Talat Mai Road,
Ban Don,
Amphoe Muang
Tel. 281828
Fax 28228.
Open 8.30am–4.30pm.

HOSPITAL
Surat-Phun Phin Road.
Tel. 272231.

TOURIST POLICE
5 Talat Mai Road
Tel. 281300.
Open 6am–12 midnight.

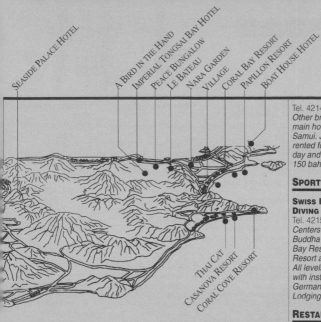

SEASIDE PALACE HOTEL
A BIRD IN THE HAND
IMPERIAL TONGSAI BAY HOTEL
PEACE BUNGALOW
LE BATEAU
NARA GARDEN VILLAGE
CORAL BAY RESORT
PAPILLON RESORT
BOAT HOUSE HOTEL

THAI CAT
CASANOVA RESORT
CORAL COVE RESORT

ATM
THAI FARMERS BANK
Na Muang Road
Tel. 282210.
Open 8.30am–3.30pm.

TRANSPORT

TRAVEL AGENCY
PHANGAN FERRY CO
2/6 Chonkasem Road,
Muang
Tel. 286461
Fax 282713.
Open 6.30am–5.30pm.

RAILWAY STATION
Phun Phin
(about 10 miles from
town)
Tel. 311213.
*Shuttle buses ply
between the station and
the town center. The
transfer is often
included in the price of
a cruise between Surat
Thani and Koh Samui.
First train for Bangkok
leaves at 11am, last at
7pm.
500 baht.*

AIRLINES
THAI AIRWAYS
3/27–8 Karoonrat Road
Tel. 272610
Open 8am–5pm.
Closed weekends.

HOTELS

SENI HOTEL
Tonpo Road
Tel. 272279.
*Small hotel close to the
port in a quiet street.
Rooms with fan or air-*

*conditioning.
130–350 baht*
⌂ 🅲 🄰

WANG THAI HOTEL
1 Talat Mai Road,
Amphoe Muang
Tel. 283020
Fax 281007
Reservations in
Bangkok:
Tel. 2556912.
*Less luxurious than it
looks from the outside
but it is clean and
pleasant. Lots of tourists
in transit for Koh Samui.
Breakfast 60 baht.
690–1,300 baht*
⌂ 🅲 ⌂ ◑ ▢ ⌁
🚗 ▭

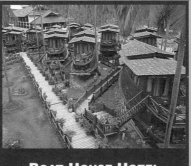

KOH SAMUI
PRACTICALITIES

ZIP CODE
84000

ATM
THAI FARMERS BANK
226 Mu 3, Taweerat-
pakdi Road, Na Thon
Open 8.30am–3.30pm.
Closed weekends.
ATM open until 9pm.

TRANSPORT

CAR AND BIKE RENTAL
AVIS
Imperial Tongsai Bay
Hotel

Tel. 421451.
*Other branches at the
main hotels in Koh
Samui. Jeeps may be
rented for 600 baht per
day and motorbikes for
150 baht per day.*

SPORTS

**SWISS INTERNATIONAL
DIVING SCHOOL**
Tel. 421538.
*Centers on Great
Buddha beach, Central
Bay Resort, Coral Cove
Resort and on Koh Tao.
All levels of coaching,
with instruction in
German and English.
Lodging included.*

RESTAURANTS

A BIRD IN THE HAND
Bo Phut Village
Open 10am–10pm.
*Small, pleasant
restaurant. Friendly
proprietor. Simple but
good food. Western
cuisine.
100–200 baht*
◑ �P

LE BATEAU
34/1 Bo Phut Village
Tel. 425297.
Open 8am to 9pm.
Closed Tues.
*In business since 1981.
Simple but pleasant
surroundings. Good
food. One-off boat and
jeep trips organized.
Thai, French and
Belgian cuisine.
100–200 baht*
◑ �P

THAI CAT
Opposite Mix Pub,
Hat Lamai.
Open 10am–10pm.
*Small, partially covered
restaurant. Friendly
proprietor and good
food. Thai and Italian
cuisine.
50–120 baht*
○ �P

HOTELS

BOAT HOUSE HOTEL
Choeng Mon Beach
Tel. 425040
Fax 425460.
*Original luxury
bungalows in the shape
of traditional crafts.
Charming and chic
Breakfast 220 baht.
3,300–5,400 baht*
🏛 ⌂ ☈ ▢ ⌁
🚗 ▭ ⚒

◆ BOAT HOUSE HOTEL ◆

Like boats at anchor, these luxury bungalows
stand on the beach at Choong Mon,
northeast of Koh Samui.

CASANOVA RESORT
124 Lamai Beach
Tel. 421425.
Well located, close to the beach (5 minutes). Large swimming pool and superb surroundings.
800–1,000 baht
🏠 ⛅ 🌊 🚗

CHATKAEO RESORT
59/4 Choeng Mon Beach
Bo Phut.
An undeniable asset here is a perfect beach. Minimal comforts. Rooms with air-conditioning cost slightly more.
400–1,200 baht
🏠 🏠 🖥 🚗

CORAL BAY RESORT
PO Box 19,
Chaweng Beach,
Yai Noi Bay
Reservations in Bangkok:
Tel. 2337711.
Beside a coral beach (the sand beach is 5 minutes away). Very pleasant atmosphere. Attractive rooms, magnificent garden.
900–1,800 baht
🏠 🏠 🖥 ⛅ 🌊 🚗 📺 🏃

CORAL COVE RESORT
Located between Chaweng and Lamai beaches. Enjoy diving on the coral reef, or take advantage of the hotel's private beach. Beautiful, immaculately clean bungalows, though few rooms with air-conditioning.
50–600 baht
🏠 🏠 🖥 ⛅ 🚗

GOLDEN SAND RESORT
124/2 Lamai Beach
Tel. 421430
Fax 421430.
Reservations in Bangkok:
Tel. 2524101
or 2524104.

IMPERIAL TONGSAI BAY HOTEL
Ban Plailaem,
Bo Phut
Tel. 425015
Fax 421462.
In the north of the island. Magnificent garden. Comfortable bungalows, some fairly isolated, some with sofa beds.

Breakfast 250 baht.
4,400–5,700 baht
🏠 🏠 🖥 ⛅ 🏠 🚗 📺 🏃

NARA GARDEN
80 Moo 4,
Bo Phut
Tel. 421364
Fax 421364.
Comfortable rooms decorated with straw and rattan, with idyllic sea views. Very breezy, so hardly anyone swims at the beach.
1,600–3,000 baht
🏠 🏠 🖥 ⛅ 🌊 🚗 📺 🏃

PAPILLON RESORT
Chaweng Beach
Fax 421387.
Very friendly proprietor. Shuttle to the airport is available on request. Small, simple but pleasant bungalows. Fans and air-conditioned rooms. Restaurant and entertainment.
400–900 baht
🏠 🏠 🖥 ⛅ 🚗

PEACE BUNGALOW
Bo Phut
Tel. 421357
Fax 425179.
Family-run business. Charming surroundings. Good restaurant. Opt for a bungalow on the beach.
60–400 baht
🏠 🏠 🖥 ⛅ 🚗 📺

PRINCESS VILLAGE
Chaweng Beach,
PO Box 25
Tel. 421382.
Teak lodges on stilts in the traditional style, with splendid views over the sandy beach and the garden. Heart-stopping.
1,100–2,000 baht
🏠 🅲 🏠 ⛅ 🚗

SEASIDE PALACE HOTEL
152 Nathon Road,
Nathon
Tel. 421080
Fax 421080.
Clean rooms with fan or air-conditioning. Pleasant surroundings with idyllic sea views.
320–500 baht
🏠 🅲 ⛅ 📺

VILLAGE
Chaweng Beach,
PO Box 25
Tel. 421382
Fax 421382.
Charming rooms. The beauty of the garden makes up for the lack of sea views. Same management as the Princess Village.
1,200–1,900 baht
🏠 🅲 🏠 ⛅ 🚗 📺

NAKHON SI THAMMARAT

PRACTICALITIES

ZIP CODE
80000

TOURIST INFORMATION OFFICE
1180 Bowon Bazaar,
Ratchadamnoen Road
Tel. 356356.
Open 8.30am–4.30pm.

CULTURE

NATIONAL MUSEUM
Ratchadamnoen Road.
Open 9am–4pm.
Closed Mon. and Tues.
Admission 10 baht.

WAT MAHATHAT
Ratchadamnoen Road,
(1 mile south of town).
Open 9am–4pm.
To get there, take a bus heading south or a songteo. Small museum inside.

SONGKHLA

CULTURE

NATIONAL MUSEUM
Between Rong Muang Road and Jana Road.
Open 9am–4pm.
Admission 10 baht.

THALE NOI RESERVE
Follow Highway N 4107 for 78 miles (exit 126), then turn off to the village of Khu Khut.
Canoes can be rented from the village and this is an ideal way to explore the nature reserve.

HOTELS

NARAI
14 Chai Khao Road
Tel. 311078.
Quiet, cozy rooms.
100–250 baht
🏠

SAMILA
1, Ratchadamnoen Road
Tel. 3113104.
All the hotel comforts you can think of. Restaurant.
700–1,800 baht
🏠 🏠 📺 🚗

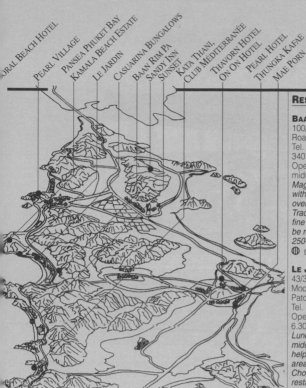

RESTAURANTS

BAAN RIM PA
100/7 Kalim Beach Road, Kathu
Tel. 17230386 or 340789.
Open 12.30pm–12 midnight.
Magnificent restaurant with a terrace overlooking Patong Bay. Traditional interior and fine Thai cuisine. Not to be missed.
250–1,000 baht
⑪ ▭ ⤬ 𝐏

LE JARDIN
43/3 Nanai Road, Moo 4,
Patong Beach
Tel. 17231187.
Open 12 noon–2.30pm, 6.30–10.30pm.
Lunch in the garden at midday. Tasty but small helpings. The terrace area opens at 6.30pm. Choice of two restaurants, offering French and Thai cuisine. Hotel accommodation available.
150–300 baht
◑ ▭ 𝐏

MAE PORN
Phangnga Road, Phuket Town
Open 11am–10pm.
Varied cuisine, including Thai dishes and seafood. Dining room with fans or air-conditioning.
80–150 baht
○

SUNSET
102/6 Patak Road, Karon Beach
Tel. 381465.
Open 8am–10.30pm.
Covered restaurant, very pleasant and romantic in the evening. Delicious food selection, including specialty seafood platter.
100–500 baht
◑ ▭

THUNGKA KAFAE
Khao Rang Hill, Phuket Town
Tel. 211500.
Open 11am–12 midnight.
Panoramic view of the town and the sea. Seafood a specialty. Terrace
140–300 baht
◑ ▭ ⤬ 𝐏

PHUKET

PRACTICALITIES

ZIP CODE
83000

TOURIST INFORMATION OFFICE
73–5 Phuket Road
Tel. 212213.
Fax 213582.
Open 8.30am–4.30pm.

HOSPITAL
MISSION HOSPITAL
Thepkasattri Road

TOURIST POLICE
Tel. 212468
Open 6am–12 midnight.

POSTAL SERVICES
Montri Road (corner of Phangnga Road)
Tel. 211020.
Open 8.30am–3.30pm, Sat. and Sun. 9am–12 noon.

TRANSPORT

AIRPORT
Tel. 311511.

AIRLINES
THAI AIRWAYS
78/1 Ranong Road
Tel. 212400
Open 8am–5pm.
Closed weekends.

THAI AIRWAYS
(INTERNAL FLIGHTS)
41/33 Montree Road
Tel. 211195
Fax 216779.
Open 7am–12 noon, 1–5pm.
Closed Sun., although some sections remain open.

CAR RENTAL
AVIS
Opposite the airport
Tel. 311358.
Open 8am–8pm.
Various other agencies in the island's hotels.

HERTZ
Premier Inter Leasing Co., opposite the airport.
Tel. 311463
Fax 311162.
Open 8am–noon, 1–5pm.

BIKE RENTAL
Phuket town and at various beaches on the island.
200–300 baht per day.

SPORTS

PHUKET DIVERS
31/1 Phoonpol Road, Muang District
Tel. 76215738.
Diving activities, with equipment rental.

PHUKET AQUATIC SAFARI
62/9 Rasada Road, Muang District
Tel. 76216562
Fax 073212 30.
Diving activities, with equipment rental.

PHUKET INTERNATIONAL DIVING CENTER
Coral Beach Hotel, Patong Beach
Tel. 76321100.
Diving and deep-sea fishing, with equipment rental.

HOTELS

CASUARINA BUNGALOWS
92/2 Taveewong Road,
Patong Beach
Tel. 340123
Fax 3401 23.
In Patong itself, facing the beach. Pleasant garden despite proximity to the road. Tidy, well-equipped rooms.
Breakfast 100 baht.
1,000–1,600 baht
🏠 🄫 ▢ 🛆 🚗 ▭

CLUB MÉDITERRANÉE
Kata Beach
Tel. 381455
Fax 3814 62.
Set in a 222-acre park. Bungalows with air-conditioning. Sports facilities include swimming pool, golf, tennis, squash, sailing, etc. Nightly or weekly stays. Travel agents sometimes have cut-price deals.
4,100 baht
🏠 🏠 ▢ ⚞ 🛆 ▭

CORAL BEACH HOTEL
104 Moo 4,
Patong Beach,
Kathu
Tel. 340106
Fax 340115.
Siam Group hotel. Very attractive rooms with all modern conveniences. Restaurants, sporting equipment. The beach, though not outstanding, is private.
Breakfast 250 baht.
1,600–3,600 baht
🏠 🏠 ▢ ⚞ 🛆 🚗 ▭ 🏃

KAMALA BEACH ESTATE
36/6 Kamala Beach,
Kathu
Tel. 230379
Fax 311481.
Reservations from Anchalee Leasing Co,
4/14 Soi Daeng Udom,
Sukhumvit 33,
Bangkok 10110.
Charming well-equipped apartments, exceptional surroundings and personalized service.
1,500–5,000 baht.
🏠 🏠 ▢ ⚞ 🛆 🚗 ▭ 🏃

KATA THANI
Kata Noi Beach
Tel. 381124

◆ CLUB MÉDITERRANÉE ◆

This elegant complex is located amid coconut trees at Kata, a beach on the coast southwest of Phuket.

Fax 381426.
Siam Group hotel. Private beach, beautiful gardens, captivating sea views. Comfortable, welcoming rooms. Restaurants and sporting equipment.
Breakfast 160 baht.
3,400–4,200 baht
🏠 🏠 ▢ ⚞ 🛆 🚗 ▭ 🏃

LE JARDIN
43/3 Nanai Road, Moo 4
Patong Beach
Tel. 17231187
Fax 340391.
A trek to the beach, rewarded with spacious and clean bungalows. Excursions can be organized upon request.
Breakfast 70 baht.
700–2,250 baht
🏠 🏠 ▢ 🛆 🚗 ▭

ON ON HOTEL
19, Phangnga Road,
Phuket Town
Tel. 211154.
The oldest hotel in town (built in April 1929) and proud of it. Inexpensive and neat rooms (fan or air-conditioning). Central.
Breakfast 50 baht.
Around 300 baht
🏠 🄫 🚗

PANSEA PHUKET BAY
118 Moo 3, Choeng
Talay,
Tulang
Tel. 32 40 18
Fax 32 42 52.
Perched on the side of a verdant hill. Private

fine-sand beach. Truly charming surroundings and atmosphere. Ideal for families and small tour groups.*
Breakfast 240 baht.
2,800–5,700 baht
🏠 🏠 ▢ ⚞ 🛆 🚗 ▭

PEARL HOTEL
Montree Road,
Phuket Town
Tel. 211044
Fax 212911.
Attractive and comfortable rooms at reasonable prices. Restaurant and nightclub. Massage room.
Breakfast 150 baht.
1,500 baht
🏠 🄫 ▢ 🛆 🚗 ▭ 🏃

PEARL VILLAGE
Nai Yang Beach,
PO Box 93
Tel. 311338
Fax 311304.
Complex within a national park. Very attractive surroundings. Well-lit and comfortable rooms. Restaurants, snooker, tennis courts and zoo.
Breakfast 225 baht.
4,500 baht
🏠 🏠 ▢ ⚞ 🛆 🚗 ▭ 🏃

PHUKET YACHT CLUB
Nai Han Beach
Tel. 381156
Fax 318164.
Idyllic atmosphere. Rooms are especially

welcoming. Relatively expensive. Restaurants.*
Breakfast 320 baht.
1,950–7,000 baht
🏠 🏠 ▢ ⚞ 🛆 🚗 ▭ 🏃

SANDY INN
102/12 Patark Road,
Karon Beach
Tel. 381935
Fax 381546.
Small but very pleasant and well-maintained hotel. 200 yards from the beach. Excursions can be organized. Quite inexpensive.
Breakfast 60 baht.
800–1,000 baht
🏠 🄫 ▢ ▭

THAVORN HOTEL
74 Rasada Road,
Phuket Town,
Amphoe Muang
Tel. 211333
Fax 211359.
All the services of a large hotel but at moderate prices. Pleasant rooms with all modern conveniences. No view.
650–1,100 baht
🏠 🄫 ▢ 🛆 🚗 ▭

PHANGNGA

PRACTICALITIES

ZIP CODE
82000

HOTELS

LAK MUANG 1
1-2 Phetkasem Road,
Amphoe Muang
Tel. 411125, 411288.
Small hotel with 24 rooms offering basic comforts.
100–150 baht
🏠 ○

LAK MUANG 2
Tambon Taichang,
Amphoe Muang
Tel. 411500.
Small hotel with 24 rooms offering basic comforts.
270 –480 baht
🏠 ○

PHANGNGA BAY RESORT
20 Tha Dan Road,
Phangnga
Tel. 411067.
Luxury hotel offering the beauty of the bay.
810–2,400 baht
🏠 ▢ ⚞ 🛆
🚗 ▭

KOH PHI PHI

HOTELS

KRABI PEE PEE RESORT
Ao Lodalam,
Koh Phi Phi Don.
Pleasant, well-equipped (shower, WC and fan) bungalows on the beach, 5 minutes' walk, north of the jetty.
300 baht

PEE PEE INTERNATIONAL RESORT
Laem Tong,
Koh Phi Phi Don
Tel. 212901
Fax 214301
Reservations in
Bangkok:
Tel. 2557600.
Luxury complex north of the island. Windsurfer rental, diving lessons, etc. Breakfast included.
1,500–3,100 baht

PEE PEE ISLAND VILLAGE
Resort complex located in the northeast on Lobako, one of the prettiest beaches on Phi Phi Don. Bungalows on stilts with air-conditioning.
950–1050 baht

KRABI

PRACTICALITIES

ATM
Utarakit Road, between
Sukhon Road and
Phattana Road.

TRANSPORT

TRAVEL AGENCIES
CHAN PHEN
Utarakit Road.
Information and reservations for bus and boat tickets.

TIP HOUSE
Prachacheun Road.
Information and reservations for bus and boat tickets.

BUS
SUNGTHEE SOUTH
STATION
Utarakit Road,
near the New Hotel.
Departures for Ao Nang beach.

◆ PHANGNGA BAY ◆

These astonishing coral pinnacles reflected in the emerald-green water are one of the most fascinating sights in Asia.

BUS TERMINUS
Talaat Kao
(3 miles north of Krabi, between Phangnga and Trang).
Take a song tao (local taxi pickup) between the terminus and Krabi. Regular departures for Surat Thani, Trang, Haadyai, Phangnga and Phuket.

BOAT
Ao Nang.
Daily departures for the Phi Phi islands between October and April.

PORT
Jao Fa Pier.
Departures for the islands and beaches (October to May only). Daily departures in the morning by express boat (2-hour crossing), two departures by ordinary boat (3-hour crossing).

HOTELS

PHRA NANG BAY VILLAGE
Hat Phra Nang
Tel. 611944.
On a beach accessible only by boat. Bungalows on stilts with shower and air-conditioning.
150–200 baht

PHRA NANG INN
119 Ao Nang
Tel. 612173
Fax 612174.
Phra Nang Inn is
situated on Ao Nang beach, overlooking the bay. It is, however, accessible by road. Bungalows with bathroom and fan from 150 baht.
Air-conditioned rooms: 700–1,000 baht.
With breakfast: 1,740 baht.

NAKHON RATCHASIMA

PRACTICALITIES

ZIP CODE
30000

TOURIST INFORMATION OFFICE
2102 Mittraphap Road,
Tambon Nai Muang
Tel. 255243
Fax 255244.
Open 8.30am–4.30pm.

POLICE
Sapphasit Road
Tel. 242010
Open 24 hours.

TRANSPORT

AIRLINES
THAI AIRWAYS
14 Manas Road
Tel. 257211.
Open 8am–5pm.
Closed weekends.

RESTAURANTS

BAAN KAEW RESTAURANT
105/17–19 Jom
Surangyat Road
Tel. 246512.
Open 10am–10pm.
Pleasant establishment. Good place for meeting Thais. Extensive menu.
80–200 baht

HOTELS

CHOMSURANG
2701/2 Mahadthai Road
Tel. 257088
Fax 252897.
Central. Comfortable rooms. TV extra. Restaurants and nightclub.
600–800 baht

DOCTOR'S HOUSE
78, Sueb Sibi Road,
3ุ 4
Tel. 255846.
A pleasant family atmosphere in this small, charming and scrupulously maintained hotel.
Breakfast 10 baht.
100–150 baht

JULDIS KHAO YAI RESORT
Thanarat Road,
Amphoe Pak Chong
Reservations in
Bangkok:
Tel. 2552480
or 2554960
Fax 2552460.
Small resort hotel with restaurant, cocktail lounge, tennis court and pool.
1,500–3,800 baht

KORAT
191 At Sadang Road,
Amphoe Muang
Tel. 242260
or 242444.
Disco and nightclub, shopping amenities.
160–650 baht

SIRI
688-69 Phoklang Road
Tel. 242831.
Midway between the station and the center of town. Cordial welcome. Well-maintained hotel with spacious rooms. Wide choice of rooms.
Breakfast 40 baht.
150–350 baht

SRI PATANA
346, Suranaree Road
Tel. 242944
Fax 246323.
*Offers single rooms for
the same price as
doubles. Modern room
facilities.
Breakfast 80 baht.
500–1,200 baht*
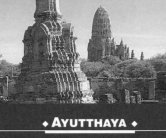

THAI POKAPHAN
106-110, Asadang
Road
Tel. 242454.
*Pleasant atmosphere.
Very clean rooms.
120–280 baht*

PRACTICALITIES

ZIP CODE
13000

CULTURE

**CHANTARAKASEM
PALACE MUSEUM**
Northeast of town,
beside the Pasak.
Open 9am–12 noon,
1–4pm. Closed Mon.
and Tues.
*Reliable town guide
available for 25 baht.*

NATIONAL MUSEUM
At the intersection of
Rojana Road and
Si Sanphet Road.
Open 9am–noon, 1–
4pm. Closed Mon, Tues.
*Also known as the Chao
Sam Phraya Museum.
Admission 10 baht.*

**BANG PA-IN
SUMMER PALACE**
About 12 miles south of
Ayutthaya.
Open 8.30am–12 noon,
1pm–4pm. Closed Mon.
*Visit included in
excursions by hotels.
Admission 10 baht.*

RESTAURANTS

PAE KRUNG KAO
K 4 Moo 2 U-Thong
Road
Tel. 241555.
Open 11am–11pm.
*Reputable eatery
beside the Pasak.
Pleasant surroundings
and good food,
including fish and
shrimp specialties .
100–200 baht*

◆ AYUTTHAYA ◆

Wat Mahathat and Wat Phra Ram
bear witness to Ayutthaya's splendid past.

HOTELS

BJ GUEST HOUSE
19/29 Naresuan Road
Tel. 246046.
*Located near principal
monuments. The
cleanest hotel in town.
Showers on each floor.
Friendly proprietors.
Food easily available.
Breakfast 50 baht.
100 baht*

CATHAY
36/5-6 U-Thong Road
Tel. 251562.
*Walk-up hotel in a
rather noisy street.
Basic but clean rooms.
100–250 baht*

SRI SAMAI
12/19 Naresuan Road
Tel. 251104.
*More comfortable than
other mid-town hotels.
Choose a room with air-
conditioning and TV. 24-
hour concierge.
350–500 baht*

U-THONG INN
210 Rojana Road
Tel. 242236
Fax 242235.
*The best hotel in
Ayutthaya, not to be
confused with the
U-Thong Hotel. A little
out of the way but with a
magnificent view.
Breakfast 150 baht.
500–1200 baht*

KAMPHAENG PHET

CULTURE

NATIONAL MUSEUM
Opposite Wat Phra
That.
Open 8.30am–4pm.
Closed Mon. and Tues.
*Classic museum
describing the evolution
of Thai art and the
objets d'art found in the
region, especially in the
Ayutthaya and
Sukhothai styles.*

OLD TOWN
*Now a historic park.
Admission 20 baht.*

LOPBURI

CULTURE

**PALACE OF KING
NARAI**
Sorasak Road,
entrance opposite Asia
Lopburi Hotel.
Open 9am–12 noon,
1–4pm. Closed Mon.
and Tues.
*Magnificent palace a
branch of the National
Museum. Pick up a
guide to the ancient
monuments of Lopburi.
Admission 10 baht.*

PHAUKLON RESIDENCE
Wichayen Road,
opposite Wat Sao
Thong Thong.
Open 9am–12 noon,
1–4pm.
Admission 20 baht.

WAT PHRA SI RATANA MAHATHAT
Na Kala Road,
opposite the station.
Open 9am–4pm.
Admission 20 baht.

PRACTICALITIES

ZIP CODE
64000

HOSPITAL
PROVINCIAL HOSPITAL
Charet Withi Thong
Road.

POLICE
Nikon Kasem Road
Tel. 6110.

POSTAL SERVICES
Nikon Kasem Road
Tel. 611645.
Open 8.30am–3.30pm.
Sat. and Sun. 9am–12
noon.

ATM
THAI FARMERS BANK
134 Charet Withi
Thong Road
Tel. 611932.
Open 8.30am–3.30pm.
Closed Sat. and Sun.

TRANSPORT

BUSES
PHITSANULOK YAN YON
TOUR
c/o Chinawat Hotel,
Nikon Kasem Road
Tel. 612134.
Open 8.30am–10pm.
BUS TERMINUS
Prasertpong Road
Tel. 611794.
WIN TOUR
Charet Withi Thong
Road
Tel. 611039.
Open 8am–11pm.

CULTURE

**RAMKHAMHAENG
NATIONAL MUSEUM**
Close to main entrance.
Open 9am–4pm.
*Excellent introduction to
the ruins of Sukhothai.*

OLD TOWN
Si Satchanalai.
*The city of potters and
second city in the
Sukhothai Kingdom.
Classified as a
historic park.
Accessible by bus or
tuk-tuk from new
Sukhothai.
Admission 20 baht.*

RUINS OF THE FORMER CAPITAL

Si Satchanalai and Chaliang.

To visit you will need an entry permit (20 baht) to each of the five areas of the historic park. The park itself is huge, so it is advisable to hire a bicycle, motorbike or even a tuk-tuk. Light, comfortable shoes are advisable for exploring on foot.

HOTELS

CHINAWAT
1-2-3 Nikon Kasem Road
Tel. 611385.
Well located. Rooms with fan or air-conditioning. Good food and service at restaurant. Various services include money-changing, rentals, reservations, phone, etc.
Breakfast 40 baht.
200–350 baht
⌂ 🅲 🚗 🖭

SUKHOTHAI HOTEL
15/5 Singhawat Road
Tel. 611133.
Clean rooms with fan. Walk-up.
150–250 baht
⌂ 🅲 🚗

PHITSANULOK

PRACTICALITIES

ZIP CODE
65000

TOURIST INFORMATION OFFICE
209/7-8,
Boromtrailoknat Road
Tel. 252743.
Open 8.30am–4.30pm.

HOSPITAL
PROVINCIAL HOSPITAL
Sithamtraipidok Road.

POLICE
Boromtrailoknat Road
Tel. 240199.
Open 24 hours.

POSTAL SERVICES
Phutta Bucha Road
Tel. 258013.
Open 8.30am–3.30pm.
Sat. and Sun. 9am–12 noon.

ATM
THAI FARMERS BANK
144/1 Boromtrailoknat

◆ LOPBURI PALACE ◆

This palace at Lopburi was built by King Narai (1666–77) and a team of French architects.

Road
Tel. 258599.
Open 8.30am–3.30pm.
Closed weekends.

TRANSPORT

RAILWAY STATION
Ekathotrod Road
Tel. 258005.

BUSES
PHITSANULOK YAN YON TOUR
194/29 Ekathotrod Road
Tel. 258647.
Especially VIP buses to Bangkok.

BUS TERMINUS
(BAW KHOW SAW)
Mittraparp Road,
Highway 12
Tel. 242430.
*Departures for Bangkok every 2 hours,
6.05am–9.40pm.
243 baht*

WIN TOUR
194/4
Boromtrailoknat Road
Tel. 24 32 22.
The largest bus company in the region.

AIRPORT
PHITSANULOK DOMESTIC AIRPORT
Sanambin Road
Tel. 258029.
Internal flights. Variable opening hours, depending on the number of flights. Enquire ahead of time.

AIRLINES
THAI AIRWAYS

209/26-28
Boromtrailoknat Road
Tel. 258020.
Open 8am–5pm.
Closed weekends.

CAR RENTAL
GOLDEN HOUSE TOUR
55/37 Sithamtraipidok Road
Tel. 259973.
Open 7.30am–6pm.
Closed Sun.
Car and minibus rental. An alternative is the Phitsanulok Tour Center, a little farther away, which offers the same services.

BICYCLE AND MOTORBIKE RENTAL
LANDI MOTOR
110/127 Phra Ong Dum Road
Tel. 242687.
Open 8am–5pm.

CULTURE

DR THAWI FOLKLORE MUSEUM
26/43 Wisuthikasartri Road,
opposite the foundry.
Open 9am–4pm.
Personal collection of handicrafts belonging to Dr Thawi. Fascinating stop for art-lovers.

RESTAURANT

RIMNAN
60 Wang Chan Road
Open 11am–11pm.
Floating restaurant. Pleasant wood décor. Good food and service.

Thai fish cuisine.
70–200 baht
◐ 🖭 ⤳

HOTELS

PAYLIN
38 Boromtrailoknat Road
Tel. 252411
Fax 258185.
Currently the most fashionable hotel in Phitsanulok. Provision for multiple tour groups. Attractive rooms. Variety of services, including massage, sauna, restaurants. Breakfast 100 baht.
900–500 baht
⌂ 🅲 🛁 ⤳ 🖵 🚗 🖭 🍴

PHITSANULOK YOUTH HOSTEL
38 Sa Nam Bin (Airport) Road
Tel. 242060
Contrasting atmosphere in the two wings of the building. Warm welcome. Quaint old beds in clean rooms. Breakfast 30 baht. Double room 100 baht
⌂ 🖭 🚗

RAJAPRUK
99/9 Phra Ong Dum Road
Tel. 258477
Fax 251395.
Lively establishment with pleasant rooms. Popular stop during peak periods, but no reduced off-peak rates. Breakfast 90 baht.
650 baht
⌂ 🛁 🖭 🖵 🍵 🚗 🖭

THEP NAKHORN
43/1 Sithamtraipidok Road
Tel. 244070
Fax 251897.
Clean hotel. Rooms plain but comfortable. Breakfast 90 baht.
950 baht
⌂ 🅲 🛁 🖭

WANG NAM YUEN RESORT
Km 46 Phitsanulok-Lom Sak Road
Tel. 252753
Reservations in Bangkok:
Tel. 3147150.
Small hotel with all conveniences.
480–2200 baht
⌂ 🖭 🍵 ◐ 🖭 🎵

PHA THAI GUEST HOUSE · CHIANG MAI YOUTH HOSTEL · LE P'TIT PARADIS · ANODARD HOTEL · AARON RAI · CHIANG MAI ORCHID · LA VILLA · JULIE GUEST HOUSE · DARET'S · CHIANG INN · ROYAL PRINCESS · GALARE GUEST HOUSE · NEW CHIANG MAI HOTEL

CHIANG MAI

PRACTICALITIES

ZIP CODE
50000

TOURIST INFORMATION OFFICE
105/1 Chiang Mai-
Lamphun Road,
Amphoe Muang
Tel. 248604
Fax 248605.
Open 8.30am–
4.30pm.

HOSPITALS
MC CORMICK HOSPITAL
Kaeo Nawarat Road
Tel. 241107.
Open 24 hours.

CHIANG MAI PROVINCIAL
HOSPITAL
Tel. 221222.

POLICE
Tel. 248130
night, Tel. 22277.
Open 6am–12 midnight.

POSTAL SERVICES
Charoen Muang Road
Tel. 245376.
Open 8.30am–4.30pm.
Sat. and Sun.,
9am–12 noon.

ATM
SIAM COMMERCIAL BANK
17 Tapae Road.

Open 8.30am–3.30pm.
Closed weekends.

MARKET

NIGHT MARKET
Chang Klan Road,
between Suriwong
Road and Tapae
Road.
Open 6–10 pm.
*Most of Thailand's
artisans make and
market their products in
Chiang Mai. Good
bargains can be had
over a wide range, but
only if you haggle.*

TRANSPORT

TRAVEL AGENCIES
SURYA SUNIE
7/3 Svondok Road,
Tambon Sutep.
*Experienced Thai guide
organizes trips to
northern region.*

UDON'S TRIBAL TREKS
Times Square Guest
House,
Your Guest House,
Julie Guest House.
*Guide Annabelle is
French and organizes
trips to the region. A
well-known Chaing Mi
establishment.*

RAILWAY STATION
27 Charoen Muang
Road

BUSES

BUS TERMINUS
Chotana Road

AIRLINES

THAI AIRWAYS
240 Phra Pokklao Road
Tel. 210044.
Open 8am–5pm.
Closed weekends.

CAR AND BIKE RENTAL

AVIS
14/14 Huay Kaeo Road
Tel. 22131316.
Open 8am–8pm.

HERTZ
12/3 Loi Khrao Road
Tel. 235496
or 235496.
Open 8am–12 noon,
1–5pm.

PC2 SERVICE
Alain Cafe,
99/2 Loi Khrao Road
Tel. 275722.
*Travel agency that also
rents out cars and
motorbikes, with
insurance.*

QUEEN BEE CAR RENTAL
5 Moonmuang Road
Tel. 275525.
Open 8am–6pm
*Travel agency that also
rents out cars and
motor bikes, with
insurance. Reasonable
rates. Recommended.*

CULTURE

**INSTITUTE FOR
TRIBAL RESEARCH**
Chiang Mai University,
3 miles west of the city.
Open 8.30am–4.30pm.
Closed weekends.
*Board bus no. 1 to visit
the small museum at
the institute.*

NATIONAL MUSEUM
Highway 11,
near Wat Ched Yod.
Open 9am–4pm.
Closed Mon. and Tues.
*Pottery exhibits and
representations of the
Buddha.
Admission 10 baht.*

DOI SUTHEP
*Accessible by song tao
from the north gate of
the city (Chiang Puak
gate).*

RESTAURANTS

**AARON RAI
RESTAURANT**
45 Kotchasarn Road
Tel. 276947.
Open 10am–10pm.
*Open-air restaurant,
established 30 years
and an institution. Warm
ambience in almost-
bare surroundings.
Excellent hot and spicy
curries. Chinese and*

regional Thai cuisine.
80–150 baht
○

**COQ AU RICO –
CHEZ JOHN**
95/25 Nimmanhemen
Road
Tel. 214346.
Open 12 noon–2pm,
6–10pm.
*This French restaurant
was opened in 1992,
but the proprietor has
been around Chiang
Mai for a long time and
his cuisine deserves
recognition. Very fine
food in especially
charming surroundings.
300–500 baht*
Ⓜ

DARET'S
4/5 Chayapoom Road
Tel. 235440.
Open 7am–10pm.
*Restaurant in a hotel
that also arranges treks.
The terrace restaurant
is inexpensive and the
knowledgeable trekking
guides have earned a
good reputation. Also
rents out motorbikes.
Thai and Western
cuisine.
50–100 baht*
○

HONG TAUW INN
95/17 18, Nantawan
Arcade,
Nimmanhemen Road,
opposite the Rincome
Hotel
Tel. 215027.
Open 11am–11pm.
*Pleasant and relaxing
surroundings. Friendly
service. Traditional Thai
cuisine.
100–200 baht*
◑ ▭

JULIE GUEST HOUSE
7/1 Phra Pokklao Road
Ratchaphakinai Road
Soi 5
Tel. 274355.
Open 8am–9.30pm.
*Terrace restaurant at
the hotel of same name.
Inexpensive fare. Thai
and French cuisine.
60–150 baht*
○ ⅍

LA VILLA
145 Ratchadamnoen
Road
Tel. 215403.
Open 11am–10pm.
*Hotel with a very
friendly atmosphere.
Italian specialties and*

excellent pizzas.
100–200 baht
◑ ⅍ Ⓟ

LE JARDIN
Times Square Guest
House,
2/10 Soi 6 Tapae Road
Tel. 282448.
Open 8am–2pm,
5–9pm.
*French terrace
restaurant. Very
pleasant atmosphere
and quality cuisine.
French and Thai food.
80–200 baht*
○ ⅍

LE P'TIT PARADIS
69 Loi Khrao Road,
Amphoe Muang
Tel. 276742.
Open 8am–10pm.
*Fine food. Generous
amounts of bread and
jam at breakfast. French
and Thai cuisine.
100–250 baht*
◑ ▭

**OLD CHIANG MAI
CULTURAL CENTER**
183 Wualai Road
Tel. 235097.
Open 7pm–10pm.
Khantoke *dinner,
with northern and hill-
tribe traditional
performances featuring
famous nail, sabre and
candle dances. Eat with
your fingers, seated on
cushions. Regional
specialties and
Burmese cuisine.
Reservations necessary.
Around 200 baht*
Ⓜ

ONCE UPON A TIME
385/2 Charoen Prathet
Road,
near Mengrai
Tel. 274932.
Open 4pm–12 midnight.
*Traditional teak house
setting. Magnificent
surroundings. Thai and
international cuisine.
180–300 baht*
◑ ▭ ⅍ Ⓟ

HOTELS

ANODARD HOTEL
57–9, Rajmankha Road
Tel. 270755
Fax 270759.
*Very friendly
atmosphere. Rooms
with fan or air-
conditioning. Clean and
comfortable.
Breakfast 100 baht.
260–480 baht*
🏨 Ⓒ ▭ ⌂ 🚗 ▭

CHIANG INN
100 Chang Klan Road
Tel. 270070
Fax 274299
Reservations in
Bangkok:
Tel. (2) 2569112.
*Attractive rooms with
superb bathrooms.
Restaurant and
cafeteria. Nightclub and
sporting facilities.
Breakfast 170 baht.
1,600–2,100 baht*
🏛 Ⓒ ⌂ ⅍ ▭ ⌂
🚗 ▭ 夫

CHIANG MAI ORCHID
100–2 Huay Kaeo Road
Tel. 222099
Fax 221625.

Good luxury hotel
slightly out of town.
Warm ambience.
Comfortable and
tastefully decorated
rooms.
Breakfast 235 baht.
2,600–3,300 baht
🏛 ⌂ ⅍ ▭ ⌂
🚗 ▭ 夫

**CHIANG MAI YOUTH
HOSTEL**
4, Ratchaphakinai Road
Tel. 272169.
*Very hospitable. Basic,
clean rooms.
Dormitories. Cafeteria.
Organizes treks.
Reductions for students
and YHA members.
Breakfast 30 baht.
110–150 baht*
⌂ Ⓒ 🚗

**DIAMOND RIVERSIDE
HOTEL**
33/10 Charoen Prathet
Road
Tel. 2700805
Fax 271482.
*By the Ping River.
Within walking distance
of commercial and
entertainment districts,
night market. Rooms
with modern facilities.
Restaurants serving
Lanna Khantoke dinner
in 100-year old teak
mansion. Other services
include tour desk, Thai
traditional massage and
convention facilities.
700–1,400 baht*
🏛 Ⓒ ▭ ⌂ 🚗 ◑
▭

**GALARE GUEST
HOUSE**
7 Charoen Prathet Road
Tel. 273885
Fax 279088.
*Beautiful house beside
the Ping River. Very
clean. Small but inviting
rooms, with fans or air-
conditioning.
Restaurant.
Breakfast 50 baht.
440–580 baht*
🏛 Ⓒ 🚗 ▭

JULIE GUEST HOUSE
7/1 Phra Pokklao Road-
Ratchaphakinai Road,
Soi 5
Tel. 274355.
*Very small rooms with
minimal facilities. Low
prices do not vary with
the season. Good
restaurant.
Breakfast 35 baht.
130–200 baht.*
⌂ Ⓒ ⌂ 🚗

◆ **ONCE UPON A TIME** ◆

This hotel in Chiang Mai is located in magnificent
green surroundings beside the Ping river.

LE P'TIT PARADIS
69 Loy Kron Road
Tel. 276742.
*Basic, clean rooms.
Very quiet, despite
proximity to the night
market.
Breakfast 60 baht.
300–600 baht*

NEW CHIANG MAI HOTEL
22 Chiyapoom Road
Tel. 236961
Fax 251531.
*Small basic rooms with
minimal facilities. Fan or
air-conditioning. The
hotel's fixed rates are a
plus for budget-
conscious travelers in
the high season.
175–250 baht*

ONCE UPON A TIME
385/2 Charoen
Prathet Road,
near Mengrai
Tel. 274932.
*Beside the Ping River.
Charming, comfortable
rooms, furnished in
traditional style. The
splendid garden
contributes to the
peaceful atmosphere of
this establishment.
Breakfast 80 baht.
800–1200 baht*

PHA THAI GUEST HOUSE
48/1 Ratchaphakinai
Road
Tel. 278013
Fax 274075.
*A real gem, as much for
the clean and
comfortable rooms as
for the ambience.
Breakfast 25 baht.
150–200 baht*

ROYAL PRINCESS
112 Chang Klan Road
Tel. 281033
Fax 281044.
*Dusit chain hotel.
Welcoming rooms with
modern conveniences.
Non-smoking levels and
classic facilities.
Breakfast 170 baht.
2000–3000 baht*

TIMES SQUARE GUEST HOUSE
2/10 Soi 6 Tapae Road
Tel. 282448.
Friendly atmosphere.

*Small room, clean and
pleasantly decorated
and with fan or air-
conditioning. Terrace
restaurant, usually very
popular.
Breakfast 50 baht.
130–250 baht*

NIGHTLIFE

DK TRADITIONAL MASSAGE
277/5 Chang Klan
Road, opposite Chiang
Mai Land
Tel. 274919.
Open 10am–12
midnight.
*Good traditional
massage with free
transport. 200 baht per
hour. Reductions for
longer stay.*

RINKAEW POVECH
183/4 Wualai Road
Tel. 274567
Open 8am–1am.
*Traditional herbal
massage. Free
transport on request.
200 baht per hour.
Also has sauna, beauty
salon and nightclub.*

THE PUB
88 Huay Kaeo Road
Tel. 211550
Open 11am–2pm,
5pm–1am. Closes at
midnight on Mon.
*In a fascinating
traditional house. One
of the best bars in the
world, according to a
1986 issue of
Newsweek.*

THE RIVERSIDE
9-11 Charoen Rat Road
Tel. 243239.
Open 10am–1am.
*Popular meeting place
with all-wood décor
beside the Ping River.
For food (Western
meals) and drinks and
soothing background
music.*

LAMPHUN
CULTURE

NATIONAL MUSEUM
Inthayongyot Road,
opposite Wat Phra That
Haripunchai.
Open 8.30am–4.30pm.
Closed Mon. and Tues.
*Collection of regional
art.
Admission 10 baht.*

CHIANG RAI
PRACTICALITIES

ZIP CODE
57000

TOURIST INFORMATION OFFICE
448/16 Singhakai Road
Tel. 717433
Fax 717434.
Open 8.30am–4.30pm.

HOSPITAL
PRACHANUKHROH
HOSPITAL
981 Muang
Satharn Prayabran
Road
Tel. 711300.
Open 8am–10pm.

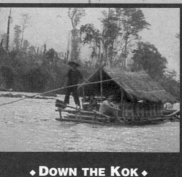

◆ DOWN THE KOK ◆

From the small village of Tha Thon,
you can follow the Kok River – with its
exhilirating rapids – all the way
to Chiang Rai.

POLICE
TOURIST POLICE
Tel. 711786.
Open 6am–12 midnight.

POSTAL SERVICES
Uttarakit Road
Tel. 713685.
Open 8.30am–3.30pm.
Sat. 9am–12 noon.
Closed Sun.

TRANSPORT

BUSES
BUS TERMINUS
Phaholyothin Road
Tel. 711224.
*Regular departures for
Bangkok every
30 minutes from
8am–7.30pm.
360 baht.*

AIRLINES
THAI AIRWAYS
870 Phaholyothin Road
Tel. 711179.
Open 8am–5pm.
Closed weekends.

CAR RENTAL
AVIS
Dusit Island Resort
Tel. 715777.
Other branches:
Baan Boran Hotel
Tel. 716678
Golden Triangle Resort
Tel. 714801.

CHIANG-RAI EKKACHAI
733/7 Phaholyothin
Road
Tel. 711358.
Open 8am–5pm.

RESTAURANTS

GOLDEN TRIANGLE INN
590 Phaholyothin Road
Tel. 711339.
Open 7am–12 midnight.
*Excellent cuisine in
pleasant surroundings.
The very informative
menu will teach you all
you want to know about
Thai cuisine. Traditional
music at weekends.
Thai and Western
cuisine.
120–200 baht*

HAWNARIGA
402/1-2
Banphapragar Road
Tel. 53711062.
Open 11am 11pm.
*Beside the clock tower.
Very famous Chiang
Mai restaurant.
Delicious food served
by courteous, efficient*

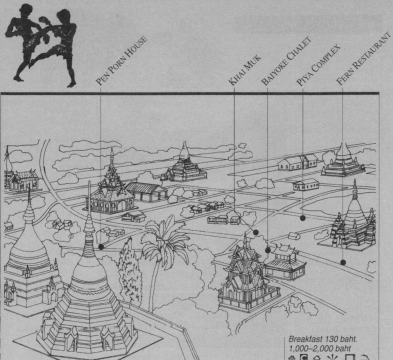

PEN PORN HOUSE · KHAI MUK · BAIYOKE CHALET · PIYA COMPLEX · FERN RESTAURANT

staff on the semi-covered terrace. Thai, Chinese and Korean barbecue cuisine.
100–200 baht
◖

HOTELS

CHAT HOUSE
3/2 Sangkaew Road
Tel. 711481.
Fifteen clean and basic rooms in all-wood house, with small restaurant. Very friendly atmosphere. The proprietor organizes good treks. Rooms with 4 beds.
Breakfast 20 baht.
80–100 baht
⌂ ▣ ⌂ 🚗

DUSIT ISLAND RESORT
1129 Kraisorasit Road
Tel. 715777
Fax 715801.
This hotel, in the time-honored style of the Dusit chain, is set in exceptionally beautiful surroundings. The view of the Kok at sunset in particular is breathtaking. Comfortable rooms, complete with all facilities.
Breakfast 200 baht.
3000–3400 baht
🏛 ▣ ⌂ ⛆ ▢ ⌿
🚗 ▭

GOLDEN TRIANGLE INN
590 Phaholyothin Road
Tel. 711339
Fax 713963.
Almost irresistible: the charms of its huge, all-wood rooms with their old furniture, soft lighting, thick curtains and small, pretty bathrooms. Breakfast is included.
550–650 baht
🏛 ▣ ⌂ 🚗 ▭

MAE HONG SON GUEST HOUSE OF CHIANG RAI
126 Singhakai Road.
Guest house at the end of a road with several hotels. Spartan but clean rooms with fans.
80–100 baht
⌂ ⌂ 🚗

WANGCOME HOTEL
869/90 Pemawibhata Road
Tel. 53711800
Fax 53712973.
Luxury hotel. Gracious ambience. Small, comfortable rooms.

Breakfast 130 baht.
1,000–2,000 baht
🏛 ▣ ⌂ ⛆ ▢ ⌿
🚗 ▭

WIANG INN
893 Phaholyothin Road, Amphoe Muang
Tel. 711533
Fax 711877
Reservations in Bangkok.
Tel. 2354030.
Luxury hotel with wide range of facilities.
900–7,000 baht
🏛 ▣ ⌂ ⛆ ▢ ⌿
🚗 ▭

MAE HONG SON

PRACTICALITIES

ZIP CODE
58000

POSTAL SERVICES
Khunlum Praphat Road, south of the town.

ATM
THAI FARMERS BANK
Khunlum Praphat Road.
Open 6.30am–3.30pm.
Closed weekends.

TRANSPORT

AIRLINES
THAI AIRWAYS
71 Singhanath-bamrung Road
Tel. 611297.
Open 8am–5pm.
Closed weekends.

RESTAURANTS

FERN RESTAURANT
87 Khunlum Praphat Road

◆ RIDE AN ELEPHANT ◆

After a visit to the elephant training center at Mae Sa, take a ride in the jungle on one of these gentle giants.

Tel. 611374.
Open 10.30am–2pm,
4.30–10pm.
*Very attractive, all-wood
décor.*
100–200 baht
◑ ▭

KHAI MUK
71 Khunlum Praphat
Road.
Open 11am–2pm,
6–11pm.
*Excellent and very
popular restaurant. The
waiters speak perfect
English and provide
good service. Generous
helpings.*
100–250 baht
◑

HOTELS

BAIYOKE CHALET
90 Khunlum Praphat
Road,
Chong Kham
Tel. 611486
Fax 611533
Reservations in
Bangkok:
Tel. 2511847.
*For a long time, it was
the most fashionable
hotel in town. Today, its
popularity has been
overshadowed by the
big hotel chains. Still
very comfortable,
though.
Breakfast 85 baht.
650 baht*
🏛 🄲 🏠 🚗 ▭

MAE HONG SON
GUEST HOUSE
Tel. 612510.
*Isolated establishment
north of Mae Hong Son,
but that is precisely its
charm. Friendly
atmosphere. Basic,
clean rooms with hot
showers outside. Fan.
50–80 baht*
🏠 🏠 🖳 🔅

PEN PORN HOUSE
*Perched on a hill, a few
minutes north of the
town center.*

Tel. 611577
Fax 611577.
*Magnificent
surroundings. Charming
ambience. Not entirely
quiet but clean rooms
with hot showers.
Breakfast, at 30 baht, is
a delight.
150–250 baht*
🏠 🄲 🔅 🚗

PIYA COMPLEX
1 Soi 3 Khunlum
Praphat Road,
Amphoe Muang
Tel. 611260.
*Pleasant hotel located
beside a small lake.
Small but clean rooms
with fan or air-
conditioning.
Breakfast 30 baht.
250–300 baht*
🏠 🏠 🔅 🚗

TARA MAE HONG SON
149 Moo 8 Tambon
Pang Moo,
Amphoe Muang
Tel. 611272
Fax 611252
*One mile from the
center of Mae Hong
Son, this deluxe*

establishment has its
own magnificent park.
Welcoming, comfortable
rooms. Sporting
equipment available.
Breakfast 190 baht.
1,900–3,000 baht
🏛 🏠 🖳 🔅 ▢ 🛶
🚗 ▭ 👤

CHIANG SAEN

RESTAURANTS

RIM KHONG
Golden Triangle Road.
Tel. 715359.
*Thai restaurant on the
Mekong. Here you will
encounter tourists en
route for the famous
Golden Triangle.
Breathtaking views.
Simple dishes but
abundant supply.
Reasonable prices.
60–100 baht*
◯ ▭ 🔅

SALATHAI
RESTAURANT
At the end of the main
street.
*Small open-air
restaurant beside the*

Mekong and right in the
center of the busy
market. Excellent Thai
dishes.
60–100 baht
◯ 🔅

HOTELS

CHIANG SAEN
GUEST HOUSE
45 Rimkong Road,
Golden Triangle Road.
*Twelve small, clean
rooms. Splendid views
over the Mekong.
Pleasant atmosphere.
100–150 baht*
🏠 🄲 🏠 🔅 🚗

GIN'S GUEST HOUSE
Golden Triangle Road.
*Pleasant atmosphere in
this small, quiet
establishment beside
the Mekong. Value for
money varies,
depending on the
season.
80–400 baht*
🏠 🏠 🖳 🚗

GOLDEN TRIANGLE
RESORT
222 Golden Triangle
Road
Tel. 777001
Fax 777005
Reservations in
Bangkok:
Tel. (2) 5123952.
*Luxury hotel
overlooking the
Mekong. For travelers
who prefer all the
modern comforts and
facilities.
Breakfast 200 baht.
2,000–4,500 baht*
🏛 🄲 🏠 🖳 🔅 ▢ 🛶
🚗 ▭ 👤

JS GUEST HOUSE
behind Chiang Saen
Post Office.
*Very well-maintained
single rooms backed by
friendly service. Rooms
with 4 beds at 30 baht
per person.
30–100 baht.*
🏠 🄲 🏠 🚗

◆ GOLDEN TRIANGLE RESORT ◆

The luxury hotel at Sop Ruak in the heart
of the fabled Golden Triangle looks out
over the Mekong River.

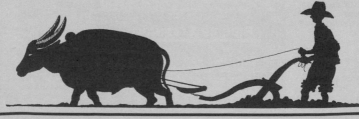

APPENDICES

◆ BIBLIOGRAPHY

ESSENTIAL
◆ READING ◆

◆ COOPER (Robert and Nanthapa): *Culture Shock! Thailand* (Kuperard Ltd, London, 1982)

◆ CUMMINGS (Joe): *Bangkok* (Lonely Planet, 1992)

◆ PAULUS (Conrad L): *Fodor's Thailand* (Fodor's Travel Publications, 1993)

◆ VAN BEET (Steve): *Chiang Mai* (APA Publications, Hong Kong, 1992)

◆ WINTERTON (Bradley): *Insider's Guide to Thailand* (Moorland Publishing, 1991)

◆ NATURE ◆

◆ BONSONG (Lekagul) and CRONIN (Edward W.): *Bird Guide of Thailand* (Ladprao Press, Bangkok, 1991)

◆ BONSONG (Lekagul) and McNEELY (Jeffrey): *Mammals of Thailand* (Ladprao Press, Bangkok, 1991)

◆ GRAY (Denis), PIPRELL (Collin) and GRAHAM (Mark): *National Parks of Thailand* (Communications Resources Thailand Ltd, Bangkok,1991)

◆ THAILAND DEVELOPMENT RESOURCE INSTITUTE: *Thailand: Natural Resources Profile* (1987)

◆ ETHNOLOGY ◆

◆ FREEMAN (Michael): *Hill Tribes of Thailand* (Asia Books, Bangkok, 1989)

◆ GRUNFELD (Frederic): *Wayfarers of the Thai Forest* (Time Life Books, London, 1982)

◆ JUMSAI (Sumet): *Naga: Cultural Origins in Siam and the West Pacific* (Oxford University Press, Singapore, 1988)

◆ LEWIS (Paul and Elaine): *Peoples of the Golden Triangle* (Thames and Hudson, London, 1984)

◆ SEIDENFADEN (Erik): *The Thai People* (Bangkok: Siam Society, 1967)

◆ SKINNER (G. William): *Chinese Society in Thailand* (Cornell University Press, Ithaca, New York, 1957)

◆ HISTORY ◆

◆ AIRES (Cristovão): *Fernão Mendez Pinto, Subsidios Para A Sua Biografia* (Lisbon, 1904)

◆ ALBUQUERQUE (Afonso Bras de): *Comentarios do Grande Afonso de Albuquerque* (Coimbra, 1923)

◆ BARROS (Joao de): *Decadas da Asia* (Lisbon, 1777)

◆ BEAUVOIR (Ludovic, Marquis de): *Java-Siam-Canton*, Paris,1869 (reproduced in *Voyage autour du Monde*, Paris, 1872)

◆ BOCK (Carl): *Temples and Elephants*, London, 1883 (Oxford University Press, 1986)

◆ BOUCAUD (André and Louis): *Burma's Golden Triangle: On the Trail of the Opium Warlords* (Asia Books, Bangkok; Asia 2000, Hong Kong, 1989)

◆ BOWRING (Sir John): *The Kingdom and People of Siam*, London, 1857 (Oxford University Press, Singapore, 1987)

◆ CHAKRABONGSE (Prince Chula): *Lords of Life* (Alvin Redman, London, 1960)

◆ CHOISY (Abbé de): *Journal du Voyage de Siam* (London/ Paris, 1687)

◆ CLARKE (Hugh V.): *A Life for Every Sleeper* (Allen & Unwin, 1986)

◆ COEDES (George): *The Indianized States of Southeast Asia* (translated by Susan Brown Cousing), Editor Walter F. Vella, East-West Center Press, Honolulu, 1968)

◆ COLLIS (Maurice): *Siamese White* (Faber, London, 1965)

◆ CORTESÃO (Armando): *A Suma Oriental of Tomes Pires* (Hakluyt Society, London, 1944)

◆ CRAWFURD (John): *Journal of an Embassy from the Governor-General of India to the Courts of Siam and Cochin-China*, London, 1828 (Oxford University Press, 1971)

◆ EARL (George Windsor): *The Eastern Seas*, London, 1837 (Oxford University Press, Singapore, 1971)

◆ FINLAYSON (George): *The Mission to Siam and Hué: the Capital of Cochin-China, in the Years 1821-1822*, London, 1826 (Oxford University Press, Singapore, 1987)

◆ GERVAISE (Nicolas): *The Natural and Political History of the Kingdom of Siam* (London, 1688)

◆ HALL (D.G.E.): *A History of South-east Asia* (Macmillan, London, 1968)

◆ HALLETT (Holt): *A Thousand Miles on an Elephant in the Shan States,* London, 1890 (White Lotus, Bangkok, 1988)

◆ HERBERT (Thomas): *Some Years Travel Into Diverse Parts of Asia and Afrique* (London, 1638)

◆ LA LOUBÈRE (Simon de): *Du Royaume de Siam* , Paris, 1691 (Modern edition *Étude Historique et Critique du Livre de Simon de la Loubère*, Editions Recherche sur les Civilisations, Paris, 1987)

◆ LE MAY (Reginald): *An Asian Arcady* (White Lotus, Bangkok, 1986)

◆ LEONOWENS (Anna) : *The English Governess at the Siamese Court* , 1870 (Oxford University Press, Singapore, 1988)

◆ McCOY (Alfred W.): *The Politics of Heroin in Southeast Asia* (Harper and Row, New York, 1972)

◆ MOUHOT (Henri): *Travels in Siam, Cambodia and Laos 1858-60,* London, 1862 (Oxford University Press, Singapore, 1989)

◆ NEALE (F.A.): *Narrative of a Residence at the Capital of the Kingdom of Siam* (London, 1852)

◆ PALLEGOIX (Mgr J-B): *Description du Royaume Thai ou Siam* (Paris, 1854)

◆ PURCHAS (Samuel): *Pilgrimage, or Relations of the World and the Religions Observed in All Ages and Places Discovered From the Creation Unto the Present* (London, 1617)

◆ SMYTH (H. Warrington): *Five Years in Siam, from 1891-96* (London, 1898)

◆ TACHARD (Father Guy): *Second Voyage du Père Tachard et des Jésuites envoyés par le Roi au Royaume de Siam* (Paris, 1869)

◆ TACHARD (Father Guy): *Voyage de Siam des Pères Jésuites envoyés par le Roi aux Indes et à la Chine* (Paris, 1686)

◆ VINCENT (Frank): *The Land of the White Elephant*, New York, 1874 (Oxford University Press, Singapore, 1987)

◆ WHITE (Joyce): *Discovery of a Lost Bronze Age: Ban Chiang* (University of Pennsylvania and Smithsonian Institution, 1982)

◆ WYATT (David K.): *Thailand: A Short History* (Yale University Press, New Haven, and London, 1982)

◆ YOUNG (Ernest): *The Kingdom of the Yellow Robe*, London, 1898 (Oxford University Press, Singapore, 1986)

◆ **ART** ◆

◆ APINAN (Poshyananda): *Modern Art in Thailand* (Oxford University Press, 1992)

◆ AUBOYER (Jeannine), BEURDELEY (Michel), BOISSELIER (Jean), ROUSSET (Huguette) and MASSONAUD (Chantal): *Oriental Art, A Handbook of Styles and Forms* (Faber, London, 1979)

◆ BOISSELIER (Jean): *The Heritage of Thai Sculpture* (New York, 1975)

◆ BOISSELIER (Jean); *La Peinture en Thailande* (Office du Livre, Fribourg, 1976)

◆ CHEESEMAN (Patricia) and SONGSAK (Prangwatthanakun): *Lanna Textiles* (Suriwong's Book Centre, Chiang Mai, 1987)

◆ HOSKIN (John): *Ten Contemporary Thai Artists* (Graphis, Bangkok, 1984)

◆ LE MAY (Reginald): *A Concise History of Buddhist Art in Siam* (Tokyo, 1963)

◆ LYONS (Elizabeth): *Thai Traditional Painting* (Bangkok, 1973)

◆ LYONS (Elizabeth): *The Tosachat in Thai Painting* (Bangkok, 1971)

◆ PAWLIN (Alfred): *Dhamma Vision* (Visual Dhamma, Bangkok, 1984)

◆ PIRIYA (Krairiksh): *Art Styles in Thailand* (Bangkok, 1977)

◆ PIRIYA (Krairiksh): *Art in Peninsular Thailand Prior to the 14th Century* (Fine Arts Department, Bangkok, 1980)

◆ PIRIYA (Krairiksh): *The Sacred Image: Sculptures from Thailand* (Museum of Oriental Art, Cologne, 1979)

◆ PIRIYA (Krairiksh): *Sculptures from Thailand* (Hong Kong, 1982)

◆ STRATTON (Carol) and SCOTT (Miriam McNair): *The Art of Sukhothai* (Oxford University Press, Kuala Lumpur, 1981)

◆ SUBHADRADIS (Diskul M.C.): *Art in Thailand: A Brief History* (D.K. Books, Bangkok, 1976)

◆ SUBHADRADIS (Diskul M.C.): *The Art of Srivijaya* (Oxford University Press, Kuala Lumpur, 1980)

◆ SUBHADRADIS (Diskul M.C.): *Sukhothai Art* (D.K. Books, Bangkok, 1978)

◆ VAN BEEK (Steve) and TETTONI (Luca Invernizzi): *The Arts of Thailand* (Thames and Hudson, London, 1991)

◆ WARREN (William): *The House on the Klong* (Weatherhill, Tokyo, 1968)

◆ WENK (Klaus): *The Art of Mother of Pearl in Thailand* (Zurich, 1980)

◆ WIYADA (Thongmitr): *Khrua In Khong's Westernised School of Thai Painting* (Thai Cultural Data Centre, Bangkok, 1979)

◆ WRAY (Joe and Elizabeth), ROSENFELD (Clare) and BAILEY (Dorothy): *Ten Lives of the Buddha; Siamese Temple Paintings and Jataka Tales* (Weatherhill, Tokyo, 1974)

◆ **RELIGION** ◆

◆ BUNNAG (Jane): *Buddhist Monk, Buddhist Layman* (Cambridge University Press, Cambridge, 1973)

◆ NIVAT (Prince Dhani): *A History of Buddhism in Siam* (Bangkok Siam Society, 1965)

◆ **LITERATURE/ GENERAL** ◆

◆ BURUMA (Ian): *God's Dust* (Vintage, London, 1989)

◆ CONRAD (Joseph): *The Shadow-Line* (Penguin Classics, London, 1986)

◆ COOPER (Robert and Nanthapa): *Culture Shock: Thailand* (Times Books, Singapore, 1982)

◆ HO (Minfong): *Rice Without Rain* (Times Books International, 1986)

◆ HOLLINGER (Carol): *Mai pen rai Means Never Mind* (Houghton Mifflin, Boston)

◆ IYER (Pico): *Video Night in Kathmandu* (Vintage Books, New York, 1988)

◆ LULOFS (Madelon H.): *Rubber*, London, 1933 (Oxford University Press, Singapore, 1987)

◆ MAUGHAM (Somerset): *The Gentleman in the Parlour*, London, 1930 (Penguin, London)

◆ MISHIMA (Yukio): *The Temple of Dawn* (Alfred Knopf, New York, 1973)

◆ PERELMAN (S.J.): *The Most of S. J. Perelman* (Simon & Schuster, New York, 1978)

◆ PHU (Sunthorn): *Nirat Phra Prathom* (translated by Montri Umarijari, The Amarin Press, Bangkok, 1986)

◆ REYNOLDS (Jack): *A Woman of Bangkok*, London, 1956, (D.K. Books, Bangkok,1985)

◆ SAUL (John Ralston): *The Paradise Eater* (Grafton Books, London, 1989)

◆ SEGALLER (Dennis): *Thai Ways* (Post Publishing, Bangkok, 1985)

◆ SHEARER (Alistair): *The Lotus Kingdom* (John Murray, London, 1989)

◆ THEROUX (Paul): *The Great Railway Bazaar* (Penguin Books, London, 1977)

◆ WARREN (William): *The Legendary American* (Houghton Mifflin, Boston, 1970)

Photographer: Luca Invernizzi Tettoni, unless stated otherwise.
1 Son of King Rama V, Robert Lenz, c. 1890.
2–3 Elephant hunt at Ayutthaya, Robert Lenz, c. 1890.
4–5 Chao Phraya River, Robert Lenz, c. 1890. Wat Arun gate, Robert Lenz, c. 1890.
6–7 Floating houses, Bangkok, Robert Lenz, c. 1890.
9 Phra Mongkol Bopit, Ayutthaya, photogravure from photograph taken by Martin Hürliman, from *Burma, Ceylon, Indo-China*, 1930.
12–13 Illustrator, Bruce Granquist.
15–30 Illustrators: Osman Asari, Seah Kam Chuan, Cheong Yim Mui, Manfred Winkler, Soong Ching Yee, Anuar Bin Abdul Rahim.
28–29 All photographs, except nest collection, by Lawrence Lim.
31 Page from manuscript on Thai military art, National Museum Bangkok.
32 Thai people at Si Satchanalai, old photograph, c. 1900. Siamese People, from H. Mouhot, *Travels in Siam, Cambodia and Laos 1858–60*, London, 1862.
Siamese woman, from *Guide to Bangkok*, Royal Railways, 1927. Siamese man (center), Robert Lenz, c. 1890. Northern Thai women at Chiang Mai, old photograph c. 1900.
33 Laotian girls, from H. Mouhot, *Travels in Siam, Cambodia and Laos 1855–60*, London, 1862.
Shan women, old photograph from Milne and Cochrane, *The Shans at Home*, London, 1910.
Muslim traders, mural painting in Wat Bowornivet, Bangkok. Karen, from C. Bock, *Temples and Elephants*, London, 1883.
Lawa, old photograph, from E. Seidenfaden, *The Thai Peoples*, Bangkok Siam Society, 1967.
34 Hunting scene, cave painting from Khao Chan-Ngam, from *The Stone and Metal Ages in Thailand*, Bangkok, 1988.
Three-legged pot, from

Ban Kao 2000 B.C., Bangkok National Museum.
Ban Chiang bronze bracelets, Suan Pakaad Palace collection, Bangkok.
Drawing of a Ban Chiang pot.
35 Vishnu from Wiang Sa, Bangkok National Museum.
Srivijaya votive tablet, Bangkok National Museum.
Wheel of the Law, Dvaravati period, 7th century, Bangkok National Museum.
Phimai Temple.
36 Elephant and soldiers, celadon ware, Bangkok National Museum.
Monument to Ramkhamhaeng, Sukhothai Archeological Park.
Illustration from *The Romance of the Rose* by King Rama VI.
Gold rings, Ayutthaya period, Ayutthaya National Museum.
Miniature gold fan, Ayutthaya period, Ayutthaya National Museum.
37 Louis XIV receiving Thai ambassadors in Paris, in Chakri Throne Hall, Bangkok.
Rama IV, from Sir J. Bowring, *The Kingdom and People of Siam*, London, 1857.
Rama V and family, painting by Edoardo Gelli, 1899, Royal Palace, Bangkok.
38 Bodhi tree, lacquer on wood from Wat Pong Yangkok, Lampang Luang.
Buddha images, Wat Chamadevi, Lamphun. Wat Ched Yod, Chiang Mai.
A Burmese prince (center), painting on wood, Seng Muang Ma, Lampang.
39 Detail of Lanna woodcarving.
Old walls of Chiang Mai, old photograph.
Last king of Chiang Mai, old photograph.
40 Rama VII in state, old photograph.
Rama VII entering Chiang Mai on an elephant, old photograph.
Field Marshal Pibul (left), from *The Bangkok Post*.
Dr Pridi Panomyong (right), from *The Bangkok Post*.
41 Siamese flags.
Portrait of King Ananda

(Rama VIII).
Early portrait of King Bhumibol.
42 Postcard of Ananda Samakhom Throne Hall, c. 1915.
Contemporary stamps. State opening of Parliament.
43 Page from astrology manuscript, 19th century, William Warren collection.
44 Old map, Michael Sweet, Antiques of the Orient, Singapore.
Stone Buddha head, late 18th century, National Museum, Lopburi.
Wheel of Law and deer, Dvaravati period, 7th century, Bangkok National Museum.
Mural depicting the Buddha cutting his hair, Buddhaisawan Chapel, Bangkok.
Gold Buddha, Chao Sam Phraya National Museum, Ayutthaya.
45 Stone bodhi tree, Ayutthaya, 17th century, Bangkok National Museum.
Bronze Padmapani bodhisattva, Chaiya, 9th–10th century, National Museum, Bangkok.
Sandstone eight-armed bodhisattva, Prasat Muang Singh in Kanchanaburi, late 12th–early 13th century, National Museum, Bangkok.
Detail of mural from Wat Thong Thammachat, Bangkok.
Detail of mural from the Lacquer Pavilion, Suan Pakkad Palace, Bangkok.
46 Monk contemplating death, Robert Lenz, c. 1890.
47 The Buddha collecting alms, lacquer panel, Suan Pakkad The Palace.
The Buddha in meditation, contemporary sculpture in Wat Thammakai, Bangkok.
Serenity, painting by Surasit Souakong, oil on canvas, © Visual Dhamma Art Gallery.
48–49 Flower arrangements.
50–51 Offerings and spirit houses.
51 Spirit house (top right), photograph by Alberto Cassio.
52 Elephant, carving on bullock cart.
Ivory tusks carved with the Buddha and other Buddhist motifs, Robert

Lenz, c. 1890.
Elephant hunt in Pattani, engraving from *De Bree Voyages*, Frankfurt, 1607.
Page from treatise on elephant training showing capture of wild elephants, manuscript from the Second Reign, Bangkok National Library.
53 Detail from 19th-century manuscript (top), National Library.
Elephant parade, old postcard.
Page from treatise on elephant training showing mythical elephants, manuscript from the Second Reign, Bangkok National Library.
Page from a treatise on elephants showing a hunting scene, 19th century, National Library, Bangkok.
Howdahs, from Father G. Tachard, *Voyages de Siam des Pères Jésuites envoyés par le Roi aux Indes et à la Chine*, Paris, 1686.
White elephant, engraving, 19th century.
54 Royal oarsman.
Royal barges (center), c. 1900.
55 From manuscript showing royal barge procession, 19th century, Bangkok National Library.
Royal barge, old postcard.
Royal barges (right), engravings, from Father G. Tachard, *Voyage de Siam des Pères Jésuites envoyés par le Roi aux Indes et à la Chine*, Paris, 1686.
Royal barges used in fighting, S. de la Loubère, *Du Royaume de Siam*, Paris, 1691.
56 Woman going to a festival (top right), detail from mural, Wat Bowornivet, Bangkok.
Women adorning themselves (center), detail from mural, Wat Suthat, Bangkok.
Woman wearing a jongkrabane, Robert Lenz, c. 1890.
Group of men wearing loin cloth, from 19th-century manuscript *The Pilgrimage to Saraburi*, National Library, Bangkok.
57 Farmer wearing a *mor hom*, cigarette card, c. 1930.
Men with cropped hair, from mural from Wat Phumin, Nan, late 19th century.

Yim-Mui, Soong Ching-Yee, Anuar Bin Abdul Rahim

Nature :
16-17 : Osman Asari, Anuar Bin Abdul Rahim.
18-19 : Osman Asari, Anuar Bin Abdul Rahim.
20-21 : Cheong Yim-Mui, Soong Ching-Yee, Anuar Bin Abdul Rahim.
22-23 : Manfred Winkler, Anuar Bin Abdul Rahim.
24-25 : Seah Kam-Chuan, Anuar Bin Abdul Rahim.
26-27 : Jimmy Chan, Cheong Yim-Mui, Anuar Bin Abdul Rahim.
28-29 : Soong Ching-Yee, Anuar Bin Abdul Rahim.
30 : Soong Ching-Yee, Anuar Bin Abdul Rahim.

Arts and traditions:
48-49, 70 : Anuar Bin Abdul Rahim.
74-75 : Paul Yip.

Architecture :
Bruce Granquist
Kittisak Nualvilai

Itineraries :
180, 184, 203, 212 : Anuar Bin Abdul Rahim.
232 : Julian Davison.
233 : Julian Davison, Tan Tat Ghee.
235 : Tan Tat Ghee.

Practical information and useful addresses :
Maurice Pommier.

Maps :
Anuar Bin Abdul Rahim : 202–3, 210–11, 218–9, 222–3, 230–1, 236–7, 276–7, 302–3.
Julian Davison : 282-283
Bruce Granquist : 12-13, 138–9, 148–9, 154–55, 168–9, 194–5, 242–3, 252–3, 256–7, 260–1, 286–7, back cover.
Brigitte Moriset : maps for Useful Addresses.

Labels :
Paul Coulbois
Laurent Gourdon
Danièle Guitton

We have not been able to trace the heirs or publishers of certain documents. An account is being held open for them at our offices.

INDEX

BANGKOK

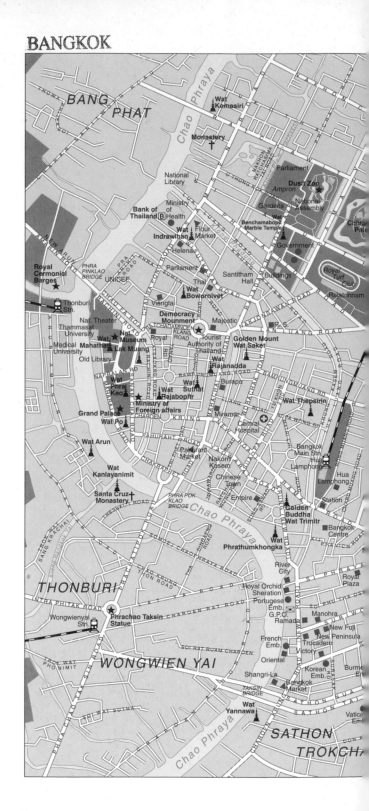